AF255732

Destruction *of* Paradise

DESTRUCTION *of* PARADISE

Triumph, Tragedy and
The Sack of the Summer Palace

John A. Roote

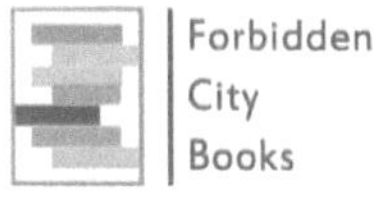

Forbidden City Books

Destruction of Paradise
First edition, 2017
Forbidden City Books, Dallas, Texas

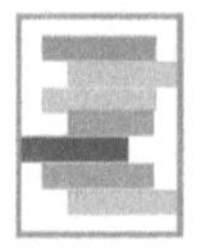

Design and typesetting, *Bookwrights*
Cover design, *Forbidden City Books*
Set in Garamond

ISBN 978-0-9994046-9-0

For Kathy

Contents

ix   The Summer Palace

xiii   Language

xv   Select Chronology

xix   Maps

1   Opium Wars

7   Invasion of the Celestial Realm—*James Hope Grant*

47   Palace of Palaces—*Robert M'Ghee*

73   A Scramble for Loot—*John Hart Dunne*

99   The French Have Arrived—*Charles Du Pin*

121   Around the World and Then to China—*Antoine Fauchery*

141   Exploring China and the Summer Palace—*Robert Swinhoe*

163   Describing Paradise—*Maurice Irisson*

193   An Artist's View—*Felice Beato*

211   Reporting from China—*T. W. Bowlby*

237   The Soldier's Eye—*Garnet Wolseley*

253   India—*Dighton Macnaghton Probyn*

267   The Wand of Victory—*Charles 'Chinese' Gordon*

283   Burning of a Palace—*James Bruce, Earl of Elgin*

315   A Scene of Destruction

323   Acknowledgments

The Summer Palace

"Nothing in our Europe can give an idea of equal luxury, and it is impossible for me in these few lines to describe the spendour of it, especially under the impression of bewilderment caused by my view of these marvels."

—James Hope Grant

First begun under the emperor Kangxi in 1709, then greatly enlarged by emperors Yongzheng and Qianlong, the Summer Palace, or *Yuen-ming-yuen* in Chinese, was without doubt the finest, most luxuriant, and arguably the most important palace ever built in China.

Situated five miles northwest of the ancient walled city of Peking, the Palace was the principal royal residence from 1725 to 1860, and designed for the exclusive enjoyment of the emperor. Its 860 enclosed acres, five times the size of the Forbidden City, comprised hundreds of buildings—public audience halls, private apartments, studios, libraries, temples, theatres and pavilions, even a series of European style palaces, placed in their own landscape settings.

The Yongzheng and Qianlong emperors constructed each Palace 'scene' with exquisite care, as a unique work of art, imitating a vision from mythology, or copying a wonderful garden from South China. It was a paradise, built at colossal expense, using the finest materials and crafts-people available—a masterpiece—the pinnacle of Chinese architectural and artistic achievement. Because of the deliberate manner of its construction and the rarity of the materials used, the Yuen-ming-yuen was, quite literally, irreplaceable.

Yuen-ming-yuen translates as *Garden of Perfect Brightness*, and a large portion of the imperial jewels, art collection and books were housed at the Palace. It was, in effect, a museum overflowing with priceless works of art and the finest furniture—pieces created especially for the emperor or given as tribute by foreign monarchs and grateful subjects.

This is the incredible and poignant story of the looting and destruction of the Summer Palace, in October 1860, by an Anglo-French army, as seen through the eyes of members of that expedition. Their accounts of this cultural catastrophe provide rare, and in some cases unique, insights into the imperial residence before it was destroyed,[1] and detail the enormous haul of artworks that were carted away to Europe.

Thirteen Witnesses

There were literally thousands of Europeans, Indians and local Chinese who witnessed the destruction of the Summer Palace and took part in the looting. Here are the stories of thirteen—three Frenchmen, three Scots, three Irishmen, one Englishman, one Anglo-Indian, one Welshman, and one Italian. They were diplomats, photographers, journalists, military officers, and a religious minister. Since almost all came from the European officer class, this would appear to open the door to criticism. The principal limiting factor is that there are only a handful of published accounts that provide substantive eye-witness material. There are no accounts in Chinese that have emerged.

It was a Chinese friend who suggested that I research and write a book that explains the actions of the Europeans, the architects of the looting and destruction. And although the thirteen individuals I have chosen may lack social and racial diversity, they were all intimately connected with these events, making their testimony unique and authentic.

---

[1] Paradoxically, because it was a sequestered place, the destroyers were among the few to see the Palace and write about it

This book considers who these men were, and how they came to be in China and have unrestricted access to a cultural masterpiece. It is a series of intimate portraits of a remarkable collection of individuals, that translates a momentous historical event to a human level, and explains definitively what happened and why.

The Author
July 17, 2017
Bournemouth,
England

Language

A few notes are necessary in order to explain use of language, naming conventions, and format.

In British and French eye-witness accounts there are a profusion of spellings of Chinese place names. In 1860 there was as yet no standard format in the West for place names in China, and writers simply did the best they could. We felt it would be confusing to have multiple spellings of the same palace or city. At the same time, we wanted to maintain as much of the 'flavor' of the original French and English accounts as possible. To this end, we have adopted a set of standard spellings based on 19th century European usage, rather than modern Pinyin. Thus, the Summer Palace is frequently referred to as the *Yuen-ming-yuen* (as it is to this day in France, rather than the Pinyin standard *Yuanming Yuan*); the Chinese capital is *Peking* (not the antiquated *Pekin*, nor the modern *Beijing*); the southern Chinese city on the Pearl River is *Canton* (rather than *Guangzhou*); and the port city in North China is *Tientsin* (rather than *Tianjin*). Original texts have been amended, where appropriate, to conform with these standard spellings.

Except in quotes from British and French sources, American English spelling and punctuation has been used. In a few isolated cases spelling errors or misnomers in the original texts have been corrected (for example, 'gadestone' has been replaced by 'jade stone'). Dates have been made to follow the American format—month, day, year—wherever possible, again for consistency. Quotations follow double quotation marks or have been indented in blocks. Words of emphasis and foreign words have been placed in italics or in single quotation marks.

Several of the actors that make up this story wrote their accounts in French. Mr. Colin Youngs M.A. (Oxon.) has kindly translated Maurice Irisson's memoir. In other cases I have performed the translations myself.

". . . a great black mass, outburst a
hundred flames, the smoke obscures
the sun, and temple, palace, buildings
and all, hallowed by age, if age can
hallow, and by beauty, if it can make
sacred, are swept to destruction, with
all their contents, monuments of
imperial taste and luxury. A pang of
sorrow seizes upon you, you cannot
help it, no eye will ever again gaze
upon those buildings which have
been doubtless the admiration of
ages, records of by-gone skill and
taste, of which the world contains
not the like. You have seen them
once and for ever, they are dead and
gone, man cannot reproduce them."

—Robert M'Ghee

Select
Chronology

1709–1820	Construction of the Yuen-ming-yuen by a succession of Chinese emperors
1793	Lord Macartney's embassy to China fails to produce a trade agreement
1816	Lord Amherst's embassy to China fails to produce an audience with the emperor or a trade agreement
1839–1842	Mandarin Lin tries to eradicate the opium trade and burns British 'factories' outside Canton. The First 'Opium War' between Britain and China ensues
1842	Treaty of Nanking—Hong Kong is ceded to Britain and five Chinese 'treaty ports' are opened for commerce with British merchant ships
1856	Seizure of a merchant ship flying a British flag ignites the Second Opium War
1858	After the bombardment of Canton and the capture of the Peiho forts, China is forced to sign the Treaty of Tientsin
1859	British emissaries are barred from proceeding from Tientsin to Peking. Hostilities resume. The British are defeated at the Taku forts
1860	Britain, joined by France, send armies to North China for the final phase of the Second Opium War:
July 28	Anglo-French forces land on the North Chinese coast, capture the city of Pehtang
August 21	Allies attack and capture the Taku forts

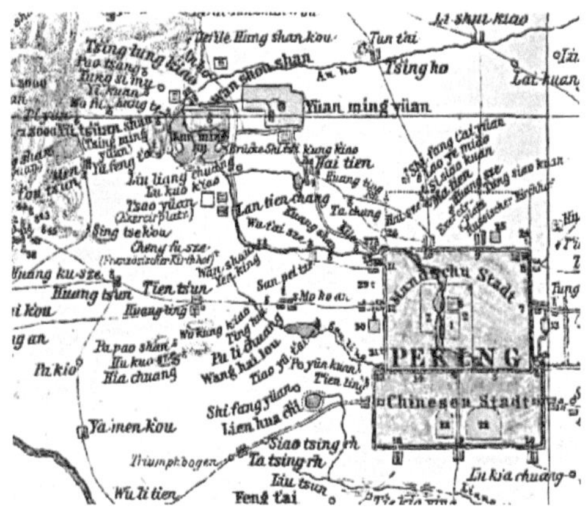

Peking and the Yuen-ming-yuen

Peking as it appeared in 1860. The Yuen-ming-yuen is northwest of the city. Further west and northwest are a range of mountains known as the Western Hills

September 8	After a period of negotiation the Anglo-French army begins to march on Peking
September 18	Negotiations break down and Allied emissaries are captured and imprisoned. Battle of Tungchow
September 21	Battle of Palikao—Allies defeat the main Chinese army who are forced to retreat north of Peking
October 6	Allies reach Peking, but the city is well defended. The French army advances to the gates of the Summer Palace and drives off a small party of retainers
October 7	French begin looting the Palace. British headquarters staff advance to the Palace at midday
October 8	Looting of the Palace continues
October 9	French army leaves the Palace and camps to the west of Peking
October 11–13	British conduct a 'prize sale' amongst themselves to raise cash for distribution to the troops
October 13	Peace negotiations with Prince Gong commence
October 18–19	British troops burn the Summer Palace as a reprisal for Chinese murder of Allied emissaries
October 19	Prince Gong agrees to terms for peace
October 24	Convention of Peking signed by China and Britain

October 25	Convention of Peking signed by China and France
November 1	French troops vacate Peking
November 10	British ambassador—Frederick Bruce—arrives in Peking.
	British troops vacate Peking. A portion of the army winters in Tientsin
1862	Loot from the Summer Palace is exhibited in Paris
1863	Loot is exhibited in London
1873	The Guangxu emperor begins to rebuild the Summer Palace
1874	Rebuilding efforts are halted for lack of funds. The Emperor instead focuses on rebuilding the Yihe Yuan palace, also burned in 1860
1873	The first known photographs are taken of the ruins of the Summer Palace by amateur photographer Ernst Ohlmer
1912–1939	After the fall of the Qing dynasty the Summer Palace ruins are indiscriminately plundered for building materials
1985	The Old Summer Palace park opens to the public

Maps

xvii   Peking and the Yuen-ming-yuen

xx   Eastern China under the Qing

19   The Allied Attack on the Taku Forts

24   The Route from Tientsin to Peking

27   Advance on Peking and the Yuen-ming-yuen

54   Plan of the Yuen-ming-yuen

55   Plan of the Imperial Apartments

232   Area Around the Russian Cemetery

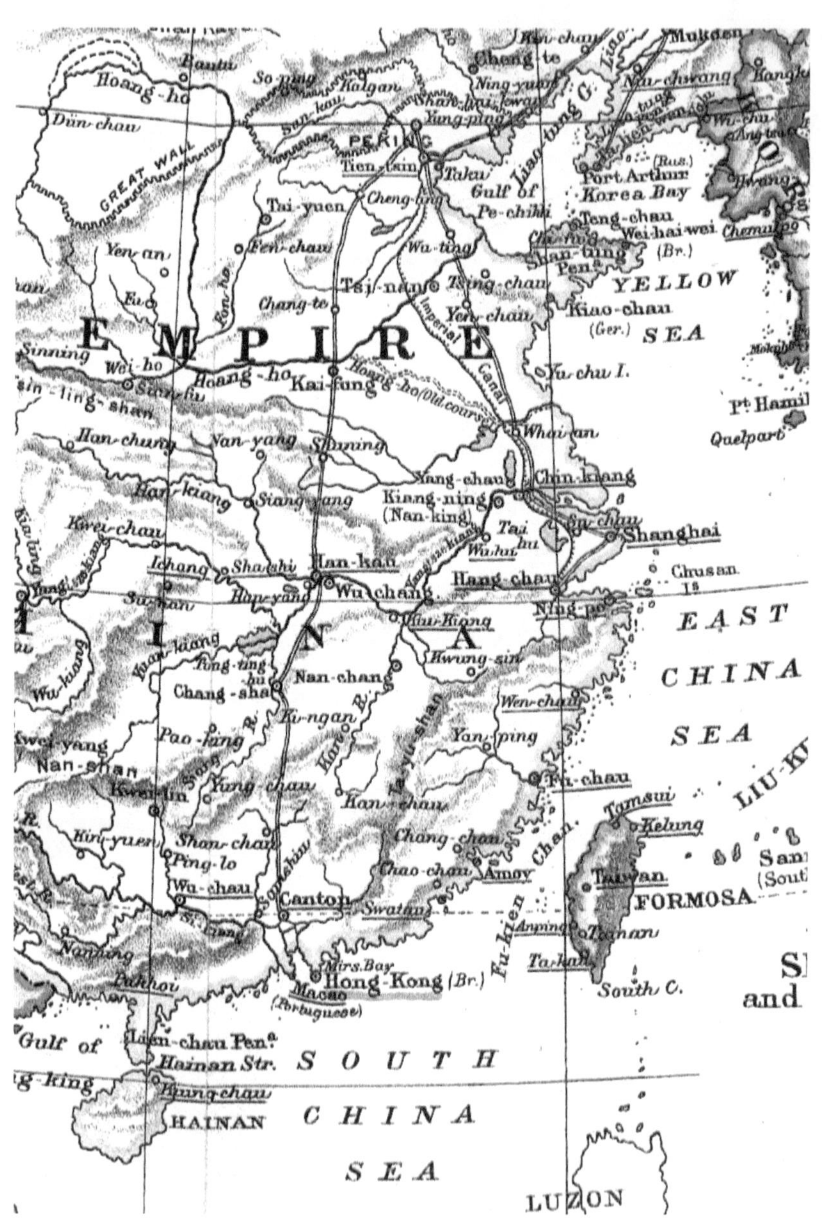

Eastern China under the Qing

Opium Wars

"Man had here imagined a whole region, quite unreal, and of great perfection, corresponding with his most refined tastes. In its time of glory it must have been an incredible place. The Yuen-ming-yuen is what the Chinese dream of when they think of a perfect garden: a collection of many different and surprising buildings, each in its own setting among trees, rocks, and flowing water, at the edge of the shores of a lake, and under the open sky."

—George N. Kates

The hostilities that brought an Anglo-French army to Peking in 1860 were the climax of the First and Second Opium Wars waged between Britain and China. In a larger sense, they were the culmination of millennia of mutual isolation.

Perhaps more than any major nation, long ago the Chinese developed a self-sufficiency, both material and intellectual. The wide plain stretching from the China Sea to the western mountains is a fertile crescent, distinct from the mountains and high plateaus of Central Asia. China was endowed with a rich bounty of foods which, combined with the natural intelligence and ingenuity of the Chinese people, helped create a large population and a vibrant civilization. This geographical isolation and terrestrial bounty resulted in a resilient and self-sufficient nation that for thousands of years led the world in riches and technology.

Since the 16th century China had been selling porcelain to Europe in large quantities; very much a one-sided affair. Europe, and especially Britain as she advanced technologically, was eager to sell their manufactured goods back to China. However, efforts made to establish reciprocal trade relations between the two countries were without success. In 1793 Lord Macartney and a large party of British representatives came to Peking bearing lavish gifts from George III, but failed to make an impression on the powerful Qianlong Emperor. Lord Amherst's embassy in 1816 proved even more futile and humiliating for the British. China did not want or need goods from Britain and, as she had every right to do, she kept Britain's merchants at arm's length. As late as 1838 the only point of contact the British had with China was on the mud flats of the Pearl River outside Canton, where ships of the East India Company were loaded with porcelain, brought across land from Jingdezhen, and tea transported from Fujian Province.

It was *Tea* that became the primary bone of contention between the two nations. In the 18th and 19th centuries Britain imported vast quantities of Chinese tea. It had become her largest import and a product desired by all classes of British society. In time, the Indian sub-continent became the principal source of tea for Britain and North America, but in the early 19th century tea was still grown exclusively in China, shipped to India, and then sold on to Britain. The trade was very beneficial to both China and Britain. However, in an age before international credit instruments, goods had to be paid for in hard currency, which meant in this case, *silver*. This trade, in the late 18th and early 19th centuries, requiring a vast transfer of silver from West to East, became a problem for Britain as she rapidly depleted her reserves.

A solution inadvertently presented itself in the form of *opium*, a drug made from Indian poppy seeds. The Yongzheng Emperor had the vision to foresee the problem with this addictive substance, and in 1729 he made its purchase illegal. But the trade was hard to control, and illusive in the attempts to stop it. Chinese consumers wanted opium and South Chinese smugglers were willing to defy the emperor and unload it surreptitiously from British ships. On a small scale this would not have been a major international problem, and indeed opium had been brought to China for centuries along the Silk Road, though in comparatively minute quantities. With each passing year the illegal opium trade grew larger, eventually giving Britain a significant inflow of silver with which to purchase the annual tea crop. The tables were now turned, and by 1840 China was importing 30,000 chests of Indian opium. The sheer scale of the opium trade began to disrupt Chinese society, causing addiction and lost productivity. It also had become a major drain on China's coffers. Something, the Daoguang Emperor (r. 1820–1850) felt, had to be done.

In the late 1830s Daoguang appointed Lin as his special representative in Canton, with the specific task of stamping out the opium trade once-and-for-all. Though opium was stored outside the walls of coastal Canton, the British were not permitted to live in or even enter the city. But they traded in opium and tea from their warehouses, and although illegal, local officials had been bribed to turn a blind eye to the trade. Lin was a resourceful administrator, and made a strong statement by burning 20,000 cases of opium in the British warehouses outside Canton, and enforcing the ban on its import through the port city. This represented a major financial loss to the opium dealers and severely disrupted the trade for the better part of two years.

Unwittingly, Lin had unleashed some powerful forces against himself and China. By burning the opium and treating the British representatives as 'barbarians', he disrespected what had become the most powerful empire in the world, with the best and most effective navy. His underestimation of British military power and her ability to retaliate proved a disastrous course of action for him personally and for the Chinese Emperor.

The 'Establishment' in London actually did not much care for the opium trade. There were many British politicians who opposed it as an immoral exercise that caused addiction among innocent Chinese people for financial gain. However, the tea trade was *very* important to the British economy and to her tax revenues,[2] and the opium trade was essentially facilitating the import of tea. By 1840 the opium traders had become a very powerful political interest group, and Britain had become dependent on the silver that was earned through its sale. For reasons of national prestige, political pressure, and economic necessity, London would not tolerate the ill treatment of her merchants and diplomatic representatives at Canton.

So Britain sent a combined army and naval force to Canton to 'protect her interests' and, at a minimum, restore the status quo in tea and opium trading. The First Opium War of 1839–42 was the result. The British navy bombarded Canton, and her marines captured the city and later taking the city of Ningpo before sailing up the Yangtse to the gates of Nanking, and threatening to take control of the Grand Canal. In the resulting Treaty of Nanking (1842), the Chinese Government was

---

[2] By 1840, import duties on tea were responsible for 10% of the British government's annual tax revenue

forced to open five treaty ports to trade in British goods and to grant her a 150 year lease of a rocky, barren, island at the mouth of the Pearl River—Hong Kong. The opium trade remained illegal, but China agreed not to interfere with British merchant ships and, critically, agreed to re-examine and renegotiate terms of trade in 12 years' time, a point that Britain intended to use as a lever to further expand trade.

The Xianfeng Emperor (r. 1850–1861) disliked and hoped to avoid the terms of the Treaty of Nanking. For him, the agreement represented a humiliating defeat and the complete antithesis of his vision for the Chinese Empire. Opium began to flow again into China, in ever increasing quantities, after 1842. It was the cause of addiction and illness in the Chinese population, especially the government officials who were among those who could afford to purchase the drug.

The Chinese, however, still did not accept British merchants or consuls as equals, and did not want to deal with them diplomatically. The British had, therefore, not succeeded in finding a peaceful way to deal with the Chinese. If they reached an agreement with officials in, say, Canton, they would often find that more senior officials in Peking would not honor the arrangement. The only means they had found to get the attention of the Chinese government was by force of arms. And, the cultural divide was as wide as ever—the British felt they had nothing to learn from the Chinese, and the Chinese felt they had nothing to learn from the Europeans.

In 1856, after the failure of the Chinese to re-engage in diplomatic discussion about trade, an argument about the import of opium on a British registered boat of Chinese origin (the *Arrow*) caused the conflict to reignite. To avenge the inference, the British sent a military force to the mouth of the Peiho River, originating close to Peking, which flowed to the important trading city of Tientsin. The mouth of the river was guarded by a series of forts, armed with cannon, and with a chain barrier across the mouth of the estuary preventing ocean-going ships from freely entering. The British captured the forts and concluded hostilities with the Treaty of Tientsin (1858), which gave Britain additional trading rights and the ability to maintain a diplomatic presence in Peking. Lord Elgin, who had been the British representative in charge of the campaign, returned to Britain satisfied that his work was complete. But, once again, the Chinese only signed the treaty under duress and sought every way possible to avoid compliance.

In 1859 British diplomatic representatives attempting to proceed up the Peiho to Tientsin and Peking were prevented from doing so by Chinese officials, and hostilities resumed once more. A British naval force attempted to force their way into the Peiho, and a landing party of marines attacked the forts, but were repulsed, and the Chinese sank several British gunboats. Much to his frustration, the British government called again upon Lord Elgin to go back to China, this time to get her to comply with the terms of the Treaty of Tientsin.

The expedition that was launched in the spring of 1860 was a much more serious and substantial military operation, drawing on regiments stationed in India as well as Great Britain. The campaign that followed, in due course, brought the Anglo-French into conflict with China's main armies, and they fought all the way to the heart of the Chinese Empire—Peking.

Bibliography

Opium Regimes, Edited by Timothy Brook and Bob Tadashi Waka-bayashi, University of California Press, Berkeley and Los Angeles, 2000

Invasion of the Celestial Realm

James Hope Grant

"In the distance we at last perceived the Palace, beautifully situated amidst gardens and woods."

—James Hope Grant

The men who are the storytellers in this book, are truly an extraordinarily talented and accomplished group of individuals. Today this seems paradoxical when one considers that most of them had a direct hand in either looting or destroying the great artistic and architectural gem that was the Summer Palace. It is however, a fact. James Hope Grant, the first individual to tell his story, is no exception. He was perhaps the most successful field commander in the British Army during the Victorian Era, who in the course of his career 're-wrote the book' on British army training and tactics.

Grant was a brave and well-respected general and he was chosen to command the British expeditionary force assembled to invade North China at the culmination of the Second Opium War. As the commander-in-chief, Grant explains the sequence of battles and logistical challenges that led the Allied army all the way to the gates of Peking. His clear and direct account of these events has much to commend it, and it provides an excellent introduction to the campaign and the thorny issues of diplomacy.

[Author's Note—Whilst some readers may not be overly concerned with the details of the military campaign, they are important because they shaped the mindset of the Allies with regard to the subsequent looting and destruction of the Summer Palace]

The Grant family has its origins in Scotland. The name *Grant* first appears in northern Scotland in the early part of the 13th century: Sir Laurence *Le Grant* was Sheriff of Inverness in 1258.[3] The Grant clan motto, appropriately, is 'stand fast'. James Hope Grant was born July 22, 1808, the fifth and youngest son of Francis Grant of Kilgraston House, Perthshire, a Scottish landowning gentleman of comparatively modest means, and Anne Oliphant. His grandfather was Patrick Grant, born in Scotland in 1704. His elder brother John Grant, born in 1798, inherited the Kilgraston estate when their father died, and James, as a younger son, was destined for a career in government service. James purchased for himself a commission as a 'cornet' in the 9th Lancers, in 1826, and was promoted to lieutenant in 1828.

In 1835 Hope Grant was promoted to captain with the Lancers, and in 1841 Lord Saltoun appointed him his Brigade-Major to go to China as part of the First Opium War. "In July 1842 he was present at the hardest fought action of the First China War, the capture of Chinkiang, and next took part in the landing before Nanking, which induced the Chinese to sue for peace."[4] As a reward, Grant was appointed Assistant Adjutant General and promoted to major. In 1843 he was made a Companion of the Bath for his services in China, and in 1844 he rejoined his regiment at Cawnpore, for what would prove to be sixteen years' continuous service in India. In 1847, while in India, Grant married Elizabeth Helen Taylor, daughter of Benjamin Taylor of the Bengal civil service.

At the start of the Second Sikh War in 1848, the 9th Lancers marched from Meerut to join Gough's Army in the Punjab, and fought the Sikhs at Chilianwala. For his service in the Sikh War, Hope Grant was promoted brevet lieutenant-colonel, in April 1850, and put in command of the regiment. The Lancers were posted to Ambala, where they remained until the outbreak of the Indian Mutiny. In May 1857 Grant was made brigadier of the cavalry brigade that was formed in Ambala. "On . . . campaign, he was to be accompanied by his 'enormous violincello', the very sight of which made the natives run away, crying 'Shaitan' (Satan)."[5]

The cavalry were soon in action during the Mutiny. In June 1857, Grant was in the fighting north of Delhi and showed great courage, as one biographer noted, "Late on June 19, just as dark began to fall, one

---

[3] Research on the Grant Clan from Scotlandinoils.com

[4] Sotheby's, catalog, London, September 17, 2004

[5] Sotheby's, catalog, London, September 17, 2004

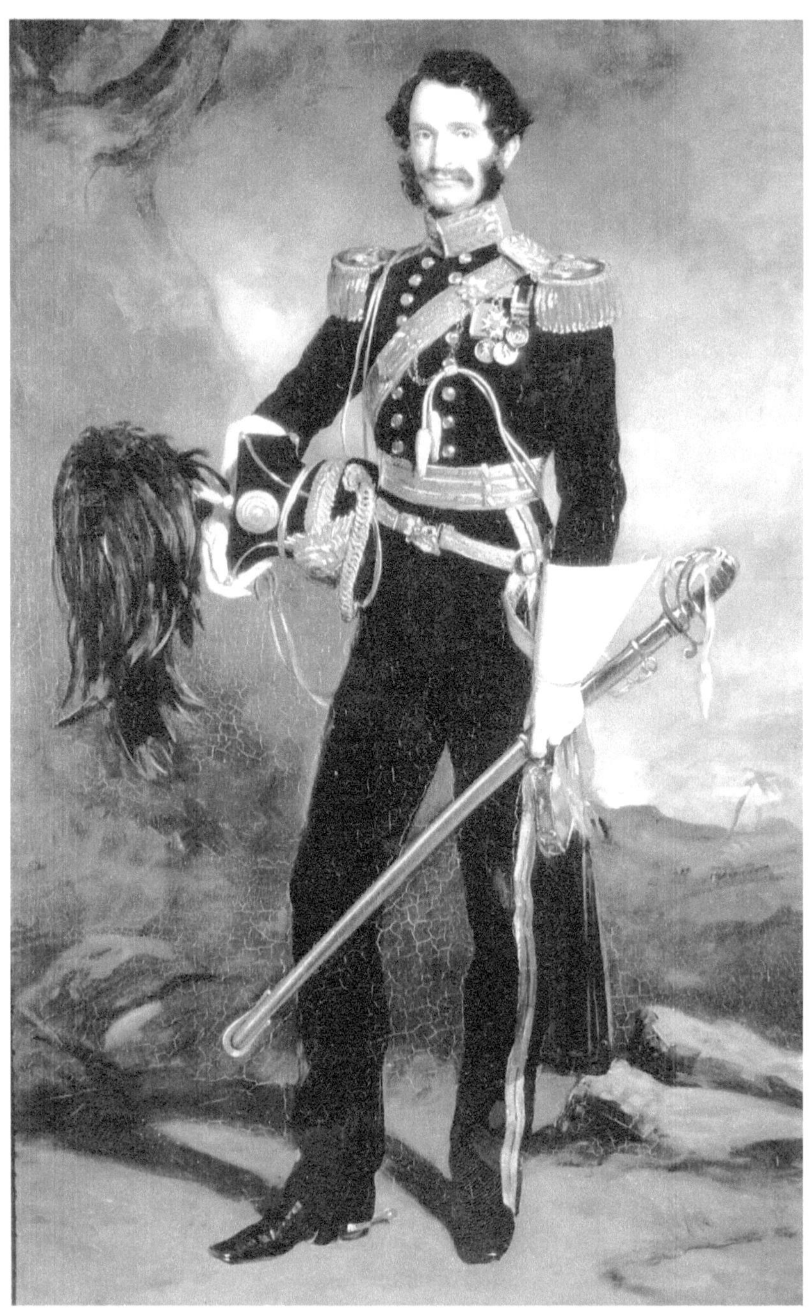

James Hope Grant, painting 1850s, by his brother Francis Grant, RA

of the many desperate hand-to-hand conflicts took place, with the muti-
neers and rebels issuing from the city and attacking the rear of the British camp. Hope Grant turned out with a squadron of the 9th Lancers
and six guns to counter the threat. As long as daylight lasted the rebels
were driven back, but when darkness set in they got round our flanks;
and two of our guns were in jeopardy. Grant collected a few men and
charged the rebels; a Sepoy five yards from him shot his horse, and he
was left dismounted in the middle of the enemy. Three men stuck to
him—his native orderly, of the 4th Irregulars, Rooper Khan; Privates
Thomas Hancock and James Purcell . . . Hancock and Rooper Khan both
tried to induce Hope Grant to take their horses [which he refused], but
he eventually took hold of Rooper Khan's horse's tail and was dragged
out of the crowd."[6]

China

Grant was not involved in the early phases of the Second Opium War
but was selected as commander of the elite Anglo-Indian army that was
sent to invade North China in 1860. The expedition was to be carried out
in conjunction with the French, whose force was commanded by Napoleon III's flamboyant and temperamental cousin, General Montauban.
"In the month of October I received a letter from Lord Clyde. . . . He
informed me that the home authorities had decided to nominate me to
the command of the British force about to proceed to China . . . I was
greatly pleased at this information."[7] "I appreciated my nomination to
the command . . . the more, because I had sought for it neither directly
nor indirectly."[8]

For Hope Grant and the War Department back in London, wag-
ing an effective campaign 10,000 miles from home, a journey of several
months by sea, was not going to be easy. Transporting the best troops and
horses safely from Europe and India simultaneously, with the appropriate
supplies and matériel, was a logistical nightmare. Hope Grant's efficiency
as a leader was one of the primary reasons for his selection for command.
His task was to procure all of the necessary supplies and supporting personnel in Hong Kong and coordinate the movement of the army up the

---

[6] Ibid.

[7] Hope Grant in Knollys, *Life of Sir Hope Grant*, p. 45

[8] Hope Grant in Knollys, *Life of Sir Hope Grant*, p. 48

Chinese coast to Tientsin. This process was to take several months. Since there was a dual command between British and French forces, the two countries had to coordinate their efforts so that both had their forces in position at the same time ready to deploy on Chinese soil. One saving grace was that China did not have an effective navy, which allowed the Allies to make their preparations in their toe-holds on the Chinese coast, unmolested.

Grant's sojourn to China started peaceably enough, he sailed from Calcutta to Hong Kong where the British expeditionary force was to assemble:

> We reached Hong Kong on March 13, 1860. Admiral Hope, who was there in command of the fleet, carried his flag on board the *Chesapeake*, and I at once proceeded to make his acquaintance. He was a tall noble-looking man, with a prepossessing and most gentleman-like appearance, and we were not long in becoming excellent friends. From him I learnt that Lieut.-General Cousin de Montauban, the French military commander-in-chief, had gone to Shanghai ... [once on land] I was most hospitably welcomed at Government House by the governor, Sir Hercules Robinson, whose residence was beautifully furnished in English fashion.[9]

Task and Assumptions

The task entrusted to the Anglo-French expeditionary force was to compel the Chinese emperor to ratify the 1858 Treaty of Tientsin. Britain dispatched an army to North China, and France 'volunteered' to participate in the campaign in order to open her own trade with China. It was hoped that the objectives of the mission could be accomplished with little or no fighting. However, the invasion army, a hand-picked military force, was prepared to go all the way to Peking if necessary.

One of the primary constraints on Grant was that the campaign be accomplished during the 1860 combat 'season', i.e. quickly. In part this was due to problems of supply, in part to minimize expense, and in part because a protracted campaign would allow the Chinese to concentrate a force large enough to defeat the Allies or at least effectively block their

---

[9] Hope Grant, in Knollys, *Life of Sir Hope Grant*, p. 49

path to the capital; and in part because of weather. Weather was to be a key factor in the destruction of the Summer Palace that autumn. The summer months in North China were known to be very hot and August believed to be accompanied by heavy rains which would turn roads into mud and make transportation of guns and movement of supply carts very difficult. The winter, December to March, was considered too cold for European troops to operate effectively. The ideal period for an attack was considered to be either June/July or September to November, when weather would be clement and conducive to military action. Grant had this all very much in mind as he planned the campaign from Hong Kong and later Shanghai.

It is often assumed that European success in the Second Opium War was a forgone conclusion, which gives the impression of not only a barbaric invasion of China, but an imperious one. For those in charge of the operation this was far from the truth. In fact the previous British invasion force had been defeated in 1859 trying to capture the Peiho forts and the Canton merchants had laid a wager that the 1860 campaign would end similarly before the Allies could even establish a bridgehead on land.

It was easy for the British government to make the political decision to fight a war in Asia, but the military challenges were many. The Chinese army was numerically far superior, fighting on their own soil, their morale was high, they were highly mobile, and equipped with substantial artillery. The forts dominating the entrance to the Peiho River were formidable and with a vast hinterland to retreat into, the Chinese military forces had considerable room for maneuver. Their main disadvantage was their arms, which were primitive or weak and no match for the modern rifle or Armstrong Gun. Never-the-less, 10,000 miles from home the Europeans faced considerable problems of supply and combat in a territory with which they were entirely unfamiliar.

The stakes were high. If Hope Grant failed, the defeat would bring down the British government. He and Montauban had to get their men, horses and guns in position off the China coast, successfully land them, together with all necessary matériel, establish a secure bridgehead on the mainland, capture the Chinese coastal forts and then deploy their forces in the field against the Chinese army. If an extended campaign was required, including an advance to Peking, the army had to be moved, together with their artillery, one hundred miles, largely on foot, across potentially hostile territory where they would be exposed to the elements for days at a time (no tents for shelter or sleeping), and then kept supplied with appropriate food, water and ammunition for the duration of the campaign. The army then needed to be returned safely to their base of operations and supply ships and transported back to India and Europe in a healthy condition. If winter were to set in, the troops, like Napoleon's army of 1812 would be without the appropriate clothing. They would also be unable to conduct a lengthy siege of Peking, and if forced to winter in China would likely run out of supplies and lose the morale of the troops.

Whilst, with hindsight, it is quite possible to see how the superior technology of the European forces and their professionalism, experience and extensive training allowed them to defeat the Chinese army, at the outset the outcome of the campaign was by no means certain. Britain's success in a series of battles, against a far larger foe, was in no small part the result of excellent military leadership by Hope Grant and his staff. The fact that the war has been much criticized in this century was not foreseeable in 1860 and was not the concern of the commanding general whose task it was to win the war.

Preparations

Once the British army had assembled in Hong Kong, they were to proceed up the South China coast to Shanghai and then advance in force to the mouth of the Peiho River, which was the gateway to Peking. The British sent soldiers from England as well as calling on Indian and British troops based in India.

"On March 31, 1860 we set sail from Hong Kong for Shanghai," notes Hope Grant, "where we arrived on April 6; and I at once went to call on General de Montauban and Mr. Bruce."[10]

> The latter was our plenipotentiary in China; but his brother, Lord Elgin, was shortly expected to take over the management of affairs during the war. I had formerly known Frederick Bruce well. In disposition he was a fine, upright, honourable fellow, and in appearance tall and strong made, with a remarkably good expression of countenance. I was sorry to find that the chief diplomatic power was to be taken out of his hands; but Lord Elgin had more experience, and had been in China before. General

---

[10] Hope Grant, in Knollys, *Life of Sir Hope Grant*, p. 52

de Montauban was a fine, handsome, soldier-like-looking man, apparently under sixty years of age, with a pleasant expression, and in general appearance quite the *beau sabreur* [gallant warrior].[11]

April 23, I . . . returned to Hong-Kong where there was a great deal of work awaiting me . . . Nearly all our force was now concentrated on the newly-acquired promontory of Kowloon [directly across the bay from Hong Kong island]. Its total strength was 13,116 men, of whom about 1,000 were cavalry. The two irregular cavalry regiments were really magnificent. They were composed of fine handsome men—Sikhs—becomingly dressed, well mounted, and commanded by two excellent officers—Major Fane a cavalry officer of great repute during the Indian Mutiny and Major Probyn, both of whom I had known well in India during the Mutiny. Probyn's Irregulars were the admiration of everyone. The King's Dragoon Guards was also one of the finest regiments in the service; and, altogether, I had reason to be proud of my little cavalry force. It was commanded by Brigadier Pattle, of the King's Dragoon Guards . . . The two generals of divisions were Major-General Sir John Michel and Major-General Sir Robert Napier—both excellent officers.[12]

Grant was pleased with the progress being made: "Thus far everything had gone wonderfully well with us. The men were in excellent health; and our cavalry and artillery horses were assembled in capital condition. W's had purchased and collected, from various places, numbers of ponies and mules; and had also organised a coolie corps. I must also mention that two batteries of the newly-invented Armstrong guns had arrived from England; and, it was in a great measure owing to the scarcity of draught animals experienced by the French that the armies were unable to take the field until so late a date that, as will be subsequently seen, Peking was captured but just before the severe winter set in. But for the strenuous efforts which were made to hasten the preparations, there is reason to suppose that the operations of the expedition

---

[11] Hope Grant, in Knollys, *Life of Sir Hope Grant*, p. 53

[12] Hope Grant, in Knollys, *Life of Sir Hope Grant*, p. 58

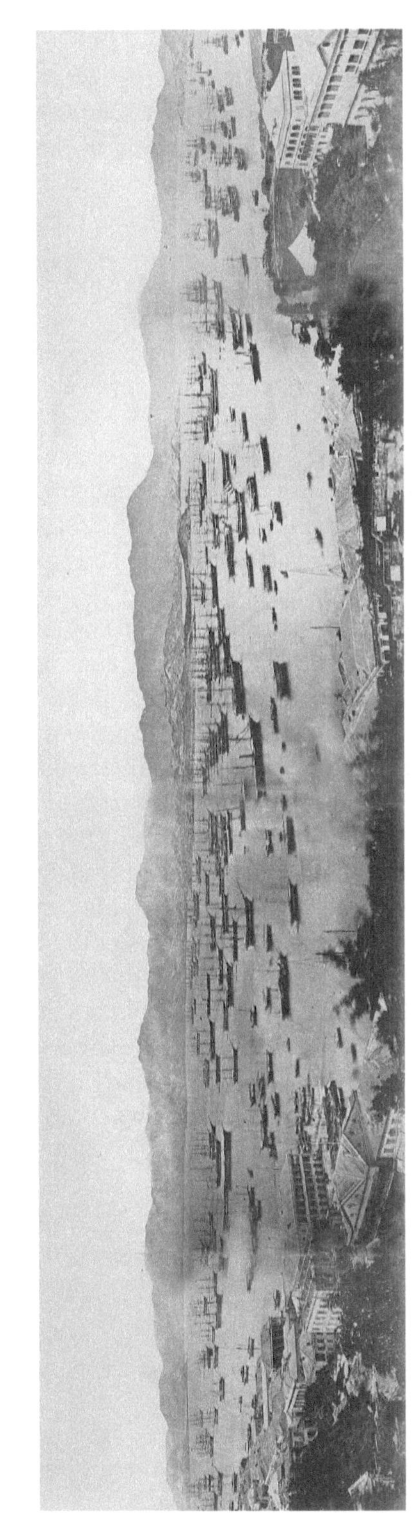

The British fleet in Hong Kong Harbor, June or July 1860, Felice Beato

would have been prolonged into another year. Our embarrassments were increased by the ignorance of all foreigners as to the resources of the country—thus requiring an accumulation of every sort of supplies."[13]

Advance to North China

"On June 11 I sailed from Hong Kong for Shanghai, which we reached on the June 16; and I immediately went on shore . . . General de Montauban laid before us his plan of attacking the Taku defences:"[14]

> He [Montauban] proposed to land at a spot twenty-five miles south of the large fort which had done so much damage to our fleets the previous year, and then to march up along the coast through a wretched semi-barren country, taking with him his light guns only . . . This scheme appeared to me very hazardous . . . Before attending the conference I had consulted with Admiral Hope, and we both came to the conclusion that our most judicious course would be to proceed up the river Pehtang, eight miles north of the Peiho, capture the town of Pehtang, and there establish a base for future operations. The Taku forts were four in number, two small upper and two large lower works—a large and a small fort being on each side of the river. In front of the lower forts, near the mouth of the Peiho, were fixed two very strong chain-barriers, impassable for ships under fire; and on each side of the river was a salt-marsh. The plan which I proposed to the French general was first to attack Pehtang, the defences of which were, so far as we could ascertain, of a less formidable description. Here, too, there was, it is true, a fort on each side of the river, but there were no barriers thrown across; and by landing near the town of Pehtang we could attack in rear the Taku forts.[15]

[13] Hope Grant, in Knollys, *Life of Sir Hope Grant*, pp. 63–65

[14] Hope Grant, in Knollys, *Life of Sir Hope Grant*, p. 67

[15] Hope Grant, in Knollys, *Life of Sir Hope Grant*, pp. 67–69

Montauban reluctantly agreed to Grant's plan. However:

> My satisfaction was marred by the French general's statement
> that he could not be ready to begin operations until the July 15.
> This delay was serious, as by that date the rainy season would
> in all probability have set in, and would have so inundated the
> country as to render it almost impassable for troops. We were
> prepared to open operations on 1st July, but the French very
> naturally insisted on a simultaneous start; and as I had received
> strict injunctions from home to act in unison with our allies,
> I had no alternative but to wait patiently.[16]

Preparing to send his force north for the final part of their journey, Grant
noted, "The men were in excellent health, and the horses in first-rate
condition; though they had travelled so far over a troubled sea . . . On
July 9 Lord Elgin arrived, and I immediately went on board to pay my
respects. My eldest brother was married to his sister, Lady Lucy Bruce,
and in former days I had known him well. Twenty years at least had
intervened since we had last met, and we were, of course, both much
changed; his hair had become perfectly white, and mine was well sprin-
kled with grey. We renewed our old acquaintance, and he told me how
he and Baron Gros, the new French ambassador, had been wrecked in
the harbour of Galle."[17]

Of his Indian contingent, Grant was well satisfied:

> The force had been conveyed a distance of 5,000 miles from
> India . . . Each English soldier was a splendid fellow, and looked
> as though he were a thoroughbred gentleman—powerful and
> strong enough to contend with any men the world could pro-
> duce. The Sikhs, too, with their beautiful turbans wound grace-
> fully over their ears and drooping down the backs of their heads,
> were almost equally splendid, and looked as if they intended to
> vie in acts of daring with the British. I need scarcely add that
> the Royal Artillery was, as usual, in the most beautiful order.
> And then the horses were turned out in a manner which did
> credit to both branches of the service. They had been taken from

---

[16] Hope Grant, in Knollys, *Life of Sir Hope Grant*, p. 69
[17] Hope Grant, in Knollys, *Life of Sir Hope Grant*, p. 78

the stud-depots of India; and having recently had plenty of rest and good food, they looked handsome, imposing, and full of breeding.[18]

Our force amounted, in round numbers, to about 11,000 men; that of the French 6,700. (Summary of expeditionary forces, as arrived at Ta-lien-wan Bay up to July 9, 1860: officers, 419; men, 10,491; horses, 1731). On July 26, 1860 our fleet got under weigh. It consisted of 173 vessels, some of which were sailing-ships, and the others steamers, drawn up in two lines. The French fleet, composed of 40 transports and men-of-war, formed the third line.[19]

Landing at Pehtang

Several days later the fleet anchored just twenty miles from the Taku forts, which loomed large in the distance. The army prepared for a landing:

A total of 2,000 troops, in equal numbers of French and English, were forthwith landed; and as we had the prospect of wading through at least two miles of mud, I took off my boots and stockings, tucked up my trousers, and pushed forward at the head of my men towards a raised causeway, which led apparently from the gate of Pehtang to the Taku forts ... At last all our wading difficulties were got over; our men reached the causeway, which was found sound and dry, and were ordered to bivouac on it for the night. I arranged with Admiral Hope and the French that at daybreak we should make a simultaneous attack on Pehtang from the road. At the same hour the gunboats were to steam up past the forts and support us with their fire.[20]

The next day Pehtang was captured:

Very early in the morning we entered Pehtang, and found that our gunboats had taken up the position previously assigned to

---

[18] Hope Grant, in Knollys, *Life of Sir Hope Grant*, p. 80
[19] Hope Grant, in Knollys, *Life of Sir Hope Grant*, p. 83
[20] Hope Grant, in Knollys, *Life of Sir Hope Grant*, p. 86

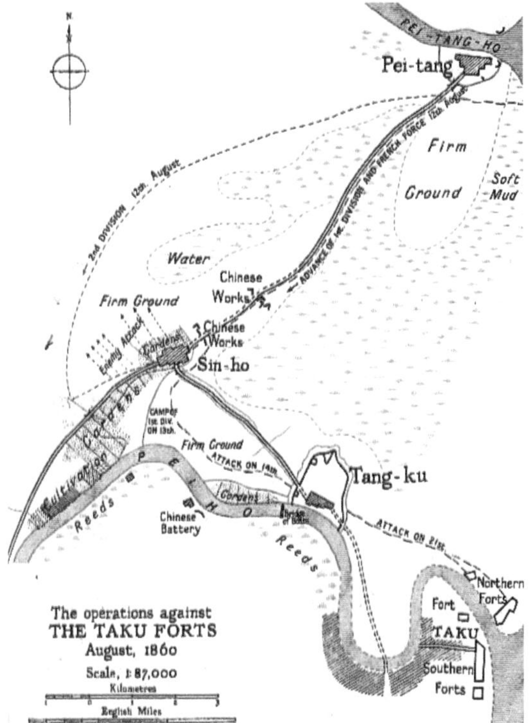

The Allied Attack on the Taku Forts

them. The Chinese coolies, of whom we had a large number—about 2,500—were for the most part atrocious villains, though extremely useful; and in the first instance, when they could be comparatively but little controlled, the robberies and crimes they committed in the town were fearful.[21]

"On August 12 the Allied force moved against the village of Sinho, which was connected to Pehtang by a narrow causeway nine yards wide," notes biography Henry Knollys. "When about a mile from Sinho, a large body of some several thousand Chinese cavalry, under Prince Seng [or Sengge], appeared in order to oppose the advance,"[22] but under fire from the Armstrong guns, the Chinese retreated and the town fell.

---

[21] Hope Grant, in Knollys, *Life of Sir Hope Grant*, p. 87

[22] Sotheby's catalogue, London, September 17, 2004

Hope Grant and Montauban again disagreed, this time on how to attack the forts that defended the entrance to the Peiho River:

> Montauban considered Hope Grant's plan riskily unorthodox, but Hope Grant stuck to his guns and by August 20 had won the debate, though in doing so Hope Grant carried a great responsibility. There was already considerable political pressure to reach Peking. A second reverse at Taku would not only finish his own career, but probably break up the Anglo-French alliance, and more than likely bring down the British Government.[23]

Hope Grant describes the attack on the first fort, which surrounded the town of Tang-ku:

> Our attack was directed against the side of the work at right-angles to the river, where the ditches and walls were of weaker profile. The heavy fire from our 36 guns soon knocked the intrenchment to pieces ... Meanwhile some companies of the 1st Royals and 60th Rifles crept through some sedges along the banks of the river, reached the foot of the fort, and succeeded in forcing their way in. An entrance once effected, the Chinese abandoned the whole of their works, turned, and fled. The French met with obstinate resistance at the point they had selected for their attack, a little to our left; but, gallantly led by Colonel Schmitz, the French chief of staff, they scaled the walls about the same time as ourselves ... During the engagement Sir John Michel had his horse killed under him. We were now well sheltered in the large village of Tang-ku, which lay within the enceinte of the works.[24]

> The French general now proposed to me that both our armies should cross the river, and attack the town of Taku, which was intrenched, and the large southern fort on the right bank. This plan, upon further consideration, appeared to me very hazardous ... I therefore determined to adhere to my original intention,

---

[23] Ibid.

[24] Hope Grant, in Knollys, *Life of Sir Hope Grant*, pp. 100–101

and endeavoured to convince General de Montauban that by gaining possession of the upper northern fort, we should be able to command all the others. In vain: he remained unmoved, but told me that if I was determined to carry out my plan, he of course would give me his assistance—but that he should feel obliged to write a protest against it.[25]

The Allies attacked the first fort, as Hope Grant intended:

At five o'clock on the morning of the August 21, the enemy opened on us a heavy fire from the two upper forts, one on either side of the river. Our guns quickly responded, and a cannonade from our forty-seven pieces was maintained with great vigour for three hours. Our shot fell thick upon the doomed fort, and at about 6 o'clock A.M., an 8-inch shell falling on their powder-magazine blew it up with a terrific explosion. For some time the fort was so shrouded in dense clouds of vapour and smoke, that it appeared to have been entirely destroyed; but by degrees it cleared away—the enemy recommenced fire, and seemed determined not to give up the place without a desperate struggle. Inside the work was a high cavalier from which heavy guns were opened on us, but we soon succeeded in silencing them. The general direction of our attack was against the enemy's rear . . .

Our storming-party consisted of the 44th and 67th Regiments. Some of our men swam across the ditch, and others got over with the French. On reaching the escarp they were sheltered from fire. The French placed their ladders against the parapet and endeavoured to get over; but the defenders offered a vigorous resistance with their swords and pikes, and knocked them off the crest as soon as they showed themselves. At last my aide-de-camp, Anson, gallantly succeeded in clambering across a drawbridge which had been hauled up over the ditch in front of my force, and with his sword cut the supporting ropes . . . The bridge fell into its proper position, and afforded to our men a means of crossing. Some of our officers perceived a small breach

---

[25] Hope Grant, in Knollys, *Life of Sir Hope Grant*, p. 105

which we had effected in the wall close to the gate, and here Lieutenant Burslem of the 67th Regiment forced his way in, but was driven back. Lieutenant Rogers was the next to enter, but was wounded. The French, who behaved as gallantly as possible—worthy of the great nation to which they belonged—entered the breach at the same time as our men, and their great ambition was to plant their standard first upon the walls; but young Chaplinz of the 67th Regiment, who carried the colours of his corps, out-did them, and placed the British standard upon the highest part of the works. He was wounded in three places ... Sir Robert Napier, whose conduct was very gallant, was struck by shot in five places, but was not actually wounded.[26]

The other forts, as Hope Grant had imagined, surrendered:

> The next day, August 22, I sent over Sir Robert Napier to take possession of the forts on the right bank. They were all handed over to him in due form, including 600 guns. The same day Admiral Hope broke away the chains and barriers which had been placed across the river [the Peiho].[27]

On August 24 the Allies moved up the Peiho and occupied the town of Tientsin:

> After our easy conquest of the other forts, he [the Chinese general] thought to retreat forthwith with his army, and the place [Tientsin] was denuded of troops. The inhabitants at first were frightened; but finding that far from molesting them, we treated them with kindness, they soon gained courage, and brought up in plentiful supplies, amongst which were fine fat sheep weighing 70 or 80 lb. each, fat oxen, apples, pears, grapes, peaches, and the great luxury of enormous blocks of ice.[28]

---

[26] Hope Grant, in Knollys, *Life of Sir Hope Grant*, p. 112

[27] Hope Grant, in Knollys, *Life of Sir Hope Grant*, p. 116

[28] Hope Grant, in Knollys, *Life of Sir Hope Grant*, p. 117

After a delay of some days in Tientsin negotiating with the Chinese imperial commissioners, Lord Elgin ordered the army to march on Peking:

> On August 31, three [Imperial] Commissioners arrived from Peking with a view to stop our advance. They gave out that they were entrusted with full powers; but this turned out to be false. They were only mandarins of small importance; and therefore, when on September 7 they brought forward pretended terms of a convention, Lord Elgin and Baron Gros instantly broke off negotiations, stating their resolution not to conclude a treaty before reaching Tungchow, fifteen miles from Peking.
>
> On September 8 we recommenced our march . . . Lord Elgin and I set out, and overtook them on the 9th. During the third night after our start the rain came down in a deluge, whereupon nearly the whole of our drivers, Chinese cart-men, together with their mules and ponies, conveying our baggage, absconded.[29]

After several days' march the army had made considerable progress towards their objective:

> On the September 13 we reached the pretty little town of Ho Si Wu, half-way between Peking and Tientsin, and on the 16th I was joined by Sir John Michel's division, raising our force to 2,300 infantry, a company and a half of engineers, three batteries of artillery, and the whole of the cavalry. The French with 1,200 men marched into the town the day after ourselves. Sir Robert Napier's division remained behind to hold Tientsin, forty miles to our rear.[30]

By September 14 a peace plan appeared to have been formulated to the satisfaction of all parties: the two European armies were to advance but stop short of the town of Tungchow. Elgin and Gros were to be permitted

---

[29] Hope Grant, in Knollys, *Life of Sir Hope Grant*, p. 130
[30] Hope Grant, in Knollys, *Life of Sir Hope Grant*, p. 131

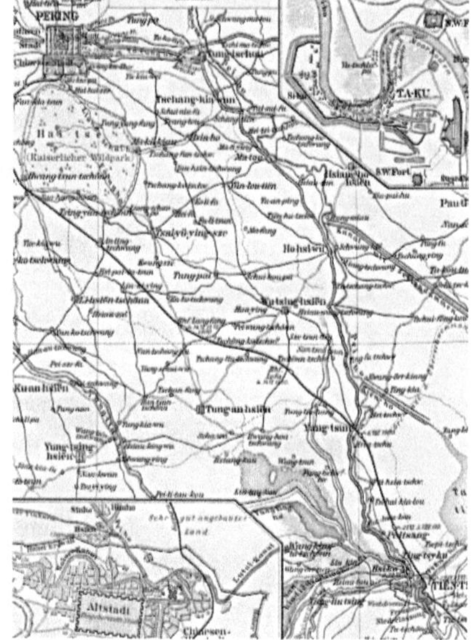

The Route from Tientsin to Peking (from a map dated c. 1900). Tientsin is bottom right. The Peiho River leads north, to the east side of Peking. Tungchow is located just east of Peking. Ho Si Wu is two-thirds of the way up the Peiho.

Capture of the British Emissaries

On September 17 Harry Parkes, the chief British emissary, went ahead to Tungchow to select a site for encampment and to procure supplies and settle final details for signing the peace treaty. Parkes was British Consul at Canton, "Although of comparatively low diplomatic rank, twenty-nine year-old Parkes was an old China hand well known to the Chinese as the British official with whom they most often had to deal. Indeed the Cantonese rated him above 'the barbarian commander', placing a price on his head six times greater than that offered for Hope Grant's. Parkes was accompanied by Elgin's secretary, Harry Loch, Bowlby of *The Times*, two British officers, and an escort of half a dozen Dragoons and about twenty Sikhs from Fane's Horse. Likewise, a party of French officers and others went forward on behalf of Baron Gros,"[31] recalls Knollys.

After spending the night inside the Chinese lines and having been well treated, the British party noted that the Chinese general, Prince Seng, had sent a large body of cavalry forward toward the British positions. Parkes protested but was promptly made prisoner by the prince.

---

[31] Knollys, *Life of Sir Hope Grant*, p. 131

All the other British, French and Sikh personnel remaining inside Chinese lines were likewise captured. Prince Seng, it transpired, was against signing the peace treaty and favored defeating the Europeans in battle. He effectively nullified and countermanded the previous actions by the more passive Chinese 'commissioners' who had negotiated the truce.

Seng not only captured the Europeans (who were operating under a flag of truce—something recognized by the Europeans and Chinese alike), but had them imprisoned as common criminals. They were taken back to Peking and treated in the most brutal manner. This aggressive gamble would backfire as the Europeans produced a series of military victories, and it infused them with a sense of revenge.

"The French, on learning of the capture of the emissaries favored an immediate attack on the Chinese army," notes Knollys. "Hope Grant was more cautious in the face of a much larger enemy force. Another emissary, Wade, was sent to the Chinese, under a flag of truce, to demand the return of the prisoners. Wade was fired upon and retreated."[32]

Advance to Peking

On September 18 the Allies continued marching north and met the substantial Chinese army at the battle of Tungchow, south of that city. "General de Montauban," states Hope Grant,

> Advanced, and soon got on the left flank of the Chinese . . . He then brought up his artillery and opened an enfilading fire upon them, from which they must have suffered considerably, as they had not apparently the power of moving their guns, and were unable to reply. They therefore attacked him with their cavalry, and for a short time the French guns were in jeopardy . . . Our gallant little force of cavalry, with about half-a-dozen troopers which General de Montauban had with him, the whole led by Colonel Foley, the Commissioner with the French, now charged the Tartars,[33] and, though a handful compared with them, used

---

[32] Ibid.

[33] 'Tartar' or 'Manchu' refers to the fact that the Qing dynasty (1644–1911) was made up of rulers from Manchuria, a region to the North-East of China, which thereafter became part of the Chinese empire. A portion of the Qing army in 1860 was made up of Manchurian warriors, including the cavalry

their sharp swords with such effect that the enemy was compelled to retreat. I had already ordered the 9-pounder battery to open fire, which diverted the attention of the Chinese from the French flank attack, which was further supported by the 99th Regiment and the Dragoon Guards . . .[34]

Hope Grant continues. The Allies were able to overcome the large numbers of Chinese cavalry:

Sir John Michel encountered such heavy masses on his left . . . Probyn, who had only 100 of his regiment with him at the time, was ordered to charge to the front, which he did in most gallant style, riding in amongst them with such vigour and determination that they could not withstand his attack for a moment, and fled in utter consternation . . . The whole of their position was now captured, and I sent a message to the French, who had made a long circuit, to say that I intended to advance and take the town of Chan-chia-wan; but General de Montauban replied that his men were so knocked up that he did not propose to advance any further.[35]

Having defeated the Chinese in this major encounter, Grant notes:

I sent the Irregular Cavalry to make a reconnaissance up to Peking; and on their return, Probyn, who was in command, told me that, along the whole distance, he had seen neither troops nor camps, but that report stated that the Chinese army was in position to the north of the town. He had ridden up to within 200 yards of the walls, which he described as being very high and in excellent repair.[36]

General Ignatief, the Russian ambassador [to Peking], who had throughout followed us up in our march, was now on his way

---

34 Hope Grant, in Knollys, *Life of Sir Hope Grant*, p. 138
35 Hope Grant, in Knollys, *Life of Sir Hope Grant*, p. 138
36 Hope Grant, in Knollys, *Life of Sir Hope Grant*, p. 144

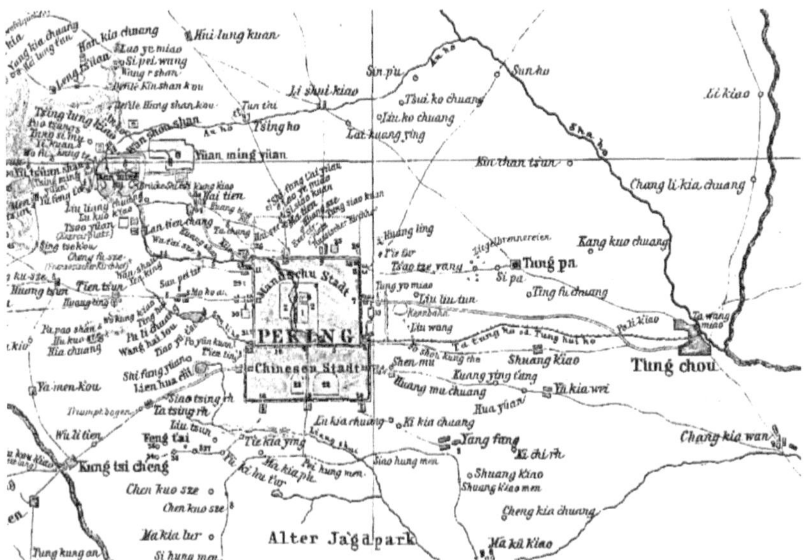

Advance on Peking and the Yuen-ming-yuen. The Allies captured the town of Tungchow (right) then circled north of the city, the British camping there, the French continuing west until they reached the Yuen-ming-yuen (top left)

to Tungchow. He received us very cordially, and showed us an excellent map which he had caused to be made of Peking, wherein was represented every street and house of importance . . . I had it photographed by Signor Beato, whom I had specially allowed to accompany the expedition, and who had previously photographed scenes in India and the Crimea.[37]

After a few days of preparation, the advance to Peking continued:

On the morning of October 5 we marched, the men carrying three days' rations. The country was so intersected with houses and trees that our progress often became difficult. We only

---

[37] Hope Grant, in Knollys, *Life of Sir Hope Grant*, p. 145

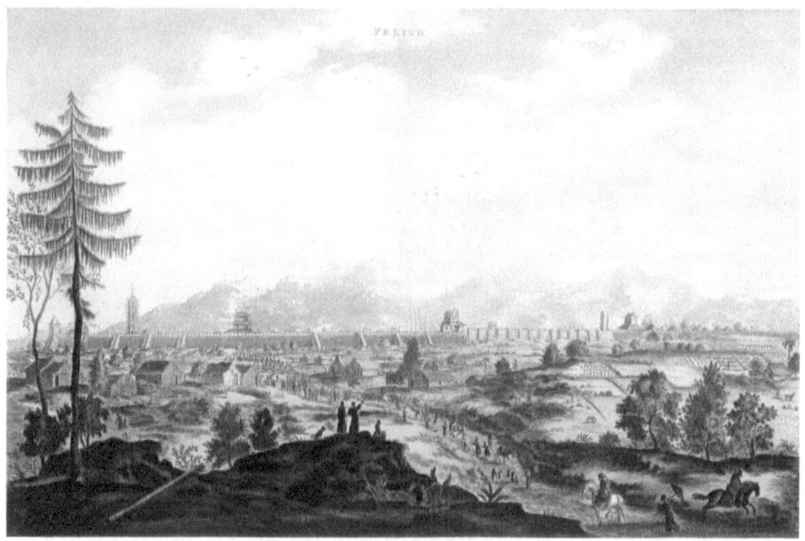

18th century image of Peking, artist unknown

accomplished about five miles, and then encamped round some old brick-kilns about three miles from the north-east angle of Peking. On October 6, after a couple of hours' march, we came upon a large grass-covered ruined rampart [the Yuan Dynasty city wall] where the men halted for breakfast, and where General de Montauban and I agreed that as the army of Seng had apparently retreated, we should make for the Summer Palace, where we should probably find the Emperor or principal Government officials.[38]

Hope Grant sets forth the following account of the capture and looting of the Summer Palace:[39]

---

[38] Hope Grant, in Knollys, *Life of Sir Hope Grant*, pp. 148–49
[39] Hope Grant in Knollys, *Incidents in the China War of 1860*, pp. 126–223 (except as noted)

Capture of the Summer Palace

October 6, 1860:

> It was reported to me that a strong force of Tartar cavalry was moving ahead of us. They retreated, however, so quickly, that we soon lost sight of them amongst the trees and houses; but I was determined to follow them up, and moved my force along a road which led up to a rampart, forming part of the same ruined fortifications before mentioned. Our troops were now much fatigued; and I gave orders for them to encamp near some fine temples situated on a large open plain within the line of works, while I myself went in search of the French general, whom we supposed to be on our left, for the purposes of holding a conference with him. But he was nowhere to be found, and the cavalry which I had sent out as flankers had also disappeared. He and his force must have lost us in the enclosed country. I rode all along the line of ramparts to try and find them, but in vain. It had no doubt been arranged between us that we should ultimately march to the Summer Palace, but I expected that in the first instance the French would follow us.[40]

> Lord Elgin and I took up our quarters in a handsome old temple dedicated to Confucius. As soon as it became dark, I ordered large fires to be lighted to indicate to the French and to our cavalry the position of our camp, in the event of their having lost their way; and the following morning, October 7, I caused a salute of 21 guns to be fired on some rising ground outside the rampart with the same object. Even this was of no avail, and so I sent a squadron of the King's Dragoon Guards to find out the exact position of the Summer Palace, and to ascertain if the French and our cavalry were there. Wolseley, Deputy Assistant Quarter-master General, went with this party, and at 9 A.M. returned with the information that he had found them at Yuen-ming-yuen, the Chinese name of the palace. The French during

---

[40] Hope Grant, in Knollys, *Incidents in the China War*, p. 126

their march had missed our track, and had therefore proceeded
to the Palace.[41]

The Palace, Looting

Hope Grant describes the scene when he arrived at the Palace around
midday on October 7, 1860:

After breakfast Lord Elgin and I rode over to see General de
Montauban. In the distance we at last perceived the Palace beautifully situated amidst gardens and woods, and a range of large
suburbs in front. We passed the park walls by a fine old stately
gateway, and proceeding up an avenue, came to a range of handsome dwellings roofed over with yellow tiles, turned up at the
ends, Chinese fashion. In different parts of the grounds were
forty separate small palaces, in beautiful situations [the true
number of 'scenes' or palace sections in the Yuen-ming-yuen was
over 100]. The park was carefully kept—the footpaths and roads
clean and in excellent order, and there were various pretty pieces
of ornamental water. We found that the French had encamped
near the entrance of the great Audience Hall, and it was pitiful
to see the way in which everything was being robbed.

[*Here, five lines of text in Hope Grant's original journal relating to
the looting of the palace by the French were redacted by Knollys in
his account, as they were, presumably, a strongly worded criticism
of the French*]

The principal palace was filled with beautiful jade stone of
great value and carved in a most elaborate manner—splendid
old China jars, enamels, bronzes, and numerous handsome
clocks and watches, many of which were presents given by Lord
Macartney [British ambassador to China in 1793] and ambassadors from other countries. In a building close to the main palace

---

[41] Hope Grant, in Knollys, *Incidents in the China War*, p.127

were two mounted howitzers which had been made at Woolwich and likewise presented by Lord Macartney to the Emperor. They had apparently been kept as curiosities and never used. They were afterwards sent back to Woolwich. One room only in the Palace was untouched. General de Montauban informed me he had reserved any valuables it might contain for equal division between the English and French. The walls of it were covered with jade stones, and with ornaments of various descriptions.

General de Montauban told me that the only opposition the French had met with was from a small guard at the Palace gates, where two of his officers had been wounded in forcing an entrance. The Emperor and all his grandees had taken flight only a short time previously, and had carried little or nothing away with them.

General de Montauban and I agreed that all that remained of prize property should be divided between both armies. A quantity of articles was set aside for us, and I determined to sell them for the benefit of our officers and men. The French general told me that he had found two 'joes', or staves of office, made of gold and green jade-stone, one of which he would give me as a present to Queen Victoria, the other he intended for the Emperor Napoleon. In a stable we found eleven of Fane's horses, two of Probyn's, and one belonging to the King's Dragoon Guards, all of which had been taken from the escort sent with Parkes.

The next day, October 8, a quantity of gold and silver was discovered in one of the temples of the Summer Palace, and a room full of the richest silks and furs. This treasure was divided in two equal portions between the French and ourselves.[42]

On the same day that the French army left Yuen-ming-yuen [October 9], the Palace was re-occupied by the Chinese authorities, and five Chinese who were taken pillaging were executed by these authorities. My patrols have since found the enclosure constantly closed and the houses not destroyed.

---

[42] Hope Grant, in Knollys, *Incidents in the China War*, pp. 127–130

The Prize Sale

Hope Grant held a sale amongst the British to generate cash to pay his soldiers as 'booty', their reward for winning the campaign. It was common for European armies to be given their share of the 'spoils of war' when a foreign nation was defeated:

> A great change in temperature now took place, and on October 9 the rain fell, and a cold north-east wind set in like the blasts of Edinburgh in March. I went to Sir Robert Napier's quarters, and in the course of the conversation he told me that his aide-de-camp had brought away from the Summer Palace a large piece of gold, which he had found lying on the ground, and which at first had taken for brass ... I therefore decided to issue an order *directing the officers to give up any valuables they might have obtained from the Summer Palace for the purpose of putting them into a general stock* [emphasis added], which would afterwards be divided equally. These directions were accordingly promulgated; and I was greatly pleased to find that a quantity of articles of value were given up by a number of gentlemen who, when they found the French making such havoc among the treasures, had thought there could be no harm in appropriating a few things to themselves. I felt very proud of their liberal and honourable behaviour; and I therefore resolved to take a great responsibility upon myself, and at once to divide the spoil amongst the officers and men of the British force at that moment at Peking. It was sold by auction and, together with what had been handed over to us by the French, realised a good round sum. Colonel Walker, Captain Wilmot, and Captain Anson were appointed prize agents. Their task was a difficult and an arduous one, but they performed it with great ability. Wilmot took sole charge of the accounts, and kept them with admirable regularity.
>
> I declined to take my own share of the proceeds of the sale; and the two generals of division, Sir John Michel and Sir Robert Napier, in the handsomest way waived their claims. Strictly speaking, I had of course no right to take this step [technically any loot belonged to the British Crown]; but considering the lenient laws of France on the subject, and the strict way in which

I had as much as possible prevented the men from plundering, I thought I was justified in thus acting. I wrote to Mr. Sidney Herbert, Secretary of State for War, informing him of my intention, which I hoped, I said, would be approved of. In course of time I received an answer from Lord John Russell, saying that 'I had taken a grave responsibility upon myself'; but her Majesty had, under the circumstances stated by me, approved of what I had done. The sum realised by the sale amounted to about 8,000 pounds, which with 18,000 in specie, handed over to us by the French, was divided into three shares. One share was reserved for distribution among the officers at a more convenient date, and the other two were on the spot divided among the men, so that by the October 16 every private soldier with the army before Peking received about 4 pounds;[43] and thus for the first time, perhaps, British troops rejoiced in the speedy apportionment of the spoils of war.

Numbers of beautiful ornaments were now put up for sale; and the officers, knowing they were to get their prize-money, at once bid freely, and the articles sold for great prices. A small yellow Chinese tea-cup realised 22 pounds. I bought several beautiful jade stones, and also a necklace of the finest green jade, with rubies, which, by a label attached to it, we ascertained had been presented to the Emperor by a famous Tartar chief. Nobody seemed to take a fancy to the ornament, and I paid for it only fifty dollars. I also bought a fine carving of lapis lazuli. The prize committee secured a beautiful gold jug, from which the Emperor of China used to pour rose-water upon his delicate hands, and this they presented to me in a very handsome manner. There were two beautiful large enamel vases which had been given up by Major Probyn,[44] and they were so handsome that I requested him and the prize committee to allow me to send them to the Queen, to which they readily agreed.[45]

---

[43] In 1860 the wage of the private British soldier was 1 shilling per day. 4 pounds therefore represented almost 3 months' pay

[44] Taken from the Audience Hall of the Palace, according to Robert M'Ghee

[45] Hope Grant, in Knollys, *Incidents in the China War*, pp. 190–194

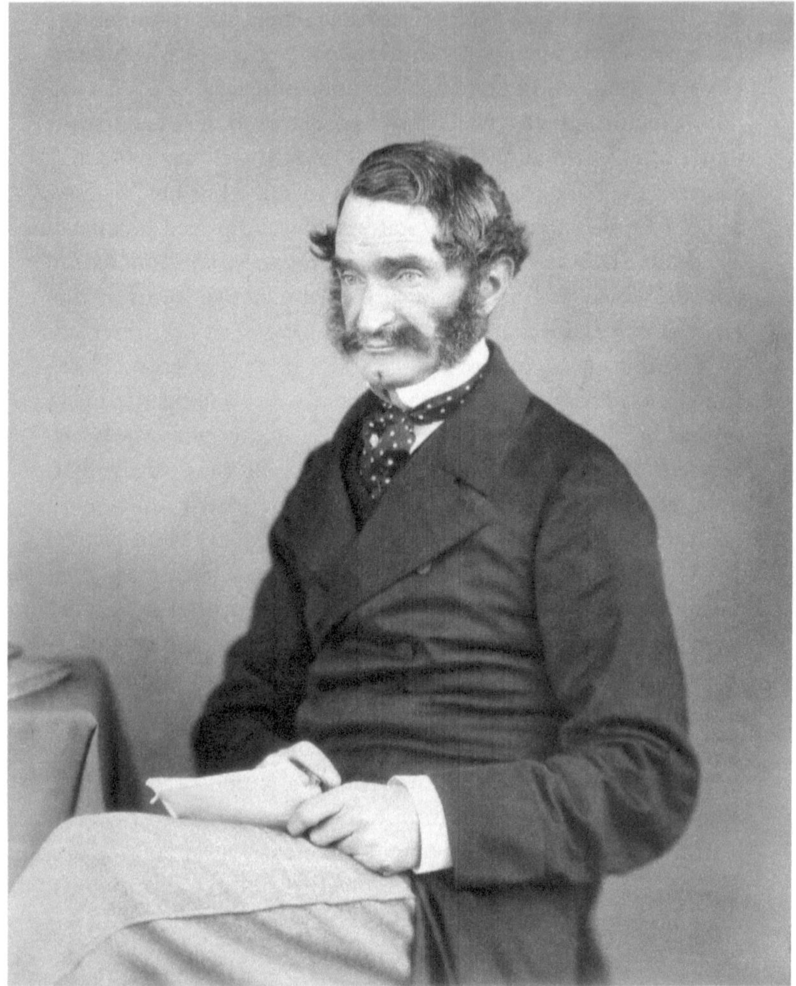

James Hope Grant, 1860, Felice Beato

Aftermath of the Looting

On October 10, the Commissioner Hang-ki begged to be allowed to visit the Summer Palace in company with Parkes. I consented and gave him an escort. Parkes told me it was most distressing to see the poor man. He seated himself upon the edge of one of the little lakes, put his head in between his hands, and burst into tears, saying that everything was lost, and that he should destroy himself . . .

This day, October 10, General de Montauban and I, with the approval of Lord Elgin and Barron Gros, sent a letter to Prince Gong,[46] informing him that unless he chose to give us up one of the gates of the Tartar town, we should batter down an entrance for ourselves . . . The French general and I then started off to the Anting Gate to reconnoiter. White flags were hoisted in every direction and Tartar soldiers lined the parapets; but they took no notice of us, and I rode so close up to the walls that I was able to let my horse drink out of the ditch [a large moat surrounded old Peking].

Late in the evening of the 12th, a letter arrived from Prince Gong for Lord Elgin, wherein he bitterly complained of the state to which the Summer Palace had been reduced, the more unjustifiable, he said, because peace had been concluded. This was false, because it was as yet by no means even certain that the terms would be agreed to. However, by noon on the October 13, the Anting Gate was given up, and Sir Robert Napier marched in with 300 of the 67th Regiment, and with 100 of the 8th Punjab Infantry. The wall round the town, which, as far as I could ascertain, extended over a circumference of sixteen miles, was indeed a wonderful sight. Ancient history tells us the walls of Babylon were so broad that several chariots could be driven abreast on the top of them; but I really think those of Peking must have exceeded them. They were upwards of 50 feet in breadth, very nearly the same in height, in excellent repair, and paved on the top, where, I am sure, five coaches-and-four[47] could with a little management have been driven abreast.[48]

---

[46] In the latter stages of the negotiations Prince Gong, the emperor's younger brother, represented the Chinese government

[47] A 'coach-and-four' was a coach pulled by four horses

[48] Hope Grant, in Knollys, *Incidents in the China War*, pp. 194–195

Funeral of the Prisoners

On October 17 the funeral took place. General de Montauban and his staff were present, The Russian ambassador was, owing to indisposition, unable to attend, but was represented by his suite. Lord Elgin and I were the chief mourners; and a procession, consisting of a troop of the King's Dragoon Guards, a troop of Fane's Horse, and one officer with 25 men from each English regiment, followed in the cartage. The band was furnished by the 6th Rifles. I shall never forget the bitter cold of that day, the hills were white with snow, and a northeast wind blew with the cold piercing blast of winter. We marched down to the cemetery, which was situated just outside the walls of Peking; the coffins were laid in one large grave; the burial service was read without any pomp or display; and we then left the bodies of our poor countrymen in their last sad resting-place.

General de Montauban was not prepared for such a simple ceremony, and expressed his surprise when it was concluded. It was certainly a contrast to the funeral of the French soldiers, which took place on October 28. Of course I attended with many of my officers; and I also sent a squadron of the King's Dragoon Guards. General Ignatieff, his staff, and that of the British embassy, accompanied the procession; but Lord Elgin, owing to a severe attack of influenza, was confined to his house. We passed under the walls of the city, which by this time was in our possession, and through the suburbs, to the old French Jesuit cemetery, a handsome enclosure, wherein was dug one large deep grave, with a ramp down which the coffins were conveyed, thus sparing the awkwardness and annoyance of lowering by ropes, and laid side by side.

Then the ceremony was begun by an old French *abbé*, who had been so long at Peking that he had almost forgotten his own language. Sundry other priests, attended by Chinese boys, assisted all in full canonicals. One of them came forward and made an oration on the merits of the deceased; this was followed by reading the service, accompanied by continual tinklings of bells ... Next Colonel de Bentzman read a funeral oration; and General de Montauban made an excellent speech, winding up by saying, '*Adieu, mes amis, adieu!*' Now came the most singular part of the whole ceremony. Every French soldier present marched past the tomb singly, firing his rifle against the coffins, which in a short time were covered with exploded cartridge-papers. This concluded the funeral.

On October 18, Sir John Michel's division, with the greater part of the cavalry brigade, were marched to the Palace, and set the whole pile of buildings on fire. It was a magnificent sight. I could not but grieve at the destruction of so much ancient grandeur, and felt that it was an uncivilised proceeding; but I believed it to be necessary as a future warning to the Chinese against the murder of European envoys, and the violation of the laws of nations.[49]

The Convention of Peking

October 24:

Lord Elgin started in the afternoon, accompanied by myself and 400 infantry, 100 cavalry, and two bands playing at the head of the procession. I rode alongside our ambassador, who was conveyed in a richly-ornamented sedan-chair to the hall, a distance of three miles. The main street was broad and handsome, but the roadway was atrocious.[50] The centre was raised high and much broken, and was flanked by two minor tracks, almost impassable from holes and pools of water. There was a vast concourse of spectators, men, women, and children, but none of them showed the slightest animosity against us. It took us about an hour to reach the Hall of Ceremonies [inside the Forbidden City], where the treaty was to be signed, and which was quite separate from the Tartar portion of the town. We entered the gates of the hall, marched through gardens, up the paved way, and on approaching the grand entrance were met by Prince Gong and about 500 mandarins, some of whom were princely looking fellows, dressed in silk robes of state.

---

[49] Hope Grant, in Knollys, *Incidents in the China War*, pp. 201–202
[50] Inside the city of Peking

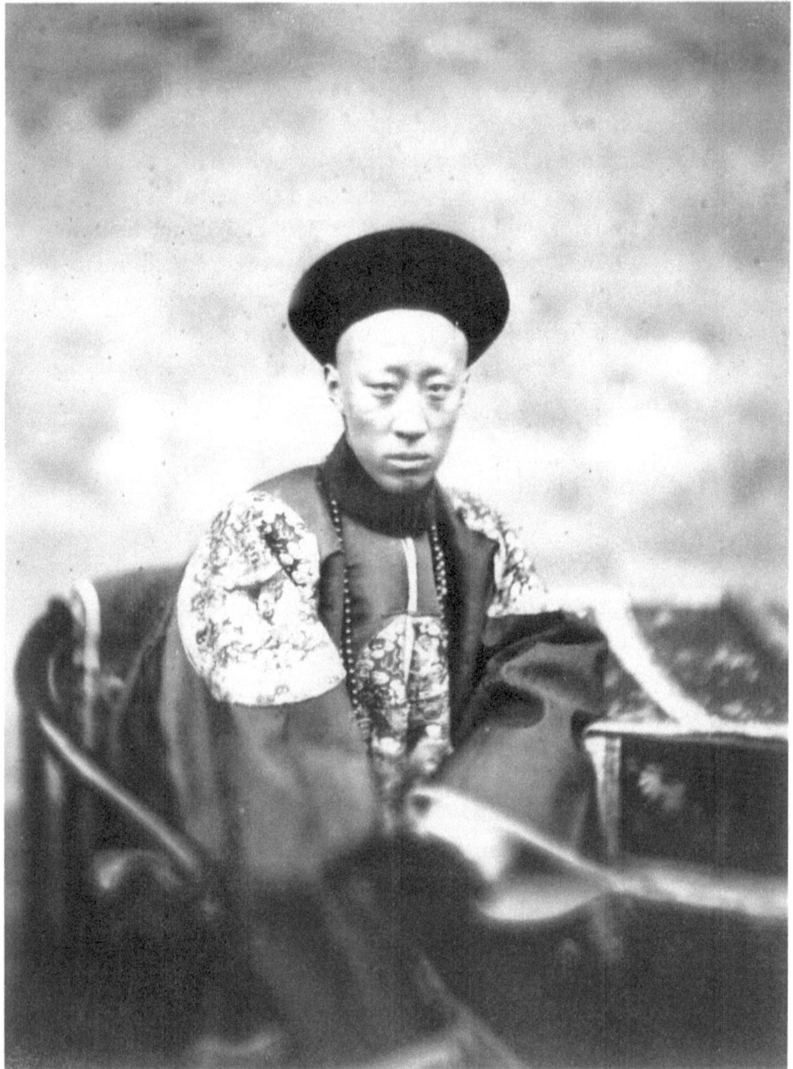

Prince Gong, Peking, November 2, 1860, Felice Beato

The Prince came up and closed his hands in front of his face, according to the Chinese salute; but Lord Elgin returned him a proud contemptuous look, and merely bowed slight, which must have made the blood run cold in poor Gong's veins. He was a delicate gentlemanlike-looking man, evidently overpowered with fear. We were placed in chairs of state, in the most honourable position, the left-hand side, and the convention was laid before the Imperial Commissioner, who on this occasion was invested with full powers. After talking over several points, he signed it and ratified the former treaty [the Treaty of Tientsin, 1858].[51]

Withdrawal of Troops from Peking

The war was now at an end, and the good tidings were conveyed home by my aide-de-camp, Anson. The weather became bitterly cold, some of the hills being covered with snow; and as-according to the information which General Ignatieff, with his usual extreme kindness, furnished me the Peiho would soon become frozen up, and as it would be unsafe to linger at Peking, I was anxious to return as soon as possible to Tientsin, there to make preparations for embarking our troops. In the first instance, therefore, I settled to staff in our return journey on the November 1; but Lord Elgin was very desirous that we should remain eight or ten days longer-by which time, it was hoped, an edict would have arrived from the Emperor at Gehol [modern Chengde, where the Qing emperors had another palace], on the north side of the great wall of Tartary, and 130 miles from Peking, to which he had retreated. Without this edict the proclamation of peace could not be published; and Lord Elgin was very anxious that the terms should be made known to the Chinese at Peking before his departure. I therefore agreed to postpone our march until the 7th and 8th November.

The French General, however, would not wait, and started on the November 1, leaving a battalion of 450 men as a guard for Baron Gros, who had taken up his residence in the town. As a general rule, our soldiers were not allowed to enter Peking, but commanding officers were empowered to give passes to non-commissioned officers and very steady men. Thus order was maintained, and the inhabitants soon gained confidence. In this, as in all Chinese cities, there was a street occupied by

---

[51] Hope Grant, in Knollys, *Life of Sir Hope Grant*, p. 192

curiosity-shops, and it was amusing to see the way these houses were beset with English and French purchasers; and the sums they paid away must have been very great. There were quaint articles of antiquity in arrived silk, jade-stones, enamels, porcelain, and bronzes.[52]

After the treaty was confirmed by the Chinese emperor, Grant recounts the withdrawal from Peking:

On the 9th [November], I marched away from the place with the remaining (Sir John Michel's) division—as did likewise Baron Gros with his escort. Both forces moved off without any attempt to annoy us on the part of the people, who indeed seemed rather sorry than otherwise at our departure. At the end of the third day's march, I hastened on to Tientsin, the place of embarkation, and on the arrival of the infantry, I instantly sent them off. It was fortunate that I thus acted, as, shortly after their departure, the frost set in with such intensity, that in three days the river was frozen over, and navigation rendered impossible. The cavalry waited to the last, as I intended to march them down from Tientsin to Taku, 34 miles distant, in two days, where they were to embark. A severe snowstorm, accompanied with frost, came on, with symptoms of the water communication being closed, and I became very anxious to hurry them down as soon as possible.

I therefore gave orders that the whole distance should be accomplished in one day's march—somewhat to Brigadier Pattle's dismay, who was apprehensive for the wellbeing of his horses. I was confident the journey would not hurt them; and on the November 23, the two regiments—King's Dragoon Guards and Probyn's Horse, I marched independently, each commanding officer taking his own time and making his own arrangements. Every man and horse reached their destination the same evening, although the roads were certainly in a fearful state; and in two days after they were all safely on board ship. The Taku Forts, Tientsin, Shanghai, Hong-Kong, and Canton, were, for

---

[52] Hope Grant, in Knollys, *Life of Sir Hope Grant*, p. 194

the present, occupied by strong garrisons.[53] [Note, Fane's Horse, with some other troops, remained at Tientsin for the winter]

Controversy over Looting by French

On arriving at the Summer Palace, the French Commander-in-Chief persuaded the Brigadier to move on with the English cavalry to more open ground, while the French encamped just outside the Palace, and French guards were put over the entrances to the Palace instead of joint French and English guards, as might easily have been done. [Quoting General Montauban:] 'It was only fair that when we had driven away the Tartars who took refuge at the extremity of the enclosure, I had sentries posted, and directed two officers, with two companies of marine infantry, to protect the Palace from depredation, and to allow nothing to be removed until the arrival of the English commanders, to whom I immediately sent.' Thus there could be no pillage. 'Nothing', the General distinctly asserted, 'had been touched in the Palace when the English arrived.' Evidence to the contrary, however, exists in overwhelming abundance.[54]

Major-General Foley, who was with the French on the night of October 6, asserts: 'I cannot agree that the Palace was not sacked. It is true that General de Montauban gave orders that nothing should be touched until the arrival of Sir Hope Grant; but I saw a woeful difference in the appearance of the wonderously magnificent collections which met the eye upon the first entrance into the Palace, at 6 A.M. on October 7, of General de Montauban, his staff, and myself, and that which presented itself upon our return to the Palace after breakfast about 11:30 A.M. Sir Hope Grant arrived about 1 P.M. Eyewitness: 'At the Palace I found looting going on everywhere. Officers of the French army of all ranks . . . were looting systematically.'[55]

---

[53] Hope Grant, in Knollys, *Life of Sir Hope Grant*, pp. 196–197

[54] Hope Grant, in Knollys, *Life of Sir Hope Grant*, p. 200

[55] Knollys, *Life of Sir Hope Grant*, p. 201

An officer from the headquarters staff stated in his notes that, 'October 7—The General and Lord Elgin rode over to the Palace. The French were looting it from end to end. October 8—The looting in the Palace (is being carried on) to a frightful extent to-day. Many of the things put aside for the Queen had been looted by the French.'[56]

Reaction in Britain

Although often regarded today as an imperialist travesty, at the time the Second China War was viewed as a great success in Britain. According to Knollys: "It is scarcely too much to say that the China War of 1860 may be considered the most successful and the best carried out of England's 'little wars', if indeed the latter term be not a misnomer."[57]

The War Office was concerned about the withdrawal of the British troops:

December 10, 1860

I fear the winter is rigid; but with the stores of Peking under your hand, I hope there is no danger of your being short. I can only wish you God-speed with all my heart. I have perfect confidence in your judgment, and will do my utmost for your assistance, so far as at this distance can be done. The performances of the force under your command are fully appreciated here.

Believe me, &c., Sidney Herbert.[58] [Minister for War]

And they gave a succinct summary of British reaction to the campaign:

January 10, 1861

The public here are, I think, very much pleased at the way in which everything has been done in China—firmness, temper, skill, success. But they are puzzled as to the future. They doubt

---

[56] Knollys, *Life of Sir Hope Grant*, p. 202

[57] Newspaper obituary, publication unknown

[58] Knollys, *Life of Sir Hope Grant*, p. 169

the stability of any treaty, and have a growing and inaccurate assumption. The prisoners had been murdered before the Summer Palace was destroyed. 'Objection to wars which succeed in obtaining indemnities, but which cost far more than the indemnities recovered. I trust, however, that the severity of the lesson, the appearance of a hostile force in Peking, and the rapidity and completeness of the campaign, may produce a lasting effect. In the mean-while, the whole thing has been so well done that, provided it does not recur, everyone seems satisfied.

Believe me, &c., Sidney Herbert[59]

From the point of view of the British Army, the invasion of North China under Hope Grant's command could scarcely have been more successful. The army had won a series of military victories against an adversary numerically far superior. Lines of communication had been maintained and the army well supplied despite being thousands of miles from home, and put ashore with some logistical difficulties. Few men had died in battle or from disease. The objectives for the mission set by the Government had been accomplished. The military units had been withdrawn successfully with only a modest garrison left in China. The army had a further boost to its morale and the public had conquests to celebrate. Most of these accomplishments were credited, appropriately, to Hope Grant.

After his great success in China, Hope Grant was rewarded with the title K.C.B. (Knight Commander, British Empire). After a short stay in the UK which included a return to Scotland and some golf at St Andrews, Hope Grant was quickly given his next command. This was the life of a capable field officer serving in the British Army in the 19th century. He returned to India as the general in command of the Madras Army. In 1865 his long service abroad came to an end and he was recalled to London to serve as Quartermaster General of the home forces in London.

In 1870 Grant became head of the Army at the Aldershot Division in Hampshire. There he set about training the home troops in skills that he knew from his wide field experience in combat were of value. In 1872 he was promoted to the rank of General. In 1874 while still serving in Aldershot, at the age of 67, he became ill. On "November 14, 1874. He

---

[59] Knollys, *Life of Sir Hope Grant*, pp. 170–71

moved up to London for medical treatment, and then it was found that an organic disease, attributable to the privations of campaigns and to prolonged service in the tropics, was rapidly bringing his life to a conclusion. During the last few weeks of his life he was continually occupied in revising with his former A.D.C. the proof-sheets of *The China War*. When he realised his condition, he said, 'I should like to live, but I am quite willing to bow to God's decree that I must die.' He patiently endured much pain, and when the Prince of Wales and the Duke of Cambridge separately intimated a wish to see him, the weary sufferer at first declined, but afterwards altering his mind, said, 'Yes, let them come. It will do them no harm to visit a dying man, and perhaps I may be able to say something to them which will do them good.' Accordingly the interviews took place."[60]

> An hour before he died, a clergyman of the Church of England read to him some of the ministrations for the sick, at the conclusion of which Sir Hope asked for a prayer. Then his mind wandered, and he was once more in India in desperate combat with the sepoys. 'Is there any difficulty in clearing them out?' he frequently and anxiously asked, and was only appeased when his delusion was humoured, and he was assured that all the enemy had been driven away. 'Three times in one day!' he exclaimed, manifestly dwelling on the conflicts of June 19, 1857 before Delhi, of which he was wont to speak as constituting the hardest personal fighting in which he had ever been engaged. 'That position is inaccessible', was his last audible utterance. Shortly after he died—March 7, 1875.
>
> Sir Hope Grant was buried in the Grange Cemetery, Edinburgh. The pall-bearers at the military funeral were his old companions in arms, Generals Sir Frederick Stephenson, Sir John Douglas, Sir Archibald Little, and Generals M'Cleverty, Primrose, and Anderson"[61]

On Grant's tombstone are inscribed the words "A Good Soldier of Jesus Christ."

---

[60] Knollys, *Life of Sir Hope Grant*, p. 340
[61] Knollys, *Life of Sir Hope Grant*, p. 341

Bibliography

Knollys, Henry, *Incidents In The China War Of 1860, Compiled From The Private Journals Of General Sir Hope Grant G.C.B. Commander Of The English Expedition*, Blackwood, Edinburgh, 1875

Knollys, Henry, *Life of General Sir Hope Grant*, Blackwood, Edinburgh, 1894

Palace of Palaces

Robert M'Ghee

"I wandered one day for hours through its cool shades and winding paths, from building to building, and here and there a terrace on the side of a hill, with summer-houses, so cool, each containing suits of richly-furnished apartments, now deserted . . ."

—Robert M'Ghee

"During the winter of 1859–60, I was sitting one evening reading with a companion, by a comfortable fire, in my quarters at home, feeling very well content . . . when the post arrived; I opened one letter, the handwriting of which I knew well to be of a good and firm friend, when, to my dismay, I discovered in the first few lines that I was to join the Chinese expedition . . . If a shell had fallen at my feet through the roof I could hardly have been more startled. 'China for me', I said, holding up the letter; [to] my companion . . . neither of us spoke for some minutes,"[62] Robert M'Ghee. M'Ghee was a chaplain attached to the British Army, and he had received an order to join the ten-thousand-strong British military force that was assembling for a campaign in China. He joined the headquarters staff of General Hope Grant. And, like a number of members of the British and French army, he responded to public interest in the campaign by publishing his memoir of events in China. Each of these memoirs, of which a number are examined in this book, offer first-hand accounts of the Summer Palace

---

[62] M'Ghee, pp. 2–3

before its destruction. M'Ghee's memoir and his detailed description of the Palace, was a revelation in Britain when it was published in 1862.

Robert James Leslie M'Ghee[63] was born in Carlow, Ireland, about fifty miles from Dublin, in 1819. His parents were the Reverend Robert J. M'Ghee, and Mary Andrews William Stanley. The family were of the Protestant faith and therefore most likely of Scots-Irish descent. M'Ghee's father was a prominent member of the (Protestant) Church of Ireland and in the 1830's he campaigned strongly against the influence of the Catholic Church. The elder M'Ghee was educated at Trinity College, Dublin and Robert followed in his father's footsteps, graduating with a degree in theology in 1841. His life would probably have passed unnoticed by history had it not been for his involvement in the Second Opium War.

In 1839, at the age of twenty, M'Ghee married Eleanor Calhour. Upon graduation in 1841 he was ordained as a minister and was appointed curate of the parish of Tydavnet. In 1842, he moved jobs and became the chaplain of the Magdalen Asylum in Dublin. In 1844, through further studies, he received his M.A. degree from Trinity. That same year he became pastor at the Parish Church at Mullavilly.

In 1850 the restless M'Ghee moved to England and took up the positon of rector of High Roding in Essex. Then in 1855, he joined the British Army with the rank of Assistant Chaplain to the Forces. In 1858 he was promoted to Chaplain to the Forces. It was in this capacity that he heard the news that he was to be assigned to the expeditionary force leaving for China. He was, it seems, a reluctant participant in the campaign.

Getting to China

In the spring of 1860, like the other members of the expedition that were posted from England to China, M'Ghee began a long sea voyage from Southampton, England to Hong Kong. Here he describes a portion of that journey, across Egypt to the Red Sea:

> At Alexandria it was hot, although but a few days before we had
> left France, bound in a most severe frost; at Cairo, where we

---

[63] Whilst several sources state the reverend's name as *McGhee*, in his book he spells it as *M'Ghee*, therefore this is the correct spelling

were detained two days, it was hotter still. Our delay arose from a storm on the Red Sea so violent that our ship could not receive the mails or passengers until it abated. Of course I was not sorry for the detention, which gave me an opportunity of seeing something of the first Eastern city which I had ever entered.[64]

M'Ghee had never left the British Isles. All of the sights and experiences were new. Having sailed down the Red Sea, the fleet reached Aden and from there, on to the Indian Ocean:

Aden appeared to me more like the evil part of Hades, as one's imagination paints it, than any other place. Its sterile rocks evidently of volcanic formation, and those innumerable black boys, like imps of darkness.[65]

The fleet ported at Galle, Ceylon, which was unfamiliarly tropical:

Galle . . . was my first introduction to tropical life . . . all that I had read of it and the pictures and illustrations which I had seen, failed to give any adequate idea of its luxuriance, its deep colouring, and the load of varied vegetable life. The steaming soil must groan as it produces it. Towering above all are seen the tall coconut trees laden with fruit and standing close, as their stem is branchless. Underneath [was] a matted jungle of spice trees and towering shrubs, rich in various colours and in fragrance.[66]

In North China

As the senior pastor with the British expeditionary force, M'Ghee was attached to commander-in-chief, General Grant. As described earlier, in that role he was at hand in October 1860 when the general's headquarters staff were the first amongst the British to visit the captured Summer Palace. Because of that privilege M'Ghee has left for posterity what is perhaps the best account of the Palace from any British writer. While Lord

---

[64] M'Ghee, p. 5

[65] M'Ghee, p. 8

[66] M'Ghee, p. 9

Elgin and his generals were busy trying to determine the next military steps to defeat the Chinese, how to protect and deploy their troops and how to divide up loot, M'Ghee (and one or two other members of the staff) were free to wander and observe the great Yuen-ming-yuen palace and take detailed notes that he later turned into his account of the campaign. As a man of God, M'Ghee was more concerned about observing the Palace and its grounds than looting them and enriching himself in the process, or it would seem so.

The morning of October 7:

> Early next morning a salute of twenty-one guns was fired from the bund in order to let the allies know our whereabouts, and to find, if possible, our lost cavalry, but a more certain method was adopted at the same time. Colonel Wolseley, with an escort of sowars [sikh soldiers], is sent off to the Yuen-ming-yuen to seek for them, as it is just possible the French may have gone there. Nothing loth, he starts off at daybreak. He only knows the direction of the Palace; that is quite enough for him, rather more, in fact, than he requires; if there is an officer in the army that can find his way, he is the man. The Tartars may be in force in the neighbourhood; no doubt they may. It would give double pleasure to his ride if there was a good smack of danger about it. He returned with the news that he has found the French at the Yuen-ming-yuen, and our cavalry in the neighbourhood.[67]

M'Ghee was one of the party who rode out to meet the French at the Palace later on the morning of October 7:

> Between twelve and one o'clock on Sunday Lord Elgin [Chief British Minister in China] and Sir H. Grant rode out to the Yuen-ming-yuen with a strong escort of sowars and some of the King's Dragoon Guards. Lord Elgin was accompanied by his suite, and Sir H. Grant by his personal staff, Sir R. Napier and staff, and General Crofton and staff, one or two of the Head-quarter staff, and some naval officers. After a brisk ride

---

[67] M'Ghee, p. 201

of some six miles, guided by Colonel Wolseley, they arrived at the Palace.[68]

The party who accompanied Lord Elgin and Sir H. Grant on the first visit to the Palace were detained beside the water for several hours at General Montauban's [the French commanding officer] request; he sent a message to Sir Hope, begging that he would not bring a large party into the Palace, as none of the French officers had yet been permitted to enter [this was not quite accurate, as it transpires] . . . The Commander-in-Chief had a long conference with General Montauban, and was assured that nothing had been touched. It was agreed that, prize agents being appointed, they should select such articles as they deemed fitting as prize for each army, and that, when their selection was complete, the rest of the property might be taken as individual spoil.[69]

M'Ghee describes the approach to the Palace and the magnificent Audience Hall which stood directly inside the front gate:

It [the Palace] is approached by a grand causeway road, which divides a large sheet of water. The outer gate is not very imposing, it is of the same form as that used for all large public buildings in China . . . Inside the first entrance-gate there is a large, flagged courtyard, some hundred yards wide by eighty deep; at each side, both within and without, are guard-rooms. Fronting the grand entrance stands another gate of similar construction; then another court, in which stands the 'Hall of Audience', a magnificent building, in which, in his imperial chair, the Emperor gave audience to those few and great ones who were honoured by admission into the 'Vermillion' presence . . . This hall [measured] . . . about 120 feet, its breadth about 80 . . .

A large and most elaborate plan of the Palace gardens nearly covered the wall at one end of the room.[70] About half way down

---

[68] M'Ghee, p. 202

[69] M'Ghee, p. 205

[70] This plan of the garden was painted by the Jesuit priest Castiglione for the Qianlong emperor

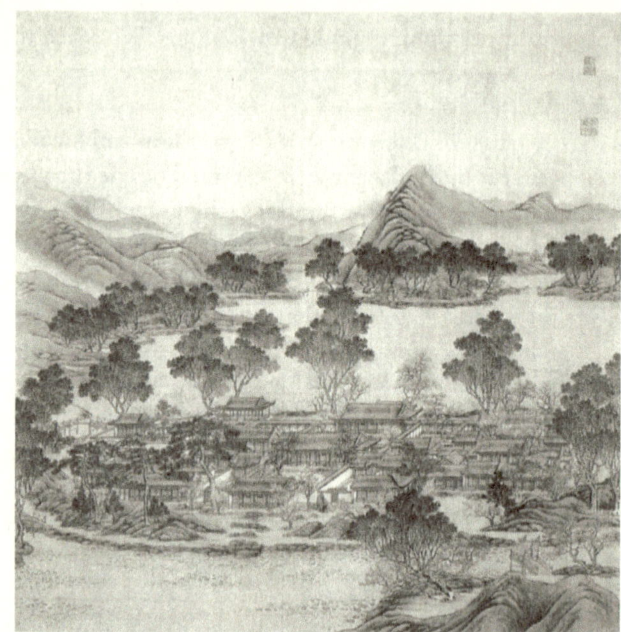

The Imperial Island, home to the emperor's private apartments, one of the Forty Views of the Yuen-ming-yuen, 1744

one side stood the imperial dais, which was ascended by three steps, and upon it was placed the chair of state, richly carved in dark wood, and cushioned in rich embroidery. The ceiling was of wood, deeply carved, very rich and massive; and there was an air of state, a solemn dignity, about the place which impressed you not a little, and rendered it most suitable to the purpose for which it had been built."[71]

The Imperial Apartments

The party moved past the Audience Hall to the so called 'Imperial Island', which contained the Imperial Apartments:[72]

---

[71] M'Ghee, pp. 203–204

[72] When originally designed by the Yongzheng Emperor, this section of the palace was laid out as 'nine islands', which symbolized the nine continents of the Chinese world. The islands were built around a central lake (the 'Back Lake') and each island had a special purpose. The 'imperial' island was the principal island and it contained the private apartments of the imperial family

Behind this hall [the Audience Hall] was a passage leading to the right and left, one side of it being formed by the wall of the Hall of Audience, the other by a large rockery. Following the path to the right you found yourself in a labyrinth of courtyards and buildings, full of all sorts of curiosities, silks, and stores of every kind of property; while proceeding to the left, and turning again to the front, you arrived at an artificial piece of water,[73] one of hundreds in the grounds, and nearly all connected by a slow-flowing stream, surrounded by rockeries and bridged at each end, where it narrowed.

I need hardly say that all around noble trees of various sorts cast their luxurious shade; and on the opposite side of this miniature lake [the Front Lake] stood the imperial apartments, entered by none save members of the imperial family. If you can imagine fairies to be the size of ordinary mortals, this then was fairy-land. Never have I beheld a scene which realized one's ideas of an enchanted land before.[74]

And now let us take a look at the Palace [i.e. at the imperial apartments]. They were built, as every Chinese house is, from the lowest to the highest, in what I must call the courtyard plan. You enter through a passage and one or two doors, one of the state-rooms, furnished in the richest manner with tables and seats of black or very dark wood—ebony, or a wood of equal beauty[75]—carved in the most elaborate manner, so that figures and landscapes are made to stand out completely, and are often only attached to the background by some one or two points, which you do not see until you look for them.

No more perfect display of the art of wood-carving could be conceived. Wainscots of the same adorned the walls, while the seats and couches were draped with the richest silk-embroidery, all of the imperial yellow, and adorned with dragons in gold.

---

[73] The 'Front Lake'

[74] M'Ghee, pp. 204–205

[75] Either zitan, the most precious of woods in imperial China, reserved for the emperor, or Indian rosewood; both of which are almost black in color

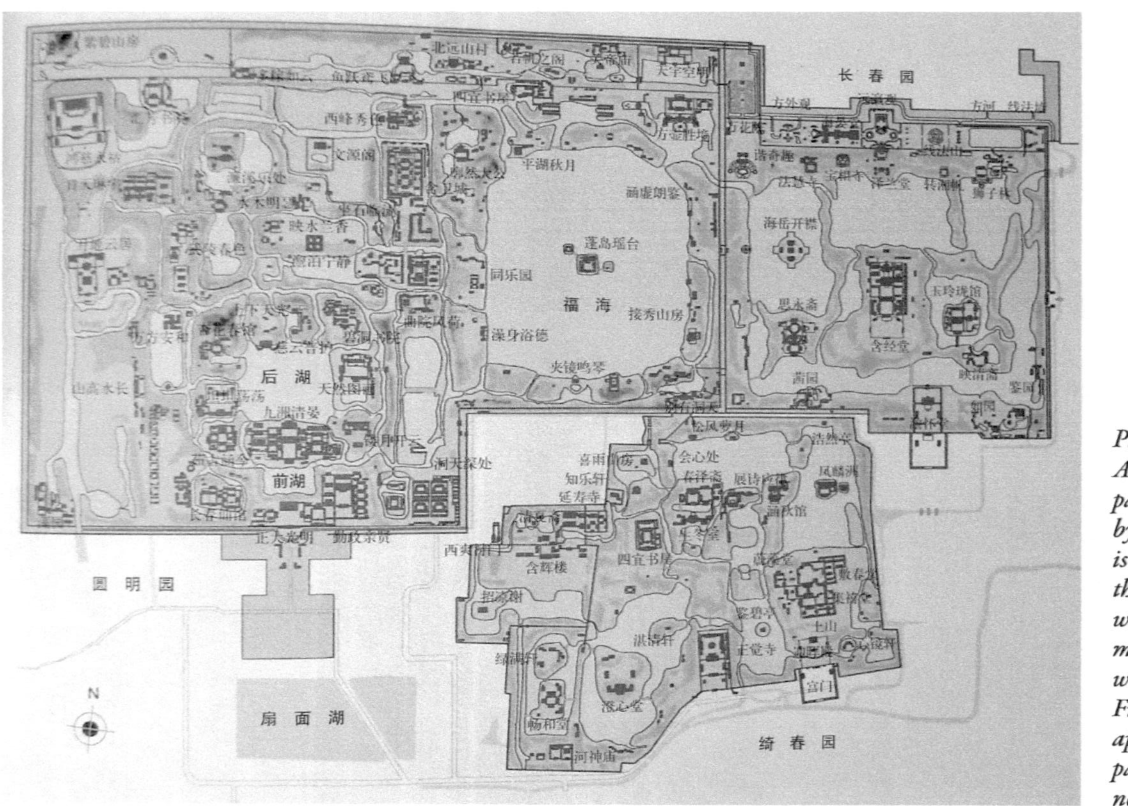

Plan of the Yuen-ming-yuen. A vast series of gardens and palace 'scenes' surrounded by walls. The main entrance is shown on the left half of the plan, one third of the way up the plan. Behind the main gate, in a direct line were: the Audience Hall, the Front Lake and the imperial apartments. The European palaces were to be found in the northeast (upper right) corner

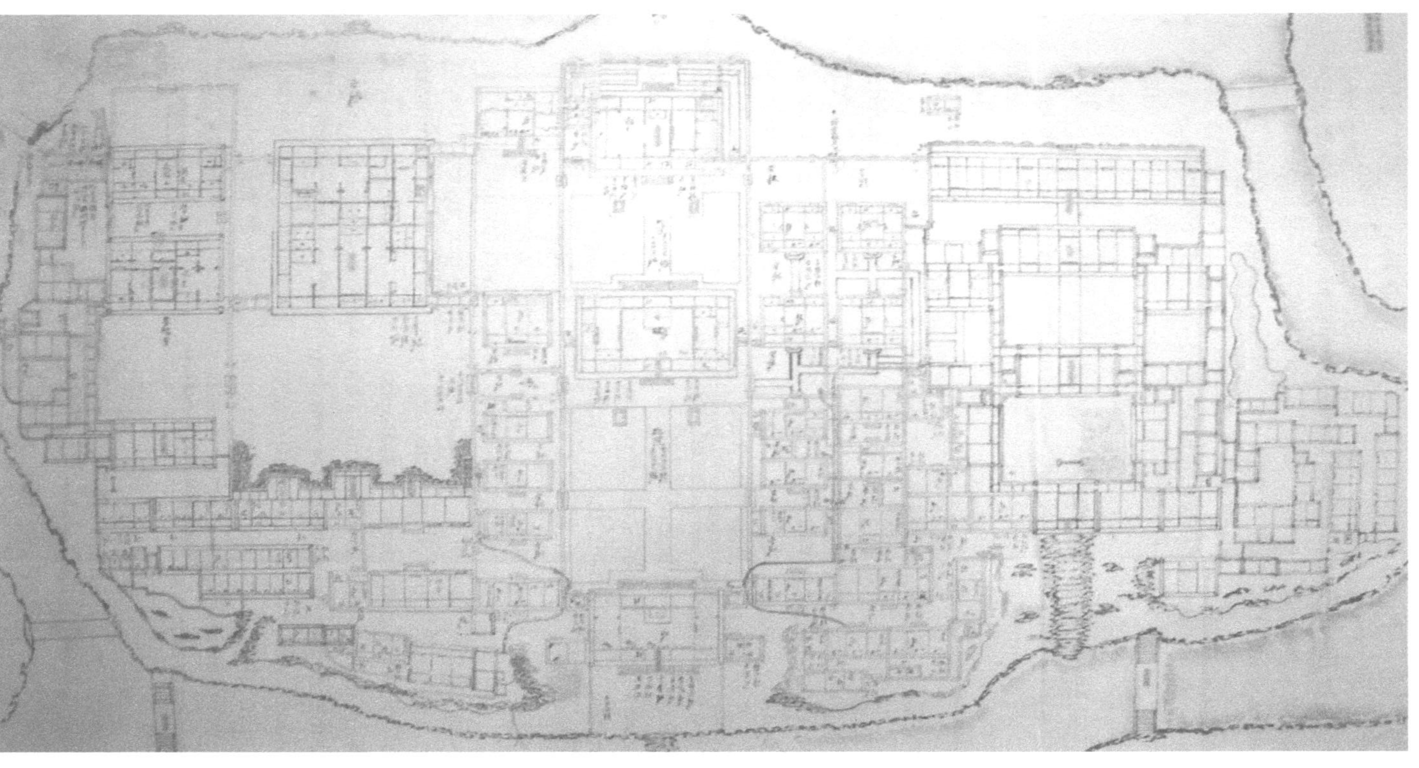

Plan of the Imperial Apartments

On the opposite side of the courtyard, about fifty feet square, and flagged with marble, stood another room, of larger dimensions, and furnished in a similar manner; and all round it, on tables and stands, were placed vases and cups of the most choice and beautiful jade stone, china, and enamel, clocks, gilt and many of gold, several of French manufacture; mirrors of large size set in costly frames, while splendid glass chandeliers hung from the ceilings. Room here opened off room; and while they varied in size and shape, the style and furniture were similar.[76]

This suite of apartments stretched right and left; the extreme left of the building was sacred to the ladies of the court; and here were some exquisite boudoirs, fitted up with the perfection of Eastern luxury and taste; and a spiral staircase, the only one in the building, led to a similar suite of apartments over-head, a great part of whose ornament consisted in the most rare and costly of Chinese works of art, with a few French in manufacture as in design and taste. These suites of apartments fronted another sheet of water [the Back Lake], surrounded by rockeries on a gigantic scale (all planted), and opened out upon a graveled walk or drive, while, behind them, small courtyards innumerable were surrounded by store-rooms filled with boxes of furs, china, embroidered dresses, shoes (which proved that the ladies of the palace were not cursed with small feet—I mean Chinese small feet[77]).[78]

The furs were ermine (but not valued much by us, as the tails were wanting), sables, squirrel, un-born camel, a very curious and beautiful grey skin with very minute curls of hair, unborn lamb, black astrakhan, and others which none of us appeared even to have seen before, and which we were unable to name. But the imperial robes; how am I to describe them? Rich silk, blue or yellow, brown or purple, covered with delicately-worked embroidery, exquisite in colour and shading, as unrivalled in execution, with the golden, five-clawed dragon blazoned over the embroidery. Truly these imperial dresses were a sight which

---

[76] M'Ghee, p. 208

[77] Han Chinese women had their feet bound in order to make them smaller. Manchu and Mongolian women did not practice foot binding

[78] M'Ghee, pp. 208–209

conveyed lofty ideas of the splendor of the court to which they belonged.[79]

To the right of the imperial apartments the buildings of the Palace stretched for about half-a-mile, and consisted of the residences of officials, with servants' apartments, and rooms full of silk dresses, in which, having been pulled out of their boxes and thrown on the floor, you would sink above your knees as you entered the room.[80]

Large rooms there were too, with shelves divided into compartments all round, and in each compartment was placed some work of Chinese art, in jade stone, enamel, bronze, or china, or some valued gift of the 'barbarian' relics of an English mission of the last century, or some importation from France through Russia, each article carefully labelled, and the label describing, not only its age and origin, but the exact position in the room which was assigned to it.

In this wing of the building also the silk was stored, and there seemed to be enough of it to clothe half the population of Peking. When the Palace was opened to indiscriminate plunder, these rolls of silk attracted much attention from the Sikhs, who carried them off in cartloads; they sold them in camp for two dollars a roll at first, but their value was soon raised to from ten to twenty dollars. Various were its colours and texture, satin or silk, plain or figured, white, blue, yellow (the Imperial colour), purple, stone, or fawn colour; there they were to be had for carrying away, or if you chose to buy them, 8s. 4d. for fifteen or twenty yards; all good husbands who were there have no doubt got a supply for their wives; brothers and cousins, too, have no doubt done likewise for the fair ones who belong to them at home. Oh! What a pleasure it is to look at a gift, whatever it may be, which you intend to present to some dear one at home, and to imagine the pleasure with which it will be received.[81]

---

[79] M'Ghee, p. 209

[80] M'Ghee, p. 210

[81] M'Ghee, pp. 210–211. This passage suggests that M'Ghee was a customer for silk

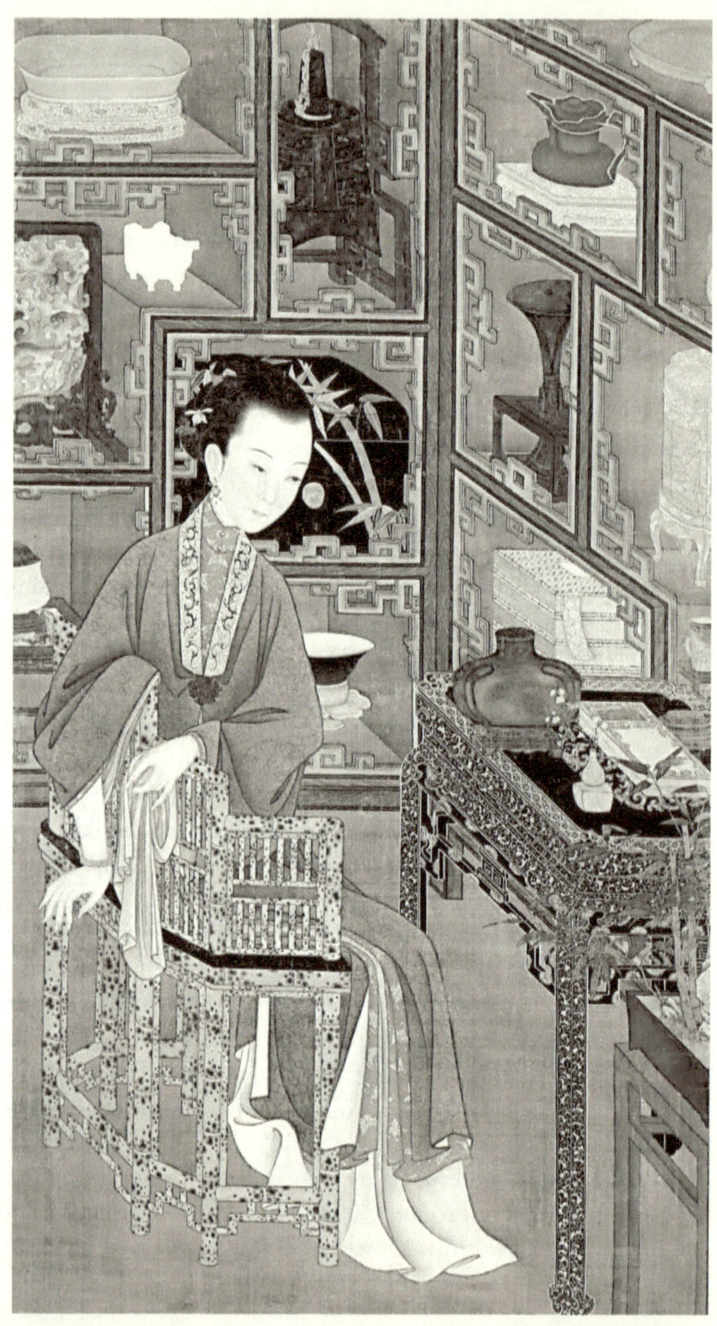

The Imperial Apartments. Painting entitled: One of the Twelve Beauties, concubines of Yongzheng, before he became emperor—early 18th century

The Imperial Park

Wandering beyond the Imperial Island, M'Ghee recorded his observations of the balance of the Yuen-ming-yuen palaces and gardens:

> The grounds extended for six or seven miles in every direction, and further towards the hills.
>
> If you can, you must imagine a vast labyrinth of picturesque rocks and noble timber, lakes and streams, summer-houses roofed with porcelain of the imperial yellow, theatres and their store-houses, filled with all the paraphernalia for masquerades upon a gigantic scale, one theatre and its belongings covering from five to ten acres of ground, all richly planted around; temples more numerous still, full of quaint deities (some of them, as it has since turned out, of gold), and every building within view of at least one other, and all these filled with works of Chinese art of great age, beauty, and value, and in the background a range of hills, their outline cut clear against the sky [the Western Hills]; you must think of all the best gifts of nature, in colour and in form, of trees, shrubs, and wild flowers; wood, water, rock, hill, and mountain, you must add; then deck the scene with all the world-famed skill of the Celestial in landscape gardening, thrown in here and there so well that it looks like nature's own hand; scatter those beautiful buildings round, with their gorgeous roofs peeping through the dark forest timber; see, there is an imperial stag bounding across your paths; conjure up the quaint old Chinese bridge here and there, to carry you across the feeder of some placid lake, with its ornamental waterfowl: and you may be able to form some very faint and indistinct idea of the Yuen-ming-yuen, which you can no more conceive than I can describe.[82]
>
> I wandered one day for hours through its cool shades and winding paths, from building to building, and here and there a terrace on the side of a hill, with summer-houses, so cool, each containing suites of richly-furnished apartments, now deserted, most of them untouched, although I met scores of Chinese carrying away heavy loads of plunder from the outbuildings of the

---

[82] M'Ghee, pp. 211–212

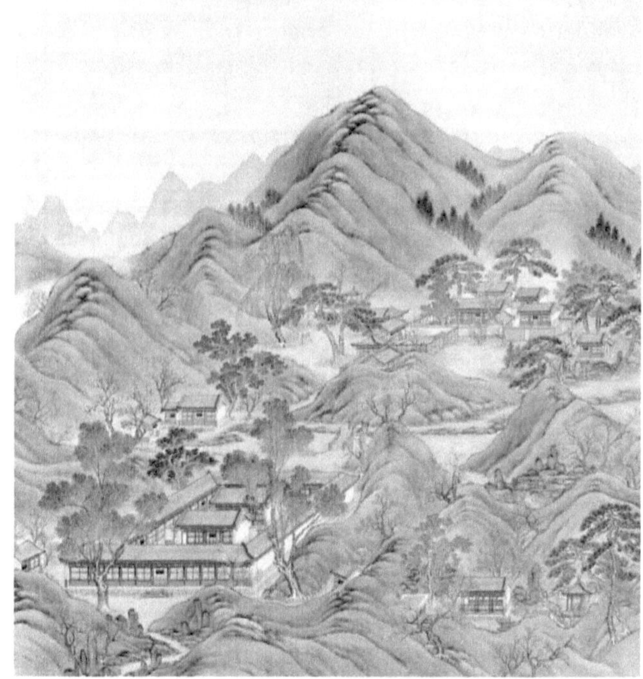

*One of
the Forty
Views of the
Yuen-ming-
yuen, 1744*

Palace (chiefly cloth and china). 'Come,' I said to S, who was
with me, 'let us look at this place.' We ascended a flight of some
seventy or eighty marble steps, a gentle stream of water at each
side falling into a large marble basin at the bottom, bridged with
marble also; we reached a terrace surrounded by dark pine trees
[this scene was in the northeast of the Palace, bordering the
European Palace section]; in the centre stood a temple, a large
circular building; we entered it, there was the triple Buddha,
and before him the ashes of the sticks of incense, the last that
ever were to smoke at his shrine; he was, or rather they were,
huge, and in gilded wood; numerous smaller shrines were placed
round the building, with smaller deities.

'What is this?' said S;[83] 'gold, is it not?' taking up with some
little difficulty a deity about two feet high.

---

[83] Could this be Robert Swinhoe, another member of Hope Grant's staff?

'Gold, my dear fellow, do you think gold is so plentiful in China that they have golden gods in a remote temple like this, where anyone might carry them off?'

'It's precious heavy then,' he said, 'if it is not gold, let us smash him and see;' and down went the divinity, with a heavy thud on the marble floor, but no sign of a smash in him.

'I'm sure it is gold,' said S.

'Bring it home then,' said I, laughing.

'I wish I had that lazy Sikh here,' was his rejoinder, as he stood looking at his idol, 'I should make him carry it.'

So we left it there, but when the burning came it was found, or another like it, and was brought home, and it made a fortune. I feel sure that multitudes of such things were thrown away and burnt, because it was incredible that they could be made of gold, and yet they were. On another shrine the incense-burners were of iron, plated with gold; on another, of rich enamel of every colour in the rainbow, with gilded mounting, while every shrine was draped and curtained with yellow satin, richly embroidered.[84]

Proceeding along the terrace we arrived at a summer-house embosomed in shade—and by a summer-house I don't mean a small octagonal or hexagonal building, with a deal table and some benches for the convenience of a picnic party, distempered walls, rectangular windows (such as Ruskin loves), and a slate roof. Nor do I mean a bower covered with moss, and roses and jessamine trained over it, and thatched with reeds or heather. No, I mean a house with ten or twenty rooms in it, sleeping rooms and sitting rooms, all fully furnished and fit for the immediate reception of a nobleman's or gentle man's family; yes, or of an emperor—for to some one of these cool retreats we are told that Hein Fung [Xianfeng] loved to retire and pass his

---

[84] M'Ghee, pp. 212–213

days with one or more of the reigning favourites. Let us enter. The door is fastened inside, never mind, a vigorous kick sends it flying open from the centre, and we stand in a marble courtyard.

Two small rooms, one on each side, where the wooden sword denotes the eunuch's dwelling; three steps of marble opposite bring us to another door. 'Your turn now, S'; and in it goes, for S has a strong leg. Another marble courtyard, larger than the first, and steps ascending, for it is built on the face of a hill, and the house is terraced; two long buildings at each side containing three rooms each, those at the ends opening off the centre one, which is a sitting-room furnished just like the Palace, dark or black carved wood and crimson or yellow embroidered satin, knickknacks and ornaments the same. What would Wardour Street say if it were here? Why the furniture of this one summer-house would sell, at home, for a prince's ransom. One larger building fronts the entrance of the courtyard; bang goes the door; in we go.

Much larger rooms, three of them on the same plan, a splendid French clock in gold enamel, the furniture is more gorgeous, the ornaments more rare, and in a carved cupboard in the wall there are boxes of the imperial yellow china, each cup wrapped in soft paper and in a compartment by itself, so precious is it deemed. Some, of the finest 'crackle',[85] so minute that you must get a good light to see it in. Some with the five-clawed dragon finely worked in it, not visible when you look directly at it. Some curious old grey 'crackle', too; imperial scepters in green and white jade stone; two tall jars in porcelain, painted in the richest colours, representing a series of hunting scenes in which the tiger and stag are pursued. Tablets adorn the walls, one or two yards square, in which sylvan scenes of landscape or of hunting are represented, in which the figures, trees, water, beasts, &c, are made of jade stone, green and white, and of other coloured stones.

Sleeping-rooms to the right and left, satin embroidered hangings, and the raised bed-place universal in China, which

---

[85] A form of glaze used on some pieces of Chinese porcelain that created a 'crackled' appearance. In 1860 Western understanding of the Chinese arts was generally quite simplistic

doubtless the imperial person has e'er now pressed. A garden adorns the centre of the courtyard; some of the shrubs are still in flower. Trees from outside over hang it all, while a stream, cool as the rock it springs from, flows through it, caught here and there in deep, pure white marble basins. To the right and left passages leading to other buildings of similar stamp, and some storerooms, one filled by several gilded chairs of state, another with large enamels, a third with quaint masks and lanterns for an evening entertainment; but if I was to write a whole book on the subject I could not describe it, nor could you even then imagine it. Reluctantly we descended again from the terrace and fairy palace, and wandered along the shores of a lake; but time (in our case) was short and art was long.

Here, lying at the bottom near the shore, were porcelain jars and vases which had been thrown there by some overloaded plunderer, to be brought away at some more convenient time; and standing above his middle in water, is an unfortunate coolie, bleeding from a wound in his chest, which he has received who can tell how, but no signs that we can make will induce him to come on shore. As we near the Palace again, we meet large parties of Chinese, plundering their own Emperor; we examine their baskets and bundles—china vases, felt, and coarse wadded clothing, are all that we can find; they have not got into the best buildings; they are afraid of us, or else they have gone in for the things which will be most useful to themselves, or are least likely to be recognized, in which case, off go their heads at once. But we must get back to Peking for this time; we shall see the Palace more than once perhaps again.[86]

Looting

On the first afternoon, when the advance party entered the Imperial Apartments, the British began to loot:

Sir H. Grant gave permission to such officers as were of the party to carry away a memento with them—anything they

---

[86] M'Ghee, pp. 213–216

pleased, provided that the prize-agents did not object. Of this privilege everyone appeared to avail themselves; and while one became enamoured of a jade stone vase, another lost his heart to an embroidered robe, while a third, with an eye to the future, selected a fur-coat. Strange, is it not, but nevertheless true, that we sometimes cannot see things that are being done under our very nose! General Montauban was no doubt sincere in his assertion, that 'nothing had been touched'; but it was passing strange that he could not have seen that his own camp outside the palace-gate was blazing with silk of every hue, and the richest embroidery; nor did he know that, at the same moment, you could buy a richly-jewelled watch, enamelled and set round with pearls or brilliants, or with both, for five or six and twenty dollars.

How cheap must watches have been in France when the army started for China! for how could they have got them from the Palace when General Montauban declared that he had placed sentries all round it? But how came it that when the officers who accompanied Sir H. Grant were detained outside the imperial apartments, they were accosted by French officers passing and repassing them, thus, 'Mais pourquoi n'entrez-vous pas, messieurs, ce n'est pas de tendu d'entrer, mais regardez;' and diving into the capacious pockets of his overalls, he would produce a bar or plate of gold. 'C'est d'or, voyez-vous', and he would proceed to bend it to prove its ductility. Now, General Montauban did not know a word of all this, although it went on under (as I have said) his very nose; nor did he know that although not in the imperial apartments, never-the-less in other rooms of the Palace in which there was valuable property to any amount, the French gunner was to be seen with a large sack, filling it with all sorts of things which struck his fancy.[87]

And while on this subject, which has been so much canvassed at home, I add and am moreover prepared to assert that by far the greatest part of the property acquired by officers and soldiers in the English force was purchased from the French; so that were you to ask an officer where he had procured such or such a curio, or dress, or watch, the chances were five to one

---

[87] M'Ghee, pp. 206–207

that he would tell you that he bought it in the French camp.
We had Indian allowances, and they had the plunder, and we
bought some of it; with very few exceptions, no officer or soldier
in the English force got a single article of intrinsic value from
the Palace; although everything that came from the place has no
doubt a decided value from its associations; but the difference
was just this, that while the British officer looked for articles of
virtue, as a memento of the place for himself, or for his friends
at home, the Frenchman had an eye to more solid advantages,
and he reaped them.[88]

After the looting was complete, by order of General Sir Hope Grant
there was a prize sale in the British camp on October 11 and 12, the proceeds of which were to be distributed among officers and men. M'Ghee
describes the goings on:

Sir H. Grant … gave up all share in the matter himself, an
example followed by both the generals of division … Every
officer who had visited the Palace had brought away something
with him as a memento of the place, and had probably not forgotten the 'old folks back home', as everyone would expect a
trophy of some sort or another. These things were all called in
by the Commander-in-Chief, and ordered to be sold by auction, the proceeds to be distributed in prize-money. Two non-
commissioned officers were selected as auctioneers; the prize
agents … in a few days arranged everything; a few articles were
returned to each officer at a valuation, if he chose to take them,
and everything else was ticketed for sale.
There was the usual amount of amusement that an auction
affords when everyone knows everyone else; it went off very mer-
rily, and though the things appeared to sell for very high prices,
still they did not reach anything like the value they would bear
in Europe. Ten, twenty, or thirty pounds for a piece of jade stone,
a bowl, or a cup, perhaps, was nothing extraordinary; enamels
too, were in request, and as one gallant officer was understood
to have an unlimited commission from Baron Rothschild, you
may suppose that there was a good deal of competition, and fur

---

[88] M'Ghee, p. 207

dresses were sold from ten pounds up to fifty. The rolls of silk which had been taken from the store-rooms were assorted in lots, an imperial yellow or a silk of more than ordinary value was placed in.[89]

Treatment of the Prisoners

M'Ghee tells of the release of the prisoners who had survived captivity:

I never saw a more pitiable sight than the return of the sowars [Indian soldiers]; having read their own statements, you can well imagine the state of those who survived such brutal and cruel treatment. Hardly able to walk they dragged their legs along and held their hands before their breasts in a posture denoting great suffering, and such hands as they were, crumpled up and distorted in every possible way, some with running sores at the wrists, some in which the bloated appearance caused by the cords had not yet gone away, and some were shriveled like a bird's claw and appeared be dead and withered.[90]

Funeral of the Prisoners

Several of the British emissaries and their guard had died in captivity. When their bodies were returned, M'Ghee, as the senior pastor, presided over their funeral service:

On Wednesday, October 17, the funeral of Messrs. Bowlby, Anderson, De Norman and private Phipps took place. The Russian Embassy had given permission in the kindest manner that their burial-ground should be used to the interment of those unfortunate victims of Chinese treachery and barbarity ... The Russian burial-ground is outside the north wall of the city, about a quarter mile from it ... it is walled and plastered and an old Chinaman lives there and takes care of it ... The funeral was an impressive sight. Lord Elgin and Sir H. Grant were chief

---

[89] M'Ghee, pp. 293–294
[90] M'Ghee, p. 252

mourners; every one made a point of attending . . . The funeral service was read by me, as principal chaplain, and the priest of the Russian church having requested me to take part in the service, bore the cross . . . while the service was being read.[91]

No mention is made of what happened to the bodies of the Sikh soldiers.

Destruction

On October 18 and 19 the British burned the Summer Palace. M'Ghee gives the most complete description of this tragic event:

Winter seemed to have set in that day [October 17]; the heavens were black, and bitter was the cold north wind, which cut into the very marrow of our bones, as it swept from the snow-capped mountains down over the plain. But the sun shone brightly on the next day, when by the General's order the First Division marched out under command of Sir John Michel to burn the Yuen-ming-yuen.

My duties did not permit me to be present on the first day when this work of destruction was begun [October 18]; the troops were spread over the country by one and two companies, and fired every building in four palatial 'gardens', as they are called, beginning with the Yuen-ming-yuen; next, and to the west the Wan-shan-yuen; then the Chin-ming-yuen; and last the Heang-shan, which mean respectively, 'the enclosed and beautiful garden', 'the birthday garden', 'the golden and brilliant garden', and the 'fragrant hills'. On the second day I arrived at eight o'clock in the morning, at the Yuen-ming-yuen, and started with Fane's and Probyn's Horse, three guns, and the Queen's to the farthest of these places, the Heang-shan. We marched through scenery of the most enchanting beauty, planted hills, lakes, temples, with villages interspersed, which were the abodes of the Imperial troops; many a matchlock was to be seen in their houses, but they thought only of conciliating

---

[91] M'Ghee, pp. 256–258

us by 'chin-chining', 'kowtowing' and offering hot tea and cold water.[92]

I never experienced more mingled feelings than upon this occasion. As I rode along through scenes which (if anything can compensate for the absence of those 'looks that we love', as Moore calls them) it was worthwhile coming all the way from home to see; I could not help giving to them all the admiration of my heart which their beauty demanded. A tribute so due that you must perforce pay it. I turned the corner of a high wall round which the paved road led, and before me was a dense mass of smoke, and the fierce blaze of the raging fire towering above it, and far above the trees. A temple, which means not one building, but a whole cluster of separate edifices, circling round one great shrine, was in flames, and communicating destruction to the noble trees in and around it, which had shed their grateful shade over it for many a generation: its gilded beams and porcelain roof of many colours, in which of course the Imperial yellow claimed the superiority—all, all, a prey to the devouring element.

You could not but feel that although devoid of sympathy for its deity, there was a sacrilege in devoting to destruction structures which had been reared many, many hundred years ago; nor was it the buildings only, adorning as they did the scenery, which claimed your sympathy, but every building was a repository of ancient and curious art, enamels made before the present dynasty of China, books to no end, engravings of all sorts of scenes, historical, illustrating the wars of the Chinese and Tartars, some the production of purely native talent, and others by Jesuit missionaries, and drawn in the Chinese style. These missionaries are generally learned in something else besides religion, and thus they beat ours out of the field altogether. Embroidered hangings of enormous value, altar furniture plated with gold, things, which, apart altogether from their value, were full of interest from their beauty and rarity, all devoted to destruction; some few were saved by officers, but as carriage was difficult, but few.[93]

---

92 M'Ghee, p. 283
93 M'Ghee, pp. 284–285

Take them all, they will be burned in half-an-hour if you don't; this is a case of 'salvage', not plunder. More jade stone, more books, carpets, pictures, enamels, everything you can imagine. There are the Sikhs, carrying off any amount of thick cloth and carpet for warm sheeting for their horses, for the nights are cold now.

What campaigners those fellows are, fit to go anywhere; and when led by such men as Probyn and Fane, fit to do anything. The troops are halted here for about an hour, and the various corps receive their orders from Sir J. Michel as to where they are to carry on the work of destruction. Looking up from the entrance of the park, the groups of buildings which were scattered through the thickly wooded hollow in the hill-side extended for about a mile and a half up the hill, and reached about half-a-mile right and left of the entrance; soon after the order was given, you saw a wreath of smoke curling up through the trees that shaded a vast temple of great antiquity, which was near the centre of the park, and roofed with yellow tiles that glistened in the sun, moulded as they were in every grotesque form that only a Chinese imagination could conceive; in a few minutes other wreaths of smoke arose from half-a-hundred different places, each like the smoke from some gamekeeper's cottage, hidden in the woods on a hill side in some park at home. Soon the wreath becomes a volume, a great black mass, outburst a hundred flames, the smoke obscures the sun, and temple, Palace, buildings and all, hallowed by age, if age can hallow, and by beauty, if it can make sacred, are swept to destruction, with all their contents, monuments of imperial taste and luxury.

A pang of sorrow seizes upon you, you cannot help it, no eye will ever again gaze upon those buildings which have been doubtless the administration of ages, records of by-gone skill and taste, of which the world contains not the like. You have seen them once and for ever, they are dead and gone, man cannot reproduce them. You turn away from the sight; but before you arises the vision of a sad, solemn, slow procession. Mark that most touching sight, the dashing charger led, not ridden; the saddle is empty, the boot is in the stirrup, but it is empty also; the limb that filled it forms now a part of the skeleton that lies in the coffin on that gun-carriage. You saw that sight two days ago, you see a vision of it now; you turn back and gaze with satisfaction on the ruin from which you had hidden your face, and say, 'Yes, thank God, we can make them feel something of the measure of their guilt'; and if there were another building left to burn, you would carry the brand to it yourself.

Fane, with a troop or two of his sowars, takes a circuit on our return, and fires some outlying buildings which had escaped on the march out, and on our return to the Yuen-ming-yuen we find that the 60th Rifles and Punjabis had made the best use of their time and burned far and wide, and all that now remained was the Hall of Audience already described, and the lodges and buildings between that and the grand entrance; they were spared to the last, as in them the troops had been quartered. It is three o'clock, and we have to march back to Peking; the order is given, fire soon found, and a few smart rifle men soon set the Audience Hall in a blaze; its pomp and state, and it was a noble chamber, are going fast before the devouring flame; the roof must soon go in, it has been alight some time, you feel the heat a hundred yards off; there down it goes, with a terrific crash. Now for the gate and the lodges, don't leave one, no, not one—not a vestige remains of the palace of palaces, the Yuen-ming-yuen. Now back again to Peking, a good work has been done.

Yes, a good work, I repeat it, though I write it with regret, with sorrow; stern and dire was the need that a blow should be struck which should be felt at the very heart's core of the Government of China, and it was done. It was a sacrifice of all that was most ancient and most beautiful, but it was offered to the manes of the true, the honest, and the valiant, and it was not too costly, oh no! one of such lives was worth it all. It is gone, but I do not know how to tear myself from it. I love to linger over the recollection and to picture it to myself, but I cannot make you see it. A man must be a poet, a painter, an historian, a virtuoso, a Chinese scholar, and I don't know how many other things besides, to give you even an idea of it, and I am not an approach to any one of them. But whenever I think of beauty and taste, of skill and antiquity, while I live, I shall see before my mind's eye some scene from those grounds, those palaces, and ever regret the stern but just necessity which laid them in ashes.[94]

---

[94] M'Ghee, pp. 285–289

Aftermath

After the Peking portion of the campaign was complete, the army withdrew to Tientsin and M'Ghee spent the winter of 1860/61 with the garrison that was left in that city. He had formed good relationships with the other members of the headquarters staff and was disappointed to see them depart for England: "It was with heartfelt sorrow that I took leave of the Headquarters staff, my companions during the campaign," M'Ghee notes of their departure in November 1860. He was to live with the 60th Regiment in Tientsin for almost a year.

M'Ghee summed up the feeling of most British people of the time about the China War: "We were . . . bound by the motives of the most ordinary prudence, bound for peace sake, for our own honour sake, even for the spread of civilization, and the sake and cause of religion, to insist most firmly upon a free entrance for our Minister into Peking, I cannot see the shadow of a doubt, and I believe that this one point would never have been really yielded unless the Government of China had been taught to feel that it was not in their power to prevent it."[95] M'Ghee felt that the opening of trade would benefit both Britain and China. It was a common sentiment among the British that the Emperor of China, a Manchu, was a tyrant holding back the Chinese people from trade that they desired, and could benefit from. M'Ghee also believed that the British had made a favorable impression on the Chinese people, that they had "impressed them with an idea of our dignity and strength."[96]

Amazingly, items taken from the Palace by Chinese looters found their way to Tientsin to be sold to the garrison:

> Numbers of jade stones and enamels found their way from the Yuen-ming-yuen down to Tientsin, and were exposed for sale in the shops. At first the vendors strenuously denied that these pieces had come from the Palace, but they soon found out we were not to be deceived, and made no further secret of the matter, and only laughed when we told them that they would have their heads cut off if these things were found with them, as a proclamation had been issued in Peking, threatening with death any person who exposed imperial property for sale. This threat, however, had no effect, as although when we first came down

---

[95] M'Ghee, p. 358
[96] M'Ghee, p. 362

from the capital the natives would kow-tow to a piece of imperial silk which a Sikh carried in the street.[97]

M'Ghee did not leave Tientsin until October 1861. After China he finished out his career with the British Army in various locations. In 1861 he was promoted to Chaplain Second Class. In Dublin in June 1862 he completed his memoir of the campaign and it was published that year. In 1866 he was created Chaplain First Class and in 1872 he was appointed principal chaplain to the British army base in Gibraltar. In 1878 he retired on half pay and went to live in London. M'Ghee was living in London according to the 1891 UK census.

M'Ghee died May 7, 1897, and his address was given as "The Reverend Robert James Leslie Mc Ghee [*sic*] of Rose Cottage, Mill Hill Park, Acton, Middlesex." He left his estate to "Robert James Mc Ghee [*sic*], retired Lieutenant-colonel in her Majesty's Army"[98] (this may have been M'Ghee's nephew).

Of some note for a non-combatant, it is stated that M'Ghee won a Distinguished Conduct Medal in China. The DCM was established in 1855 for "distinguished, gallant and good conduct in the field" for all ranks below commissioned officers in the British Army. However, no official confirmation can be found of this fact and the London Gazette, which was responsible for such announcements, mentions M'Ghee's promotions but does not record him receiving this award.

Bibliography

M'Ghee, The Reverend R. J. L., *How We Got to Peking, Narrative of the Campaign in China of 1860*, Richard Bentley, London, 1862

---

[97] M'Ghee, p. 341
[98] UK probate records

A Scramble for Loot

John Hart Dunne

"When I went into the Palace it was in a frightful state of disorder. Everything that could not be moved was being smashed, and property that the Chinese would have ransomed for a million was being carried away or destroyed."

—John Hart Dunne

John Dunne was a young captain with the 99th Regiment of Foot at the time of the North China campaign. He has a left a remarkable account of how he and his regiment got from Calcutta to Peking and how he took part in the sacking of the Summer Palace. Dunne was a brave officer and at the sharp end of much of the fighting that brought the British to Peking. His account of the looting of the Palace on October 8, 1860, is of special note, with unique specificity and candor about what occurred that day.

Like Robert M'Ghee, Hart Dunne was born an Irishman, in December 1835, the son of John Dunne of Cartron, County Roscommon, and Marianne, the daughter of Colonel Hart. Dunne was educated privately and at the age of seventeen obtained a junior commission in the 62nd Regiment, the old Scots Fusiliers. In January 1854 he transferred into the 21st Regiment. On war being declared against Russia he went out with his regiment to the Crimea as a lieutenant. He was present at the Battle of Alma and after that Balaclava, and then in the thick of combat in the terrible fighting at Inkerman, in the trenches before Sebastopol, and then ultimately at the assault on the Redan in June 1855. In Russia he was promoted to captain. For his conduct in the campaign he was awarded the Fifth Class of the Order of the Medjidieh, and the Turkish medal, by the Ottoman Sultan.

In 1856 Dunne transferred to the 99th Regiment of Foot—*the Nines*—as they were affectionately known by the regiment, with whom he was destined to go to China. "The 99th was formed for general service in Glasgow in 1824 following the request of the Governor of Mauritius for reinforcements. It became the 99th (Lanarkshire) Regiment in 1832."[99] Subsequently, the regiment was sent to India and Dunne was stationed in steaming Calcutta. When they were selected to be part of the expedition to China in 1860, Dunne was attached to the army headquarters during the advance and capture of the Taku forts.

From Calcutta to Peking

Dunne's text of the China Campaign, published in 1861, is both charming and grounded. His openness shines through in all his descriptions, which were written *in situ*, *en route* to or in China. It has, with some justice, been termed a *masterpiece*:

> These Notes were not written with any intention of publishing them; but were merely entered in a book for the amusement of some relatives. The Author has not now either time or opportunity to correct or revise them, or even to read them over, as they are going by the present mail to England. Should the interest shown at home in one of the most perfect little armies that England ever possessed justify their publication, it is hoped this statement will save them from a very severe criticism.

> [Aboard the] Transport 'Bosphorus', December 4, 1860.[100]

They are in fact much more than mere 'notes'. The following are exerts from the text:

---

[99] Description per *The Wardrobe*—home of the infantry regiments of Berkshire and Wiltshire www.thewardrobe.org

[100] Dunne, *Preface*

February 5, 1860: Last night I rode my last ride on the Calcutta course. They [the members of Calcutta society] will naturally class me amongst that too numerous class of British officers who, after having got all they can in the way of amusement out of the people of a place—after having dined with the governors, flirted with their wives, and made love to their daughters—go away, and only remember them for the sake of laughing at some weakness of the man's, or abusing his wines and dinners, or telling stories about his wife, or talking flippantly about his daughters. These same young gentlemen, by the way, sometimes wonder why they are not received with open arms by every father of a family. Were I in the position of *pater familias*, I confess I should be careful before opening the road to my cellar or my daughter's affections to any one of them.[101]

After sailing across the Bay of Bengal, the 99th landed at Singapore:

We directed our *gharry*[102] to take us to the *Hotel de l'Esperance*, where we ordered dinner. Whilst waiting, the doctor . . . and myself walked along the Esplanade, on which there are some handsome houses. Whatever other hopes the *Esperance* may hold out, there are certainly none of getting a decent dinner there. Ours was vile; nothing eatable except the fish, and one could have hardly swallowed the wine if it had not been for the ice. 'Ate some prawn curry with a Malay chutnie. This latter is handed about in a large circular board, something like a roulette-table. It is divided into ten compartments, besides one in the centre, containing cucumber. The other ten ingredients, of which one takes a spoonful of each, were mostly unknown to me, but I recognized garlic, onions, salt fish, eggs, etc. Madame Esperanza, who chatted away with us, says there is nothing going on here.

They seem a 'do nothing' lot, and I suspect it is almost as dull as an Indian station. We afterwards migrated to the Masonic Hotel, where there is one of the best American bowling alleys

---

[101] Dunne, pp. 1–2

[102] A form of horse drawn carriage used in India and other parts of the Far East

that I ever saw; then we got into a *gharry*, and started for the Chinese theatre. It is a very large wooden building, and seemed capable of holding two thousand people; but there were not more than five hundred present. Every man had his own stall; we, however, were given seats on one side of the immense stage. This stage was lighted by some large braziers full of oil, which were hung from the roof above, and had to be continually lowered and replenished. All the rest of the house was in comparative darkness. The actors were in the front part of the stage, with the band in the rear of them. What it all meant is more than I can say, for there were no scenes; all they did in that way was every now and then to move a few chairs, etc. Having an enormous case of cheroots, I managed, by the judicious distribution of some, to get an entree to the green-room. We had been considerably disgusted by noticing that the prima donna, whilst on the stage, took a cup of some concoction at intervals, and after making some horrid guttural noise squirted it out of her mouth in a most un-lady-like manner. We saw this charmer soon after come behind, and I was rather pleased to discover, as the disrobing took place, that it was a common John Chinaman, with his tail complete; for even in Singapore one does not like one's ideal standard of woman to be lowered.[103]

After a very trying and mostly uncomfortable voyage from Singapore, the regiment eventually arrived at Hong Kong:

March 31: One can never write anything during the hurry and confusion that goes on in a transport [ship] in harbour. We got into Hong Kong just a week ago. Found that Sir Hope Grant and all the head-quarter staff had arrived. The place was swarming with staff, artillery, and engineers. The harbour crowded with men-of-war, gunboats, and transports. The 44th were encamped at Kowloon, the Royals in the barracks, the 3rd at Canton, and the 67th on their way down from Whampoa. If it had not been that the three ships containing the regiment came in together, we should have been sent to Canton, as the junior regiment. It is now decided that we are to go on at once to the island of Chusan, where our colonel is to have a brigade.

---

[103] Dunne, pp. 18–20

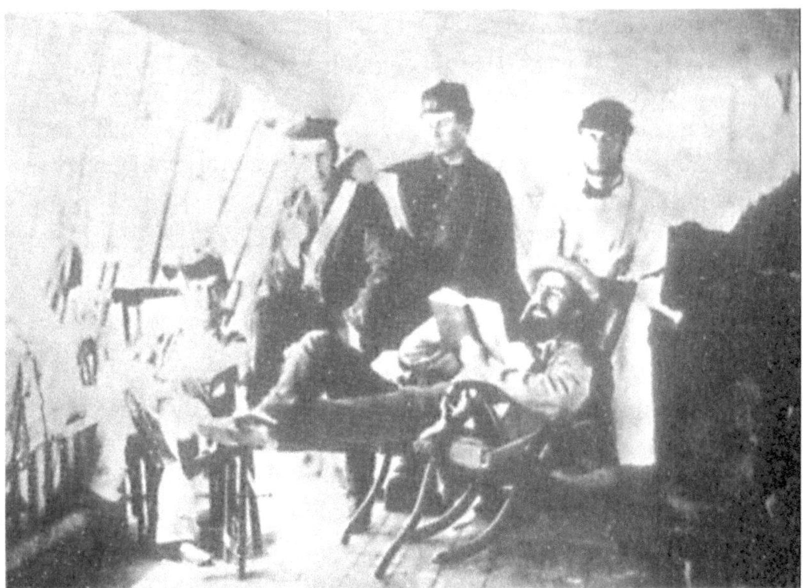

Officers of the 99th Regiment on board ship en route to China. Captain Hart Dunne is seated, right, photographer unknown

Everything is gloriously uncertain, and many say even now that there will be no war. An ultimatum has been sent to the Emperor; and it is supposed that the occupation of Chusan may bring him to reason. It would be, I suspect, a disappointment to some hundreds, who are looking forward to promotion by the row [i.e. the upcoming war]. Even Guardsmen have not been above coming out in order to get their share of the rewards. As to Hong Kong, I never saw a place that appears to have been more unfairly maligned. It is certainly now under its most favourable aspect. We all came to the conclusion that it was far preferable to many Indian stations. The Royals have a perfect little theatre, fitted up with boxes, galleries, and pit-stalls, just like a London one, and the acting is by no means bad. At Calcutta, with all its wealth, they have nothing to be compared to it. Then there is the Hong Kong Club, an establishment whose praises have been sung by Albert Smith, Wingrove Cooke, and all strangers visiting this distant colony. However, when we praised the place, everyone laughed, and said it was only on account of our having been so long at sea. Perhaps it was, but I think not.

It is confidently expected that there will be no fighting at Chusan, and the inhabitants, it is said, will be only too glad to receive us. All the mess plate and heavy baggage of the regiment has been put into store at Hong Kong. They are establishing a coolie corps for the campaign, to which we have had to give a certain number of men as overseers. Hong Kong is to be garrisoned by a depot battalion, formed by detachments from various regiments. We have left some officers and all sickly men.

A large quantity of stores have come on board, beside extra ammunition, in case of the Chusanites being troublesome. Yesterday was an awful scene of confusion. Dagg's company, which was sent on from India before us, came on board, and half another company disembarked from us to the *Octavia*. Then there were compradors with accounts, and Sanpan boatmen waiting to be paid, and three or four young ladies with our clean linen, bright, wicked looking eyes, and no very fixed moral principles, all crowding about the entrance of the cuddy at the same time; whilst inside were our own servants, trying to stow away all sorts of tin pots and kettles, purchased for campaigning; captains and pay-sergeants still at accounts; subalterns grumbling at the price of tents,[104] and comparing their previous night's adventures . . .

April 8: Easter Sunday—Such a time as we have had since writing the above! When the *Simoon* left us to our own devices, there was a 'fresh breeze' blowing, which presently increased to 'half a gale', even by the captain's confession, and this has continued, more or less, ever since, until yesterday evening. Except making a good deal of 'easting' we have done nothing during the last week, which has seemed at least a month to everyone on board, so wretched have we been. Every bone in one's body aches with the numerous bumps we have daily endured. We are quite accustomed to seas coming in mid-ships, but when one big one flooded the cuddy, it became past a joke. Happily, at the

---

[104] Officers, at their own expense, slept in tents while in the field in China. Enlisted men had no form of shelter and slept beneath the stars. Only when occupying local towns did the troops get billeted in houses and temples

present moment, it is calm, and we are quietly working round the south-east corner of the island of Formosa.[105]

Having advanced all the way up the coast from Hong Kong to North China, the 99th was involved in several of the ensuing battles:

August 13: Last night, when the French occupied Sinho, they looted it frightfully. It is very hard on our men that they should always have such an example shown them. The women and children, and old men, took refuge in some junks and boats in a creek that runs through the place, and we put a guard on them to save them from the tender mercies of our allies. Poor wretches, they were huddled together in the most helpless manner, when I saw them this morning.[106]

Bowlby, the Times' correspondent, is a very good fellow; he lives with us, and is one of the Headquarter mess.[107]

Dunne describes the British attack on the Pehtang forts and some fierce fighting:

August 22: We had a union jack all ready to be hoisted; but it was lost in the confusion. Luckily I had another one, belonging to the quartermaster-general's department, so when we saw the French *drapeau* [flag] going in, and that there was none of ours, I ran in with mine, got up to a shed on the top of the cavalier, and seeing that there was a high pole attached to the roof, climbed up, and with some trouble sent our flag flying. Having rashly divested myself of my sword-belt and flask, whilst doing this, a Frenchman, who cared, I suppose, more for brandy than glory, quietly walked off with the latter. The whole of the ramparts were strewn with their dead and wounded, some of them frightfully disfigured.[108]

---

[105] Dunne, pp. 28–33

[106] Dunne, p. 78

[107] Dunne, pp. 80–81

[108] Dunne, p. 89

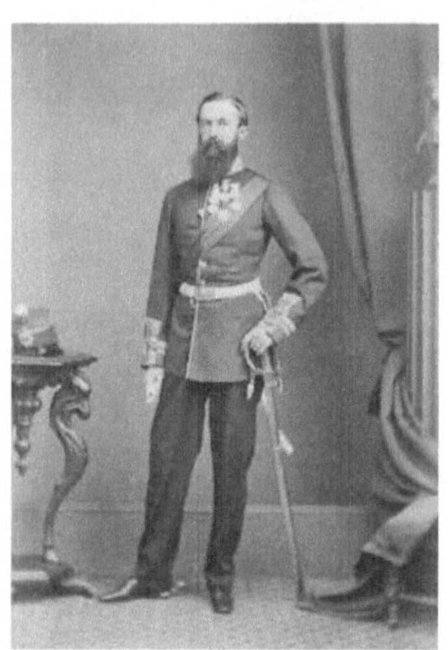

John Hart Dunne,
China, 1860, Felice Beato

> Our casualties . . . amounted to about two hundred killed and
> wounded. The French lost three or four officers killed, and about
> an equal number of men with us. They were about one thousand
> strong, and we had under fifteen hundred.[109]

It was beginning to look like the war was over and the Chinese representatives ('commissioners') were agreeable to signing a peace treaty, but
then on September 8:

> It appears that, after the convention had been drawn up, and
> everything arranged for signing, the commissioners declared
> that they had not power to sign a treaty of that description;
> so Lord Elgin said, 'Very well, then we will go to Peking, and
> arrange matters there.'[110]

> September 12: We had a very pleasant march this morning of
> seven miles or so, and are now about thirty from Tientsin. There
> are many more groves of large trees, and altogether the country

---

[109] Dunne, p. 90

[110] Dunne, p. 99

looks far better than it did nearer the sea. Today we first saw the mountains near Peking.[111]

Bowlby, however, says we shall all be back in Tientsin before this day month. Fellows talk of putting on their 'war paint' tomorrow; but, for my part, I don't believe in our friends making another fight of it.[112]

We have first the change and the complete novelty of the country, and then it is something to be one of the first English army that has ever penetrated into the interior of China. Everyone, individually, feels he is doing and seeing what has never been done or seen before, and that alone has a great charm in it now-a-days, when everyone goes everywhere.[113]

Ho Si Woo, September 14: This day six years, we landed in the Crimea. Then I was a boy. Now I am a somewhat used-up old captain. A long march of twelve miles and 'a bit' brought us to this town, which we kept a little to our left, and pitched our tents on the grass alongside the road, about a quarter of a mile from it. Managed to get our tent put up in a tope of trees, and I write this on the grass under their shade, with a delicious cool breeze passing through them.[114]

British Officers Plunder Ho Si Woo, Battle

September 16: Ho Si Woo, was discovered, owing to a lot of low natives trying to plunder it. They did get in, but were quickly driven out, and a guard put on, with orders that no one but officers were to be allowed to enter. But, alas! for the probity of the British officer, it is said that they looted to a man. I cannot swear to any general joining in the Sack; but field-officers, I hear, were almost as eager and as plentiful as ensigns. Yesterday morning we rode down to our Chinese uncle's. There were about fifteen rooms. One large one was devoted to gold and silver ornaments, pearls, etc.; whilst the others contained thousands of packages

---

[111] Dunne, p. 102

[112] Dunne, p. 103

[113] Ibid.

[114] Dunne, pp. 103–104

of fur coats, silk dresses, and mandarin clothes of every description; also common blue cotton dresses, and one room full of cash. I am not going to criminate my friends; we will drop a veil over all yesterday's transactions.[115]

September 18: With the 15th Punjaubees, Brigadier Reeves with the marines and ourselves were to hold the centre; and we had artillery, the King's Dragoon Guards, and the French on our right; Probyn's people were on our left flank; Major Dowbiggin with two of our companies went forward and occupied some houses in front of the Tartar position. By bringing forward the left, until we had outflanked them, our plan of attack must have forced them either to retire through the town of Chang-chia-wan, or fight our centre and right. After an hour's firing, and our gradually pushing on, they chose the former alternative. In our part of the field, they did not come forward much. Our two companies opened a scattered fire on their centre, to which they replied by throwing *gingal*[116] balls up at the main body of our column. It was a great day for the colours of the 99th; the first time they were ever under fire. Storms of shot went over our heads, and a few fell close amongst us.[117]

September 23: The Battle of Palikao: We advanced in column, and as we went on the Tartars galloped out in swarms to meet us. We took ground to the left of the marines, and the latter formed squares. As they came on, our leading company gave them one volley, and instantaneously they turned round and trotted back to their original position. Sir John Michel just then rode up and ordered us to deploy, and from that time until the end of the day he was almost always with the regiment. There were still masses of cavalry in our front and extending far to our left. Suddenly we saw the King's Dragoon Guards emerge from a cloud of dust, and fall upon them, like a wall of iron. It was a magnificent sight. The Tartars opened showers of gingal balls,

---

[115] Dunne, p. 106

[116] A type of musket mounted on a swivel

[117] Dunne, p. 110

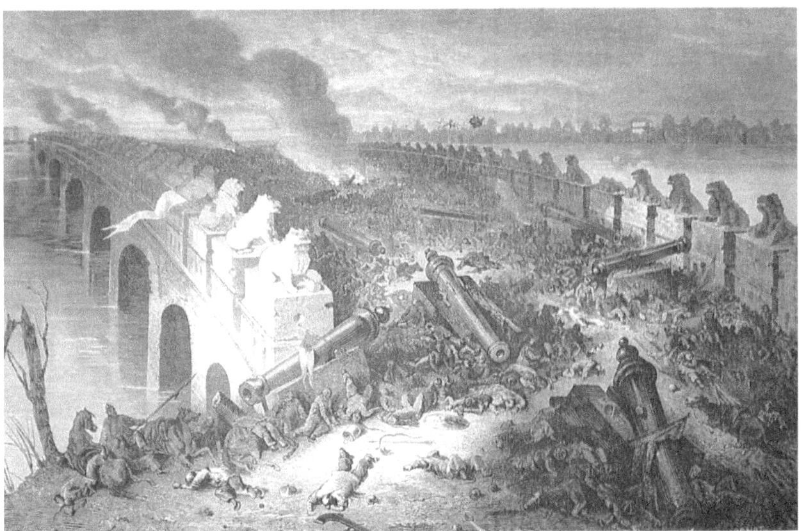

The battle of Palikao, September 23, 1860, artist unknown

and stood very fairly; but what could withstand the weight and pluck of British Dragoons?[118]

On we pushed, and whenever the Tartar cavalry attempted to stand, our artillery opened upon them. Just before we reached one of their largest camps, they made a good deal of show of holding their ground, and I was sent out with two companies to skirmish. Whilst riding forward with Sir John Michel, my pony put his foot in a drain, fell, and rolled over me. I was up again in a minute, but somehow lost my sword, although I did not miss it at the time. Another company was sent out to reinforce these two, and for a few minutes we opened fire, but the enemy retreated to a village on our left, behind a tope of trees. Sir Hope Grant, who had come up, sent Major Dowbiggin with two companies after them, and, after a short delay, I was sent to occupy a village on the right with the remainder of the regiment. We met with no resistance on our side, and halted near a well of water.[119]

---

[118] Dunne, p. 116

[119] Dunne, pp. 117–118

> September 28: Poor Bowlby never would believe that they
> would make another fight of it after Taku, and told me so as we
> were riding together into Ho Si Woo. I only hope he may live to
> acknowledge the error of his opinion.[120] [Bowlby was captured
> by the Chinese]

The British advanced to a position just north of Peking, where they
camped:

> October 7, 1860: 7 P.M., the commander-in-chief has just come
> in, having discovered Pattle's brigade and our gallant allies. The
> French, either accidently or purposely, pushed on yesterday to
> the Emperor's summer palace, about four miles off. They have
> plundered it tremendously, and now, it is said, that they have
> watches, and clocks, and jewelry absolutely lying about their
> camp. M, who was over there, says the things inside are mag-
> nificent, and he has brought in some splendid dresses and bits
> of jade stone, so we have mustered as many dollars as we can
> collect, and are off to the French camp, and, if possible, to the
> Palace also, in the morning. General Montauban, I hear, declares
> that everything is being guarded most carefully by him, so we
> must suppose that his men are merely keeping the things in their
> tents and knapsacks for safety.[121]

> Monday, October 8: A memorable day in the history of plun-
> der and destruction. Off soon after daylight with a select little
> party, and a parson as 'dux' [the Reverend Robert M'Ghee, per-
> haps]. We got to a village near the Palace at about eight. Here
> I was induced to join Reboul, and left the others, thinking that
> he ought to be the best guide. Instead of that, I had not got
> more than a quarter of a mile with him when he declared he
> had lost the way. Being too proud to retrace my steps, I, alone
> and unguided, struck out a path for myself. I knew one land-
> mark, as I thought, and also knew that there was a paved road
> leading to the Palace. At length I reached this paved road, but,

---

[120] Dunne, p. 122
[121] Dunne, pp. 127–128

without knowing it, I entered it on the other side of the Palace, and thus I rode four or five miles before discovering my mistake. Fortunately it then suddenly struck me that neither French nor English had I seen all the way, and I luckily turned, for going on much further must have brought me to a Tartar *picquet*, as I afterwards found that no one had advanced anything like so far in that direction.

Retracing my steps I came at length to the Palace-gardens, got hold of a French soldier, who did not know the way, and found myself lost in a labyrinth of paths and islands. It was nearly twelve o'clock before I got out of this maze, and found myself at the Palace gates. Saw every one clearing off, loaded with booty; and, in despair, took to buying pearls in the French camp, and a few jade stone trifles. When I went into the Palace it was in a frightful state of disorder. Everything that could not be moved was being smashed, and property that the Chinese would have ransomed for a million was being carried away or destroyed. Every officer in our army who had managed to procure leave was doing business, and the more enterprising had brought carts with them. Some confined their attention to jade stone ornaments and vases; others were in the enamel bronze line. A few took to embroidered silk and fur coats; whilst a large proportion went in exclusively for rolls of silk. Presently I saw a troop of Sikh cavalry fall-in in the courtyard. Their appearance was somewhat ludicrous, for each sowar had about twenty-four rolls of silk piled up in front and behind their saddles. These silks were of every description of colour, and the men could hardly get their hands over the pile in front so as to guide their horses.

In the French camp, where the troops expected to move that afternoon, the men had thrown rolls of silk on the ground, and, for a couple of dollars, I got as many as I could carry. Not having been at Delhi, Lucknow, or any good sack, I own to being very green about the business. Indian fellows were quite at home at the work; but with regard to the rest of us, I don't believe one man in twenty knew how to go about it; for the man who 'loots' well must have a good knowledge of minerals and metals, a quick eye, a cool head, and, above all, a determined fixedness of purpose. 'He who hesitates is lost', and half the fellows got little or nothing by first picking up one thing and then throwing it down for something else, or rushing about to inquire whether it was valuable or not. People don't plunder palaces every day, so I will try to give a notion of the scene. Imagine Christie's, Hunt and Roskell's, Howell and James's, half-a-dozen watch and clockmakers, two or three upholsterers, and that fine fan-shop in Regent Street, all being under the same roof; and then imagine, if you can, what would be your sensations when told that, without breaking the eighth commandment, you might have your run of the place for just ten minutes, and no more. I think that even ladies would be somewhat confused, and would have hardly made up their minds ere the time had expired.

Now this was the case with many of us. As for myself, after having made a fair collection, I incautiously intrusted a Chinaman to carry the greater part of it, and the villain took advantage of my stopping for a moment to look at the throne, and disappeared; so, except my purchases from the French, I had nothing but two or three coats of the Sun's brother, which I threw over my saddle. Rode back with an irregular cavalry man, who had a cart-load of silk, *cum multis aliis* [with many others]. On getting into cantonments found that 'D', having brought in two coolie loads of loot, had ridden back on a second venture. The example was contagious, and when 'M', who had only got thirty-four rolls of silk, proposed that we should go back again, and declared that he knew the direct road to the silk rooms, I was weak enough to take a pack-mule and start with him. When we got there, however, we found these rooms were completely cleared out, so we had to content ourselves with about three hundred pieces of embroidered silk, each about the size of a cushion, and beautifully worked, which have since sold for about seventy pounds. As we left the Palace it was quite dark, but flames breaking out from part of it lighted us on our homeward path. Bought a great lump of sycee-silver from a Frenchman, and he and two comrades walked with us to our house for the money. Lay down very tired, and with the conclusion that plundering a palace was, after all, anything but an amusing occupation. It brings out all the worst passions of one's nature—avarice and covetousness amongst others. Everyone is dissatisfied with what he has got, because he thinks someone else has done better; and I believe

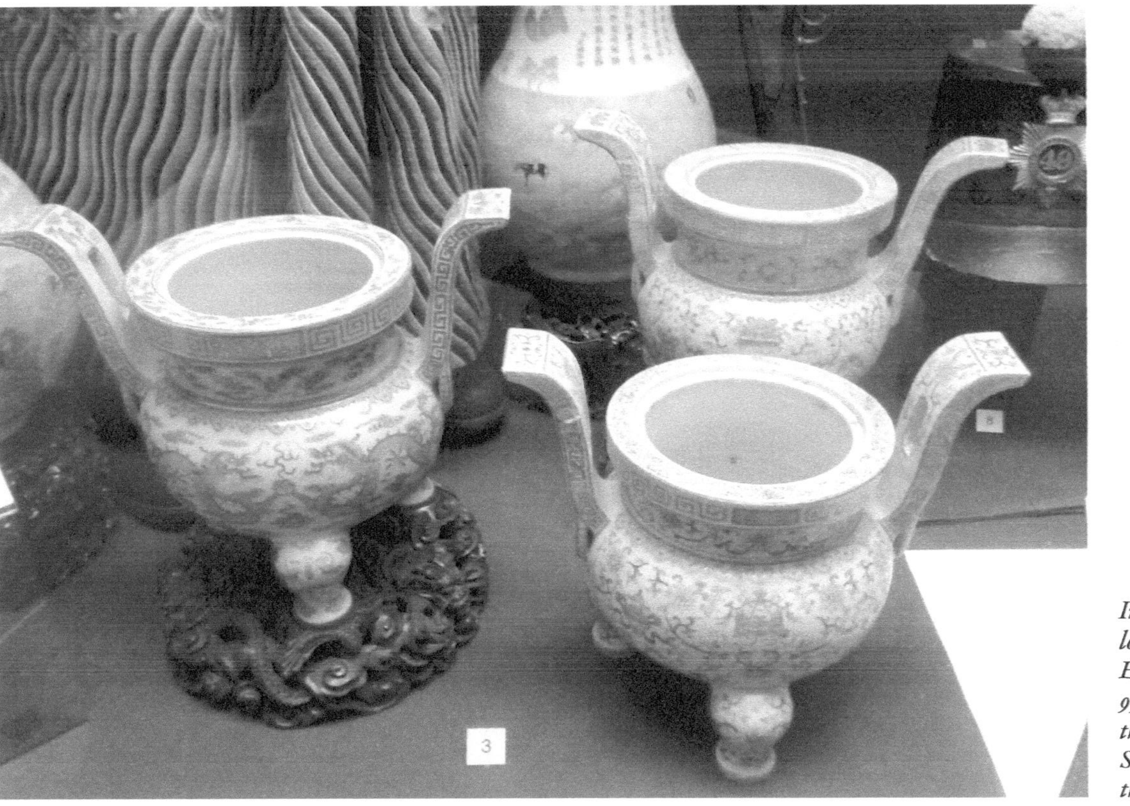

Imperial cloisonné vases—loot brought back to England by officers of the 99th Regiment, now in the regimental museum, Salisbury. Copyright the Author, 2015

everyone feels more or less lowered in his own estimation, by the inward knowledge of what his feelings are on the occasion.[122]

October 9: To-day there was a general surrender of all our ill-gotten possessions. It was decided that everything taken at the Palace should be given up, and sold for the benefit of the army. Sir Hope Grant, in a very good general order, put it entirely to the honour of the officers that they should give up everything; so, of course, there was nothing for it but to produce all. An exception was made as regarded those things purchased in the French camp. I have been able to retain a good many trifles that I bought there; also a pretty little dog, smaller than any King Charles, a real Chinese sleeve-dog. It has silver bells round its neck, and people say it is the most perfect little beauty they ever saw.

Parkes, Locke, and one French officer have been given up by the mandarins in Peking. The others, they say, are either dead or have been taken away by the Tartar army. They are still hesitating about surrendering the city; accordingly siege-guns have been brought up, and batteries are being traced.[123]

October 10: Rode over with two or three others to the French camp, to see what we could pick up. They were full of watches, jewelled snuff-boxes, and ornaments of every description; but they asked as much for many things as one would pay in Paris. The fact is, they have got so much silver that they don't care about selling anything that they can carry; and despising thoroughly the luxury of a change, their knap sacks are crammed with the spoils, of war. In one camp we saw them squatted down in parties or squads, whilst the corporals served them out ingots in the way our men get biscuit; and a sergeant assured me that every man in his company had at least one, if not two, watches apiece.[124]

---

[122] Dunne, pp. 128–133

[123] Dunne, pp. 133–134

[124] Dunne, pp. 134–135

The Prize Sale

October 11: All the things taken from the Palace were laid out in a large joss-house [temple] at headquarters, this morning, and at two o'clock the sale commenced. When we saw the quantity of enormous bronze enamel vases, China jars, and jade stone ornaments of every description, which had been collected together, with the piles of furs, silks, and satins, it was unanimously agreed that, taking into consideration their short space of time, their want of proper transport, and with so many their want of opportunity to get at the Palace, no men could have acquitted themselves more creditably than the officers of this little army. The things sold for enormous prices. One coat was knocked down for seventy-five pounds to a captain of Madras sappers; not a single fur coat of any value went for less than twenty pounds. The whole day's sale realized over three thousand pounds.[125]

October 12: At it again at ten this morning. The first thing, a gold jug, was unanimously presented by the officers of the army to the commander-in-chief. We of the Second Division afterwards bought two jade-stone vases for Sir Robert Napier, who, as well as his Excellency and Sir John Michel, had given up all claims to prize-money. They say the proceeds of this auction, together with all the gold and silver found, will amount to about thirty thousand pounds sterling, two-thirds of which go to the men and one-third to the officers.[126]

By the by, how we are ever to get all our 'annexations' down to the fleet is a problem of dubious solution.[127]

October 19

The whole sky, on the Summer Palace side of the horizon, is black with the volumes of smoke from it and the smaller palaces round it. We hope the old Emperor, in his hunting-box in the

---

[125] Dunne, pp. 135–136

[126] Dunne, p. 136

[127] Ibid.

hills, may see it. Several staff-men who went out with the First Division yesterday filled their carts with enameled bronze vases, which were still remaining.[128]

The second sack of the Palace, and the mandarins' palaces beyond it, has turned out a better thing than the first one. Harris of the Punjaubees, has brought in 300 lbs. weight of gold, valued at something like 11,000 pounds. Several people have bought up gold from the native troops for a. few dollars; in one case a piece worth at least 200 pounds.[129]

Dined with Fane's people in the evening. Saw a beautiful set of engravings found in one of the palaces the other day. It is supposed to represent the history of the war of the Tartars against the Ghoorkas [*sic* Gurkhas]; it bears underneath the name of a French priest and is dated 1765. The etching, the number of figures introduced, and the life-like way in which they are grouped make it a remarkable work.[130]

October 23: It turns out that our Tartar friends of yesterday are peaceably inclined. Spent the morning at headquarters settling my auction bill,[131] reading magazines, and looking over Signor Beato's photographs.[132]

October 26: This morning Sir John Michel rode over to the Summer Palace with a cavalry escort and since officers were allowed to accompany him, I joined the cavalcade, which was an extremely large one, and consisted of all sorts of people, dressed in all sorts of costumes and mounted on all sorts of animals. We passed by the blackened walls of the old palace, and pushed on to a pagoda situated on the highest point in the grounds, and which had escaped the fire. After dismounting at the bottom of the hill,[133] a circular path cut through the rocks brought us up to the base of the tower, which most of us then ascended. At

---

[128] Dunne, pp. 141–142

[129] Dunne, p. 143

[130] Dunne, p. 146

[131] What did he buy at the auction?

[132] Dunne, p. 146

[133] This "hill" would appear to be Wanshou Shan, part of the New Summer Palace

the top of this tower, which was about the height of one of our monuments, the view was magnificent. We could trace mountains far off which must be giants compared to the others nearby, and a walled town to the north of us lay under us, at some five or ten miles distance. There were pagodas, joss-houses, ornamental water and grounds, with bridges just like the old familiar blue willow-pattern delft, all spread out as a panorama before us; but the atmosphere towards Peking was hazy, and we could only just see the walls.

We afterwards went with Sir John Michel to several pretty grottoes and other places, and gradually the party dispersed to explore. With two others I rode, by a short cut which I knew, straight to the Palace grounds, having heard in the morning that some of the enameled vase rooms had not been burnt. We three, with an enterprising middy, got to a courtyard and house which had escaped [being burned], and closing the gate, dismounted, and proceeded to make a selection; but this was a terrible business. There were heaps of large enamel things, but no small ones. Massive bronze vessels were there, beautifully worked, and some tables also, but nothing that looked portable. Still, having always been so unlucky before, I would not, like one of my party, go off in search of the unknown, but collecting together all that looked best, endeavored to choose from the lot anything that it was possible to move. Tying my pocket-handkerchief and a piece of silk together, I made a rope; at one end fastened an old enameled vase, and at the other to a large tray of the same description. After some difficulty, found the head and tail of a large bronze enameled monster, something like a dog [a *qilin*], and finding that I could lift it, slung the other things across my saddle, filled my saddle-bags with queer small things, and with my beast in my arms, made my way with difficulty out of the ruins. It had been raining heavily for some time, and the rest of the party had taken shelter. I passed by a number of trunks [bodies] of Chinamen, with their heads hanging from the trees, who had evidently been caught following our example, by the Tartar guards. After mounting, all my enamels began clattering about, and it was almost impossible to manage my pony, or to avoid the mischance which befell the bottles of the renowned John Gilpin. Just as I had made up my mind that the greater portion of my booty must be left on the road, Graham and Stuart, who were laughing immensely at my appearance, decried a fellow with a donkey and panniers, whom I immediately took into my service, and with his assistance brought everything safe into cantonments.[134]

In the City of Peking

On the afternoon of the 8th [November], we escorted Lord Elgin on a visit to take leave of Prince Gong, and at the same time to introduce his brother. The place appointed was at a considerable distance from the Embassy, and we had a long trudge through the muddy, mazy streets of Peking. After having drawn up my guard outside, I followed up the great people through several courtyards. In the reception-room there was a long table, and two small ones flanking it. All of them were covered with little dishes of fruits, and sweetmeats of every description. Lord Elgin took his seat at the centre of the large table; Prince Gong on his right, and Mr. Bruce[135] on his left. On the right of the Prince was Mr. Parkes, and on the left of Mr. Bruce was Mr. Wade, these two gentlemen acting as interpreters; then two or three mandarins. Lord John Hay, Crealock, the attachés, and self—occupied the smaller tables, and some more mandarins plied us most assiduously with delicacies, and also with champagne, which had been sent as a present from the Embassy.

Verily, I did not march to Peking in vain, neither have I endured rheumatism, and abstained from luxury, without meeting with my reward; for with the brother of the Celestial Emperor as a host, I partook of the world-famous 'Chinese bird's-nest'. Never was a delicacy enjoyed under more favourable circumstances, yet I blush to confess that I was a little disappointed, and almost preferred the almond soup which followed it. The conversation, which passed somewhat tardily between Lord Elgin and the Prince, through the medium of Mr. Parkes, was all of an exceedingly polite and friendly character. No allusion whatever was made to any unpleasant topic.

---

[134] Dunne, pp. 148–150

[135] The new British minister to the Court of Peking, and Elgin's younger brother

The Ambassador expressed a hope that the Emperor would send an envoy to England hereafter. The Prince replied that it would be a mark of great friendship on the part of the Chinese if they did so; that he would represent that, and everything else which had taken place, to the Emperor, with whom the decision must rest.

There was some talk about ships to convey them to England, and the Prince thanked Lord Elgin for his photograph. Lord Elgin informed the Prince that he intended to take his departure on the following morning. The Prince declared his great sorrow, and said he must send him some presents, and pay a visit in the morning. The hour of the visit was then named, and after that, as a naval man remarked, 'the Embassy Extraordinary hauled down its colours', by Lord Elgin declaring that his mission was ended, and getting up out of his chair, he placed Mr. Bruce in it, and introduced him as the future representative of England at Peking. Then there was some more soft talk. Although Mr. Bruce is quite gray, the Prince trusted that so young a man would quickly acquire the Chinese language; and Lord Elgin mentioned that the English had no object in China except the welfare of the Emperor and his people. Something was said about the house which Mr. Bruce would occupy next March, and Mr. Adkins, who alone forms our advanced guard in China, by living in this house during the winter, was introduced. Then arrangements were made about giving over the gates in the morning, and just before dark we took our departure. Prince Gong, is quite a young man, looks intelligent, and has a very good manner.[136]

The British departed, and re-traced their steps to the sea:

The following night we halted and pitched tents outside Tientsin. Entering the town in the morning, we sold off our carts and mules for anything they would fetch, and at noon next day went on board a gun-boat. 'Spent two cold days and nights coming down the river in this gun boat and the junk attached to it, and were by no means sorry when yesterday morning we

---

[136] Dunne, pp. 155–158

found ourselves safely put on board the *Bosphorus*, one of the largest and most comfortable transports in the fleet. Our baggage is safe on board a ship close by us, and I trust will soon be on board this one, for our wardrobes are scanty, and our clothes in a very seedy condition. The men are in high spirits, and so are we, at having finished our little campaign so happily, and at having, I trust, taken leave forever of the muddy shores of the Gulf of Pecheli.[137]

Aftermath

Through a communications ship, Dunne was able to sign off his diary on December 4, 1860 and submit it to London for publication—perhaps the first account of the China War to emerge. He himself remained with his regiment. After the closure of the campaign, the 99th was dispatched to Canton for nearly a year. A portion were sent to Shanghai in the fight against the Taiping rebels. For its service in China, the regiment earned the moniker *Pekin 1860*. Rather than being returned to India, the 99th joined the Hong Kong garrison, securing the new Kowloon territory acquired by the Convention of Peking, and remained there until 1865.

Some of the finest pieces of Chinese art collected at the Summer Palace were done so under the guard of the 99th, and they were sent as a gift to Queen Victoria. The 99th's officers, collectively, acquired several magnificent vases, which they donated to the Regiment, and are now to be found in the regimental museum.

In his journal Dunne recorded, as noted earlier, "I have been able to retain a good many trifles that I bought in the French camp, also a pretty little dog, a real Chinese sleeve dog. It has silver bells round its neck. People say, it is the most perfect little beauty they have ever seen."[138] This dog was the first Pekinese to find its way to Britain, along with four others, it seems. Legend has it that British officers (Dunne, Lord John Hay and Sir George Fitzroy) looted a private apartment in a deserted pavilion at the Palace and found five Pekingese dogs 'guarding' the body of the Emperor's aunt, who had committed suicide when she heard the British troops were approaching. This is contradicted by Dunne's own

---

[137] Dunne, p. 159

[138] Dunne, p. 134

account. Probably all five dogs were obtained the same way—from the French camp, by various persons, including Dunne. A pair of the dogs were commandeered by Admiral John Hay and eventually found their way to Goodwood Castle, where they became the property of the Duke of Gordon. Another pair were given to the Duchess of Richmond. Dunne sent his dog as a gift to Queen Victoria. She accepted the animal and called it 'Looty'.

The New York Times reported, in an article dated February 12, 1912, that after its capture the Chinese empress was anxious about the welfare of Looty, but was assured that it was going to be given to the Queen of England. "Good feeling was thus established all around, and the little dog, bearing the name of Looty, was domiciled at Buckingham Palace. He was a very lonesome little creature, the other dogs taking exception to his oriental habits and appearance, and when the Prince and Princess of Wales returned from a Continental trip, the latter pleaded with her mother-in-law to be allowed to take Looty to Sandringham."

Evidently, Looty got over her initial culture shock, and continued to live with the Queen until the dog's death in 1872. She became quite famous and even had her portrait painted for Her Majesty.

Dunne wrote in addendum, later: "This little dog was found by me in the palace of Yuen-ming-yuen near Peking on October 6 [*sic* 8th], 1860. It is supposed to have belonged to either the Empress or one of the ladies of the Imperial Family. It is a most affectionate and intelligent little creature—it has always been accustomed to be treated as a pet and it was with the hope that it might be looked upon as such by Her Majesty and the Royal Family that I have brought it from China." J. Hart Dunne, Captain 99th Regt.

In November 1865 Dunne was promoted to the rank of lieutenant-colonel. In 1870 he was married to Julia, daughter of W.R. Chapman of Whitby. Their son John also became a soldier and fought in the Great War before becoming an aeronautical engineer of some renown.

Dunne was promoted, again, to the rank of major-general, in 1881, and in 1885 was placed in command of the 2nd Infantry Brigade at Aldershot. He was made full general in 1893. In 1898 he was made colonel of the Duke of Edinburgh's Regiment (Wiltshire)—the old 99th. After 50 years of service, he retired from the Army in 1902, and was knighted in 1906.

From 1865 to 1868, the 99th served in South Africa where they were inspected on one occasion by Prince Alfred, the Duke of Edinburgh, who was touring the colony. He was so impressed with the regiment that he took a continued interest in them for the rest of his life. In 1874, the 99th (Lanarkshire) Regiment of Foot became officially the 99th (Duke of Edinburgh's) Regiment. The unit returned to South Africa in 1878 and took part in the Zulu War. At the Battle of Gingindlovu, the 99th helped defeat Zulu impis which were trying to overrun the British laagered position. The regiment was honored for its service in the conflict by being awarded the battle honor *South Africa 1879*. In 1881, following up on the earlier Cardwell Reforms of 1872, the 99th was merged with the 62nd Regiment of Foot. The new regiment was known thereafter as The Duke of Edinburgh's (Wiltshire Regiment).

Dunne died at his home in Sidmouth, Devon in April 1921 in his 90th year. *The Times* noted: "Sir John Dunne served through the Crimean campaign and was the last survivor of the 36 of the 21st Fusiliers who landed on the Peninsular on September 14, 1854."[139] A fitting tribute to a man whose good humor and intelligence saw him through many difficult times with the Army. Dunne was one of the last survivors of the British force that went to China in 1860.

Sale of Hart Dunne's Loot

As per his notes, Dunne acquired four silk gowns belonging to the Emperor at the Yuen-ming-yuen. There is a similar gown that was looted by Captain Ely that was donated to the officers' mess of the 99th Regiment that is now on display in the regimental museum. Dunne had a hand in donating a set of ceremonial porcelain vases that now are also in the museum.

Dunne's China objects were inherited by his son J.W. Dunne. They then passed to JW's daughter Rosemary. Rosemary lived alone to a good age. When she went into a retirement home her house was burgled and many of the best objects were stolen. Some of these are unknown. Dunne's uniforms, the silk robes and Dunne's medals were bought back from an auction house by Rosemary's niece. She has Dunne's papers and all the remaining objects he brought back from China including an imperial jade seal, and a copy by the artist of Queen Victoria's painting of 'Looty'.

---

[139] *The Times*, April 21, 1924

Bibliography

Dunne, John Hart, *From Calcutta to Pekin*, Samson Low, Son & Co.,
    London, 1861

The French Have Arrived

Charles Du Pin

"The eyes were dazzled, and desires fulfilled! We circulated among these heaps of riches without touching anything. The orders of the General were strict."

—Charles Du Pin

On February 25, 1862 the Paris auctioneer M. Baudry put up for sale in Room 5 of the Hotel Drouot "three-hundred and thirty-one 'Objets Précieux' from the Summer Palace, the Yuen-ming-yuen, recently housed in the Musée Japonais et Chinois of Colonel Du Pin."[140]

"The objects discovered in the Summer Palace," noted the sale catalog, "in the secret study of the emperor and in the large pagodas, are of historical interest, which augments their value as works of art. The *Grand Album*, painted on silk, representing the 40 Views of the Imperial Palace, deserves particular attention, because it is the only rescued image of this palace, the most beautiful in China, and, before fire made it disappear.[141]

How it was that Charles Du Pin, an officer with the French expeditionary force to China, came to possess all these works of oriental art, including many from the Chinese Emperor's private quarters, requires some explanation. As a soldier he was a dynamic and highly charismatic individual, as is evident from the description Du Pin left of the campaign.

---

[140] Baudry, Auction Catalogue, February 25, 1862, translation by the author
[141] Ibid.

His perspective as someone who was part of the French command in China, and who therefore had greater access to the Summer Palace than his British counter-parts is full of valuable details, including an account of the capture of the Palace on the evening of October 6. Du Pin was also one of the 'commissioners' chosen by his general to gather up and evaluate the finest treasures from the Palace for Napoleon III. He therefore had a keen insight into the looting that ensued and the art that was collected.

Writing in 1862, Du Pin comments: "It is too early to judge the expedition to China and even to hazard an opinion on its effect on the future. But barring some great political and commercial event, there is no doubt that the entry of a French army into Peking, will remain as the most extraordinary adventure of our time."[142] Du Pin, a career army officer, was head of the French Topographical Ordinance in China. He was a most controversial officer as well as an amateur photographer. He was literate, opinionated and a first hand-observer of the events in China. As such he has left one of the best accounts of the taking of the Summer Palace.

Born in Lasgraisses in southwestern France on December 28, 1814, Du Pin was the son of the town mayor, Pierre Paul Charles Louis Du Pin (1769–1825) and Marie-Sophie de Genton de Villefranche, who were married in 1812. From the start of his career he was clearly a man of ability. He attended the prestigious military engineering school the 'Polytechnique' and later the army staff college 'Ecole d'application d'état-major'. Du Pin trained as a topographical officer, in 1836 he was appointed lieutenant, and showed sufficient promise that he was promoted to captain in 1842. That was the year that he was posted to a cavalry regiment in Algeria where France was engaged in a war of colonial conquest. It was in Africa that Du Pin began to carve out a reputation for himself as a dashing officer in exotic locations. He participated in the taking of d'Abd el-Kader in 1843 with some heroism, saving the life of a senior officer. Later he fought in the battle of Smalain. On his return to France, Du Pin was made aide-de-camp to a general and subsequently promoted to cavalry major. In 1853 he was posted back in Algeria as part of the Zouave Expedition.

With the outbreak of the Crimean War in 1854, Du Pin sailed to the Russian peninsular. He was shortly thereafter promoted to lieutenant-colonel. In 1859 he was staff officer with a cavalry division fighting against Austria. During his early career he was awarded two *Legions d'Honneur*,

---

[142] Du Pin, Expédition de Chine, 1862, p. 5, translation by the author

France's highest honor for valor, as well as a number of other decorations. By the time he was sent to China in 1860, Du Pin was a cavalry officer in charge of the topographical department. After the Battle of the Taku forts he was promoted to the rank of full colonel.

It is not clear how and where Du Pin learned the technique of *photography*, but by 1860 he was already a capable amateur and brought his own camera with him to China. He also had under his command Antoine Fauchery, a civilian employed to photograph the events of the expedition. The two men became friends. Du Pin's role as topographical head appears to have been to advise the commander-in-chief of the lay of the land and record the geography that he observed as well as engage in scouting sorties. With a very large Chinese cavalry force at large around Peking, this proved a dangerous assignment.

Evidently Du Pin must have kept a diary during the China campaign because his memoir of his time in the Orient, *Expedition de Chine*, published in 1862 under the pseudo-name *Paul Varin*, contains many detailed descriptions. In addition to his military duties and his diary, Du Pin also found time and opportunity to take some of the earliest photographs of North China.

The following is Du Pin's narrative of his observations of the sack of the Summer Palace:[143]

Arrival at the Palace, October 6, 1860

The village where we had arrived heralded by its grandiose appearance the approach to an imperial residence. The intersecting streets and roads were paved and maintained with great care. Its gentle inhabitants, more astonished than frightened by our presence, watched quietly the passing of our troops and establishing their bivouac. The marine companies under the captain of the frigate *Jauréguiberry* were at the head of the column. They advanced two kilometers into the village, following a sunken road, bordered by high walls, and arrived at a large square planted with large trees, bounded on one side by a lake, and on the other by the Imperial Palace, which was preceded by an avenue bordered on each side by uniform buildings, no

---

[143] Du Pin, *Expédition de Chine*, 1862, pp. 226–247, inclusive, (except as noted) translation by the author

doubt for lodging the Emperor's retainers. The entrance to the square was blocked by entanglements; we destroyed them, and our troops, as and when they arrived, there set up their bivouacs. In front of the Palace gate stood, under an awning, a post consisting of ten men armed with bows and muskets. At the sight of our leading troops entering the square, these brave Chinese fled, leaving behind their bows and even lighted matches on their guns. The mandarin who commanded them had forgotten in his haste to take his hat, decorated with a white jade bowl and a beautiful peacock feather.

The sun had been down for some time, and we started to distinguish objects with difficulty, when the commander in chief gave the order to Commander Campenon to send a party into the Palace to ensure it was indeed abandoned.

The officer enlisted a company of marines commanded by M. de Kenny, naval lieutenant, to accompany him on this mission. They broke into the first enclosure of the Palace by way of some side doors—the central front gate was strongly barricaded inside with wood beams. After a court of three hundred meters in size, they met a second enclosure, which they crossed, like the first, without seeing anyone, and emerged into a vast courtyard intersected in its final stages by a white marble canal traversed by a bridge, also of marble, supporting a gallery-like wood covering. Everything seemed deserted; the most profound silence reigned in the vast courtyards. A third compound followed; and like the central grand entrance was closed. It is neglected, and on they marched—divided into two groups headed toward the two side doors, which they equally found barred. We thought we heard behind these doors the sound of voices,[144] and began to push on the gates, while several agile sailors climbed the four meter high wall.

The darkness was profound. Two small doors a few hundred meters apart, gave way about the same time under the force of the men, and we piled-in in two columns. At the head of the left was M. de Pina, a naval lieutenant, aide of the commanding officer, chief ordinance officer to the commander-in-chief [Du Pin himself!], who was there, but an amateur. This officer

---

[144] Du Pin personally accompanied the advance party

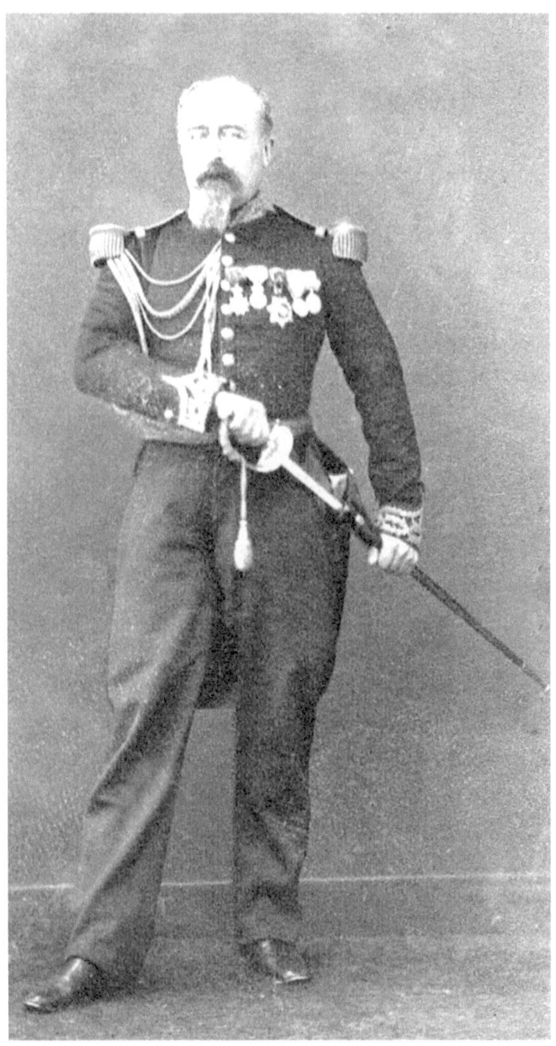

General de Montauban, China, 1860, by Charles Du Pin or Antoine Fauchery

was advancing, revolver in hand, when he suddenly received a violent saber blow to his wrist, while a marine NCO, having jumped over the wall, tumbled into the courtyard and shot a Chinese armed with a lance. That shot was followed by five or six others, fired at the Chinese we thought we saw fleeing into the darkness, followed by a volley from the column on the right. Soon the two troops, alive to the sound, and not discerning their mutual position, exchanged gunfire, requiring all the authority of chiefs to stop it. This mistake, which could have had dire consequences, fortunately did no harm . . .

We were sure that the Palace was abandoned. Meanwhile, an unfortunate incident happened in the great courtyard square where all our columns were arriving in succession. When the first shots rang out in the Palace, an employee of the treasury, who had had the unfortunate idea to follow the company of marines, ran with fear toward the camp, yelling at the top of his voice: 'General, help! The marines are surrounded! Help!' These cries of alarm, thrown out in the middle of the darkness and following a fusillade which we did not know the cause, spread fear among the troops. Soon after, the arrival of Monsieur de Pina, with a bloody wrist, produced a strange confusion. They [the troops] thought it was a night attack by the enemy. Firearms were discharged as if by themselves, and balls crossed in every direction. Reconnaissance followed and was greeted with shots fired in our direction. The voice of the leaders finally came to dominate the confusion, and order was resumed.

M. Vivenot, a midshipman, had received a serious hip injury. The horse squadron leader, staff officer, was hit by a bullet which appeared to be small caliber, perhaps from a revolver. The Tartars prowling around the Palace, took advantage of the disorder to unload their guns at our camp.

Entering the Palace

At daybreak [October 7] we heard a volley of cannon shots from somewhere close to Peking, that, because of its regularity, we assumed to have come from the British army. As a result, Brigadier Pattle [commander of the British cavalry division that had accompanied the French to the Palace], who had bivouacked near us with his cavalry, sent out a reconnaissance party and learned that the English army had become lost on the previous day's march, and too tired to go to the appointed *rendez-vous*, had spent the night inside some earthen ramparts in front of the western gate of the north side of the city.

At eight in the morning, General de Montauban followed by his staff, department heads, escorted by the marine infantry, went to visit the palace Yuen-ming-yuen. Brigadier Pattle and his officers accompanied him. This officer [Pattle], in accordance with the wishes of General de Montauban, had communicated our position to General Grant, and invited him to advance to our position along with Lord Elgin, in order to agree about the disposition of the booty that we expected to find in the Palace. Prior to his visit, General de Montauban told the officers who surrounded him that he counted on their honor to respect and preserve the Palace untouched until the arrival of the English.

We proceeded to the front door of the Palace by way of a paved square adorned on each side by a giant bronze lion resting on a pedestal of white marble, three meters high. (*Note, these beautiful statues were of colossal proportions and of such great weight, we had to give up the idea of carrying them away, as we had thought we might. We later took the two dragons in gilt bronze which we found on the white marble bridge over the canal, located in the penultimate courtyard in front of the Palace*). After crossing the courtyard where we found the Chinese killed from the day before. We visitors arrived at a building in the shape of a parallelogram [the Audience Hall]. We climbed the wide, white marble steps and entered a huge hall. At the far side stood a throne made out of black wood, marvelously sculpted, a wonderful work of prodigious size. One approached the throne by degrees, between a row of cloisonné incense burners and huge glazed vases, on which were depicted all kinds of animals. The left wall of the room was covered in its entirety by a single picture painted on silk offering a view of the full extent of the Imperial Palace. All around the room, and on shelves, were a profusion of vases, sculptures, cloisonné pieces, enamels, all of an extraordinary beauty and size; piles of albums containing drawings done with care, patience and precision, which the Chinese alone have the secret; and books, written in the hand of emperors, bound in carved red Peking lacquer, and enclosed in carefully worked boxes.

The decorations of the first throne room, its grand character, indicated that it was indeed the sacred place where the sovereign of so many millions of men, surrounded by his first dignitaries, dressed in gold-embroidered costume and sparkling jewels, deigned to greet ambassadors. Before him they struck the earth with their foreheads! [the kowtow] A short distance away, and behind the first building, there was a second throne room, less imposing, but more elegant than the first, where without doubt there were less formal receptions. The apartments attached to this room were crammed with gold objects, or silver adorned with precious stones; richly inlaid weapons; green and white jade bowls; goblets of gold or silver, inlaid with turquoise and pearls, statues of idols made from solid gold; of flowers, clusters of fine pearls, ornaments, trees twisted and augmented by the most precious materials.

The eyes were dazzled, and desires fulfilled! We circulated among these heaps of riches without touching anything. The orders of General were strict. We reached, together, in front of an artificial lake surrounded by rocks and rising mountains [the so called 'Front Lake'], which was bordered by a sandy road. We crossed a bridge which threw itself across the feeder canal to the lake and found ourselves in a third throne room, smaller than the previous one, also elegant, but of an intimate elegance. Due to the proportions of this room, its ornaments, and its furnishings, one felt that under these gilded ceilings the Emperor had become a mere mortal for his parents or close friends. Behind, followed parlors and apartments of all sizes; to the right was a storeroom for furs and robes; in front the apartments of the Emperor; to the left, those of the Empress.

The Imperial Apartments

It is a renunciation to describe the contents of these apartments. Let words paint the picture of the rich materials and artistry. What we had seen until now was a miserable specimen compared to this. It was a vision of the *Thousand and One Nights*, such enchantment, a delirious imagination that one cannot dream of compared to the palpable reality before us! All was going according to the requirements of the general Montauban, when the British officers who followed brigadier Pattle, unable to contain themselves, began by operating, what was later called 'removal'. The ice was broken. Although the presence of the general served as a brake, each man set his sights on a particular art object, so the material value was absolutely not a cause for disdain. In sum, in the first visit, which lasted until ten in the morning, we took very little. Moreover, the general had allowed each chief of service to choose an object to his liking, as a souvenir. However, greedy passions were singularly excited; the marine infantry company set up as a guard to the Palace became insufficient; and, it must be said, the temptation was too great, she won over the officers and soldiers on guard as well! One felt that these riches were the price of blood, the fruit of conquest; that we were the first to arrive at the *rendez-vous*; that in our place the English would not bring such delicacy; did they wait to share when they were at Ho Si Wu and Tchang-kia-Ouang?[145]

Looting

Then began the disassembling of the Palace, but a partial disassembling, very different from what would have certainly been practiced by the English army, well used to doing this wherever they are; because our soldiers, more squanderers than interested looters, contented themselves with the *feeling* of plunder rather than incur the sense of shame they would never forget under their noble flag, did not take more than one tenth of the wealth that they had at their disposal. And the proof is that so few of them thought to make a fortune when in their place is was easy to amass a considerable one. In this circumstance, therefore, where everything was possible, as everything is relative, good and evil, according to the environment where you find yourself, leaving something was a virtue, and as such, our troops showed a real disinterest in grabbing anything they could remove from the Palace. Among the many tales which mark the violation of the Palace, it is one that deserves to be told.

---

[145] Du Pin seems to be saying that when the British looted these villages that they did not concern themselves with sharing with their French brother-in-arms, so why now should the French worry about equally sharing this prize with the British

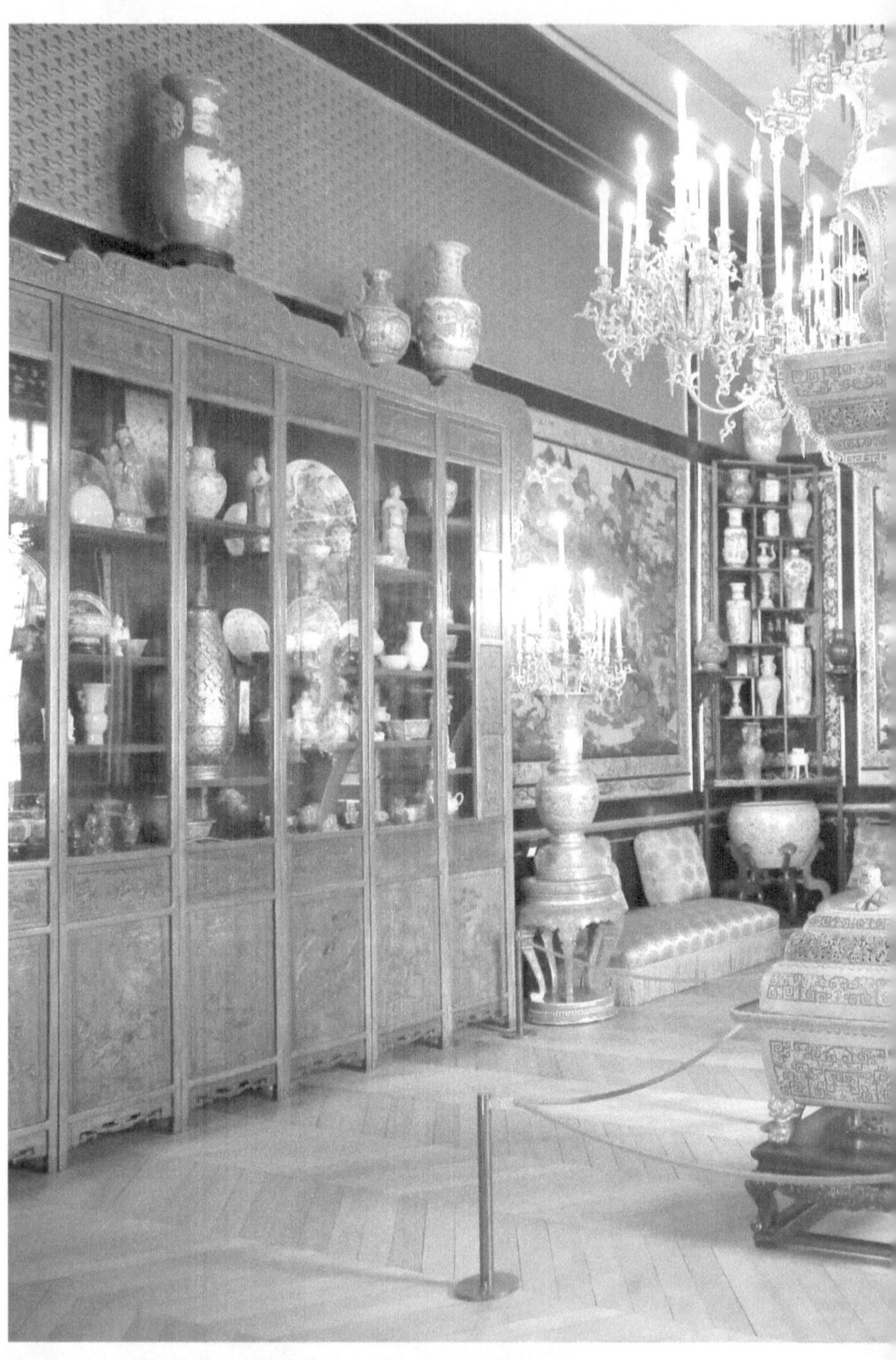

Treasures from the Yuen-ming-yuen. Palais de Fontainebleau.
Copyright the Author, 2016.

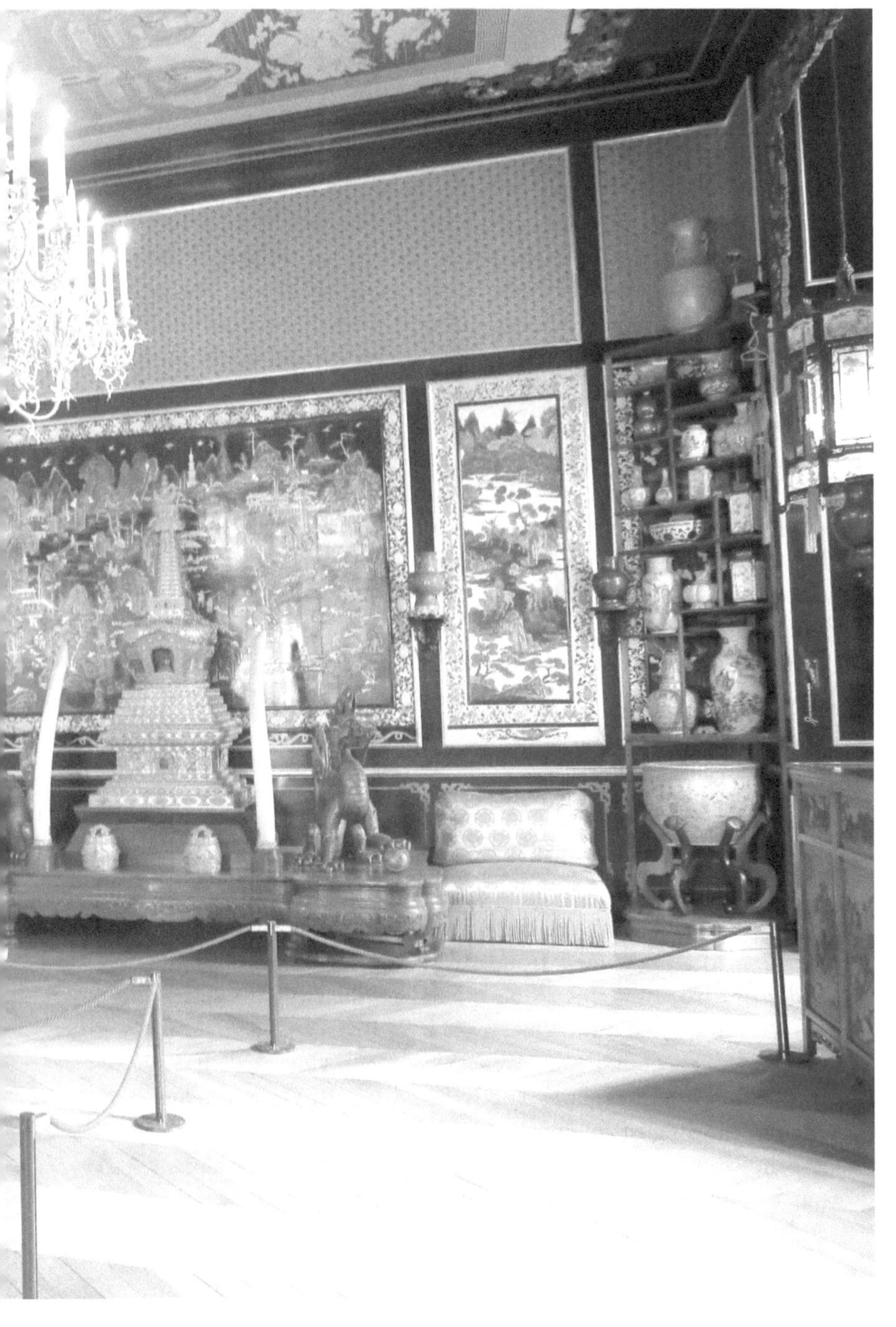

An officer emerging from a dark corridor, in an enforced situation, darker still, and lost in the darkness, resorted to the redeeming light of a match to find himself [this 'officer' was Du Pin himself]. He was in a room, in an instant flooded with clarity, thanks to numerous candelabra laden with candles with which it was adorned. Then arose in his eyes the most splendid of spectacles! To left and right of this room stood two beautifully adorned altars on which, and next to them, were incense burners, chandeliers and solid gold vases, carved and inlaid with pearls and precious stones. At the center of one of these altars, there was a small shrine in gold, adorned with turquoise, green with antiquity, and holding a black stone idol, topped with an animal head, wolf or fox. The shrine bore four inscriptions in the Chinese, Mongolian, Tibetan and Manchu languages, indicating that it had been offered by a great military leader, to some emperor dead for a thousand years. To left and right of the shrine glittering with jewels were two human skulls mounted in the form of cups. The brilliance of illumination soon attracted others into the room, which became that what was at that hour of all things in the palace of the Emperor of China. It was his private chapel.

Arrival of the British

About two o'clock the commanding general of the British army arrived. A commission composed of a colonel and two officers, was immediately named from each army in order to choose and share worthy items to be offered to their highnesses the French Emperor and the Queen of Great Britain. The members of the French commission were Lieutenant Colonel Du Pin [the author!] and captains Foerster and Cools; Colonel Foley chaired the English Commission. Together they proceeded in the choice and dividing up of the remaining objects; but already much and more precious things had disappeared. The operation ended at nightfall.[146]

---

[146] Du Pin, p. 239

The European Palaces and Tibetan Town

Note, the European Palaces were a small part of the overall Yuen-ming-yuen, in the north-eastern section of the park. They were designed by Jesuit missionaries resident at the court of Qianlong during the second half of the 18th century. After the burning, being made of brick and stone, these buildings survived much better than their counterparts made largely of wood. In the park today the ruins of the European Palaces are some of the extant remains. Du Pin is one of the few witnesses to describe this portion of the Palace:

It will profit us in the few moments that remain to us, to complete the overview of the Summer Palace, before fire made it into little more than a memory. Behind the Palace lay a lake much larger than the one we have mentioned [the 'Back Lake'], which was surrounded by three buildings [*sic* nine]; one on the right serving as chancellery and containing, among heaps of writings and boxes of Chinese ink, some artistic objects, and 'basketfuls' of furniture and valuable fabrics. Then we went into a huge maze of canals, lakes, and mountains, all man made, and scattered with secondary palaces, long abandoned and turned into store rooms. In one of these palaces, built in the style of Louis XV, one could see a series of rooms lined with Gobelins tapestries, the arms of France, and the walls of which were hung length-wise with portraits of the beauties of the court of France, with their names at the bottom [these were the European Palaces]. But the tapestries and tables were dilapidated, gouged and showing signs of long abandonment. Further, a huge pagoda, whose walls were eight meters high, ran its parallelogram eight hundred meters of land on its long sides and five hundred on the shorter side. The interior was covered with small temples full of the richest offerings. It was in one of these temples, they found a splendid armor whose helmet was adorned with a crest, with a fine pearl, most oriental and as big as a pigeon's egg. [Note, this armor was given to the Emperor; Unfortunately, the pearl was lost/stolen in transit].

The walls of the pagoda, forming at the top a very large gallery, raised three meters, was divided into an infinite number of small niches adorned with gilded bronze statuettes. We could count, without exaggeration, more than seven or eight hundred. This was, without doubt, the workshop of idols of worship of the cult of the Buddha, very widespread in the Chinese Empire. In front of the pagoda, was almost as extensive a palace, but turned into a warehouse and filled with silk, velvet and satin robes with gold brocade and decorated with the five-clawed dragon. Finally, we arrived at a large lake, surrounding the clear waters of the palace of the emperor's concubines [the Fou Hai, or Happy Sea]. All that was fantastic and feminine that one can dream of, most rare, more valuable, and even more extravagant, was there together.

Overview of the Palace

These lakes, these mountains, these palaces, these courts, these pagodas, covering a huge area, rendered useless any surveillance that tried to examine it. Countless bands of Chinese, driven to one side, spread through these splendid buildings, looting and destroying all the objects that they could not carry away, either because of the volume of these objects, or due to the Imperial Dragon that they carried as a sacred mark. These depredations carried out by these indigenous looters were considerable.

In the afternoon, General de Montauban went to visit several pagodas located three kilometers from our camp. One of them, in white marble, built on a mound, stood as high as the Pantheon in Paris, and sheltered under its dome a colossal statue, with a woman's head in Greek profile, and a body from which came forth nine great arms, which gave birth to nine hundred other smaller arms, forming a range.

Departure

The 9th, in the morning, was fixed as our departure [from the Summer Palace]. The camp of the French army offered as strange a tableau and as animated as one can imagine. Outside and inside the tents were piled the most diverse and valuable objects, riches of a recent day which and on which had lulled so many dreams that now the drum sound had dissipated. We had seen the trooper, naive as a child. He had the foresight and the destructive instinct, without thinking of the fatigue of the road, stuff his pieces of silk clothes and velvet, as if he had a stage to take to make tribute to his country; then, those that he could not take away. They were everywhere, sumptuous furniture, silk, gold brocaded imperial robes, and, above that, that pitiful faces to be separated. As for silver, it was so abundant that it was almost disdained because of its excessive weight. More than one soldier gave an ingot of 480 fr., or thereabouts, for a few bottles of water spirits or absinthe. At eight o'clock we had to say goodbye to this ephemeral opulence, and, although there had been no distribution of food since yesterday, there was no murmur from the ranks; everyone was happy and light under the burden of his booty. The grenadiers had wrapped red silk bands around their headgear; outfielders, true to their colors, yellow silk bands; the center had adopted blue. Hungry Chinese, in large numbers, had drawn close to our soldiers, following them as servants, the pay a piece of bread. These poor devils, each attached by his long braided hair tail on the lapel or shoulder strap of its singular patron, he frivolously followed, without flinching under the weight of baggage which he had been charged. It was dressed in this way and in this burlesque order that the army began to march.

Once they had completed their mission in Peking, the French army sailed south to Shanghai. In January 1861 Dupin joined Antoine Fauchery on a photographic expedition to Japan. They sailed from Shanghai to Yokohama. Presumably he was granted some form of leave to do this, or perhaps it was an official visit. There Du Pin took a series of photographs in Edo and Yokohama. He left Japan in May 1861 and returned to Paris.

As discussed in the chapter concerning Antoine Fauchery, there are in existence at least two series of photographs, both stereoscopic, taken by personnel from the French expeditionary force in China. Based on the preponderance of evidence, both of these series appear to be the work of Charles Du Pin. Research done by Terry Bennett indicates that on returning to France after his time in Asia, Du Pin not only published a series of photographs of China and Japan but also held a small exhibition to display them. There was also a set of images given to Queen Victoria by Du Pin.[147] There is little doubt that Du Pin took some, if not all, of the extant images taken by French photographers who were part of the expedition. As discussed elsewhere, it is quite possible, likely even, that Fauchery also took his own set of photographs that either have been lost or have not yet been identified.

There were other potential photographers, part of the French force, that did not produce any photographs of the Peking area. Baron Gros, the diplomatic representative of Napoleon III brought with him a full set of photographic equipment, but when the ship carrying him and Lord Elgin was sunk off Ceylon, as Elgin notes in his letters, all of the Baron's equipment was lost. There was also Paul-Emile Berranger a French naval commander who took photographs during the first phase of the Second Opium War (a number of these images are in the collection of Terry Bennett and it is he who has researched the involvement of Berranger in photographing activities during the China campaign). However, Berranger was not involved in the second phase of the war. So his collection of images, whilst very interesting and important, are confined to scenes along the Chinese coast. Legrand, a French commercial photographer in Shanghai was also expected to take images of the campaign but decided it would be more profitable to sell liquor to the troops during the expedition, and left his camera behind.

Thus, in spite of his busy military duties and collecting while on campaign, Du Pin is currently the only Frenchman from whom there are identified photographic images of the China expedition. However, significantly, he omitted to take any picture of the Summer Palace. As is the case with Antoine Fauchery, the official photographer, this is a cause of frustration among scholars because Du Pin was so close to the action and had privileged access to the Palace on October 7 and 8. Du Pin, it seems, as head of the French committee that set aside loot for the French and British heads of state, used his access to the Palace to avail himself of a hefty selection of loot and was distracted.

Shortly after he returned to Paris, Du Pin held an auction to dispose of his discoveries, and this fact brought him considerable attention and criticism. His collection became quite famous because of some of the

---

[147] Enquiries by Mr. Bennett and by the author have failed to reveal the presence of the Du Pin photographs, or indeed any photographs of the 1860 campaign, in the Royal Collection

wonderful works of art he obtained, and his acquisition of it notorious in Parisian society.

There is an extant advertisement of the Du Pin sale and also sale records. Some of the Colonel's loot was purchased by the Wallace family, Marquesses of Hertford, and are now part of the *Wallace Collection* in London. Du Pin had the foresight to acquire the extremely important and very beautiful book of *The Forty Views*—watercolors of the Emperor Qianlong's favorite forty views of the Summer Palace that were commissioned by him in 1744, and evidently 'rescued' by Du Pin. These, Du Pin put up for sale in Paris. But before they could be sold, Napoleon III intervened and they were eventually acquired by the Biblioteque National, where they can be found today. So given Du Pin's looting and his other official responsibilities on October 7 and 8, it is not at all surprising that he failed to take pictures of the Palace. He was after all an *amateur* photographer and his engagement with the booty of the Palace was a lucrative aspect of the French campaign, and he was able to benefit substantially from it.

Before embarking for China, Du Pin had run up considerable debts. His gallant lifestyle of women and gambling left him in financial difficulties, and it seems he used his Summer Palace loot as a way of setting matters straight. Again thanks to the research of Terry Bennett, it is known that his very public sale of loot, right after the French Army returned home, in the wake of the condemnation of the sacking of the Palace by Victor Hugo, was highly controversial. Important members of the military establishment felt Du Pin, especially given his role on Montauban's staff, had abused his position and brought the French Army into disrepute. He was severely rebuked for his actions. His next military appointment was rescinded and he was placed on inactive service.

Undoubtedly Du Pin was a remarkable man, if at times a rascal. He was intelligent and talented. He was valued by the commanders under whom he served both for his bravery and his effectiveness, performing duties under very different sets of conditions. His observations of the China campaign reflect his ideas and point of view. He was a patriot, a loyal son of France. His journal is full of defenses of the French army and its looting. According to Du Pin, the French were essentially entitled to loot the Palace and had no obligation to wait for the British to arrive or to share equally with them. He claims that the French soldiers were 'moderate' or restrained in their looting and destruction of imperial property, which seems to stretch credulity. He is quick to place blame at

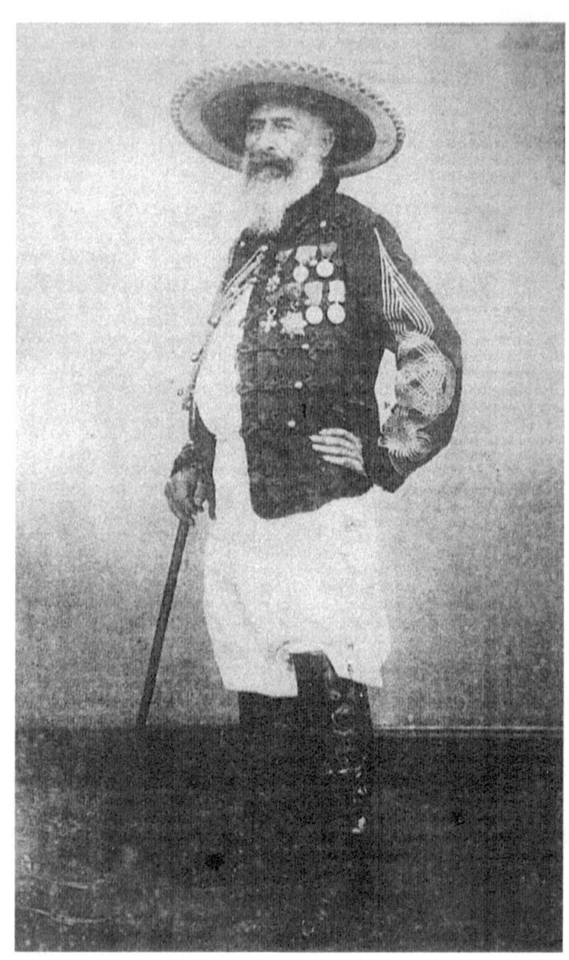

Charles Du Pin, most probably in Mexico, in his red jacket, photographer unknown

the door of the British and the local Chinese citizens for more thorough looting and extensive destruction. He clearly loved the French soldier, and by all accounts, they seemed to have loved him back.

Du Pin was a larger-than-life character with a vision that extended beyond that of most officers. He was quick to make enemies, but was appreciated by his commanders-in-chief. Later, in Mexico, he revealed himself to be a ruthless tyrant, but in China he was at worst a great plunderer. It is said that he appreciated the art that he found in the Palace and the Palace itself. That is probably true. But one should not over-emphasize his romanticism for the material world. He was romantic in his view of French destiny, and looking back at him after 150 years that appears pompous and 'puffed-up', but in the context of the mid-19th century to which he belonged, he was merely a product of the empire that Napoleon III created. It is in that context that he and his observations should be judged.

Mexico

Du Pin's military career, in spite of the scandal that rocked it, was not over after China. His reputation as an effective officer was known to the Emperor and he personally recalled Du Pin to active service in 1863. He was made part of the army sent to conquer Mexico and to put Napoleon's cousin on the throne.

Du Pin became infamous in Mexico. He was known as 'The Red Devil' for his ruthless tactics. After the French had placed Maximillian on the throne of Mexico, there was tremendous resentment in the country against France and guerilla activity was rife. Du Pin was made chief of counter-insurgency, answerable directly to the French commander-in-chief. He became, much to the resentment of other officers, essentially a law unto himself. And this seems to have suited Du Pin. His intelligence and understanding of topography made him a wily foe. He developed a band of loyal irregular troops and adopted an eccentric form of dress which included a red coat. But at the same time, he made enemies in the military establishment and with the Emperor Maximillian himself. Du Pin took 800 local banditos, trained them, and took them north into the Mexican desert to face the worst of the geographic conditions and the guerillas. His ruthless suppression of opposition to French rule became notorious and his execution of guerillas scandalous. Mexico seemed to bring out a brutal side of Du Pin that was not seen in China.

Du Pin was recalled to France in 1865 and investigated for exceeding his authority, but cleared. He briefly returned to Mexico in 1866, before all French troops were recalled to France in 1867. He became sick and died in France in 1868. He was only 54, but his excessive lifestyle and years of campaigning had exhausted his body. Du Pin remains a very controversial figure and at the same time a valuable source of information and images from the China of 1860.

Du Pin's Loot

Du Pin returned to France with a fabulous haul of loot and he exhibited his famous collection in Paris in 1861. As discussed, he also returned to France with financial problems. In order to pay off his debtors was forced to sell his collection from China and Japan. The auction was held on February 26, 1862. The catalogue states:

> The objects found in the summer palace Yuen-ming-yuen, in the secret anteroom of the emperor and in the large pagodas, are of historic interest which augments their value as works of art. The Grand Album, painted on silk, representing the forty views of the Imperial Palace, will attract particular attention, because it is only here where one can find the images of the Summer Palace, beautifully made in China, which fire has destroyed.[148]

Of the 331 items auctioned by Du Pin, 49 were stated as coming from the Summer Palace. The *piece de resistance* was a solid gold wine cup, taken from the Emperor's private 'chapel'. The following details of Du Pin's loot and item numbers are from the auctioneer's annotated catalog, as well as other sources:

Item 282: Solid Gold Cup, decorated with large, fine pearls, rubies, and sapphires. Made in the Qianlong period (1736–95); sold for 8,010 francs. According to the Wallace Collection, Sir Richard Wallace acquired this cup, as well as the pair of gold incense burners (below) in Paris at the sale of a collector called Allegre, in May 1872. The 1872 sale catalog described them as having Summer Palace provenance. The base on which the cup is mounted has a label stating it is from the collection of Colonel Du Pin.

Item 283: a 'reliquary' in solid gold, decorated in ancient turquoise, made on the 25th day of the 11th month of the 42nd year of the reign of Qianlong. Inscribed in Chinese, Mongolian, Manchu and Tibetan. Also found in the Emperor's private chapel.

Item 288: a pair of incense burners, in bronze covered with gold. They were at the foot of the emperor's throne in the 3rd throne room of the Yuen-ming-yuen. Sold for 9,050 francs.

---

[148] Du Pin auction catalogue, (Baudry, auctioneer) February 26, 1862. Translation by the author

> Item 316: a square-sided 'spinach jade' vase with sculpted lid, mounted
> at the top with the imperial dragon. Sold for 5,200 francs.
> Item 329: Grand Album representing the 40 views of the palace
> Yuen-ming-yuen, painted on silk, with a description of each
> palace, 40 double leaves. Withdrawn from sale.

The French establishment was furious. The feeling was that French officers should not be on campaign to acquire wealth and if they did they
should do so discreetly. Du Pin's very public exhibition and then sale of
his collection was an embarrassment for the government and the army,
especially since Du Pin was the man responsible for evaluating the art
works that should be brought back to France for Napoleon III.

"The expedition to China is a huge revelation," proclaimed Du Pin,
less concerned with the morality of the actions of the Allies and more
focused on their efficacy, "One believes in dreams when you think that
only a few thousand Europeans were able to dictate terms to an empire
of four to five hundred million people. The ease with which they overthrew the many and brave armies, would leave no doubt about the fate
of this vast Empire . . . Was armed intervention a real benefit; you might
say, what advantage can result from this intervention? What advantage?
That of having increased our influence . . . finally to have marked our
place on the world's biggest marketplace. The government and the army
prepared the way. French trade will you dare to engage in it? There is the
question!"[149]

Bibliography

Du Pin, Charles, *Paul Varin, Expédition de Chine*, Levy, Paris, 1862

---

[149] Du Pin, *Expédition de Chine*, 1862, p. 307, translation by the author

Around the World and Then to China

Antoine Fauchery

"Never, in military memory, had he [the soldier] passed through prospects so sparkling, and the palaces of Yuen-ming-yuen made him forget all the hardships and privations of the road, never weary of the memory of brilliant gold, silver and silk, like the reading of a tale from the Arabian Nights . . ."

—Antoine Fauchery

"During the war in China, Fauchery obtained, through M. Dalloz, a position as part of the expedition, with an official title, and to be the correspondent for *Le Moniteur*. At the Summer Palace, he saw at his feet twenty times the fortune he had sought in vain; but it seemed to him less easy to excavate there than to pick at a miserly lode. Fauchery, who so well represented the French press in China, has died in Japan at the time he was implementing the materials of a great work on these little-known countries. An honorable position, a well-deserved reward awaited in France, but too late, as always. He left a reputation for wit, of gaiety, of bravery that will not be extinguished."[150]

Antoine Fauchery has been described as a man of mystery. Certainly in death that is the case. For a man of both letters and photographs he

---

[150] *Revue anecdotique des lettres et des arts: documents biographiques de toute nature, nouvelles des librairies*, p. 90, translation by the author

tantalizes us with insight into the Summer Palace as well as the holes in the surviving record of his time with the French expedition to North China. Fauchery came to China as a journalist and photographer, part of the French headquarters staff. Although his personal diaries and papers have been lost, he submitted reports to a French journal which give a lively and unique record of his observations of the Summer Palace. As a photographer, frustratingly, this talented and observant individual seems to have left no visual record of Peking, or tantalizingly, none have emerged.

He was born *Antoine Julien Nicolas Fauchery* in Paris on November 15, 1823, second child of Julien Fauchery, a merchant, and Sophie Gilberte, née Soré. He was baptized at the church of St Germain l'Auxerrois. Little is known of his early years other than that he was educated at the Lycée and trained in several of the arts, including architecture, painting and wood-engraving. As a young man he studied art under the great French painting teacher Leon Cogniet, who was master to many accomplished artists, but became impatient, abandoning painting and tried his hand at engraving. Dissatisfied with this too, the Frenchman turned to writing. He was introduced to Théodore de Banville, the son of a captain in the French navy, and an up-and-coming writer, who published a volume of verse in 1842 and *Les Stalactites* in 1846.

Through Banville, Fauchery met a number of prominent Parisian men of letters, including, Henri Mürger, Champfleury, Charles Baudelaire and Gérard de Nerval. Friendship with Banville seemed to inspire Fauchery who began writing for *Le Corsaire-Satan*, a popular newspaper, for which he produced a number of articles. He became part of Banville's group of literary friends and began living something of a bohemian life; so much so that he was immortalized as the painter *Marcel* in Murger's *La Vie de Bohème*, a character in Pucini's opera *La Bohème*. "Antoine Fauchery, a fine boy, spiritual and charming, who Murger cast as the painter Marcel in *La Vie de Bohème*, was the most gay company of the friends of my youth," noted de Banville later in life.[151] As a writer, it was said, "Fauchery . . . took a lot of care, time and trouble to complete a short work more than he ever loved literature."[152]

---

[151] *Oeuvres de Théodore de Banville. Odes funambulesques, suivies d'un commentaire*, p.354, translation by the author

[152] *Revue anecdotique des lettres et des arts: documents biographiques de toute nature, nouvelles des librairies*, p. 90, translation by the author

In Paris, Fauchery also developed a close friendship with Gaspard-Félix Tournachon (known as 'Nadar'), an important and innovative early French photographer. It appears that Fauchery learned the new and somewhat demanding photographic technique that he was to practice in France, Australia and Asia, from Tournachon.

Fauchery had a restlessness and a strong spirit for adventure. He and Tournachon joined a group of French idealists and emigré Poles who left Paris in 1848 in order to help liberate Poland from Russian rule: "One evening, among others, at the Café de Buci, we were talking for the thousandth time, and still with the same feeling of anguish, when suddenly, like a very thunderbolt, we saw and felt, falling into our arms with tears, embracing us like brothers, not Fauchery and Nadar, but, as their passports said, Nadarski and Faucheriski . . ."[153] The two desperados traveled west through Germany where they were briefly imprisoned before returning to Paris. They did not reach Poland.

Eighteen forty-eight was a year of revolution throughout Europe. It would be surprising, given his revolutionary zeal, if Fauchery did not play a supporting role in the French Revolution of 1848 which overthrew once-and-for-all the French monarchy and ushered in the Second Republic headed by Louis-Napoleon, later Napoleon III, the man who was the political head of the France that invaded China in 1860. The poet Alphonse de Lamartine was head of the French Republic for three months in 1848.

Fauchery continued to write during the period 1848 to 1852 and authored a series of pamphlets, serials and short plays for the journals *Le Corsaire*, *Journal pour rire*, *Dix Décembre* and *L'Evénement*. He also wrote a biography of the Archbishop of Paris, Denis-Auguste Affre, who was martyred at the revolutionary barricades in 1848.

Antipodean Voyage

In July, 1852, Fauchery responded to the call of adventure again and, together with his girlfriend Louise, set off for Australia in pursuit of gold, which had been discovered in the State of Victoria. He hoped he could make his fortune and that would allow him to live the life of a man of letters back in Europe, which was his ambition. The two lovers

---

[153] Nadar, in Dianne Reilly, *Sun Pictures of Victoria*

undertook the long sea passage from London to Melbourne. Fauchery's observations of life at sea have survived and are quite amusing. He sketches a vivid picture of life on board for 160 passengers during their four-month long ordeal:

> It is in this cellar, or rather in this oven, that two thirds of the passengers stay during most of the day; through a dense vapour their silhouettes move incessantly and with fantastic jerks . . . the children cry out, the crockery rattles, while sick folk moan and others get drunk; from all this hurly-burly comes a nauseating smell complicated by the heavy perfumes of the musk-flavoured liqueurs with which, alas, the over-voluptuous Englishwomen inundate themselves . . . Phew! Let us go [above deck] as quickly as we can.[154]

After a short stint in Melbourne the young French couple set out for the Ballarat goldfields. Eventually Fauchery was to conclude that nothing but heartbreak and disappointment lay at the bottom of the mines, but in the meantime he kept a diary in which he recorded his observations of activities in the rough mining town: "The mine! that is the one centre of attraction, the goal of all hopes, the dreamland where the sun rises! . . . It's the gold-fever; the fever for pure gold . . . driving all those who are stricken with it to throw up suddenly the most lucrative positions to run away and look for the uncertain."[155] He himself chanced upon a nugget of nearly 4 ounces, poking up between the roots of the grass, but overall was unsuccessful as a miner.

One party, working a shaft next to Fauchery, uncovered a huge nugget on their second day at the diggings, "Suddenly the sound of two metals meeting rang out from the point of his pick; he stooped down: a shining yellow spot had been laid bare! . . . it was a mass with the volume of a big paving-stone, a piece of gold set right in the middle of a hole, a piece of gold weighing 132 pounds! I was not on the spot at the moment when the man who made this wonderful find came up from the hole; I saw him only an hour later. He was a negro . . . He was speaking very softly, like a man who has just committed a crime. His white partners were in little better case than he was; they were stunned by success . . .

---

[154] Fauchery, *Lettres d'un mineur en australie*
[155] Ibid.

The day after this memorable event the five partners . . . announced their intention of making back for Europe immediately. And actually, having gone back to town, they embarked on the same steamer that had brought them out, taking with them on one hand two hundred thousand francs' worth of gold, and on the other hand the memory of having been miners for two days." (Fauchery and Daintree Collection : "Prospecteurs, les chercheurs d'or").

After two years at the diggings Fauchery returned to Melbourne in 1854 with little to show for his efforts. He reflected on the changes he observed in the young city:

> I found Melbourne modified, practically transformed. Canvas Town and the bazaar on the banks of the Yara-Yara no longer existed. The government had replaced the canvas city with vast, spacious board huts for the use of newcomers with no resources . . . The town had developed, the shops had grown bigger, the takings in the hotels and public houses had increased tenfold. Two theatres, elegantly constructed, one for dramas, the other for equestrian feats, had replaced the old circus, that modest tent in which I had heard the Ethiopian harmonists from the Gaîté theatre delighting the colonial audience. In the streets, the blue and red shirts, the muddy trousers and the big gendarme-boots had become rare, and the consideration once accorded to this costume now seemed to be given entirely to black coats and white collars. The miners themselves, coming down from the mines, hastened instinctively and unanimously to shed the dusty livery of labour, to rank as citizens by putting on the garb of the regular gentleman.[156]

With £60 in his pocket, he opened the *Café Estaminet Français*, a French café at 76 Little Bourke Street East, a retreat for immigrants who "lacked any sort of social milieu and sought in vain a little corner where they could sit in comfort," according to Dianne Reilly. He invested in a French billiards table, glasses, plates and a coffee pot. His advertisement stated, "BILLARDS, SOFAS, LUNCHES, COLD SUPPERS, You can

---

[156] Fauchery, *Lettres d'un mineur en australie*, in Dianne Reilly, *Antoine Fauchery, 1823–1861 Photographer and Journalist par Excellence*, La Trobe Library web site

play pool!"[157] But despite his best efforts to offer a genial environment the venture was not a success. He notes, "I shall not regret Melbourne, though I found it a small city and am leaving it a large one, with shops . . . gas lighting . . . and with five new theatres [including] a lyric theatre where the company made up of people from all countries, sings the same opera in French, English, German and Italian."[158] Undeterred, the Frenchman returned to the diggings once more, this time to the Jim Crow goldfield, near Daylesford. He became a storekeeper. But again success eluded him, and he left Daylesford broke after just six months in business. Fauchery trekked back to Melbourne on foot, recording in his letters sensitive impressions of the scenery, the Aboriginal people, and the various squatters he observed en route.

With no money left Fauchery sailed back to France in March 1856. His comedy *Calino* which he had written with Théodore Barrière was staged that spring in Paris. His dairy from which *Lettres d'un mineur en Australie* was derived, was published by *Le Moniteur Universel* in fifteen instalments from January 9 to February 8, 1857 and was then published in book form by Poulet Malassis et de Broise. "Antoine Fauchery's account of his time in Australia is overshadowed by his remarkable photographs, but his written account is a lively tale of minor successes and failures in the new colony," notes his biographer Reilly.

On January 15, 1857 Fauchery married his girlfriend Louise-Joséphine Gatineau at the Church of St. Pierre de Montmartre. In attendance was his friend Dr. Gérard Piogey to whom he had dedicated the publication of the *Lettres*.

Fauchery's remarkable antipodean efforts had achieved for him recognition in official circles. In April 1857 he applied for and received a commission from the French government to return to Australia with the purpose of recording his impressions as part of an official *photographic* mission to Australia, India and China. He was awarded 500 francs to accomplish the task.

Fauchery left France and Europe forever, in July 1857, when he sailed from London to Australia for the last time. Equipped with a camera, official governmental accreditation, and funds for travel further afield, his goal was to send home his written impressions and photographic records of various countries in the East.

---

[157] Ibid.

[158] Ibid.

On arriving in Melbourne in November, 1857 he set up shop as a photographer at 132 Collins Street East. James Smith, a prominent Melbourne writer, records his observations of Fauchery at this time:

In a small four-roomed cottage, standing a little back from the south side of Collins-street East, on the block of land now covered by the Austral Buildings, I found a French gentleman domiciled as a photographer, who, accompanied by his wife, was cheerfully reconciling himself to the discomforts of colonial life at that time, and exhibiting a vivacity and buoyancy of spirits all the more remarkable as he had occupied a prominent position in Paris as a man of letters. This was M. Antoine Fauchery.[159]

Fauchery advertised his services in the *Illustrated Melbourne News*:

Mr. A. Fauchery, just returned from Paris, begs to inform his friends and the public that he has brought with him a splendid collection of PHOTOGRAPHIC PORTRAITS AND ENGRAVINGS, executed by himself during his sojourn there, and for which he solicits their early inspection at his rooms, No. 132 Collins-street East. Mr. A. F. is ready to take portraits, Landscapes, and Views of Public Buildings or Private Residences, in large sizes, by quite a new process; and also to operate the reproductions of Portraits, Engravings, or Pictures into as many copies as desired. Likenesses taken after death.[160]

Early in 1858 Fauchery began a connection and collaboration with Richard Daintree (1832–1878), a public school educated English geologist who had recently developed an interest in photography. Daintree came to Victoria in the hope of using photography in geological fieldwork. Together, Daintree and Fauchery re-visited the Victoria goldfields and captured images of life there; and toured parts of South Australia recording some of the finest early photography of the region. "Their different backgrounds—Fauchery the artist, and Daintree the geologist—combined to produce remarkably high-quality images so early in the history

---

[159] *Illustrated Melbourne News*, January 16, 1858, p.38, in Dianne Reilly, *Antoine Fauchery, 1823–1861 Photographer and Journalist par Excellence*, La Trobe Library web site
[160] Research by Dianne Reilly

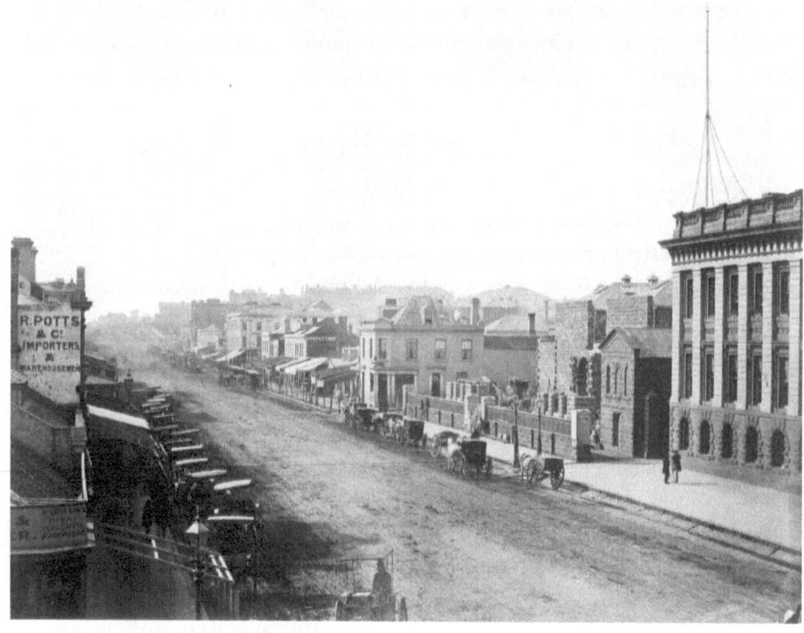

Swanston Street, Melbourne, Antoine Fauchery, 1858

of photography, providing a rare and invaluable record of life in Victoria in the late 1850s,"[161] according to Dianne Reilly who is an authority on Fauchery's Australian photographic journey.

The Fauchery-Daintree collaboration produced some remarkable photographs which they sold as albums of views, or studies, similar to those offered by photographers in Hong Kong. Throughout 1858 Fauchery worked as a photographer in South Australia. The 53 images in the *Fauchery-Daintree Album*, which is to be found at the La Trobe Library, were made in the studio of Fauchery using the collodian wet-plate process that produced wonderful large format albumen silver prints. An album, entitled 'Australia', featuring images of Melbourne and Victoria, was favorably reviewed by the *Argus* on August 13, 1858 as 'the Sun Pictures of Victoria'. The reviewer noted, "The collection under notice are admirable specimens of this branch of art, for art it is; as, irrespective of the skill requisite to manipulate successfully, the manipulators must

---

[161] Reilly, Dianne, *Sun Pictures of Victoria*

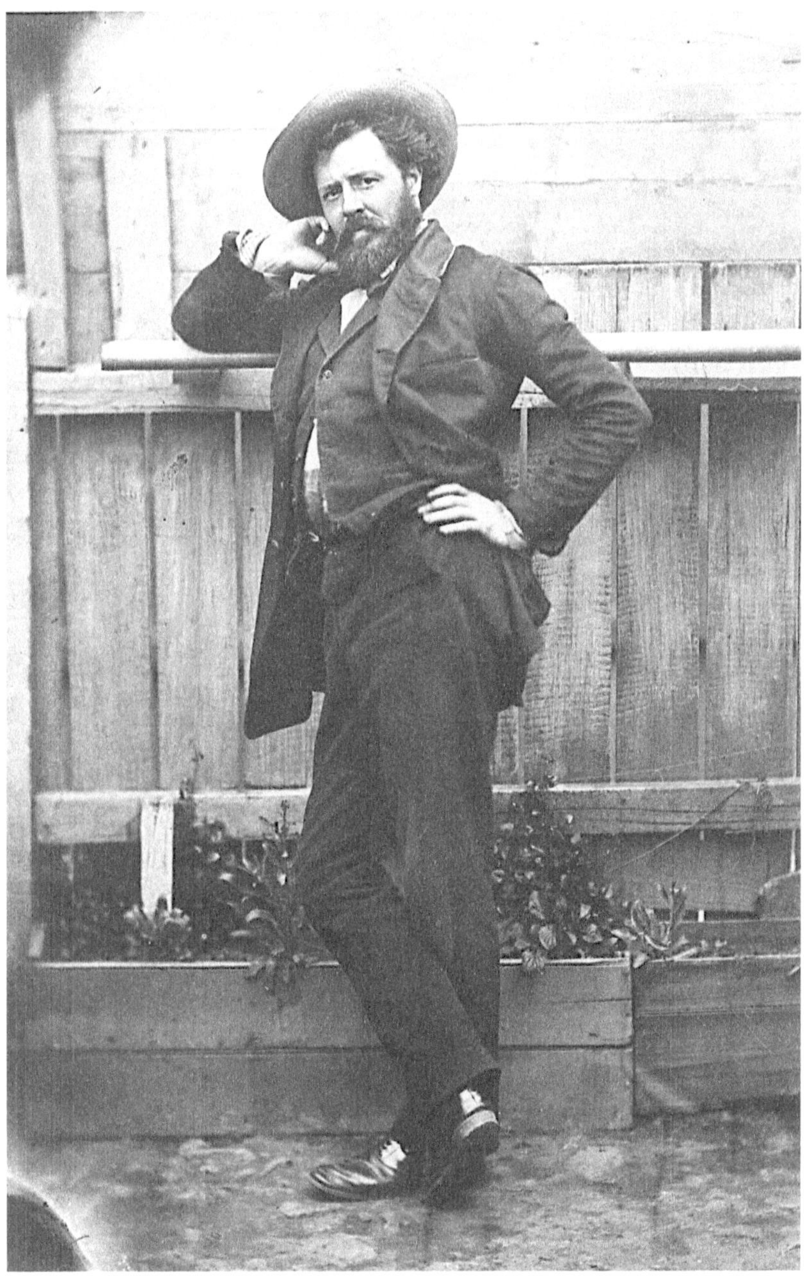

Antoine Fauchery, Australia, 1858,
photographer unknown (perhaps Richard Daintr)

also possess the artistic faculty in choice of subjects, in the selection of the most picturesque point of view, and in discerning the most favourable aspects or accidental dispositions of light and shade."[162] These were amongst the first photographs of Melbourne. His photographic portraits on paper using collodion negatives were exhibited. At the March 1858 *Victoria Industrial Society's Eighth Annual Exhibition of Manufactures, Produce, Machinery and Fine Arts* where he won a gold medal. Fauchery had at last found professional success! Clearly this was an occupation that suited the Frenchman. In terms of technique he had learned his lessons well back in Paris from the pioneer Nadar.

There is no additional information about Fauchery's activities in Melbourne, except for his presence at the death-bed of his friend Lionel Moréton de Chabrillan, the first French consul-general in the city. His partnership with Daintree, who went on to fame exploring the northern portion of Queensland, came to an end sometime in early 1859.

Onward to the Orient

In March 1859 Fauchery left Melbourne, sailing to Hong Kong, which he reached on May 13. From there he and his wife journeyed to Manila on June 9.[163] There exist, somewhere, images that Fauchery took in the Philippines, as recorded in his obituary, but their whereabouts are not known today. What *is* known is that Louise Fauchery died after a short illness in the Philippines in late 1859, leaving her husband alone and devastated.[164]

There are few details of how Fauchery occupied his time in the Philippines. It is speculated that he was working as a spy for the French Government at a time when French expansionist activity was starting to ferment. But there is really no evidence to support this conclusion other than a lack of tangible work output. In late 1859 Fauchery requested funds from the French government to go to China, and in early 1860 he received approval and a payment of 1,000 francs from the French embassy in Manila to take photographs and write reports of what he saw in China. When he learned that the French were launching an attack on Peking, Fauchery contacted *Le Moniteur* asking to be their

---

[162] Ibid.

[163] Research by Terry Bennett, see Bennett *History of Photography in China 1842–1860*, p. 94

[164] Ibid.

correspondent, to which they agreed. Accordingly, Fauchery sailed from Manila to Chefoo, mainland China, arriving there on July 8, 1860, and joining the French troops.[165]

In China, Fauchery became acquainted with Charles Du Pin the head of the Topographical Service with the French force. The two men became friends. Du Pin, was a photographer in his own right and, like Fauchery, an adventurer. Du Pin brought with him to China his own camera and photographic equipment (he has been confirmed as the author of at least one series of images taken during the campaign). Fauchery, consistent with his practice of taking photographs, and his charge from the French government, can be said, with all but certainty, to also have his camera with him when he arrived in China. There was, therefore, between the two friends, at least one, probably two, cameras and one assumes they had availed themselves of enough chemicals and glass plates to capture images in China. This rather dispels the myth that the reason for the lack of images coming from the 1860 French expedition to China was the lack of photographic equipment.

There are two series of photographs that exist in known collections taken by Frenchmen connected with the expedition. One—a series of stereoscopic images[166] that cover Peking, Shanghai and the captured Chinese forts—was in the collection of collector and author Terry Bennett. It is clearly attributable to Charles Du Pin (rather than Fauchery), as is discussed in the chapter covering Du Pin's work. This leaves another series that was collected by Clarke Worswick and is now at the Getty Museum in California. This series of 10 images includes subjects ranging from a patrol of the 102nd infantry regiment, to scenes that appear to have been shot in Shanghai—schools and the temple of Zikawei. Interestingly the *numbering* of the images suggests that there were originally at least thirty-nine in the series, although there are only ten at the Getty. The author's research has confirmed that the 102nd regiment was part of the French expeditionary force and were not in China at any other time in the 19th century, so these appear to be images captured in 1860.

Zikawei is near Shanghai, where the French were stationed *en route* to North China. Crucially, Fauchery did not join the force until *after*

---

[165] Ibid.

[166] Stereoscopic images are duplicate pictures, side-by-side, that when looked at through a specially designed stereo viewfinder produced a 3-D effect. They are normally printed on card and to the naked eye they appear as two identical images side-by-side

they had sailed further north, to Chefoo, and so it is unlikely that he was the author of this series (although he did sail back to Shanghai after the peace treaty was signed). Also, the pictures in question appear at times poorly composed and are more likely the work of an amateur (such as Du Pin) rather than the accomplished Fauchery. There is also an image of the French *te deum* service (part of a set of 24 images discovered by Régine Thiriez), in remembrance of the men killed in captivity by the Chinese, at the French cathedral in Peking. This has no obvious attribution other than it was taken by a Frenchman and so cannot be allotted definitely to either Du Pin or Fauchery.

Fauchery, as evidenced by his correspondence during the war and accounts of him at the Palace on October 7, was present at every phase of the campaign, including at the Summer Palace when it was captured and looted. The subject matter of all of this was clearly important and clearly marketable—for Fauchery needed to make a living. He had his camera, and even if something had happened to damage it, he could potentially have used Du Pin's, or perhaps one of the other officers in the Topographical Service. There was enough time during various lulls in the fighting, during the time at the Summer Palace, and after the cessation of hostilities, for photographs to be taken, if not of the military operation, then certainly of the country and the cities; as was amply demonstrated by Felice Beato who produced a series of remarkable pictures. So what happened?

War Correspondent

During the course of the China conflict Fauchery was to submit fifteen reports, as letters, to *Le Moniteur Universel* which were published in Paris between October 12, 1860 and February 3, 1861 as the *Lettres de Chine*. If Fauchery kept a diary during his time in China, it has not survived. We must rely on his dispatches to France, which he apparently wrote at night in his tent, for his impressions of the events and sightings in Peking. They provide a valuable firsthand account, from a non-military observer, of what happened immediately before and during the occupation of the Summer Palace from the perspective of the French expeditionary force:

"General Grant learned from his spies that the Tartar army had withdrawn to Yuen-ming-yuen," Fauchery notes in a letter dated October 6,

1860, quoting General Montauban, regarding the French army's approach to the Summer Palace:

> [A] . . . magnificent imperial residence, a mile and a half from where we were, and he proposed me to march against it: the time was not late, the troops were not tired, they were full of ardor; a mile and a half in these conditions shall be promptly taken. After [what turned out to be] a long and difficult march, we arrived at seven o'clock at the villas Yuen-ming-yuen (Haitien); we followed a road of paved granite and we crossed a magnificent bridge that leads to the imperial palace, located 200 meters from the bridge, and whose entrance is opposite. The road between the bridge and the Palace is lined on the left with thick trees and beautiful sites; to the right, a large square bordered by a row of fine houses, home to the principal mandarins. Before settling in camp, General de Montauban wished to search the entrance of the Palace, which was believed to be occupied by part of the Tartar army. But who would have guessed? Twenty armed man with bows and arrows, spears, was the extent of the resistance. As the evening was advanced, the French general made a secure occupation of the first court, for fear of some surprise during the night, and the troops rested quietly.[167]

When he had chance to see it in daylight on October 7, Fauchery was astonished by the turn of events and the sumptuousness of the Yuen-ming-yuen:

> It's really amazing, cries here the eyewitness, that we find ourselves in this situation, but yet that's the way it is, but since we find ourselves in China you are not so surprised. Nowhere else, assuredly, would one see the head of a great empire comparable to Europe and commander of three hundred million subjects, run away before six or seven thousand soldiers, and allow them to go shopping in the center of his government, his throne and the prestige attached to it; abandon everything behind him; his capital, his palaces, his treasures, altogether until then his

---

[167] Fauchery, *Les Lettres de Chine*, as recorded in *Cochinchine*, p. 118, translation by the author

favorite retreat, the largest and most sumptuous of his residences, the Chinese 'Versailles' or Saint-Cloud, and leave it in the custody of a few men armed with arrows and spears.[168]

As part of the French force, Fauchery had two days to wander around the Palace and he had some very definite reactions to what he saw. Perhaps influenced by his socialist leanings, perhaps the Palace was just not to his taste, he found the rooms grotesque in their opulence:

> In our quick tour through the meanderings of the Yuen-ming-yuen park, we discovered large buildings like the shops of the City of France or the City of Paris, true warehouses, each filled with nothing but rolls of silk of all colors, staggered along the walls ten rows deep, stacked throughout the extent of the warehouses leaving only a narrow corridor for traffic! Other stores, crowded under the same conditions, contained cotton fabrics, Russian linens, furs; in each, enough to clothe the whole of China! In the other remaining principal buildings were scented sachets, necklaces, watches, pipes. In one of them we found over ten thousand gods of a single identical model, and in another pastries and (spoiled) preserves to fill a ship! What a profusion of superflousness![169]

He found the valuables that the Palace apartments contained over-done and not to his taste—Fauchery was not fond of Chinese art—while at the same time acknowledging their obvious value and appeal to the ordinary soldier:

> Ecstasy is not possible where the extreme carelessness and bad taste present indelible stains that result in tarnishing too much the luster of such rare magnificence, and unfortunately you cannot take a step through these Chinese splendours without the injury to the eye by the rough, clumsy, artless, way that these objects of incredible luxury are laid out . . . in the halls, narrow passageways, the hallways, you collide with antique treasures ever the more dazzling: monstrous porcelain creations from the

---

[168] Ibid.

[169] Ibid.

good climes of Nanjing, vases and incense stands the height of a man in silver or massive in gold, boxes, furniture and chests of all shapes and sizes, in Peking red lacquer, so rare today and so sought today by collectors, of green and white jade shaped a thousand ways, lace, ivory, agate and coral, festoons of sandalwood, roots fashioned in crazy ways, Canton brushes, peals from Ceylon and jewels as big as hazelnuts and sown everywhere! And heaps of little things yet invaluable, of impossible nomenclature, scaffolded from floor to ceiling on shelving of great incoherence, in the most grotesque fashion! . . . this entire mass of objects represent assuredly a good many millions in actual value, but where confusion and even profusion confuse the look, sometime dazzle, but does not charm. In short, when you leave this Palace, this eighth wonder as sung by the poets of the heavenly entourage, you carry a violent headache and the vague memory of a Babel built upside down!

As for the soldier, who did not look so close, it was at the height of his wishes. Never, in military memory, had he passed through prospects so sparkling, and the palaces of Yuen-ming-yuen made him forget all the hardships and privations of the road, never weary of the memory of brilliant gold, silver and silk, like the reading of a tale from the Arabian Nights could give.[170]

All-in-all Fauchery's account gives a very different views of the Palace and its contents, but is consistent with the course of events recorded elsewhere. He did not find the museum of Chinese valuables to his liking, either in principle or practice.

Photographs

Did Antoine Fauchery take photographs in China, and if so, did they survive? This is an important question that has been debated by scholars. Almost certainly, he did, but probably not at the Summer Palace. Firstly, there is no doubt that Fauchery was tasked by the French government with taking photographs during the expedition, and in one of his early

---

[170] Fauchery, *Lettres de Chine*, as recorded in *Cochinchine*, pp. 117–118, translation by the author

letters to *Le Moniteur* he acknowledges this, although in subsequent letters he never speaks of actually taking any. The French public were anxious to see the first pictures of the famous Summer Palace and of Peking itself. Several photographers were part of the French expeditionary force, as is discussed in the chapter concerning Charles Du Pin. Fauchery is recorded in his obituary as having taken photographs in the Philippines, and since the funding he received from the French government specifically required photography, there is every reason to assume that when he arrived in China with camera in hand, that this was his objective. There was plenty of material to photograph in China, and Fauchery had the time to take images.

Robert Swinhoe, the translator with the English army, was a French speaker and corroborates in his memoir the presence of Fauchery at the Palace, and tells of spending time with him. Regarding October 7, Swinhoe notes, "After breakfast the Moniteur correspondent got me a pass to accompany him into the Palace . . . and we had not been long in before Sir Hope Grant and Staff arrived . . . [Later] *The Moniteur* correspondent, myself, and the eunuch, continued our rambles through the palaces."[171] There is no indication at all here that Fauchery was taking pictures—which surely would have been noteworthy. And no pictures have emerged that were taken during the French occupation of the Palace. On that same day General Montauban actually complains in his memoir of not having a photographer on hand to photograph the Palace. It has been suggested that in view of the extensive looting, the French be sensitive to images captured of the scenes of rampage.

The most likely explanation is that General Montauban did not want photographs taken of the looting, and so he explicitly forbade it, and in any case, with all the chaos that ensued on October 7 and 8, photography was farthest from the minds of the French. It was probably also not the first thought of the photographers themselves. Fauchery was healthy during the Chinese phase of the expedition with both an incredible spectacle to admire, and the clear prospect of acquiring valuable loot. In his obituary it states that Fauchery was present at the looting but did not partake himself. Given his strongly held principles and his unconventional character, that is certainly possible, although it seems curious that the writer of the obituary would say such a thing. Fauchery was not a man of any means and if he did not loot he was one of the very few who

---

[171] Swinhoe, p. 300

did not. One is left to conclude that he either spent the days of October 7 and 8, when he had no military duties to perform (unlike some of his army colleagues), either wandering through the Palace and critiquing it or that he, like everyone else, including his friend Du Pin, was taken up with at least some looting. Either way, no photographs of the Palace taken by Fauchery have emerged, which is frustrating for the historian and contributes to the huge gap in the visual record of this amazing palace complex.

If Fauchery did capture images throughout the campaign, even including the Summer Palace what happened to them? Whilst the series of stereoscopic images discussed earlier seem to be both sequentially wrong for Fauchery's schedule of movements and in terms of composition and technique not the work of a professional, the answer to Fauchery's work may lie in what he did after the peace was signed.

Death in Japan

Leaving North China, both Fauchery and Dupin sailed to Shanghai with the rest of the French military force. Evidently Fauchery was still serious about completing his work for the French government of documenting the mysterious countries in the Far East. It seems he must have had a camera with him, or he could not possibly take pictures in Japan. Again he to the wrote *Le Moniteur*, this time requesting that he be their correspondent in *Japan*, to which they replied in the affirmative.[172] Du Pin and Fauchery embarked together from Shanghai for Yokohama on January 10, 1861. But once on land Fauchery became very sick. He notes in his last letter to *Le Moniteur* dated March 1861, "During my travels I had defied illness and epidemics for too long and my luck ran out . . . In Japan I have been suffering from an indeterminate illness that I caught whilst in Shanghai. Thinking that the sea would improve matters, and spurred on by my desire to travel, I arrived with a bad case of dysentery and gastritis."[173]

Contrary to his hopes, Fauchery did not recover. He remained more-or-less bed-bound during his time in Japan and died in Yokohama on April 27, 1861. He was just 38. Father Mounicou, a French priest living

---

[172] Research by Terry Bennett, see Bennett *History of Photography in China 1842–1860*, p. 95

[173] Fauchery, letter dated March 1861, research and translation by Terry Bennett

in Japan noted in his diary, "April 27: A Frenchman, named Antoine Faucherie [*sic*], recently attached to the French Legation, died in the hospital, after having refused the consolations of the church."[174] The Frenchman was buried in the Yokohama Foreign General Cemetery, which was at the time the only burial ground available to foreigners. Research by Harold S. Williams, an Australian living in Japan, indicates that he has been unable to identify Fauchery's grave (which probably had no marker), or any photographs that he might have taken in Japan in the Japanese archives. It is highly likely that Fauchery took images in Asia and had intended to publish them when he returned to France, but his untimely death undid his plan and the photographs along with his notes and papers were left in Japan and probably discarded.

It is impossible to imagine that such an artistic man would not find much of interest in North China and Shanghai. He also could have used his situation to take images that could be sold commercially. Fauchery had the skill, the means, motive and opportunity to take some artistically beautiful images of what to him was the strange and wonderful land of China and its people, a country he might never see again. It is also the case that if he did take photographs they do not appear to have been developed into prints because of the photographer's ill health and premature death. Fauchery, at least for now, continues his reputation for being a man of mystery.

A Paris periodical recorded: "He was a man of letters of an adventurous nature and with a chivalrous character, who lived and died impoverished." His friend Banville noted sorrowfully of the death of the heart-broken Fauchery: "I do not remember anyone who has been to me, with a higher degree than he, the most elegant and sympathetic, quick of comprehension and of supreme grace."[175]

Bibliography

Fauchery, Antoine, *Les lettres d'un mineur en Australie*, Paris, 1857
Fauchery, Antoine, *Lettres de Chine*, *Le Moniteur*, Paris, 1860–1861
Lefort, L., *La Chine et Cochinchine*, Lille, 1862

---

[174] Mounicou, research and translation by Dianne Reilly

[175] *Oeuvres de Théodore de Banville. Odes funambulesques, suivies d'un commentaire*, p. 355, translation by the author

Reilly, Dianne, *The Mysterious Antoine Fauchery*, *The La Trobe Journal*, Melbourne, April 1984
Reilly, Dianne, *The Sun Pictures of Victoria*, Currey O'Neil Ross, Melbourne, 1983
Thiriez, Régine, *Through the Barbarian Lens*, Routledge, Abingdon, 1998

Exploring China and the Summer Palace

Robert Swinhoe

"Ere long a dense column of smoke rising to the sky indicated that the work had commenced . . . As we approached the Palace the crackling and rushing noise of fire was appalling, and the sun shining through the masses of smoke gave a sickly hue to every plant and tree, and the red flame gleaming on the faces of the troops engaged made them appear like demons glorying in the destruction of what they could not replace."

—Robert Swinhoe

One of the very best accounts of the events surrounding the sacking of the emperor's Summer Palace was compiled by a young interpreter with the British consular service—Robert Swinhoe. Swinhoe was born in Calcutta in 1836 to Robert and Caroline Swinhoe (née Anderson), one of ten children. Robert senior, a lawyer, was also born in Calcutta in 1798 and Caroline in Ceylon [Sri Lanka] in 1810. They were a family that over several generations were connected with the Empire and the colonial service. A picture has survived by Felice Beato of Swinhoe in 1860. Based on his dark looks and the fact that the family had been several generations in India, perhaps Swinhoe was Anglo-Indian (a mix of English and Indian heritage) which was very common in the British service in India.

Swinhoe is best-known not for his involvement in the China War but as a naturalist. As a trained observer and a sensitive man not given over to wild looting, Swinhoe has left one of the most detailed and nuanced accounts of the Summer Palace in all its glory, before it was destroyed. He was one of the first from the British force to enter the Palace and had unobstructed access, before the mayhem of looting and destruction commenced. He also gives valuable details of the looting that ensued.

Swinhoe developed an interest in birds early in life and when he lived in China discovered many species hitherto unknown in the West. Both of Robert's parents died in 1845, probably from a disease epidemic, leaving him an orphan. Shortly thereafter he was sent back to England to the custody of his grandparents. Like many children born in the colonies, Swinhoe was a stranger in England, but it was there that he attended school (he was resident in London in 1851, living with his grandparents) and later studied at London University where he graduated in 1853. He must have been a talented student as in 1863 he was elected as a fellow of King's College London.

In 1854, at the age of eighteen, Swinhoe applied for and was admitted to the Chinese section of the British consular service and was sent to Hong Kong. Evidently considered a gifted linguist, he was assigned to be an interpreter. In 1855 he was posted to Amoy in southeastern China. There he became proficient in both Mandarin Chinese and the local dialect. He also became interested in exploration and pursued his interest in the birds and wildlife of East Asia. In 1856 Swinhoe made his first trip to Formosa (Taiwan) where he began making observations of the wildlife and collecting samples. In Amoy the potential for encountering a European woman must have been slim, but Swinhoe succeeding in meeting the eighteen year-old daughter of a Scottish missionary, and they were married in 1858:

> [marriage] "On Oct. 27, at the British Consulate, Amoy, China . . . by the Rev. John Stronach, uncle of the bride, Robert Swinhoe, Esq. . . . of H.M.'s Consular Service, to Christina Lochie, eldest daughter of the Rev. A. Stronach."[176]

In 1858 Swinhoe was assigned to *HMS Inflexible* which circumnavigated Formosa in search of British captives. The same year he was transferred

---

[176] Birth, Marriage and Deaths in England and Wales

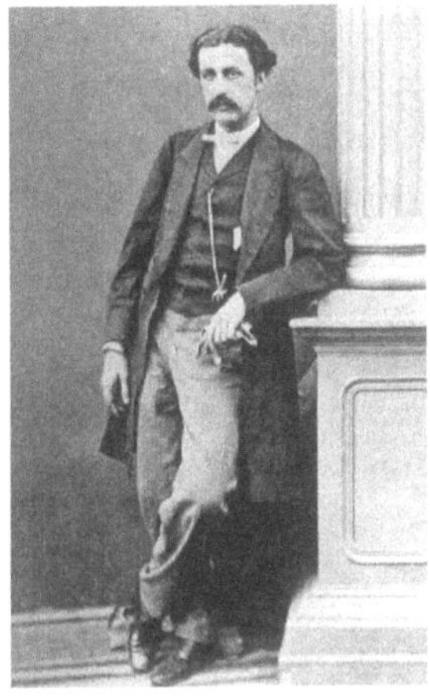

Robert Swinhoe, date unknown,
photographer unknown

to Shanghai. Interpreters were invaluable to the British Expeditionary Force, and when hostilities resumed between Britain and China in 1860 the talented young consular officer was posted to the staff of Sir Robert Napier, commander of the 2nd Division of infantry in China, and in the latter stages of the campaign to General Sir Hope Grant, the commander-in-chief. It was as a key member of Hope Grant's staff that Swinhoe was able to witness first-hand so many of the actions pivotal to the fate of the Summer Palace.

Swinhoe's account of his adventures during the war is entitled *Narrative of the North China Campaign of 1860*. It was written in early 1861, immediately after the conclusion of hostilities, while the author was still in China. It was then published the same year, in London, and provides a crisp, animated account of the happenings among the British forces. The narrative covers the entire campaign, although the focus here is on the activities related to the Summer Palace.

Swinhoe begins his account by explaining his surprise at being called into service as part of the expedition:

> I had procured three months' leave of absence from Amoy, and was enjoying myself to the best of my ability at Canton, in rambling through its narrow painted and gilded streets, and inspecting its old yamuns [*yamun*: an official Chinese residence], temples, and pagodas, when one morning it was announced to me that I was placed by Mr. Bruce at the disposal of Sir Hope

> Grant, for the time being, as interpreter. Accordingly, I went down by the first boat to Hong Kong; where all was bustle and preparation for the intended expedition to the north. Ships were being chartered by the score; troops were arriving by shiploads almost every day.[177]

The army traveled north by stages to Peking, as has been described. Swinhoe was assigned to Brigadier Pattle's command in the advance to the Summer Palace and was part of the first group, with the French, to enter the garden. The interpreter begins by describing the road to the Yuen-ming-yuen:

The Narrative

> The stone-way runs through this group of ugly hovels [the village of Haitien] on to a broad road with the pavement through its centre. Stone garden walls stand to the right and left as you advance, enclosing the grounds of nobles and imperial connections. You advance, *suivant le pave*, across a stone bridge, take a sweep to the left, and the road brings you between two large pieces of water in front of the grand entrance to the palace of Yuen-ming-yuen. It was here under the trees that the French were encamped. After the capture of the entrance the French posted a guard at the gate, and bivouacked under the trees.[178]

General Montauban, the commander in chief of the French division personally took Swinhoe and some of the officers from the British party into the Palace grounds, "General Montauban led us into the Palace, solemnly protesting all the while that he had strictly prohibited his troops from entering within its walls, as he had determined that no looting should take place before the British came up, that all might have an equal chance. We entered through the central gateway upon a large paved courtyard."[179] The principal building at the entrance to the Palace was the Audience Hall where the Emperor received official visitors and they paid their respects to him and presented gifts:

---

[177] Swinhoe, p. 1

[178] Swinhoe, p. 293

[179] Swinhoe, p. 294

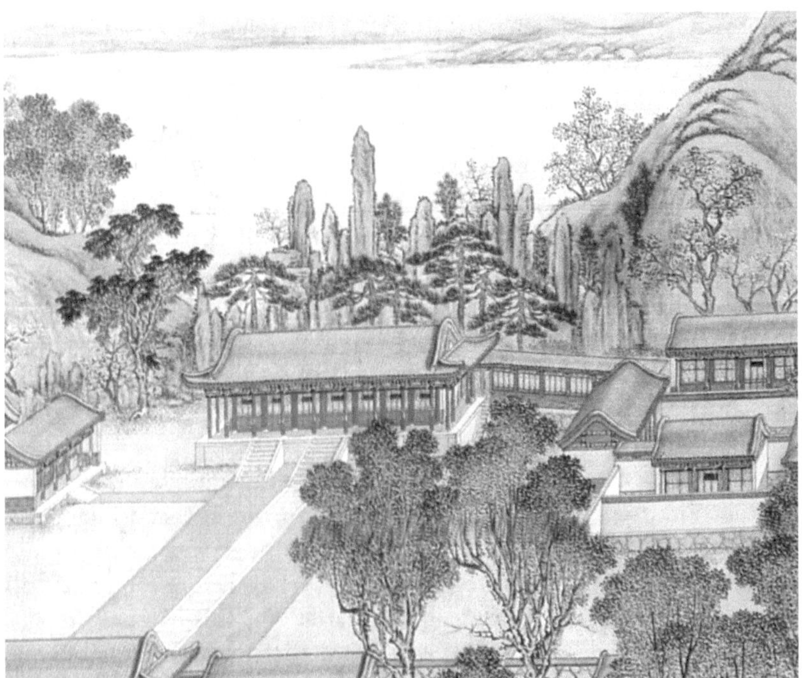

The Audience Hall. One of the Forty Views of the Yuen-ming-yuen, 1744

On the centre of the pavement, and facing the gate, stood the grand reception hall, a large Chinese building, well adorned exteriorly with paint and gilding, and netted with iron wire under the fretted eaves to keep the birds off. We entered its central door, and found ourselves on a smooth marble floor, in front of the Emperor's ebony throne. The carvings on the throne consisted of dragons in various attitudes, and was quite a work of art . . . The left side of the room was covered with one extensive picture, representing the grounds of the Summer Palace. Side-tables were covered with books in yellow silk binding and articles of virtue. There was somehow an air of reverence throughout this simple but neat hall, and we could well imagine the awe that it was calculated to inspire on the chosen few who were privileged to draw near on ceremonial days, and render their obeisance before the much-dreaded Brother of the Sun and Moon.[180]

The French had begun to assemble some of the best Imperial treasures: "The hall filled with crowds of a foreign soldiery, and the throne floor covered with the Celestial Emperor's choicest curios, but destined as gifts for two far more worthy monarchs. 'See here,' said General Montauban, pointing to them, 'I have had a few of the most brilliant things selected, to be divided between the Queen of Great Britain and the Emperor French.'"[181] Subsequently a portion of these were taken by French troops, a portion were sold at the Prize Sale, and only a few items were actually presented to the Queen (some additional items were presented to Her Majesty by individual officers).

Swinhoe exited the great audience hall and continued to explore: "Behind the grand hall was a rockery, and in front of that again a large pond, so that a pebbled path leading over a bridge and taking a semi-circular sweep of half the water had to be traversed before you visited the next hall. The distance was about 500 yards."[182] "This hall was smaller, and not got up with such care: yellow sedan chairs and one mountain chair stood close to the throne; on the right and left were small rooms adjoining, with images of Buddha."[183]

Swinhoe and the officers from the British party were given the first tour of the Emperor's private apartments:

Behind stood another reception hall, and in rear of that again a third; and on the left the Emperor's private rooms, beautifully got up, the tables spread with all manner of precious articles, many of which were English or French. The house was small, and consisted chiefly of one moderately sized room, with a large double-seated throne, covered with gaudily coloured cloth, and having red drapery in rear, which formed a curtain to a waiting recess. A large glass chandelier hung from the roof, and large ornamented clocks and statuettes stood about the floor.

---

[180] Swinhoe, pp. 294–295

[181] Swinhoe, p. 296

[182] Ibid.

[183] Ibid.

Opposite the door was a carved wooden wainscoting, which formed by partition from the hall a narrow passage leading on the left to two small rooms with a spiral staircase in the rearmost of them, conveying you to two other small rooms above, which appeared from their shelves of books to have been the Emperor's studio.

A window in each of these rooms, of large single panes of glass, enabled you to look down into the hall. On the right of the passage were the Emperor's two retiring rooms. A banging blind over the entrance being withdrawn, you could enter the foremost of these rooms, which communicated again, by means of a doorway and another banging blind, with the room in rear, his Majesty's bedroom. A large niche in the wall, curtained over and covered with silk mattresses, served for the bed; and a sloping platform enabled his Majesty to mount into it. A small silk handkerchief, with sundry writings in the vermilion pencil about the barbarians, was under the imperial pillow, and pipes and other Chinese luxuries were on a table close by ... The greater part of the curiosities lay about these rooms, and we proceeded to examine them as we would the curiosities of a museum ... He [Montauban] told the Brigadier [the British cavalry commander Pattle] that nothing should be touched until Sir Hope Grant arrived. The Brigadier then went to breakfast with General Montauban and Staff, and I sought my friends of the *Bureau Topographique*."[184]

Swinhoe continued his tour later that morning, "After breakfast the correspondent of *The Moniteur* [Antoine Fauchery, who was also part of the Bureau Topographique in China] got me a pass to accompany him into the Palace again, and we had not been long in before Sir Hope Grant and Staff arrived."[185]

The Moniteur correspondent, myself, and the eunuch, continued our rambles through the palaces. On the extreme left were the Empress's two rooms and several smaller ones for the sundry wives, but none of them in style at all approaching those of

---

[184] Swinhoe, p. 297

[185] Swinhoe, pp. 299–300

the Emperor's. Several baskets of fruit and sweetmeats lay on the Empress's table, showing that her departure was of no long date. On the right of the grand hall were houses after houses well stored with silks, curios, and luxuries of all kinds, such as birds-nests, tea, tobacco, dried fruits, etc. Then followed the houses of the retainers. Narrow painted galleries connected all the imperial rooms in endless maze intricate, perplexed.[186]

Beyond the island which contained the Emperor and Empress's private apartments lay the rest of the Palace grounds. Here the resourceful interpreter, with his love of nature, could appreciate the artistic magnificence of the imperial creation:

Behind the chief building came the summer park, the extent of wall surrounding the whole being about twelve miles. Pebbled paths led you through groves of magnificent trees, round lakes, into picturesque summer-houses, over fantastic bridges. As you wandered along, herds of deer would amble away from before you, tossing their antlered heads. Here a solitary building would rise fairy-like from the centre of a lake [the three islands in Fou Hai, the Lake of Happiness], reflecting its image on the limpid blue liquid in which it seemed to float . . .[187]

A sloping path would carry you into the heart of a mysterious cavern artificially formed of rockery, and leading out on to a grotto in the bosom of another lake. The variety of the picturesque was endless, and charming in the extreme; indeed, all that is most lovely in Chinese scenery where art contrives to cheat the rude attempts of nature into the bewitching, seemed all associated in these delightful grounds. The resources of the designer appear to have been unending, and no money spared to bring his work to perfection. All the tasteful landscapes so often viewed in the better class of Chinese paintings, and which we had hitherto looked upon as wrought out of the imagination of the artist, were here bodied forth in life. I will not, however, venture on too minute a description, as it would doubtless prove

---

[186] Swinhoe, p. 300

[187] Swinhoe, p. 301

tedious to the reader. Such spots can be better imagined than described. Just within the walls that encircled the grounds on the right and left were large handsome llama temples with yellow tiled roofs [one temple has survived]."[188]

This was the maximum extent of Swinhoe's exploration:

> In the afternoon the Brigadier called me away and we returned to our bivouac where we had to spend another night; but this time we spent the dark hours stowed away in a rude straw hut close to the threshing-floor. The farmer to whom it belonged appeared to have been a bird-fancier, for two cages hung to the roof of the hut, the one containing a hawfinch, and the other a pair of redpoles, both old acquaintances of our boyhood's early days. The next morning we found our way to the British camp before the Tih-shing gate, where the Cavalry Brigade took possession of the quarters set aside for them, and I returned to my old position in the Topographical Department, and put up with Colonel Wolseley.

Looting

From the beginning, loot and abstinence from looting were in the forefront of the conversation when Swinhoe and the French officers entered the Summer Palace. They came to the Emperor's private apartments:

> The greater part of the curiosities lay about these rooms, and we proceeded to examine them as we would the curiosities of a museum, when, to our astonishment, the French officers commenced to *arracher* [to scoop up] everything they took a fancy to. Gold watches and small valuables were whipped up by these gentlemen with amazing velocity, and as speedily disappeared into their capacious pockets. After allowing his people to load themselves as fast as they could for about ten minutes, the General insisted upon them all following him out, and kept on repeating that looting was strictly prohibited, and he would not

---

[188] Swinhoe, pp. 301–302.

allow it, although his officers were doing it without any reserve before his own eyes. He then told the Brigadier [the British Cavalry commander] that nothing should be touched until Sir Hope Grant arrived.[189]

They then made their way back out of the Palace to the front gate:

> The French camp was revelling in silks and bijouterie. Everybody had some rare curios to show me, asking me their worth, as, being an interpreter, and having the eunuch with me they looked upon me as quite a connoisseur. One French officer had a string of splendid pearls, each pearl being of the size of a marble (this he afterwards foolishly disposed of at Hong Kong for 3,000 shillings); others had pencil-cases set with diamonds; others watches and vases set with pearls. Indeed, it would be an endless task to enumerate all the valuables already appropriated from the Palace, and yet the French General had asserted that nothing had been taken, as looting was strictly prohibited![190]
>
> Sir Hope Grant and Staff arrived. General Montauban welcomed him, and positively assured him that nothing had as yet been taken from the Palace; but as Sir Hope Grant walked through the French camp his own eyes plainly told him the falsehood of such a statement. Looting still continued, but more surreptitiously . . . Lord Elgin next arrived, and strongly protested against the looting, saying, in plain terms, 'I would like a great many things that the Palace contains, but I am not a thief'.[191]

The next day looting was going on ravenously:

> On Sunday the 7th [*sic* the 8th], every one that could get permission to leave the camp repaired to the Summer Palace, as the General [Hope Grant] now made no objection to looting. Soon after breakfast I mounted my horse, and galloped across country alone, on a promise to meet some officers there. It was a bright, fresh forenoon, and the sunlight gave a youthful brightness to

---

[189] Swinhoe, p. 298

[190] Swinhoe, p. 299

[191] Swinhoe, p. 300

the decaying foliage of the groves that marked the way. A few villagers stood watchful at the doors of their domiciles, but disappeared sharply on spying me. The French camp still lay before the Palace, and the French sentries at the gate; but no pass was required, the place was open to ravages of any and all. What a terrible scene of destruction presented itself!

How disturbed now was the late quiescent state of the rooms, with their neat display of curiosities! Officers and men, English and French, were rushing about in a most unbecoming manner, each eager for the acquisition of valuables. Most of the Frenchmen were armed with large clubs, and what they could not carry away, they smashed to atoms. In one room you would face several officers and men of all ranks with their heads and hands brushing and knocking together in the same box, searching and grasping its contents. In another a scramble was going on over a collection of handsome state robes. Some would be playing pitch and toss against the large mirrors; others would be amusing themselves by taking 'cock' shots at the chandeliers. Respect for position was completely lost sight of, and the most perfect disorganization prevailed.

The love of gain is most contagious, and in every sense the *incitamentum malorum* [incitement to evil], as the Latin grammar rightly teaches us. No one just then cared for gazing tranquilly at the works of art; each one was bent on acquiring what was most valuable. That scene afforded a very good proof of the innate evil in man's nature when unrestrained by the force of law or public opinion. Licensed theft soon displays the love of greed natural to every heart; and its concomitant vices, jealousy and dissension, speedily follow. The silk warehouses on the right were burst open, and dozens rushed in over the piles of valuable rolls of silk and embroidered dresses. These were throwed out in armfuls. There were piles on piles of them; and though plunderers were conveying them away by cartloads, still the ground was strewn with them, and there was yet more in the houses.

A commission of prize agents had been formed by Sir Hope Grant for the purpose of collecting together curiosities to dispose of for the benefit of the army; and the officers composing it were busy all day in making their selections from what yet

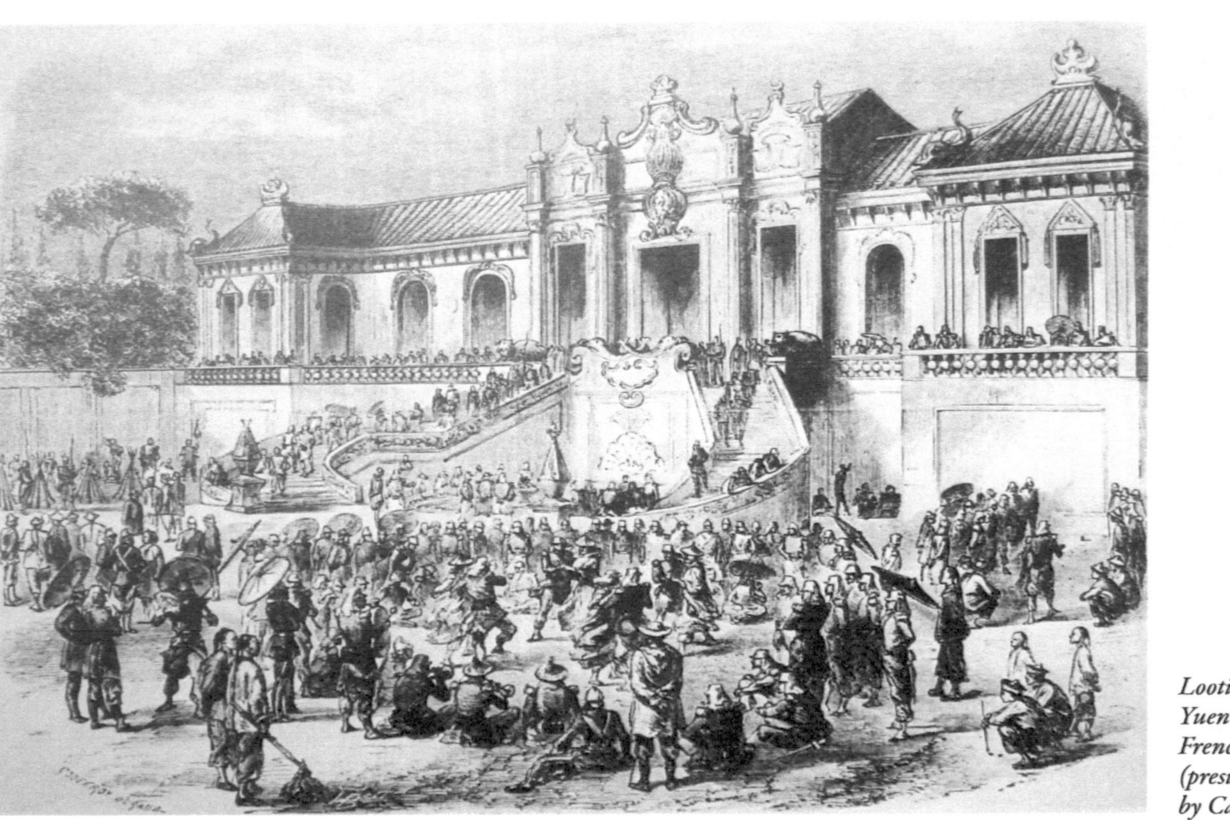

*Looting of the
Yuen-ming-yuen by
French soldiers, sketch
(presumably in situ)
by Captain Legrand*

remained undamaged; while hundreds of others were looting on their own account. New rooms were constantly being found as the marauders extended their researches, still untouched and filled with old bronzes, clocks, enamelled jars, and an infinity of jade stone curiosities. To these the plunderers rushed with eagerness. The booty was plentiful, but the means of conveyance scarce. Chinese from the surrounding villages crowded in and added their numbers to the vivacious looters, and hundreds of them were going backwards and forward forwards all day laden with bundles of spoil. After the spoliation had continued some time, light portable valuables became more rare, and the natives were soon seized upon as porters for the larger curios. An officer would be seen struggling under the weight of old jars, furs, and embroidered suits; he would meet a native similarly laden ... the native would be compelled to relinquish the remainder of his spoil and undertake the freight of the officer's burden. Soon the rumour spread that treasure had been discovered, and an excited crowd ran about to seek for the spot, but very wisely a guard had been placed over it, and the money was made over to proper hands for fair division between the English and French armies.

At the close of the day's loot it was found, as was to be expected, that much dissatisfaction occurred among the different members of the [English] army. Numbers of the officers, and nearly the whole of the men, had by their duties been deprived of participation in the spoil; and among those that were there several had fallen across articles of great value, while others had only procured trumpery 'gewgaws'. Some of General Napier's staff officers, moreover, had stripped off and brought away with them the roof of a neglected cottage, which had been mistaken for brass, but which turned out to be nearly pure gold, worth some 9,000 pounds. This they handsomely placed at the disposal of the General of their division, and it was being beaten out for distribution among the troops, when Sir Hope Grant received intelligence of the intention, and fearing the dissatisfaction that such distribution among a portion of the army was sure to produce, and in order to make matters for those whose duties prevented them from sharing in the work of spoliation, he issued orders to call in all the loot acquired by the officers, appealing to their honour as officers and gentlemen to restore faithfully all they had taken.

This measure, of course, caused great grumbling on the other side among those who had put themselves to considerable trouble in the acquisition and bringing away of what they held. One officer, in particular, who had laden his horse with his treasures and trudged all the way on foot to camp some five miles, leading his steed by the bridle, became the object of many sallies of wit when the orders were published.[192]

The Prize Sale

A sale was then appointed to take place on the 11th [October] of all the articles collected by the commission, as well as of the booty called in; but on restoring his spoil each officer had the option of redeeming it at a price fixed by the commission. When the French had finished their work of destruction in the interior of the Palace, they set the Emperor's private residence on fire, and then relinquished the grounds and removed their camp to a village in front of the Anting Gate. The Seikhs [Sikhs] and a few of the dragoons were the only privates that had found their way to the Palace, and consequently their camps, especially that of the former, were much resorted to for the purchase of silks; the price usually a one dollar (4s. 6d.) a roll, whereas the real value of the silk might have rated at from $3 to $5.

The store and canteen keepers who followed the camp consequently drove a large business in this article, receiving payment for stores and liquors supplied to the troops in silk at that rate. But for knicknacks and *bijoux* the French camp offered the greatest allurement for several days. You had only to ask the first French soldier you met if he had anything for sale, and he would soon produce gold watches, strings of jewels, jade ornaments, or furs; and numbers of British officers, who had disposable dollars, quickly found means of exchanging them for objects of greater value in the French camp. For weeks, in either camp, nothing was talked of but curiosities purloined from the Summer Palace, and what they were likely to fetch. Numbers of the

---

[192] Swinhoe, pp. 305–309

French officers had acquired tolerable fortunes, and their men were rolling in dollars, which led to much disorder and serious disturbances in their camp. For days after their return from their late bivouac their soldiers were constantly to be met with in a state of intoxication, and still carrying out the acquired spirit of plunder and spoliation to the villages in their neighbourhood.

The British share of the plunder was all arranged for exhibition in the hall of the large llama temple, where the headquarters staff were quartered, and goodly display it was: white and green jade stone ornaments of all tints, enamel-inlaid jars of antique shape, bronzes, gold and silver figures and statuettes, etc. fine collections of furs many of which were of much value, such as sable, sea-otter, ermine, Astrakhan, lamb, etc.; and court costume, among which were two or three of the Emperor's state robes of rich yellow silk, worked upon with dragons in gold thread, and beautifully woven with floss-silk embroidery on the skirts, the inside being lined with silver fur or ermine, and cuffed with glossy sable. At the end of the hall were piled immense quantities of rolls of silk and crape of various colours, with several of the beautiful imperial yellow, a kind prescribed by the Chinese law for the use of his Imperial Majesty alone.

The sale continued over three whole days, and was largely attended both by officers and men. A perfect mania of competition appeared to have seized all ranks, and the prices realized were fabulous. The most trivial article fetched two or three pounds, and one of the court robes was knocked down at the high figure of 120 pounds. Had the Emperor been present he would doubtless have felt flattered at the value set by the foreigners on any object solely because it had belonged to him. In the sale of an emperor's effects beneath the wall of the capital of his empire, and this by a people he despised as weak barbarians and talked of driving into the sea! The proceeds of the sale amounted to 32,000 dollars, and the amount of treasure secured was estimated at over 61,000 dollars, making a rough total of 93,000 dollars. Of this, two-thirds was set apart for distribution in proportionate shares to the soldiers and one-third for the officers, of all those engaged in active service during the day of the capture of the Palace. Sir Hope Grant generously made his share over to the men, and as a token of respect, the officers presented him with a gold claret jug richly chased, one of the handsomest pieces of the booty.[193]

Destruction

After several days, Swinhoe accompanied the men that went to destroy the Yuen-ming-yuen and the other palace complexes belonging to the emperor:

The First Division, under General Michel, was detailed for this work of destruction, and betimes on the 18th started for the Palace, where the buildings were apportioned to the different companies to destroy. The French refused to co-operate, as they condemned the measure as a piece of barbarism, forgetting that the chief mischief had been committed by themselves, not only in purloining and demolishing everything that the Palace contained in the way of art, but also in having permitted their men to incendiarise the choicest rooms of the Emperor.

Ere long a dense column of smoke rising to the sky indicated that the work had commenced, and as the day waned the column increased in magnitude, and grew denser and denser, wafting in the shape of a large cloud over Peking, and having the semblance of a fearful thunderstorm impending. As we approached the Palace the crackling and rushing noise of fire was appalling, and the sun shining through the masses of smoke gave a sickly hue to every plant and tree, and the red flame gleaming on the faces of the troops engaged made them appear like demons glorying in the destruction of what they could not replace. The night was a warm one, and as roof after roof crashed in, smothering the fire that devoured its sustaining walls, and belching out instead large volumes of smoke, it betokened to our minds a sad portent of the fate of this antique empire, its very entrails being consumed by internecine war, how it has compelled those nations that might have been its prop to aid in its destruction, and how, beset on all sides, with nought to turn to for succour, it at last

---

[193] Swinhoe, pp. 309–312

succumbs with a burnt of vapour, lost in the ashes of its former self. This seemed merely a portent, but it may not have been a truthful one, for there is time yet for China to regenerate herself, and by cultivating friendly relations with foreign empires, learn from them how in the present emergency of her case she may maintain order among her people, and keep pace with the march of progress.

The Yuen-ming-yuen or 'Round and Brilliant Garden', was fast becoming a scene of confusion and desolation, but there was yet much spoil within its walls, and as they were now allowed to plunder to their hearts' content, numbers of idlers were rushing about and extending their explorations to every nook and corner. In an outhouse two carriages, presented by Lord Macartney to the Emperor Taou-kwang [*sic* Qianlong], were found intact and in good order. The Emperor appears never to have used them, preferring instead the springless native cart or the sedan. Two howitzer guns, with equipment complete, the gift also of Lord Macartney, were likewise found; and among astronomical and various other scientific instruments . . . The 15th Punjaubees, who had the destruction of this most important garden, fell in with large quantities of gold, one officer alone managing to appropriate to himself as much as 9,000 pounds.[194]

Beyond the Summer Palace

A paved road leading from the left wall of the Summer Park passes close under the wall of another enclosed park named the Wan-show-yuen, or Birthday Garden [the New Summer Palace]. This consisted of a pleasantly wooded hill, not many acres in extent, and covered with magnificent temples, comprising the shrines of the three recognized superstitions of China, viz., the Confucian, the Taoist, and Buddhist, with a few yellow-tiled halls, dedicated to the Llamas of Tibet. The temples and minarets in this ground were in excellent repair, and many of them were fine specimens of art, got up with much taste, and decorated with colours of gaudy hue. Within these temples the

---

[194] Swinhoe, pp. 329–331

celestial monarchs were wont to sacrifice and pay their homage to the multitudinous deities and sages that the different sects of Chinese religionists supposed to overrule the destinies of man, on the occasion of each birthday of the 'Monarch of Endless Years', as the ruling majesty of China is designated. A view from the hill-top in this garden of its palatial temples and the country around was most perfect; you looked down on a series of quaintly picturesque buildings, grouped together with much taste; and beyond the wall, towards the south-west, a large lake, with a temple standing on its bosom, connected with the shore by a marble bridge of arches; the flat *champaign* stretched away south, speckled with groups of trees and villages, a tier of hills shut in the prospect on the right, and Peking's turrets loomed in the distance.

Continuing along the paved road, destined alone for the Emperor's use, but now blocked up at intervals with sand and stone barriers to keep passenger carts from availing themselves of it, you pass through the village of Tsing-lung-cheaow, so called from the short stone bridge it leads out on, which crosses a stream that connects the artificial waters of the park with a branch of the Peiho. The bridge past the pavement winds to the left, and finishes its graceful curve round the walls of the next garden, the Chinming-yuen, or 'Gold and Brilliant Garden'. In this are two hills enclosed by a wall, the southernmost hill being surmounted by a tall stone monument, ascended internally by a winding staircase, with loopholes in each story, admitting light on small groups of josses arranged in niches inside. This column was named the Ya-tsing Pagoda, and, from its height, could be seen at a great distance, thus affording an excellent landmark. Its destruction would, consequently, have been more noticeable, but the General was struck with its simple beauty, and spared it as a work of art. The northernmost hill was crowned with a one-spired llama temple, approached by tunnels bored through the living rock, whose sides within were carved into fantastic bas-relief images and representations of Buddha. The temple, however, was neglected, and in ruins.

The grand entrance to these gardens was by the south side, where the road widened into an outer courtyard. There were several reception halls, with thrones, within its precincts, a small lake, with a bath-house, and handsomely painted punts, a tasty little minaret, triumphal arches, and some fine temples; but the whole bore the stamp of neglect and most of the rooms appeared to have been used merely as store rooms for the reception of cast-away finery and old documents. The visits of the Emperor hitherwards must have been few and far between. It seems to have been the custom with the Chinese throughout their parks only to keep those parts in order which the imperial eyes were likely to behold. Elsewhere, bridges and other works, which cost much labour to construct, were allowed to drop to decay; and the watercourses supplying artificial basins were left choked up with dirt, and what should be a handsome piece of water to be converted into a spring was covered with rushes and dank weeds . . . Herds of deer bounded up the rocks, and halting on a projecting point would gaze with fixed and curious stare at the intruders. Large quantities of rare and costly enamels and bronzes were obtained here by many, with articles of value; but most of the precious things were so bulky and cumbersome, that they were obliged to be destroyed, because no one could carry them away.

The day was not sufficient to accomplish the work of demolition, so the troops had to bivouac out, and finish their work on the morrow. I was there on duty both days, and was enabled to take a cursory view of the different grounds of which I have endeavoured to give a short description above. But I confess I feel, what all must feel, how impossible it is to call to the mind's eye of the reader, by any display of words, what one glance of his own eye, however hastily snatched, would have conveyed to himself. Before sunset of the 19th, every place had been fired, and the troops were marched back to camp. We were among the last to leave, and we passed the Summer Palace on our return; flames and smouldering ruins deterred our passage every way, and unhappily many of the peasants' houses adjoining the contagious fire had caught, and were fast being reduced to ashes.

We passed the chief entrance to the Yuenming-yuen, and watched with mournful pleasure the dancing flames curling into grotesque festoons and wreaths, as they twined in their last embrace round the grand portal of the Palace, while the black column of smoke that rose straight up into the sky from the already roof-fallen reception-ball, formed a deep background to this living picture of active red flame that hissed and crackled as if glorying in the destruction it spread around. 'Good for evil', is a bad moral for man to learn; but however much we regretted the cruel destruction of those stately buildings, we yet could not help feeling a secret gratification that the blow bad fallen, and the murder of our hapless countrymen revenged on the cruel and perfidious author and instigator of the crime.[195]

Swinhoe was perhaps the best observer of all the events surrounding the Yuen-ming-yuen, but what is not clear is whether he himself acquired any items of loot. He was certainly in a perfect position to enrich himself, if he so chose. Did he partake of the loot that was lying all about him? Did he acquire items from the Prize Sale? Did he purchase items at bargain prices from the French camp? He portrays a disapproving picture of the looting. If he did acquire some of the Emperor's valuables he studiously avoids all mention of it; and there the trail grows cold.

Aftermath

After the war, in December 1860, Swinhoe was named British vice-consul to the island of Formosa (Taiwan). He opened up the British consulate in Tainan in southern Formosa and then moved it to the port town of Takow. In 1865 he was promoted to the position of Consul General. During the course of his time in Formosa he published several articles on his experiences as British representative, as well numerous others on the rich wildlife of this isolated island. Swinhoe has been described as "One of the most successful exploring naturalists that have ever lived." He was a prolific researcher on the relatively unknown island, where he made many observations and collected many samples. His studies there are still considered of great importance for Taiwan. Swinhoe also contributed to the theory of evolution being developed by Darwin at around this time.

In the course of his studies Swinhoe became an expert on Formosan wildlife and he published some important articles on her fauna. He named, for science, a large number of Formosan species and documented a vast number of birds, butterflies, moths and mammals. He

---

[195] Swinhoe, pp. 332–337

also 'discovered' Formosan tea, which he was instrumental in bringing to trade with Britain.

In 1865 Swinhoe was residing aboard the old Dutch frigate *Ternate* in the harbor of Takow with his young wife:

> During his stay in Takow, Swinhoe made frequent excursions onto Ape Hill where he observed macaques, eagles and a "track of flying butterflies like a river flow." Swinhoe was not only an ornithologist but also a lepidopterist. One common butterfly on Ape Hill today is the elegant brown-and-white Chocolate Tiger, *Parantica melaneus swinhoei*, named by Frederic Moore in 1883 in honour of this pioneer in the study of Taiwan's flora and fauna. Notable mammals that Swinhoe discovered during his time on Taiwan include the Formosan Black Bear, the Formosan Clouded Leopard and the Formosan Sika Deer, as well as identification of the Formosa Salmon.[196]

Swinhoe also collected live animals and specimens that he sent back to London Zoo. *Pere David's* deer, now in Europe, came from Swinhoe:

> The Taiwanese species named by Swinhoe or announced through his systematic collection encompass 227 species of birds, nearly 40 species of mammals, 246 species of plants, over 200 species of terrestrial snails and freshwater malacofauna, over 400 species of insects, and a number of amphibious reptiles, fishes and invertebrates. In memory of Swinhoe's contribution, many species are named after him, including: *Ubus swinhoei, Euploea sylvester swinhoei, Paraglenea swinhoei, Nesiohelix swinhoei, Platyrhaphe swinhoei, Japalura swinhonis, Rhabdophis swinhonis, Rana swinhoana, Naemorhedus swinhoei,* and *Lophura swinhoii.*[197]

Swinhoe stayed in Formosa until he was appointed consul in Fuzhou in 1866. Subsequently he served as consul in Ningpo from 1871. At various times he also served as 'roving consul' for the British plenipotentiary in China, Rutherford Alcock. His duties required him to visit and explore the island of Hainan, in far south China, as well as a journey up

---

[196] The Takao Club: http://www.takaoclub.com/swinhoe/

[197] *The Pioneer of Research on Taiwan's Natural History—Robert Swinhoe*, author unknown

the Yangtse River to Chungking [Chongqing], in Szechuan Province, to help to evaluate possible navigability of the river. All the while he retained the Formosan consulship, and did not relinquish it until his retirement from the service of his government, in 1875.

Around 1871 Swinhoe started suffering from paralysis and moved to Chefoo for recuperation. Ill-health eventually forced him to leave China. From his home in Chelsea he continued to publish notes about his natural history discoveries, and his last publication was the description of a new genus and species of bird *Liocichla steerii*. In 1874 he was admitted as a fellow to the Royal Society in London and was proposed by no lesser figure than Charles Darwin himself.

Swinhoe returned to England in 1875 due to his illness. He brought with him a collection of 3,700 specimens from China. His collection was eventually purchased by Henry Seebohm, and later bequeathed to the Liverpool Museum. Important Chinese species outside of Formosa named after Swinhoe, include Swinhoe's storm-petrel, the Yangtse giant softshell turtle (*Rafetus swinhoeii*), and Swinhoe's pheasant.

Swinhoe died in London in 1877 at the age of 41. It is thought he had syphilis. Perhaps his private life was an adventure. His wife, Christina, was born in Penang, Malaysia. Together they had three daughters. Christina lived in London with her daughters, before moving to Brighton, Sussex, where she died in 1914, 54 years after the destruction of the Palace.

Bibliography

Swinhoe, Robert, *Narrative of the North China Campaign of 1860*, Smith, Elder & Co. London, 1861

Describing Paradise

Maurice Irisson

*"The looting of the Summer Palace . . . lasted forty-eight hours . . .
The man who takes bread from a bread shop is a thief; the nation that
takes 5,000,000,000, that is a great nation."*

—Maurice Irisson

The ancient village of Hérisson is located in the heart of France, north of Auvergne, some 200 miles south of Paris. Situated in a loop of the Aumance River, it has the vestiges of a medieval town—fortified ramparts, stone archways, and old houses. Above the river lie the ruins of the Chateau Hérisson, a stone fortress dating from the 11th century. Maurice Irisson, born in Paris in 1839, was apparently the direct descendent of the lords of Hérisson.

He was called by one nineteenth century compendium "un homme charmant et distingué" (a charming and distinguished man).[198] In the 1860s he changed his name to *d'Irisson*. "He exercised diverse functions, effected a number of overseas voyages and is the author of numerous works under the name of *Maurice d'Irisson, comte d'Hérisson*"[199] (titles, apparently, were very important to the man). Irisson's memoir of his time at the Summer Palace, which is more extensive than any other commentator, is full of fascinating detail and it is quite distinct from any other account, full of color and theatre; and some imagination.

---

[198] *Dans l'Intermédiaire des chercheurs et curieux*, n° 1076 du 20 mai 1905

[199] Ibid.

For a man with a distinguished record of service and overseas adventures, there is remarkably little biographical information available about his life, except for his own accounts of his military adventures, of which there are several. According to French records he was born into a bourgeois family, but judging by the portrait of his grandfather and Irisson's impressive education abroad, they were well-heeled.

His father was one, Augustin Guillaume Irisson, (1790–1849), and his mother, Dorothée Julie Ernestine Maurice-Allard. Maurice, was the youngest of three children, and based on a reference to whether he might be translating Chinese or *Hebrew*,[200] contradictory as that might seem, it is possible that Irisson was also part-Jewish. He conducted his advanced studies at the universities of Leipzig and Heidelberg.

Irisson was an accomplished linguist, but it is not at all clear how or if he knew any Chinese before he set foot in China—most probably he did not. Although he was later to write an account of the state of the country, *Etudes sur la Chine Contemporaine* (1864), unlike the British interpreters who were veterans of government service in China, he was a 21 year-old who had never left Europe! But since General Montauban, who had the pick of who he wanted to accompany him on the *Expedition de Chine*, especially chose Irisson, his credentials must have been quite impressive. It is just unclear exactly what these were.

Having completed his education, Irisson, who was possessed of an adventurous spirit, joined the navy. His first voyage—to Brazil—was enough to convince him that life at sea was not for him. In 1857 he left the navy and went to Florence. As his memoir reveals, out-shone by the art, architecture and the Florentine girls was the joy he felt for the Italian reunification movement and its patriotism and infectious sense of purpose. He left Florence for Tours, where he joined the 6th Hussar regiment, that was designated part of France's army on the cusp of invading Italy and assisting Piedmont with the reunification. In his own words, he showed himself to be a young man of great romantic sense of purpose for events on the world stage:

In the spring of 1859, I found myself in Florence, I was swimming with enthusiasm. And it was not, I must admit, the splendors of

---

[200] Irisson, p. 422

art and nature concentrated in this paradise that put me in this extraordinary state. I walked on the large slabbed street without concerning myself with the palaces that lined them. I passed with indifference the Dome and marvels of the churches. The busts created by Michelangelo did not stop me for one moment. I forgot the priceless treasures and countless picture galleries. I forgot as well there was the shade of large trees, the scent of flowers and women's smiles. I concerned myself very little, in truth, with all that I had come to contemplate, had little to do with the old masters, little to do with young mistresses. It was not indeed of art and love, really! It was *the independence of Italy*. France rose to help her ally, Piedmont, with the Austrian War, and I said to myself with delight that it was essential to my happiness, and that of the world, that Italy should be free from the Alps to the Adriatic. I had no explanation at twenty, Italy and France were crazy. Today after a quarter century has passed on the memories of my youth, I still see with remarkable precision the strange spectacle of this Italian people gripped by the fever of national unity. The young and capable were all leaving to answer the call of the bugles of Piedmont.[201]

So understand that a boy of eighteen [twenty?] who had no prophetic vocation, yet wished to be in the middle of so much activity, to be helpless in the midst of so much enthusiasm. Friends from Florence went one after the other. My companions of pleasure, wrapped suddenly in supreme gravity, declared that it was finished, the laughing and having fun, and that the hour of sacrifice had come.[202]

So I chose a cavalry regiment designated to be part of 'The Army of Italy', and leaving Florence, I headed to Tours, where I soon had the honor to be part of it as second-class rider of 6th Hussars.[203]

Before Irisson's unit had the opportunity to march on Italy, he received orders from Paris:

---

[201] Irisson, pp. 3–4, translation by author

[202] Irisson, pp. 5–6, translation by author

[203] Irisson, p. 307, translation by author

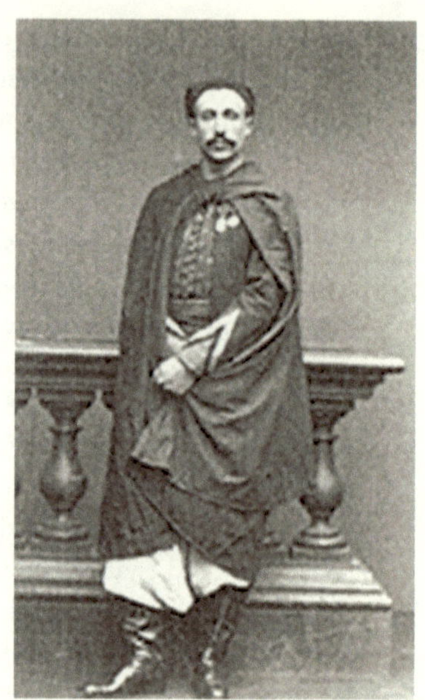

*Maurice Irisson as a young officer,
photographer unknown*

MONSIEUR,

A ministerial decision, you shall attach yourself to my person
and follow me to China, in the capacity as my private secretary-
interpreter. Please, on receipt of this letter, go to your colonel
and ask his permission, which you should receive upon presenta-
tion of this note. You leave for Paris the same day. You will find
me at the *Hotel du Danube*. Your situation will be clarified when
you arrive.

Yours, Sir,

Général de Montauban[204]

So I arrived in Paris and went to the Hotel Danube, where General de Montauban welcomed the Hussar with the greatest kindness. 'You came highly recommended to me,' he said, 'by Marshal
Pelissier and General Fleury. I know I can count on you. You

---

[204] Montauban, in Irisson, p. 11, translation by author

can assist me as something approximating a personal secretary. You will be specifically responsible for transcribing, on closed registers, correspondence with the Minister of War. Finally, as commander in chief of the English forces do not speak French [in actual fact Lord Elgin had lived in France as a boy and Hope Grant went to school in Switzerland], and, for my part, I do not speak English; and few of my staff officers know that language, you will have to serve me personally as an interpreter ... We leave France in the first days of January ... You should receive the orders to prepare to leave for China! Having been for seven months in a single unit, and now to be in general Montauban's division! What a dream for a boy of less than twenty years! I was happy with my lot, delighted with my general, delighted with my existence.[205]

Irisson embraced the new opportunity with enthusiasm, and the memoir of his Chinese campaign describes in detail the journey from Marseilles to Pehtang. For the purposes of the campaign, Irisson was attached to the 2nd Regiment of Spahis. However, he never operated as part of this regiment and he spent all his time with the commander-in-chief as his interpreter. What is of particular note in Irisson's memoir and serves as the best starting point, is his very detailed account of his observations and opinions about the Summer Palace that he gained beside General Montauban, that follows:

The Summer Palace[206]

To depict all the splendours that presented themselves to our eyes, I would now have to dissolve in liquid gold specimens of all known precious stones, and dip into it a diamond quill whose barbs would be the fantasies of an oriental poet raised on the knees of fairies and used to playing, while still a child, in their fabulous treasures.

What struck me first was this: although built in the purest and most beautiful Chinese style, the Summer Palace offered in

---

[205] Irisson, pp. 12–13, translation by author

[206] The account that follows: Irisson, pp. 307–323, has been very kindly translated into English for the author by professional translator Mr. Colin Youngs, MA (Oxon.)

its design, in its architecture and even in some of its details, singular reminiscences of the Palace of Versailles, tempered by this fact that dominates all Chinese building: that it had no upper storey and consisted throughout only of a ground floor, without lofts, without attics, without anything separating the roof from the rooms that were at ground level.

This distant resemblance is in no way inexplicable. The Jesuits who played such an important role in China; the Jesuits who gave China genuine Richelieus and no less genuine Mazarins; the Jesuits who remained honoured and more or less sovereign in Peking until 1773, the date when their order was abolished by Clement XIV; the Jesuits who were just as good administrators as they were great mathematicians; the Jesuits who had gathered together in their congregation all the talents and all the sciences; the Jesuits were in a sense the architects of the Summer Palace and the designers of its wonderful gardens.[207]

At that time, Louis XIV had just sunk so many millions into Versailles that, when the final accounts were presented to him, he ordered both, that they should be paid, and that they should be burnt, without wanting to look at them, hoping to hide from posterity and from himself his royal and crazy fantasy. Now the echo of the great king's magnificent achievements, passed from land to land, conveyed throughout the world by the mouths of men, reached the ears of the Emperor of China.

The Son of Heaven found it strange, unseemly, that there was on the surface of the globe a king who took the sacred emblem of the sun, and who had ventured to do something which he, the Son of Heaven, had not done. And what king? A kinglet, a man who ruled over a handful of human beings, 25 million people, a king who was therefore sixteen times lesser than the Celestial Emperor.

In no way envying this king for his famous crossing of the Rhine, that Napoleon called a "good joke", he wanted to rob him of the glory of having built the most beautiful palace in the world. And this is how strange, as it may seem, Versailles in

---

[207] The Jesuits were architects of the European section of palaces only. The rest of the palace was constructed by Chinese architects, in part inspired by the finest gardens in China. Irisson is a man with a wide imagination and his account must be appreciated in that way—he was not a literal observer

a sense gave birth, in another hemisphere, to the treasures and splendours of the Yuen-ming-yuen.

Construction lasted a very long time; the Jesuits were succeeded by other missionaries who were just as artistic as they were, and who merely had to embellish the original plans. But that is enough history. Let's describe it. At the far end of the first courtyard, raised up on top of three granite steps, stands an immense room, with no other decoration than a few inscriptions on the bare walls, with no furniture other than broad-backed wooden benches. This is where subjects granted the honour of approaching His Majesty waited.

Behind that room, and on the same level, is a second courtyard which separates it from the room where audiences were held. The courtyard is adorned with pots in old porcelain 1.50 metres high, which serve as containers for a large number of shrubs, each one stranger than the next.

The Chinese, torturers par excellence, like torturing nature. Everything that is strange, abnormal, extraordinary, appeals to him. Thus, the emblem of his underworld is the dragon, an example par excellence of a mythical, fantastic animal, composed of a series of natural horrors joined haphazardly together. He makes his deities monstrous. Woman, who throughout the world, among civilised nations, resembles a being intermediate between man and angel: he maims her, deforms her, makes her ridiculous.

In his fantastic mythology, he spares only one single divine creature, Koua-Him-Poussah, the Chinese virgin, whom he represents more or less with the features which we give to the Virgin Mary.

The trees which we see before us there have not been better treated than their gods or their women. Here, for example, is an oak tree: it is 200 years old. It doesn't look like a young oak tree. It is an exact, photographic, small replica of a large, ancient, forest oak tree, and it is only three feet tall. It is a perfect dwarf. Next to it stands a group of six trees of different species, planted in the same vase, a few centimetres apart, which are joined together at one metre in height, forming a single trunk from where, a bit higher up, spring leaves that it is impossible to classify. And note that the Chinese have no knowledge of grafting. These exploits are multiplied and repeated in all these large pots in various contorted shapes. Generations of scholars have devoted their lives to studying the techniques used to obtain these plant monsters.

In a short while, as we continue our visit, we will find on the shelves of ancient bookcases the fruit of their work, the results of their impossible observations, in carefully labelled and ordered volumes.

I confess that we only give vague attention to the bizarre things contained in these pots, the least of which would be worth up to 100,000 francs at the Salle Drouot (auction room). And we go straight ahead to the first audience room which opens up in front of us.

This room forms one side of a quadrilateral of buildings, in the centre of which is a garden with fountains. To its right and left, at right angles, are another two audience and ceremony rooms, and opposite it, at the other side of the quadrilateral, is the Throne Room.

As we walk through these first three rooms, extraordinary treasures begin to pass before our eyes. One must realise that in these palaces, transformed into a museum, or rather into a storehouse of splendours, the Emperor hoarded the most exquisite products of innumerable generations of the 400 million human beings for whom he was the demi-god. All the tributes in kind which his peoples were obliged to pay him, all the gifts which fear or enthusiasm snatched from both great and small, everything that he confiscated from rebellious subjects or those claimed to be.[208] One must realise that, in this immense Empire, no masterpiece was produced which did not travel naturally towards the Emperor. Nothing of value was discovered which did not fall into his hands by its own weight.

There were all the tributes in fine stones or precious fabrics offered by tributary princes, and all the things that our European kings and emperors were continually sending: ornaments, samples, curios, both to Hien-Fong and to his predecessors, everything which the simple trader, desiring to obtain access to a

---

[208] Irisson was not a student of the lives of the Qing emperors and their collecting habits. His comments are based on his imagination and assumptions, but are valuable none-the-less for their honesty and unfiltered reaction of a European to this hidden treasure house

port, selected from his goods to present to the sovereign. Everything was there, conserved with equal care and respect, from gold drapery studded with pearls, perhaps sent by the Grand Turk, to a doll that says 'daddy and mummy' taken by a captain from Marseille from his little daughter on 'present day' (1st January) and carried to China to impress the chief mandarin.

And all that overflowed from the private apartments of the sovereign and his wives, which had gradually become overfull, into these immense rooms, the size of cathedrals. The spectacle is both extraordinary and dazzling, dazzling by the richness of the objects, extraordinary by their number and their variety. Here we are in front of the Throne Room. Standing on a pedestal formed of seven steps of fine granite polished like a mirror, it is completely isolated from the surrounding buildings.

The Audience Hall

Its raised roof, which extends outwards beyond the seven granite steps by at least one metre, is supported by two rows of ironwood columns, very artistically sculpted, which resemble, in colossal proportions, those carved bamboos or ivories which, in Europe, we use to make tobacco jars or matchboxes.

No one of them resembles any other and the scenes which wind in spirals around their shafts, like on the Vendôme Column in the Place Vendôme [in Paris], are taken from national history, or from legends, or from famous novels, or from mythology. The one that I lean on, the only one of which I still have an intact memory, recounts the life of the god of wine, whose forehead is as high as the rest of his body. He is carried along calmly sitting on a buffalo, a curved stick in his hand, and before reaching the top of his column he will pass by precipices, enchanting sites, caves where monsters lie in wait for him, and under a triumphal arch surrounded by beautiful women. It is an eventful journey that this benevolent god makes there, an image of the imaginary adventures that his venerators experience after the libations of their worship.

On the shafts of the columns, all the parts of the wood which have not been chiseled, are covered with lacquer in brilliant colours; on the capitals, the imperial dragon twists and curls round on itself in all possible combinations, holding in its claws shields covered with maxims.

From the columns where we indulgently rested our glance, our eyes look up to the roof, and there meet a dazzling sight. The roof is covered with those glazed yellow tiles that are made in the small town where we slept yesterday. The roof ridges and edges are in green tiles, just as brilliant as the yellow tiles, and outline the elegant and majestic colours of the rooftop. At the four lower corners of the roof are suspended enormous dragons in green earthenware, priceless products of the city of Hang-Tchou-Fou. The enormous beasts appear to be climbing on to the ridges of the roof; they face each other in pairs, mouths open and eyes bulging out of their sockets. Finally, at each end of the roof ridge, a sea monster in green and black earthenware, climbs towards the other monster which faces it, and boldly raises towards the sky a tail, which is three metres long, ending in a fin which forms a colossal double crest to the whole building and gives it a swaggering and decisive appearance, if one can describe a monument in such terms.

In the sunshine, whose golden arrows bounce with blinding brilliance off these shining and gaily-coloured surfaces, putting sparks into the eyes of the monsters that populate them, and the darkness of caves into their gaping mouths, the superb and glorious building stands like a precious jewel enlarged to an incredible size.

Everything is neat, everything is clean, everything is intact in the ornate masterpiece on which it seems that the blue sky must close up at night like a jewel-case in azure velvet. And conservation and upkeep have been taken to such a degree that everywhere that a stray bird could place its little feet, it would find an imperceptible metal thread which would remove its desire to land and, consequently, to relieve itself on the residence of the Son of Heaven.

Access to the Throne Room is through a large opening in which there is no door. From the outside you would be able see what was happening inside, if it were not for a screen—as big as a cathedral rood screen, carved, pierced, ornate, like lace made of teak, where gods, men and horses leapt on to one other—which blocked the view, leaving a passageway on each side.

Fifty metres long, twenty metres wide and fifteen metres high: those are the dimensions of the Throne Room. They are the dimensions of one of our great temples. The throne faces the screen; it stands on top of about ten steps. It is formed of a pile of silk cushions and mattresses in an alcove that is eight metres wide, cut directly into an enormous frame of open woodwork. Imagine an alcove cut into the wooden screens of the chancels of our ancient cathedrals.

The room is almost completely in daylight, because the windows are very close together, and equipped with ventilators and louvres which, regardless of the position of the sun, allow constantly renewed and refreshing air currents to pass through. On the piers between the windows run thin strips of sculptured wood surrounding panels covered with paintings.

Almost no furniture. Behind the screen, a small altar which faces the throne; to the right of the Emperor's seat, a matching table and armchair in teak woodwork. On the table, there is still a gold sweet box, some writing brushes, a saucer full of vermillion, and paper on which characters in vermillion are written. It is His Majesty's interrupted correspondence. On the small altar, two jade perfume-burners, and porcelain saucers on which, when the Emperor is not there, fruit, tea, and flowers are placed: offerings to his spirit which, according to legend, is always present in this place. On each side of the throne, in the corners of the room, two doors have been created. Each gives access to a sort of small salon or oratory, or artists' club, as you wish. The one on the right leads to the sovereign's private apartments. It is called the Tien (Heaven).

Walls, ceilings, dressers, seats, pedestals: all is made of gold, studded with precious stones. Rows of small deities, in solid gold, are carved with such exquisite taste that their artistic value far exceeds their intrinsic value.

At the door, standing on jade pedestals, are two pagodas in enamelled gold, as big as corn chests, with their seven superimposed roofs, decorated with pear-shaped pearls in the form of little bells. Mingled with the deities, European clocks of all styles. Two of them are of the lovely type called Louis XVI, and are models of good taste, grace and fine carving. Alongside, more perfume-burners, candlesticks, candelabras, gold boxes, snuff-boxes studded with brilliants (diamonds) and decorated with enamelled miniatures. It's the dream of a feverish jeweller. In the other oratory, the one on the left, which also resembles the inside of a monstrance, are assembled all the objects intended for the daily requirements of the Son of Heaven while he is sitting in the Throne Room: his teapot, his cups, his pipes—hientaï 'smoking pipes', with golden or silver bowls and long stems decorated with coral, jade, rubies, sapphires and multi-coloured silk tassels; his ceremonial rosaries, the strings of pearls that he wears on his august chest and which are all as large as hazelnuts. Only their opalescence leaves a little to be desired.

Here also are his vermeil (gilded silver) megaphones; he uses them in certain circumstances to amplify his voice to the volume of a small thunderclap that rolls over his prostrate subjects. Then, on shelves, a large number of small silver strips, rounded at the top, 1 cm thick, 5 cm wide and 20 cm long, fairly similar in shape and dimensions to our thermometers. They bear deeply engraved and gilded characters in the carving. The inscription gives the order not to speak to the sovereign and not even to look up at his sacred person.

However if he asks: What time is it? I suppose, how do you answer him without speaking to him and without looking at him? You hand to him, head bowed, the silver tablet on which the current time is written. He looks, and knows what it means. It's very ingenious, but in his place I would much prefer a good pocket watch.

I will not describe the admiration and amazement of the barbarians who entered within these walls. Involuntarily, we spoke quietly and began to walk on tiptoe, seeing such wealth heaped up in such profusion, which human beings fight and die for in order to gain possession of them, and that their owner had calmly abandoned in his flight, like a good bourgeois who pulls the door of his residence closed behind him, and leaves his mahogany furniture exposed to the hazards of war. All that seemed so natural, so familiar, almost, so commonplace, to him, that there had been no attempt to hide these treasures.

Private Apartments

Behind the Throne Room, extending over a huge area, in the middle of the gardens, were the private apartments, also packed with *objets d'art* and luxury items, but less extraordinary ones on the whole. For, between the bedroom of an emperor and that of a private person, there is inevitably less difference than between a throne room and a sitting room.

In the Empress's quarters, the walls of the rooms and the corridors, are lined from top to bottom with racks, in which are placed above one another, like boxes of files in a lawyer's office, red boxes made of old Peking lacquer, marvelous carved objects containing jewellery, necklaces, bracelets, in pearls, in jade, in precious stones, pretty rings for the little fingers of the women, and large jade rings which the men wear on their thumbs for archery. Those that do not contain mounted jewellery are packed with *objets d'art*, with materials intended to be made into jewels, of unique specimens of transparent jade, of rock crystal, of milky jade, of dendritic stones, of rough diamonds, of fine gemstones still enclosed in their rough gangue, tea services, cups, saucers, a bazaar, a real bazaar, but not a 19-cent bazaar, a bazaar at 19,000 francs per object at least. When some of these boxes are opened in front of us, one would say that sparks and sprays of light gush out.

Further away, large wardrobes, also in old lacquer and lost in the walls of the rooms, contain the sovereign's clothes, her everyday outfits, her ceremonial outfits. There would be enough to dress from head to foot 10,000 princesses of the 1001 Nights. And the Caliph of Baghdad, who knew about such things, would not be able to find a single pin to replace or remove in their arrangement. All this is in silk, in satin, in damask, in fur, with embroidery that is sometimes as light as spider's webs but sometimes as thick as that on a bishop's cope. It is a shimmering pattern of birds, butterflies, flowers fresher than those caressed by the sun, and studded with stones that resemble dew drops in their scented chalices.

At intervals, a set of steps of strange shape allows the ladies-in-waiting to reach the highest outfits, and offers their little tortured feet steps that are padded and hollowed out like nests. His Imperial Majesty, as everyone knows, is not content with just one wife; he has concubines whose residence, quarters if you wish, is situated opposite his private apartments. These ladies, whose apartments we glance into and cast an already fatigued eye over, are, it seems to us, almost as well dressed as their sovereign, and drink their tea from services which are as precious as hers. When the Son of Heaven is going to be offered a semi-legitimate cup, he must not find the slightest difference in his pleasures.

The Park

Finally, we have finished with this tiring extravaganza. We are now face to face with nature, water, and greenery. We are now in the park. What a park! It is huge. The very high walls are about 14 kilometres round. Those who designed it set out above all to create picturesque viewpoints, an impression which is sometimes gentle and tender, and at other times violent and theatrical. They succeeded.

But they have carried out a great deal of work to assist nature, and this Yuen-ming-yuen (literally 'residence of original splendour') park contains a bit of everything, isolated palaces, temples, pavilions, pagodas, pyramids, porticos, colonnades, artificial mountains, grottos, lakes, streams, islands, thickets, mazes, observatories, kiosks. Rococo, which has been so fashionable over the last few years in our gardens around Paris, is, here, grandiose, imposing, monumental, incredible.

Here, for example, is an artificial mountain formed of rocks grouped together. The sides are carved and decorated with all the infernal deities, which grimace and twist in bushes of unbelievable plants. It dominates the whole park. Its summit is crowned by a small pagoda measuring 8 metres by 6, with its roofs on top entirely constructed of white and yellow porcelain decorated with stars. It is dedicated to the Chinese virgin, Kua-Him, who, from this culminating point, seems to extend her protection over all the palaces scattered at her feet. And I remember that in some of our towns, in the properties of fervent Catholics back home, in our native country under French skies, there is also a virgin who stretches out her arms, which bore the Son of God, over cities and isolated residences. I admire the inconceivable unity of the human brain which, disgusted by brute force, has taken refuge at the feet of the divine image of gentleness and love, and launched between the heaven which awaits humanity and the earth where it suffers and weeps, the Virgin Mother, i.e. the glorious symbol of human love, the Virgin for whom young men burn with desire, and the Mother who raises the generations, cradles and feeds them—the Virgin and Mother united in a mystic, ideal and sacred conception.

The Imperial Library

The Chinese virgin is represented by a statuette in gilded bronze, sitting in the middle of a lotus flower. On each side of her a fully-armed warrior stands guard. These two sentries display strange contortions, hideous grimaces. On the right of this artificial mountain, following a maze whose inextricable patterns allow you to get lost in an area of 50 square metres, stands a large building. It is the Imperial Library. Its roof, in yellow tiles, similar to that of the Throne Room, is also populated with a menagerie of black earthenware dragons chasing other fabulous monsters. The room is 12 metres high, 10 metres wide and 40 metres long. All its walls are lined with shelves where the most curious, the most ancient manuscripts are piled up.

In addition, it contains a few tables and armchairs for studious visitors, and two small altars, one in the north side, the other in the south, on which there still burn slowly small scented sticks in honour of Gon-Fou-Tse and Lao-Tse, whose images are reproduced on large sheets of silk suspended here and there, which can be rolled up around their sticks. Since then, we have had many specimens of such things in Europe. Here are the grottoes: they are deep, convoluted, and full of statues of gods and animals; some have creepers as an entrance curtain, others a crystal waterfall that falls from a basin above and trickles away babbling across the lawns. Here are lakes, and in the middle of the biggest one stands a small palace, which we have neither the time nor even the courage to go and visit, and which I would ask the reader to place in a corner of his memory. He will see why shortly. This palace, set on an island whose surface barely rises above the permanently constant level of the sheet of water that surrounds it, seems to rise up from the bottom of the lake.

On the edge of the lake, on the left, stands a large building in carved precious wood, completely buried under the creepers that wind around it, climb up to its roof and swirl in a plume around the dragons' tails. It is a shed. It contains carriages in gilded and carved wood, with doors painted in Martin lacquer and interiors lined with Genoa velvet, with large lanterns of chased silver, with thick seat covers spread out like the baskets of the women of Louis XIV's court, and decorated with numerous gold and silk pendants, which Lord Macartney, at the end of the last century, was instructed to offer to the Emperor of China, on behalf of George III. A memorable mission in which the English, aiming to serve the interests of their East India Company, consented to pay tribute to the Chinese Empire, and humiliated themselves before it for no gain.

These carriages, their magnificent harnesses spread out on trestles, have never been used. They are covered in dust, they mustn't be inspected too often.

Boat House

Next to the shed, the landing-stage of the imperial boats, whose roof in yellow tiles extends out over the lake. There is the boat of the emperor, the empress, those of the princes of the family, those of the grand mandarins. There is the Emperor's fishing boat, gilded, lacquered, and still equipped with its fishing tackle. It is in that boat that the Son of Heaven fishes for the innumerable varieties of fish that Chinese fish breeders, the first fish breeders in the world, have created for him. He must not have overindulged in this sport, as the fish seem to be fairly tame and, since they have no feeling of patriotism, they come to the edge of the lake to contemplate the barbarians. These shameless fish would eat their bread. Here is the golden fish, which is one foot long, whose name alone is the best of descriptions. Here are the goldfish, cousins by marriage to those that can be found in the lake in the Tuileries Gardens, the fishbowls of our dressmakers or the aquariums of our bourgeois ladies. Here are little sea monsters who have only a head and round eyes as big as man's eyes. And here are others with bodies that turn, types of seahorses, which the Chinese venerate under the name of water dragons. We may find them hideous but they find them very beautiful.

Pagoda

A bit further away stands a tower, an exact miniature copy of the famous tower of Nanjing, with innumerable roofs marking innumerable storeys. To get there, you must pass in front of a pagoda constructed in the honour of the Buddha. The statue of the god, which stands on a low pedestal, legs crossed in the Turkish or Chinese fashion, is no less than 20 metres high. A staircase that runs around the inside of the pagoda allows you to climb up as far as the head with its frizzy hair. At the first storey, you reach his knee, at the second, his navel, and so on.

This statue, which is very ancient, is in gilded bronze, but time has caused the gilding to flake off. The god's eyes, with half-closed eyelids, are made of silver, the pupil is of iron. From one knee to the other, at its base, the statue measures 15 metres. It is a fine maggot ["a seated oriental figurine, usually of porcelain or ivory, of a grotesque form," Wikipedia]. There are only two gigantic perfume-burners and an altar in this pagoda, which has been built only to serve as a plinth for the statue. It is by our introduction to this enormous gentleman that our visit to the Summer Palace ended. It had lasted several hours. We returned exhausted, worn out, our eyes burnt by all that gold and richness, our legs feeling as if they would telescope into our bodies like the tubes of opera-glasses, our heads aching, dazzled, intoxicated.

The general-in-chief had sentries posted at all the exits, so as to prevent anyone entering the Palace before the arrival of our allies, and he designated two artillery captains, Messrs Schelcher and de Brives, to see that his orders were strictly carried out.

Looting[209]

Having taken the Yuen-ming-yuen . . . The generals also decided they would choose among all these wonders [of the Summer Palace], the most worthy items to be offered to the sovereigns whose armies had made the expedition, Her Majesty Queen Victoria and His Imperial Highness Napoleon III. The [joint Anglo-French appropriations] commission immediately and quietly began its work. The removal of objects, if not the most valuable, at least the most obvious, was performed in order.

It was the middle of the afternoon [October 7], and the sentries were still at their post, the infantry was in the front of the Palace within which the commission was operating. Every moment soldiers came out loaded with trinkets, which aroused the admiration of the troopers gathered outside the secure area. After unloading, these soldiers returned and showed their passes. Amongst the troops of all kinds who were present at that first stage, French infantry, English, Chasseurs, gunners, sappers, the Queen's dragoons, Sikhs, Arabs, Chinese coolies, intermingled, a rumor circulated and grew, repeated in all the idioms of whom the representatives were crammed there, the eyes were wide and lit up, greed awakened, dry mouth.

They said, 'When the best is taken away, we will enter and have our turn. It's good at least, what the hell, that we can have our piece of the cake. We came from far enough away. Isn't that so, Martin, or Durand? And we laughed, we pressed on.' A little disorder began already. Montauban, anxious, walked to the other end of the square, leaning on a green bamboo cane that replaced his one lost in the panic of the night before. Things were not at the point that he must intervene. Suddenly a trumpet call sounds. A company call to arms. What is that? A very simple thing.

The Chinese of Haitien got into the park by climbing the walls, and they are anxious to get to the riches explored earlier. Greed was suddenly roused in them as a germ of patriotism; they said that the hour of revenge had arrived, it was a godsend, if I may word it so, to strip the Mongol dynasty and not to let the barbarians monopolise a beautiful opportunity. In addition these are low class Chinese. People are essentially thieves and

---

[209] The account that follows: Irisson, pp. 327–345, translation by the author

there was plenty to tempt them. The local peasants, proletarians of Haitien, arrived there or rather slid over the walls of the park. They approached our coolies and chatted with them.

Our coolies had ladders. The ladders were put against the walls, and a flock of fat sparrow looters with black braids fell in amongst the allies and headed toward the Palace. It was an act designed to disperse them. Hence the call to arms. They did not assemble; a second trumpet call was heard. It was a different story. In response, unarmed soldiers with cans and pots formed a line. Because we started to report the beginnings of partial fires. In China, when there things burst into fire, before thinking to protect against the flames, one thinks to protect against thieves, arriving faster than firefighters at the threatened points. As a result, the thieves habitual at exploiting fires know very well how to start them, and consider fire as a necessary ally, as the indispensable component of any profitable exercise. Also our Chinese of Haitien and our coolies had brought wicks, straw ropes, whatever it takes, in a word, to burn a palace, and had immediately begun to exercise their little industry.

Irisson defends the looting by the French:

The trooper, on learning of these new arrivals which their crude arrival exacerbates, felt anxiety give way to anger. Earlier he said these Chinese will steal everything. At that time, he added these rascals will burn everything. There was then at the guarded gates, an irresistible force. The sentries were carried away, and everyone entered with their arms and the needed helpers. Straightaway everyone began to take away what was to his liking. From the first moment, it was given me to compare the genius of the two allied nations. The French are finding good fun, good money, individually. The English, more methodical, have made it a specialty to pillage in an organised manner. They came in squads, as if a chore, men with bags, and commanded by NCOs, unbelievable detailed, rigorously exact, carrying away some touch stones.

What the hell did they find? I do not know. But I affirm that they had this primitive tool of our jewelers and our commissaries in Mont-de-Piete, and I'm not sure they did not borrow from the Chinese Mont-de-Piete. Besides the English, accustomed to living on the back of Asian populations, who, lest we forget, have only mercenary armies, that is why organised armed looting is one of the elements the war had already been proven in this respect, even in China, and I am convinced that in our place, had they arrived at Yuen-ming-yuen first, they [the British] had not expected us to begin the removal of movable objects of His Chinese Majesty. Already at Chang-Kia-Wan, they had taken strides, they had scrupulously kept without feeling obliged to inform us or to wait. First, when we arrived, we had with us the English cavalry commanded by Brigadier Pattle. Then we had walked there on the indications and the invitation of General Grant, behind his own guides. He has lost his army. It's not our fault.

Once we arrived at Yuen-ming-yuen, we did everything in our power to attract the English, firing the gun, sending acknowledgments, etc. Then, our generals did not enter the Palace with their officers. Moreover, when their commander arrived, everything was absolutely intact. Finally, when the looting began, they were with us, and more ardent than us and especially more methodical, as I just said. I resume my narrative, after this necessary digression.

So English, French, officers, soldiers, had entered the Palace, with the inhabitants of Haitien, pell-mell with our coolies (who hated northern Chinese) . . . with those bands of parasites who accompany the armed like crows, dogs or jackals, parasites, since Pehtang, sneaked in our wake, looting, stealing and destroying what we ourselves had respected . . .

Montauban, with all his energy, would have been unable to prevent his troops to go through the main gate of the Summer of Palace . . .

Personally, I imitated my comrades and went, or rather I went behind them in the Summer Palace. I even remember that I went along with the Colonel, since General, Vassoigne. Only I entered as an amateur, both hands in my pockets and firmly resolved not to touch anything. My God! I will not make me better than I am . . . I confess that I could very well take my share of the wealth of the Son of Heaven, without any qualms. I even think that I would have made my estate larger than most others because I had on many of my colleagues the advantage of perfectly discerning the value of objects, and the usual knick-knack, which would have greatly helped me to choose the most valuable and less bulky.

Interest alone held me . . . Ah! the wealth of the Summer Palace, ah! the golden pagodas, ah! diamonds, the Emperor could well keep. The others could well take them! What did it make me? . . .

So I was a spectator, disinterested spectator, but curious spectator [see comments about Irisson's loot], and I savored this strange vision, this unforgettable swarm of men of all colors, of all types, this accumulation of specimens of all races in the world dying over this heap of wealth, shouting in all the languages of the world, hastening, bumping, stumbling, falling, rising, swearing, cursing, exclaiming, each carrying something . . . There were troopers, heads buried in the red lacquer chests of the Empress, others half buried in piles of brocades and silk pieces, others who put rubies, sapphires, pearls, pieces of rock crystal in their pockets, in their shirts in their caps, and who took the necklaces of large pearls. Others were taking clocks, heavy between the arms. The engineers had brought their ax and smashed furniture for the jewels that they encrusted. There was one, seriously, who pounded on a Louis XV clock to have the dial where the hours were marked by crystal figures, he took for diamonds. Occasionally, they cried 'Fire!' We rushed, leaving everything falling down, the flame is suffocating already licked the precious walls by piling it on silks, damasks mattresses, furs. It was a hashish taker's dream. And when, after going through all the apartments looting, I came out into the lens of the spectacle of the eternally tranquil Nature, it made me shiver to get out of this furnace as if into a fresh falling shower. Our members still burning from the caress of hot steam. Here and there in the park were groups running toward the pavilions of the palace, around the pagodas, to libraries, alas!

Irisson goes on to describe how he discovered and then saved the women of the Court and later how he smuggled them out of a side gate. It is a most unlikely story, especially since another writer [Captain di Negroni] has his own account of how he saved the Empress and concubines, and improbable that the Emperor would abandon his wives, concubines and their servants to the invaders. This passage should be considered partly or wholly fantasy.

But the big lake was silent and deserted with its water palace and its stationary gondolas. I'll go see what's in there, I said to myself, looking at the island. I jump disrespectfully into a lacquered imperial gondola, inside padded with yellow silk like a glove, and I start sculling vigorously towards the palace ... I scaled three steps of white marble, I enter the main room entirely surrounded by sofas formed by mattresses of yellow damask quite similar to Turkish divans ... I listen, my hand on my sword, because I thought I heard muffled sighs. I examine the yellow mattress. It seems to me there are suspicious lumps. I give a kick; an acute cry of terror sounds, and a woman appears to me huddled, holed up like a little rabbit wearing these pajamas of precious raw silk embroidered by hand ... It crawls out of bed, falls down, hits the ground with her forehead, showing me her back, her neck and her black hair crossed with gold pins. If you have never seen a man embarrassed, just imagine the thought that you see me standing pitiful, a little silly, hand on the sword, and this woman at my feet ...

'Get up, God forgive you'. I simply say in Chinese, 'Fear not, I will not hurt you.' She stood on her two little feet. It was an adorable creature of twenty, dressed like an empress. Since no cry from the beautiful child had even indicated she had suffered the last real outrage, that is to say, death, or even the penultimate, usually rape, other humped mattress swelled gradually. Heads of women appeared, then the body. This little world rushed in, around, down around me, hitting the mat with their pretty heads. There were twenty and seven women. I had stumbled upon the harem, or at least a certain part of the harem of His Majesty. It is quite usual among the peoples of the Far East to build women's quarters in the islands, the water that surrounds them offer more solitary pleasures for the master, easier monitoring by the eunuchs. So there I was with twenty-seven women, absolutely distraught and so out of themselves ... I had all the trouble in the world to console them and to prevent them from suffering.

When I returned to camp, the night fell, the men returned loaded with plunder, dragging the most surprisingly similar items, from pots of money to the telescopes and sextants, huge material that surely they could not carry. The English camp looked the same. But everything was happening with extreme order. For us it was masquerades, gunners came wrapped in the robes of the Empress and mandarins collars. There, they had heaped in every tent the objects. Already public auctions had begun.

Here, a little anecdote of our Spahis, who served at my order, Mohammed, who had accompanied me to Tientsin, had offered me as much affection as interest. He did not leave me and nursed me like they treat a child. You are the friend of the general, he said to me often. He speaks through your mouth . . . When he returned from the Palace he brought me hands full of pearls. 'This is for you,' he said simply . . . 'Thank you, boy,' I said. 'Guard it all for you. They're worth too much money.' 'What do you want me to give you for your pearls?' The spahi said to one of my comrades. You give me a bottle of water spirits. 'Agreed.' And Mohammed gave him the pearls. The water bottle of spirits, at *Camp Yuen-ming-yuen*, sold for 100 francs by the canteen. The pearls were sold, after we left, for 35,000 francs.

Nothing tempts soldiers as clocks, and more generally the objects of spades. The Chinese, like all peoples of the East, like all the people to whom the machine is still in a rudimentary state, love mechanical objects and especially entertaining mechanics. From time immemorial, our rulers and our ambassadors have flattered them with this mania, and sent them all or brought opticians inventions, toy merchants, manufacturers of controllers. We will never know how many music boxes, *serinettes*, Barbary organs, clocks with complicated ringtones, alarm clocks, firecracker, drum rabbits, moving pictures, clocks turning the wings of a mill, pecking chickens, up and down sawyers arms— what a prodigious amount of songbirds locked in brass cages placed on a pedestal, which goes by turning a key, flute players, monkeys fiddlers, pipers trumpet, clarinet, and even bands of monkeys sitting on a pipe organ, small rope dancers, waltzing, etc., etc. were in the Summer Palace. The apartments of the

Empress, those women were literally packed. But our soldiers were divided into 'malignant' and 'malignant older children', few; big kids mostly. Malignant had made off with jewelery, specie, the dollars, the bezels, snuff boxes, gold services, pearl necklaces. The others had been tried, above all, in the middle of this pile of untold riches, for whole mechanics of European origin that had, moreover, generously been abandoned by the English. Also the second night that we passed the Summer Palace, it was impossible, insane, dizzying.

Each soldier had his bird, his music box, a monkey, his clock, waking or rabbit. It was a common bell every hour, of all kinds, jingled, continuously, accompanied, now and then, the cracking sad overworked a large spring that broke under inexperienced fingers. Multitudes of playing drum rabbits, formed a low, accompanied by cymbals monkeys, among four thousand romances and quadrilles hummed together as cranked music and *serinettes* that dominated the rou-piou-pious Birds, the rolls of Sutes, the twang of clariuettes, grinding chanterelles, *qu'entrecoupaient* an inflow of pistons and bagpipes, and also the sound of laughter of those good people so easy to amuse.

It was a nightmare. At sunrise [October 8], the looting began [again]. General tents were placed in front of one of the two pagodas. Solid gold, found in the oratory of the Emperor is intended for Napoleon. It had to be shared with the English. At this pagoda's summit shone a large diamond which launched a thousand lights. Two sentries were guarding this priceless object. They were not there for two hours and the large diamond was gone. We never knew who had taken it. We know that the looting of the Summer Palace lasted two days. Towards the end, Montauban, to stop it, found that, in colloquial language, is called a trick. He walked among the soldiers, dressed as mandarins or imperial princesses, and told them my children, so leave it all. You cannot win. And what would you do, if we meet the enemy, he still had to fight?

> 'Believe me, we will go to Peking; there will be plenty
> for everyone, you'll see.'

I heard him speak this little speech to a gunner, who, convinced, threw down what was in his arms, and took off her dress to reappear in uniform. Gunners on this occasion, it must be said, were the best placed because they had horses, boxes, cars. They used every inch of the boxes, and when the boxes were full, they filled the buckets that served them to dip the swab to clean the barrel after each shot, then they sulked the barrel itself to the muzzle. However, the little speech the general, his pious men dream, generally produced their effect, as we see, almost all soldiers imitated the Dubosclard gunner.

[sometime later, back in France] . . . I went walking through the Trianon Park. My little girl frolicking with me. I sat at the foot of a tree in the abandoned park that grows wild and that begins to look like a jungle, while the child was playing in pile of dry twigs in front of me. Mechanically, without thinking, with the match that had just served me for my cigarette, I fired the little pile of wood, and the blue smoke went up under the great trees like a bivouac . . .

'I'll issue a summons,'

Said a deep voice behind us, and a guard came out of the thicket. I was very upset. The good man was an admirable type of this species . . . On the chest of the keeper I saw the medal of China next to the Military Medal.

'Hey friend,'

I said to soften and avoid the unfortunate consequence,

'You went to China?

'Yes, what of it?'

'Me too.'

'In what body did you serve?'

'In the Spahis[210]'

'And me in the artillery. I was with the Dispot battery . . .'

The keeper from the artillery told me.

'Were you not the secretary of the general?'

'That's right.'

'How can you recognize me after twenty-five years?'

'That's because at the Summer Palace something important happened to me and I still see it. I had picked up a few items. The general said, "Don't take it. We go to Peking, there's something for everyone." You know, I obeyed. But another who was with me looting during that time, hid his loot in the bucket. I was told that there he had 300,000 francs. I do not know, but what I know is that the comrade, who had no money, is now very big owner in Cher. So you understand that that day, the General prevented me from making my fortune.'

The scene remained in my head, and I still see General de Montauban and spahi who was with him . . . I talked with that old brother in arms. What an admirable career that has featured in all the campaigns from China to Tunisia, was twice pierced from side to side, almost in the same place by a bullet, once in Algeria, once in France; had, in 1870 his leg shattered by a musket ball, was raised seven times for the Legion of Honour, and retired as adjutant of artillery, without even getting the cross. Here he had no security, he told me resignedly. I confess that hearing him speak I was ashamed of my little red ribbon. I wanted to give it to him.

The looting of the Summer Palace thus lasted forty-eight hours. I would now, in a small philosophical digression, wonder whether

----

[210] Light cavalry, recruited primarily from the indigenous populations of North Africa

these scenes, impossible to suppress, prevent, were so extraordinary that, if they were a novelty. If they were on the fringes of the international code as defined by the right people, if they were contrary to the laws of war? . . . The man who takes bread from a bread shop is a thief; the nation that takes 5,000,000,000, that is a great nation.

In China we had the right, strictly by law, the unquestionable right to take and take, being the winners, all the valuables belonging to the nation, that is to say to the Emperor to which we were fighting the war, as the Germans had the right to take our billions [during the Franco-Prussian War 1870–71], as Bonaparte had the right to take its masterpieces from a conquered Italy. So, the looting of the Summer Palace was legitimate, as far as may be legitimate what is done in wartime. The principle is indisputable. The only offense committed was a lack of detailed, application. We not only plundered, we wasted. And it is less looting than waste that was ill . . . if it were possible to govern our men we would have had to move, pack and bring all the riches of the Palace, and the palace in Peking, sharing between the two conquering nations, putting aside everything that could be put in the museum, selling the remainder, and use that sum is to reward the soldiers of the expedition, to enrich the different elements of our national budgets.

'Imitate', in a word, this was done by the Prussians in France, and, before them, Napoleon in Germany then in Italy. If they had acted with regularity, no one would have anything to say, except philosophers, dreamers and paradox manufacturers who obstinately compare war to a murder, and plunder to the fruit of a flight. This is what was not done, this is what has been done. I confess that my heart bled seeing, for example, the space between the Palace and our camp, covered in silk and precious fabrics trampled, muddy, there was the low word coming to see the millions of soldier lighting their pipes or heating the pot with the vellum of admirable and unique manuscripts; seeing, to check out and throw in the ruts to fill and put the wheels of guns and cars, cartels, lovely clocks, horological masterpieces, carved ivories, finally seeing disappear before us some of these light and splendid buildings writhing in the flames.

About 'carts', a curious detail. Arriving in Haitien, the French army had only one vehicle, that of General, which contained his tent and canteens. When she left, she had dug from, I know not where, a quantity of loaded carts such that the parade lasted an hour. As for the English baggage parade, it was incredible in length. It was a procession covering two good leagues of country. Behind us came the Chinese, not yet sated, who wiped clean and took our leftovers. Poor people do not get bored in paradise, as they say. After the expedition, the Tartar soldiers of the Emperor returned to Haitien. Houses and cottages were searched thoroughly; all that was discovered was reported to the Palace and thieves of valuables were put to the sword.

That according to Mr. Mouly, who remained at Peking after the departure of the expedition. In our so many persecutions and arrests [in China], I believe that no one case or the theft or looting did occur. In this case, some villages near Yuen-ming-yueu, which most people, if not all, had come to take part, they paid dearly later; as commander in chief, Cheng Pao, then fell upon them by night, surprise, take only what is recognized to have been taken at the palace of the Emperor; more, kill a number of people, and then destroy the villages.

I realize I have not argued, as a mitigating circumstance of our excesses, the exasperation of the soldier following the massacre, some part, if not all our unfortunate compatriots surprised and captured at Tungchow. We found in Yuen-ming-yuen, behind the throne room, the uniform of Colonel Foulon Grandchamp, the notebook, the saddle and bridle of Mr. Ader, many objects that belonged to English officers, finally fifteen full trappings of Sikh riders. All this was brought to the Son of Heaven that he might feast his eyes on barbarian spoils. By discovering this evidence of the horrible fate suffered by brothers in arms, the soldiers produced cries of rage. Had they met ten palaces commensurate with the Yuen-ming-yuen, they would have ransacked and burned heartily.

After China

After the China expedition Irisson continued his career with the French army. He had a succession of military posts. He was captain of the guard for the 7th battalion of the Seine in 1868. Then he purchased his title, but according to his own account the money had not come from the China War. In 1870 he was put in charge of a mission to America for the Ministry of Commerce and of the *Travaux Publique*. At the outbreak of the Franco-Prussian War, Irisson was made adjutant to General Truchu, military governor of Paris during the siege of the capital by the Germans. He was wounded in the siege and assisted in the peace treaty. In 1881 he was in charge of a scientific mission to Tunisia, and was in Turkey for the Ministry *d'Instruction Publique*. The resulting archaeological digs that he organized at Cathage and at Utique produced finds that were offered to the Louvre. In 1891 he served an expedition to the Congo.

Irisson died in 1898 in the French colony of Algeria. During his life he was author of more than a few books detailing his exploits on various overseas expeditions, including *Journal d'un interprète en Chine* (1882). His legacy therefore centers around this grand and remarkable account.

According to Cordier, the French historian, Irission's legimitmacy as a titled man was questioned in his later life. Cordier uncovered the following research in 1906:[211] "*Irisson* is not a pseudonym, but the name of a family that has its notice in the *Yearbook of the Nobility of France* (1870, p. 250), in the *Universal Nobility of Saint-Alais* (XIV. 418)." This source informs that "Maurice d'Hérisson . . . was born in Paris on September 25, 1839, of the marriage of Augustin-Guillaume d'Hérisson and Dorothée-Julie-Ernestine-Maurice Allard; He had an elder brother [Georges], secretary of the embassy, who died in 1874. And a sister, Madame de Saint-Pierre."[212]

The Irisson family apparently were in fact lords of the town of Hérisson but had sold their title documents in previous generations: "In 1867, the Parisian society received the circular with the exact copy made on a copy that we have before us . . . The family of *Irisson* is legitimate [as Lords of Hérisson] and the last representative sold the papers to those gentlemen who have pretended to be attached to it."[213]

---

[211] Cordier, pp. 387–388, translation by the author

[212] Ibid.

[213] Ibid.

"Mr. Georges and Mr. Maurice Irisson have the honor to inform you that, by a judgment dated April 26, 1867, rendered in the Chamber of the Council of the First Chamber of the Seine Civil Court, their ancestral name was recognized . . . and carried forth in the future as borne by their ancestors *Monsieurs D'Irisson, lords of Hérisson.*" Their coat of arms is "a crown, three roses, a hedgehog on a terrace, with the motto: 'who touches will be pricked.'"[214]

Bibliography

Cordier, Henri, *L'Expédition de Chine de 1860*, Alcan, Paris, 1906
Irisson, Maurice, Comte d'Hérisson, *Journal d'un Interprète en Chine*, Paul Ollendorff, Paris, 1882

---

[214] Ibid.

An Artist's View

Felice Beato

"Beato, the photographer whom I remembered in the Crimea and whom I knew well during the Indian Mutiny and China war is on board, as amusing as ever, his attempts to speak English—which he understands very well—being as ludicrous as formerly. He has made and lost many fortunes since I last saw him . . ."

—Garnet Wolseley

Felice Beato was the unofficial photographer for the British expeditionary force in China, and the only photographer who produced a substantial body of work during the campaign. And what a body of work! He was during his career one of the great 19th century photographers as well as being a pioneer of war photography. Beato was that rare combination of artist, technician and businessman and during his life lived in many countries attempting to make his fortune. "Felice Beato was one of the first global photographers," explains Anne Lacoste, of The Getty Museum, "No one before him was present with a camera in so many different countries to chronicle conflicts or to record their foreign cultures ranging from the Crimea, to India, to China, to Japan, to Korea, to Sudan and finally Burma."[215] As someone who did not leave an account of any kind of the Summer Palace, except through his photography, Beato's experience as we perceive it 150 years after the fact does not overlap with that of his fellow observers. But the images he

---

[215] Lacoste, Ann, *A Photographer on the Eastern Road, Introduction*

has left offer a unique record of North China in 1860: palace buildings in the vicinity of the Yuen-ming-yuen, the grand city of Peking, and by refraction a visual perspective on the Summer Palace itself.

It was a circuitous journey that brought Felice Beato to Peking in 1860. He learned about the new technology of photography as a young man and it set him on a course of seemingly perpetual travel that saw him explore and photograph much of Asia, Greece and the Crimea and also set up a variety of impromptu ventures. His biographer David Harris describes him as, "a resourceful adventurer—a peripatetic entrepreneur who traveled widely, pursuing and abandoning various businesses."[216]

Beato was born in Venice in 1832, according to research conducted by Terry Bennett. When he was a child his family lived in Corfu, then under British protection, and Beato became a de facto British citizen. When he was a teenager, Beato's family moved to Constantinople because his father was appointed to an official position there. In Constantinople Beato's sister married James Robertson, a Britisher who was superintendent of the Ottoman mint and a keen photographer. Robertson, who had toured the Middle East making landscape images, seems to have taught both Felice and his brother Antonio the science of photography. In 1853 Robertson and Felice formed a partnership and began to work together professionally. They traveled together through the Near East and Greece taking photographs, which they intended to sell. In 1855 they became the official war photographers for the British army fighting in the Crimea, where they took some important early images of military conflict.

Beginning with the Crimean War, photographers were an expected part of the ensemble of staff accompanying armies into battle. Beato served as Robertson's assistant from 1855 to 1856 in the Crimea. In 1857 the two men traveled to Jerusalem and their images are signed for the first time, *Robertson and Beato*. They went on to other places in the Turkish Empire including Constantinople where they re-shot some of the work Robertson had done in 1853. Beato took from Robertson some important techniques and methods that proved effective throughout his career. One important one was the creation of panoramic views using multiple images taken sequentially and joined as prints to form a wide view. Beato used this method a number of times in China to capture the walls of Peking as well as interior shots of the city. Shortly after this Near-Eastern tour, Beato broke free from his master and set up on his own,

---

[216] Harris, *Of Battle and Beauty*, Ch. 1, Imperial Ideology

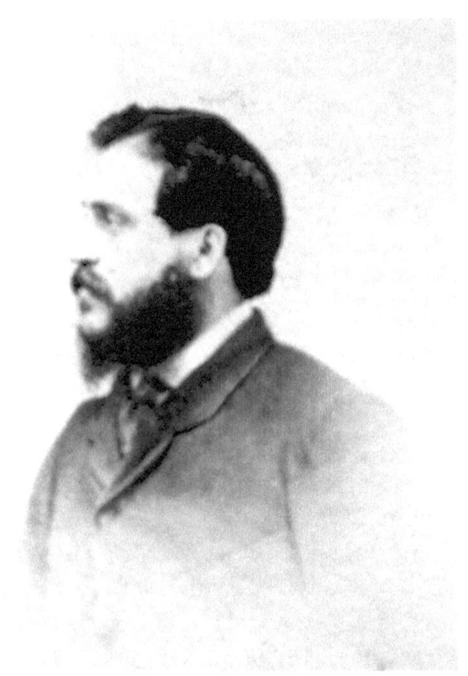

Felice Beato as
a young man,
photographer
unknown (perhaps
James Robertson)

establishing in the process his own style of photography, which perhaps can be seen to be emerging in some of his later collaborations with Robertson. Younger brother Antonio Beato may have taken Felice's place as Robertson's assistant around this time. Antonio went on to become an important photographer of the Near East and Egypt.

Beato was evidently a popular man in camp with the British officers in the Crimea. And having made these connections he used them for the rest of his career as an entrée to subsequent British military campaigns in strange lands. When a British army was assembled to go to China in 1858, Beato found a way to attach himself to it and travel with the troops. The British force sailed from Europe to India and there were diverted to fight in defense of the Indian colony. Beato accompanied the British relief army that fought in India during the Mutiny, alongside Hope Grant and many other officers who went to China in 1860.

Beato was in northern India from February 1858 until February 1860. He shot pictures in the aftermath of battle; sites where the fighting had been fiercest. Much of the conflict occurred in and around important cities where the British were besieged or in turn they besieged Indian forces. There was much destruction as well as loss of life when these cities were bombarded. Beato captured photographs of Delhi, Lucknow, and Cawnpore and also visited Agra, Benares, and Amritsar.

In India, Beato also took portraits of a number of officers. He came to know General Sir Hope Grant well and using this relationship he was able to persuade him to accompany the army traveling to China in 1860. He became a civilian attaché with no obligation to the Crown, the Army or any newspaper to provide journalistic or propaganda images. He could travel on board ship with the military and sell any photographs that he took for his own profit.

China

"The Anglo-French expedition of 1860, which concluded the Second Opium War, was the first military campaign to be recorded through photography,"[217] notes David Harris. Although several photographers accompanied the expedition, Beato was the only one to produce a meaningful body of work, tracing the various stages of the campaign. And his work, although conducted under trying circumstances, was remarkable. He employed a large format camera and the silver albumen printing technique which together produced big images full of detail. Beato shot some of the very first photographs of Peking, some of the finest images ever captured of the historic city. They represent a precious vision of Peking in 1860. Together with his images of the New Summer Palace they are a visual record of great historical importance as well as works of art. Beato also shot portraits of many of the officers on assignment in China.

Beato came to China prepared. He took over 100 photographs during his time there including early views of Hong Kong and the streets of Canton (Guangzhou). His photographs after the capture of the Peiho forts are graphic in their representation of the horrors of war. He went on to take a multitude of images of Japan and the Japanese people in the 1860s, proving that he was a versatile and sensitive witness to the alien world of East Asia.

Beato has been criticized, by Harris and others, for unconsciously (or consciously) reinforcing an 'imperial' perspective of China and recording a stereotypical and heavily Euro-centric view of East Asia: ". . . in the light of subsequent practices and the political uses of war photography, Beato's

---

[217] Ibid.

photographs of the Second Opium War appear to us as thinly veiled propaganda rather than, in any sense, factual and objective reportage."[218] This does not do Beato justice by a long chalk. In his work in 1860, and later, Beato was a businessman, not a journalist and he was not attempting to be a social historian or cultural commentator. He was in search of landscape images that he could sell to officers on campaign and the public back in Europe. In most cases, perhaps deliberately, perhaps inadvertently, his shots are devoid of Chinese (or British) figures, but not out of a sense of clinical imperialism but because this was a country at war and because when he shot landscapes his focus was on the landscape not the people who might occupy that space. Although he was always in their company and these were scenes of conquest, he deliberately avoided adding British soldiers to his images, which if he had done so would have caused him to be condemned further as distorting the cultural riches of China by superimposing European military dominance.

The idea of a critical photo-journalist free to capture images from both sides of no-man's land and free to judge either or both sets of protagonists, would not be born for another 100 years. Beato set out in China to capture the scenes of a country that happened to be at war and document the main stages of a campaign, or scenes from it, that he thought he could sell. Politics and colonialism are uppermost concerns in the 21st century mind, but were probably the farthest things from Beato's mind either consciously or unconsciously. In-spite of his commercial motivation it is very much to his credit that he was able to capture images of such purity and beauty that are invaluable both to the historian of the events of the war and of some of the great architectural works of art of the Chinese people, even in the midst of a bloody and destructive conflict. We can use our own imaginations to appreciate the perspective of a fearful Chinese population and their loss of life in an unequal struggle. We must make do with words to appreciate the looting and burning that ensued at the Summer Palaces. War is never glorious except, sometimes, in our minds.

Beato began by taking images while he was in Hong Kong and also traveled up the Pearl River to Canton. Hope Grant made sure to send Beato's pictures back to the War Office and to the Duke of Cambridge. This was most likely the arrangement that the two men had come to— that Beato could travel with the army at their expense, but Grant would

---

[218] Ibid.

get two sets of all photographs to send to London. Later in the campaign when the British were given a map of Peking prepared by Russian atta-ché, Count Ignatieff (another photographer), Hope Grant notes in his correspondence with his boss, Sidney Herbert the Minister for War:[219]

> I had [the map] photographed by Signor Beato who I had spe-cially allowed to accompany the expedition, and who previously photographed scenes in India and the Crimea.[220]

It is important to remember why Beato was in China and why he was not. He was *not* employed in any official capacity and had no official brief or over-arching duty to serve the Queen or the greater good of Britain. His personal goal was not artistic either. Although a very creative man and a highly innovative photographer, he was not driven by the desire to create *art* as such, even though he did create it. His work seems to indicate that he enjoyed his work and probably took great professional satisfaction in producing fine images, but his ultimate goal was as a busi-ness man—to make money. Later in his career he was heavily involved in real estate investment and even gave up photography to open a curio shop.

From an historical perspective those concerned with the Summer Palace are frustrated by Beato's seeming lack of interest in it as a subject, for he produced no photographs of the Yuen-ming-yuen. But the reason for this is very clear—it was neither a technical issue, as was perhaps the case with the French photographers, who photographed very little while in the Peking area, nor one of lack of equipment, for Beato managed to produce 32 excellent images of Peking, its walls, its streets, the New Sum-mer Palace and various temples, that we know of. The two issues that have stymied the historian were probably of very little concern to Beato. They were firstly, that, as has been discussed, Beato's goal was to make money and if he could do this with a portfolio of images that did *not* include the Yuen-ming-yuen—which as we shall see was the case—then so be it. Certainly for audiences back home in England the distinction between the look of the Old Summer Palace, which he did not photograph, and

---

[219] Note, as an aside, the plainness in this title. Now British and American ministers in charge of the country's military are given the more politically correct title of *Secretary of Defence*. Shades of Orwell's *1984*

[220] Hope Grant. Research by David Harris

the New Summer Palace, was meaningless. The second constraint that he had to work with was access.

The first British delegation to arrive at the Palace around midday on October 7 was that of Lord Elgin and his staff. Beato may or may not have been in this group—probably not. The delegation stayed a short while and then left. Many British officers attached to the main column did have the chance to visit the Palace on October 8, and it is highly likely that Beato took advantage of this opportunity. But in so doing he was probably more focused, like his countrymen, not on taking photographs, which of themselves would probably not have added anything incremental to his future income, but on loot! Loot had value and was freely to be had. The absence of photographs on October 8 suggests that perhaps the resourceful Beato was occupied in looting, not photography, which makes sense in the context of his overall objective in China. In addition, it is highly likely that General Montauban wishing to control opinion about the sacking of the Palace, banned all photography of it and his men in the act of looting it.

On the morning of October 9, after the Palace was vacated by the French, the Chinese Household Department took back possession of the enclosure and it was no longer available to casual observers, or photographers. The Chinese civil servants and soldiers learned of Chinese looting and sought to recover goods still in the village of Haitien. An amnesty was offered for goods returned—and a number of items were recovered in this fashion. Some Chinese found to have taken valuables and not returned them were identified and executed.

During the period between October 9 and October 17, before the Yihe Yuan was burned, Beato found time and opportunity to visit the New Summer Palace and take four hauntingly beautiful photographs of those palace buildings. Each image has been carefully researched in Europe and China, and all five are clearly of the Yihe Yuan. This is consistent with the excursions of officers in the British camp who are recorded as having gone sightseeing and hunting excursions while peace negotiations were in progress with Peking. He also took one image of the Yihe Yuan after the fire. The five images in question were labelled in his albums as "Yuen-ming-yuen", which was probably 'marketing' by Beato, not error. His album which was subsequently sold in Britain was more marketable with images of the Palace, and would probably have seemed odd if it did not include photographs with that title, and the British

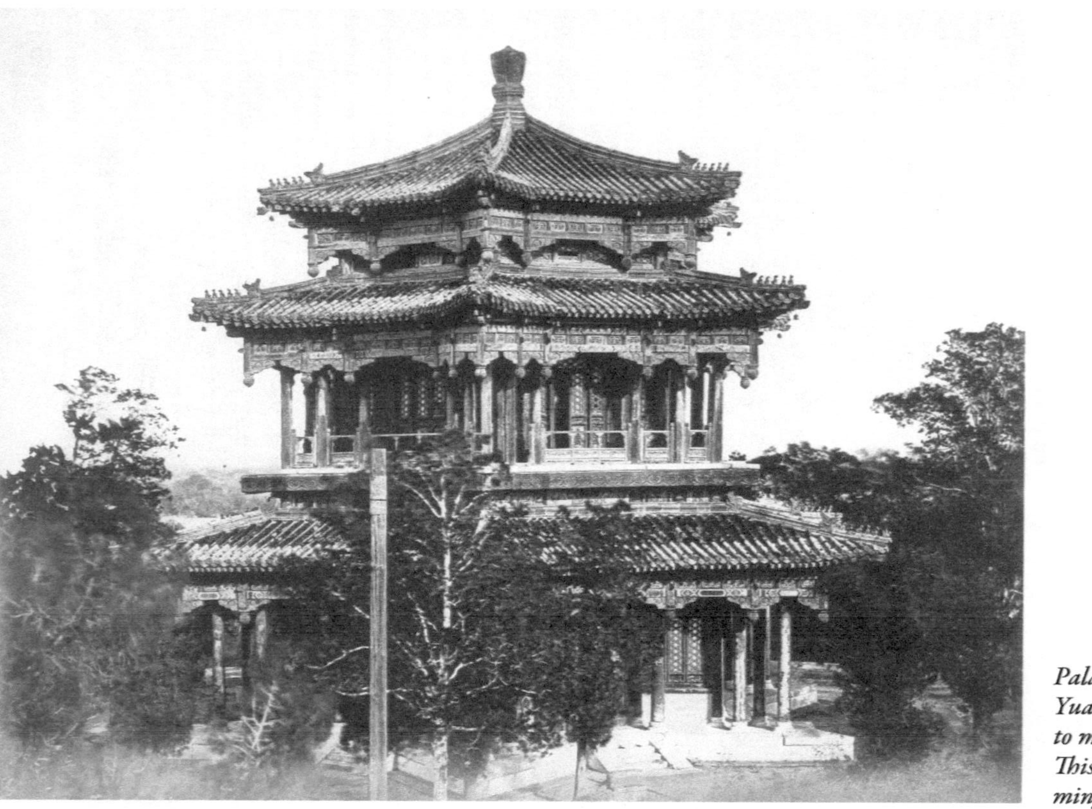

Palace building, part of the Yihe Yuan, before the destruction—early to mid-October, 1860, Felice Beato. This image was labelled "Yuen-ming-yuen" by Beato/Herring

public could not know the difference between the palace buildings of the Yihe Yuan versus the Yuen-ming-yuen.

Loot and the Fate of Beato's Photographs

In 1860 photographers in the field had with them a portable 'dark tent' of a very crude type to which they must take the glass negative after it had just been exposed. In the dark tent they would apply chemicals to 'set' the image on the glass plate and make it a stable negative. Then, the photographer could wait until he returned to his 'studio' and make prints at his leisure from the negative. In Beato's case he had no studio in China, he was a travelling photographer whose customers were at hand. In order to capture the business of the British officers who were with the expedition, he needed to use whatever space he could find to produce photographic prints from the negatives he had made and he was then able to produce a 'sample' photo album with all of his Chinese images to show to interested officers. They could select the ones they wanted and have them made up into an album of their choosing.

Between arriving in Peking and October 20 Beato assembled an album of his images, which he offered for sale to the officers. An example of a Beato album was purchased in China by Lieutenant Edward Henry Courtney of the Royal Engineers. It contained eighteen prints of images recently taken in China. Courtney himself made careful notes in the album describing the scenes. Courtney kept the album and in 1887 retired from the army and returned to England. He died at Gerrards Cross, Buckinghamshire in 1913. But the album was passed down through his family.

Lady Charlotte Canning (1817–1861), wife of Viscount Charles John Canning (1812–1862), the governor-general of India, had commissioned a complete set of Beato's China photographs. On November 15, 1860, William Wilberforce Harris Greathed (1826–1878), an aide-de-camp to Robert Napier, wrote to Lord Canning saying that he himself had ordered 38 images from Beato—architectural views of Peking and Canton—and that he paid Beato 74 dollars for them which he was to deposit in Beato's bank account in Calcutta. Lieutenant Colonel Frederick Mann noted in a letter home, "The views, Beato told me, are the first he has given although he has very numerous applicants and will probably sell thousands between officers of the force and Hong Kong people." Capt. Robert M.R. Rowley, of the Royal Horse Artillery, recorded in his diary

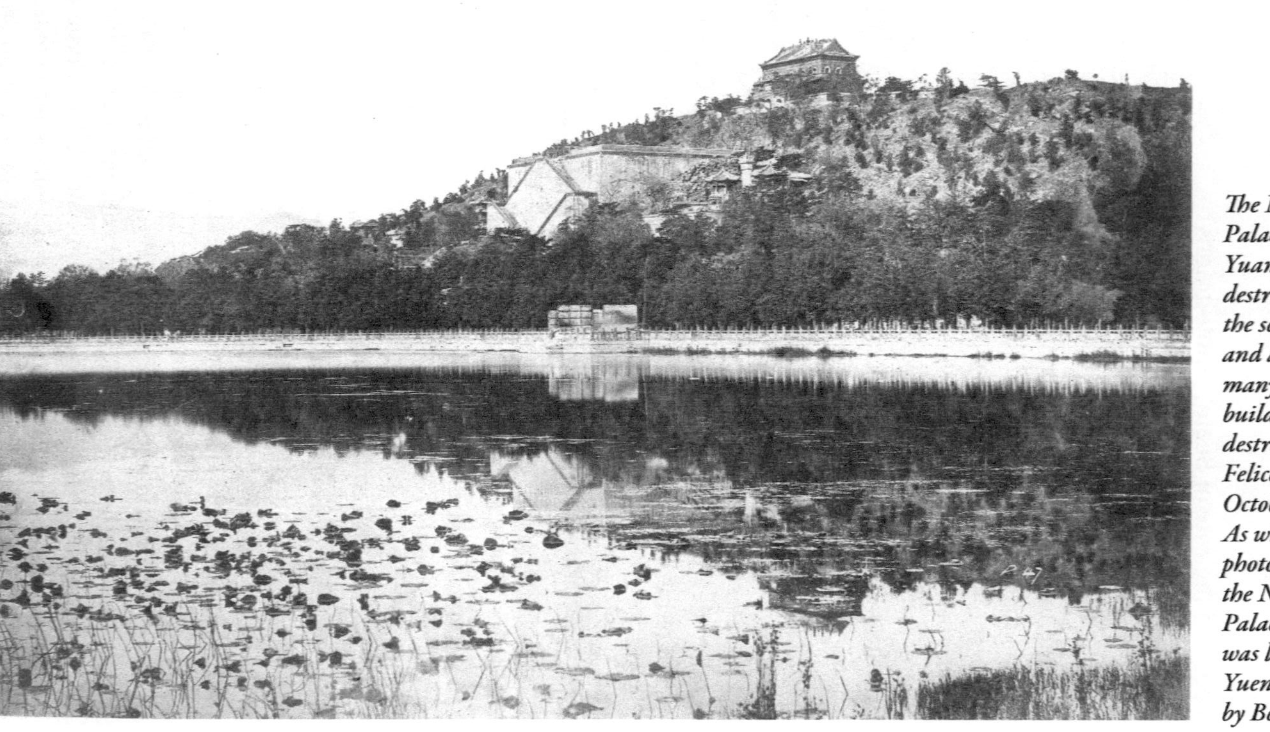

The New Summer Palace (Yihe Yuan) after the destruction. Note the scarcity of trees and absence of many of the palace buildings—all destroyed by fire. Felice Beato, late October, 1860. As with other photographs of the New Summer Palace, this image was labelled "the Yuen-ming-yuen" by Beato/Herring on November 16, 1860: "Busy all day handing over our guns to the store-keeper [at Tientsin], our serviceable horses to Probyn's Horse and our cart horses to the Military Train. I bought some railway books at a dollar each for the voyage, got my photographs from Signor Beato."[221]

On October 24, Beato was on-hand for the signing of the treaty in Peking, where, lacking adequate light, he was unable to produce images. On November 2 he shot portraits of the principal participants, Lord Elgin and Prince Gong:

> In the midst of the ceremony, the indefatigable Signor Beato, who was very anxious to take a good photograph of the signing of the Treaty, brought forward his apparatus, placed it at the entrance door, and directed the large lens of the camera full against the breast of the unhappy Prince Gong. The royal brother looked up in a state of terror, pale as death, and with his eyes turned first to Lord Elgin and then to me, expecting every moment to have his head blown off by the infernal machine opposite him—which really looked like a sort of mortar, ready to disgorge its terrible contents into his devoted body. It's explained to him that no such evil design was intended, and his anxious pale face brightened up when he was told his portrait was being taken. The treaty was signed, and the whole business went off satis-factorily, except as regards Signor Beato's picture, which was an utter failure, owing to want of proper light. Refreshments were offered to us, which Lord Elgin declined, and, after a proper amount of bowing, we took our departure. The following day the French treaty was also signed.[222]

A distinction has to be made between the prints that Beato made in the field with a fresh negative—these were of the highest quality—and images that were created in London from prints that were not quite as crisp, being a photograph of a photograph. After traveling briefly to Japan, India and Constantinople, Beato returned to London and sold

---

[221] Original research by David Harris

[222] Hope Grant in Knollys, *Life of Sir Hope Grant*, p. 192

some 400 images from the East to Henry Herring a commercial photographer. They would be the first photographic images of China ever presented to the British public. Carting 400 fragile glass plates back to London would have been impractical, and risky, especially since these original plates would have been mostly used up making prints in the field (each glass negative had a limited life as to how many prints it was capable of producing before the image on the glass wore away). It therefore seems quite likely that Beato brought safely back with him from Asia high quality prints and in London these were photographed and made into brand new glass negatives which could generate fresh photographic prints.

As has been discussed, Beato, it seems, rather dishonestly marked his images of the New Summer Palace at "Yuen-ming-yuen". This has traditionally been interpreted as honest confusion, but the marketing of Beato's images in London headline Beato's photographs of the *Old* Summer Palace, which rather skuttles that theory—either Beato or Henry Herring, the man who bought his images, knowingly claimed that the album included images of the Yuen-ming-yuen. There is no doubt that both men would have known that there were no images of this unique and distinctive complex of palaces and gardens. Beato's customers in the West were well acquainted with the fact that there was an Old Summer Palace—the principal residence of the Emperor since the reign of Yongzheng. They were also most anxious to see pictures of its much remarked upon beauty and splendour. And yet the Italian who produced 32 well composed images of the palaces, temples and walls of Peking is most notable for the absence of any pictures of the Yuen-ming-yuen. Whether it was Beato himself or Henry Herring, the portfolio that was sold in London covered the very obvious gap in his photographic record—a portfolio with coveted Old Summer Palace pictures would command a significantly higher price than one without this.

Beato with certainty did obtain loot from the Yuen-ming-yuen. There maybe some question about how he got it, but he definitely got it. Corroborating evidence was discovered by Terry Bennett who found documentation from Captain Perry Jones that Beato, "In Constantinople I ran into Senor Beato who had in his possession some fine items of loot from the Summer Palace." He sold his China loot in that city. In 1884 at the conclusion of his Japanese sojourn Beato sold his oriental antiques in London at auction, they included only Japanese items.

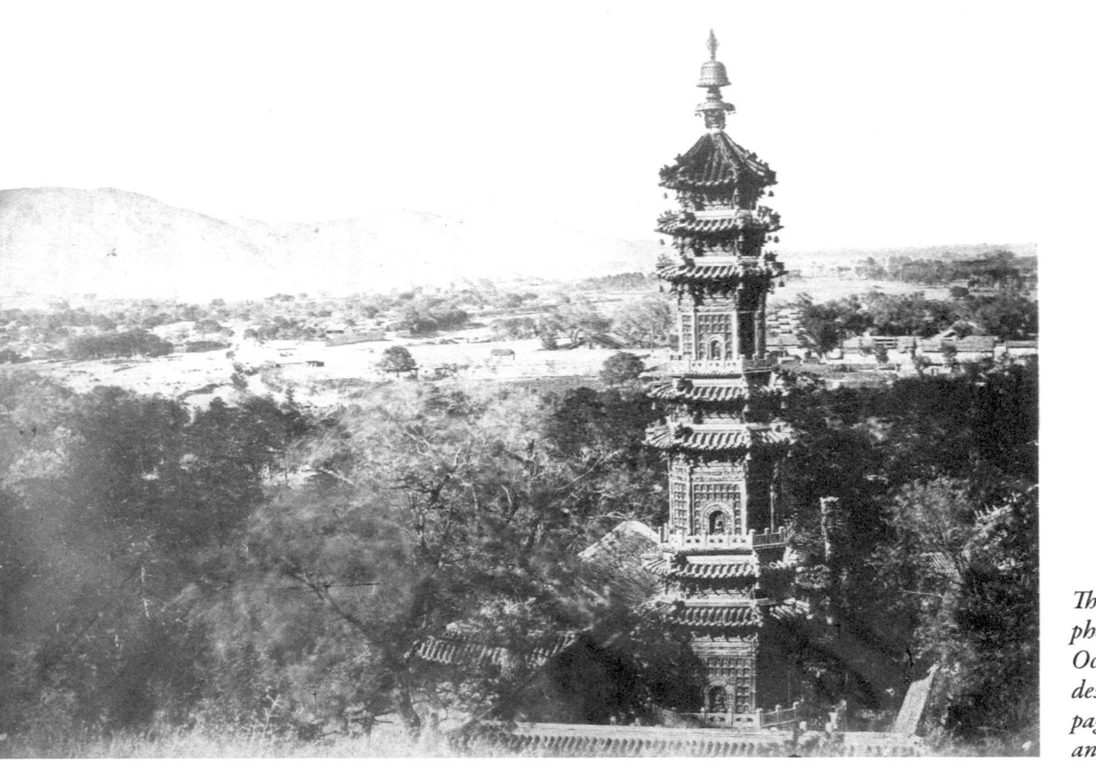

The Porcelain Pagoda, Yihe Yuan, photographed by Felice Beato, October 1860, probably before the destruction of the palace. This pagoda survived the destruction and survives to this day

In 1861 the Herring album of Beato's images of North China, went on sale for the substantial sum, at the time, of 100 pounds. It was an album of great quality, but the subject matter was what gave it such tremendous appeal. Beato's business sense was therefore well founded. Given this fact pattern, what mattered to Beato was to produce an interesting set of images of the North Chinese world and perhaps some of the leading protagonists in the conflict. The specifics of what interest us today—images of the great Yuen-ming-yuen before it was destroyed and after it was destroyed—more of journalistic and historical interest, were not Beato's concern. He could probably have sold any images that he made in Peking, regardless of the precise subject. The authorities perhaps even objected to Beato photographing the prequel and especially the acts of destruction, as politically undesirable.

Life after China

After China, Beato made his way slowly back to London. There he sold his collection of Chinese images to Henry Herring, as discussed. Beato was paid a great deal for his prints but despite the high retail price, Herring did not earn a lot of money from the process of producing the albums. Each album included 48 images selected from the 102 images that Beato had shot in China.

In 1863 Beato sailed to Japan and installed himself in Yokohama, the first 'foreign city' in Japan. He formed a photographic partnership with Charles Wirgman for several years. Japan had only just partially opened to foreigners and travel within the country was restricted. Despite this Beato produced a fine body of portraits, genre pictures and landscapes.

A fire in 1866 burned Beato's Yokohama studio to the ground destroying all of his negatives. Undeterred, he went back to many of the locations he had photographed in Edo (Tokyo) and Kyoto and re-shot the best views. Much of his work was represented in two commercial albums—one a volume of studio shot 'genre' images of Jin rickshas and geishas and another of ninety-eight landscapes. He used local artists to hand tint selected elements within the photograph to make them 'pop' and to give the photograph a different look, although his sublime silver albumen prints processed with a slight sepia tint from China come across as more pure and authentic.

In time Beato tried in vain to remove himself from the actual photography work, attempting to delegate his trade to assistants, but it did not work. His personal touch behind the camera and with customers was what the public wanted. With the money he had earned in China and any money he earned in Japan, Beato bought land on a speculatively basis. Unfortunately, although his general business sense was good, his judgment when it came to buying land and speculating on stocks and commodities was very poor, and somehow he lost all of his money through his investments. So in spite of wonderful artistic achievements in China and Japan, Beato failed in his primary objective—to build wealth. He does leave behind a wonderful collection of high quality and rare views of Japan in the Edo period. It also showed, if there was any doubt of this, that he could portray an exotic country without leaning on an imperial power or simply reproducing 'imperial' images.

In 1871 Beato accompanied the American military expedition to Korea and took some of the earliest photographs of that country. In 1877 he sold his Japanese photography business to Stillfried who went on to become a successful photographer in his own right.

As researched by David Harris, Captain Perry Jones, met Beato in Yokohama in 1879:

> I met my old friend Signor Beato here. I had first made his acquaintance whilst engaged in photography under the walls of Sebastopol; I next accosted him amidst the blood and carnage of Lucknow; and now finally I met him in the streets of Yokohama. Could anyone have chosen three more distant places, or more varied circumstances, to meet under? I have some splendid specimens of his art taken at all these places ... He was a true artist and not only manipulated well, but chose his subjects carefully and treated them artistically. He established his studio in Yokohama, but finding he had larger fish to fry, he sold his business; and I am sure scores of my old comrades will be glad to hear he is doing well.[223]

Beato left Japan for good in 1884, with very little money in hand, and returned to London where that same year he sold his collection of Japanese artworks.

---

[223] Harris, *Of Battle and Beauty*, Ch.1 Imperial Ideology

Later Years

In 1884 Beato joined yet another British expedition, this time to the Sudan where he became the official photographer of the forces led by, now General, Garnet Wolseley, another officer from China. *En route* Wolseley noted:[224]

> Beato, the photographer whom I remembered in the Crimea and whom I knew well during the Indian Mutiny and China war is on board, as amusing as ever, his attempts to speak English—which he understands very well—being as ludicrous as formerly. He has made and lost many fortunes since I last [saw] him, and now for the spell has returned to his former trade, that of photography.[225]

Mysteriously, no images from this expedition, taken in Egypt or the Sudan have emerged. Back in England Beato lectured at the Provincial Photographic Society in London on photographic technique.

Again drawn by a sense of adventure and the prospect perhaps of repeating his success in China, in 1886 Beato took passage to Burma where Britain had recently been involved in a war of conquest which she was still fighting. Again this was a mysterious and exotic land to photograph and Beato would be one of the first to do so.

Arriving in Burma after the main military operations ended, Beato still got to see more action as the invasion resulted in fighting lasting a decade. Beato was able to take a number of pictures of British military operations, of the Royal Palace in Mandalay, and other architectural marvels. He also photographed the people of Burma, soldiers and prisoners. He set up a studio in Mandalay and subsequently an antique shop, possibly quite successfully. His reputation as a fine photographer encouraged a large clientele. His images of the 'Hidden Kingdom' were emblematic of it for many years. And he remained an entrepreneur, expanding his antique business and acquiring a photographic gallery in Mandalay, as well as investments in utility companies, insurance businesses and even mines.

---

[224] Research by David Harris

[225] Harris, *Of Battle and Beauty*, Ch.1 Imperial Ideology

Death and Legacy

Beato died in Florence in 1909. As Anne Lacoste explains, Beato with all his many travels was one of the first global photographers. He was a man of great energy, the consummate adventurer, and a born entrepreneur. Beato has left us works of artistry and beauty. He remains one of the great 19th century photographers of China, perhaps the very finest. His images of China in 1860 are of great brilliance. He has been criticized by social retrospective historians for being an imperialist, creating dead images devoid of the local people. This is unfair. He wasn't trying to be a social commentator, he was what he was in China—a man capturing the sights of a country at war, in a time of fear and uncertainty. He did that job admirably. He was the first and in many ways the best photographer of Old Peking and his images capture the age. Their spareness convey a purity that over the intervening century and a half with greater haste and better technology has, with few exceptions, been lost.

Bibliography

Bennett, Terry, *History of Photography in China, 1842–1860*, Bernard Quarritch Ltd., London, 2009

Harris, David, *Of Battle and Beauty: Felice Beato's Photographs of China*, Santa Barbara Museum of Art, Santa Barbara, CA, 1999

Lacoste, Anne, *Felice Beato, A Photographer on the Eastern Road*, J Paul Getty Museum, Los Angeles, 2010

Thiriez, Régine, *Through the Barbarian Lens*, Routledge, Abingdon, 1998

Reporting from China

T. W. Bowlby

"The Chinese authorities [are] sending to us five coffins which they informed us contained the bodies of those of our prisoners who had died while in imprisonment. When these were opened one of them proved to contain, I grieve heartily to say, the remains of your poor brother."
—Captain H. Brooke

There was one man in China who might, had it not been for his dramatic demise, have provided some additional objective insight into the 1860 campaign against the Chinese emperor. He has left a fascinating account of the conflict, and his untimely death was instrumental in the burning of the Summer Palace. That man was Thomas Bowlby, correspondent for *The Times* newspaper, who accompanied the British expedition as its offical reporter.

Thomas William Bowlby came from a family, like many others of the officer corp in China, grounded in the military-clerical class. His great-grandfather was the Reverent Peter Bowlby of County Durham in the north of England, born in the first half of the eighteenth century. His grandfather was the Revened Thomas Bowlby born in 1762 in County Durham. *His* son, was Captain Thomas Bowlby of the Royal Artillery who served overseas with his regiment. The Thomas Bowlby who served in China appears to have been the only son of Captain Bowlby and Williamina Martha Arnold Balfour, daughter of Major-General William Balfour, a former Lieutenant-Governor of New Brunswick.

Bowlby was born in Gibraltar in 1818. In the 1820's the family moved to Sunderland, England, where Bowlby senior became a timber merchant. Thomas was educated privately at the Grange School, Sunderland. Upon finishing his education, he trained as a solicitor under his cousin Russell Bowlby of Sunderland, then he relocated to London where he worked for some years as a salaried law clerk. In 1846 he became a partner in the firm of Lawrence, Crowdy and Bowlby. However, some time later Bowlby was drawn to a career in writing. In September, 1848, he married an heiress, Frances Marion Mein, the youngest daughter of Pulteney Mein, of Canonbie, Dumfriesshire, Surgeon to the 73rd Regiment, and with her he had seven children.

Bowlby remained a partner in his law firm until 1854 but in 1848 went to Berlin as special correspondent for *The Times* to cover the continental revolutions. The underlying reason for his European adventures was a financial crisis. The period of the early expansion of the railways was known as 'railway mania' and Bowlby made some imprudent investments, running up debts that he could not pay. He had to leave England to avoid his debtors. Finally, he made arrangements for all of his future earnings to be applied toward the liquidation of his debts. Bowlby also went to Smyrna, where he worked on the construction of a railway. After his financial debacle he effectively became a freelance journalist, traveling to foreign countries, and was a frequent contributor to *The Times*. In April 1860 he accepted the appointment of Special Correspondent for *The Times* with the British expedition to China.

Bowlby is unique, not because of his accounts of the Summer Palace, about which his thoughts were never written, but because he was captured in September 1860, taken to the Palace, and subsequently died of ill-treatment. He has left accounts of events leading up to the capture of the Palace both in diary form and in reports submitted to *The Times*, and his death, along with his fellow captives was one of the ostensible reasons for the burning of the imperial residence.

Perhaps not surprisingly—for this was his profession and his assignment—Bowlby provides some excellent descriptions of the North China campaign. It is a somewhat confusing military operation, but Bowlby gives account of events large and small in the advance toward Peking.

As has been described in other chapters, the Allied army reached the waters off North China in August 1860 from where they had to capture a series of defensive forts and occupied serveral Chinese towns, including

212

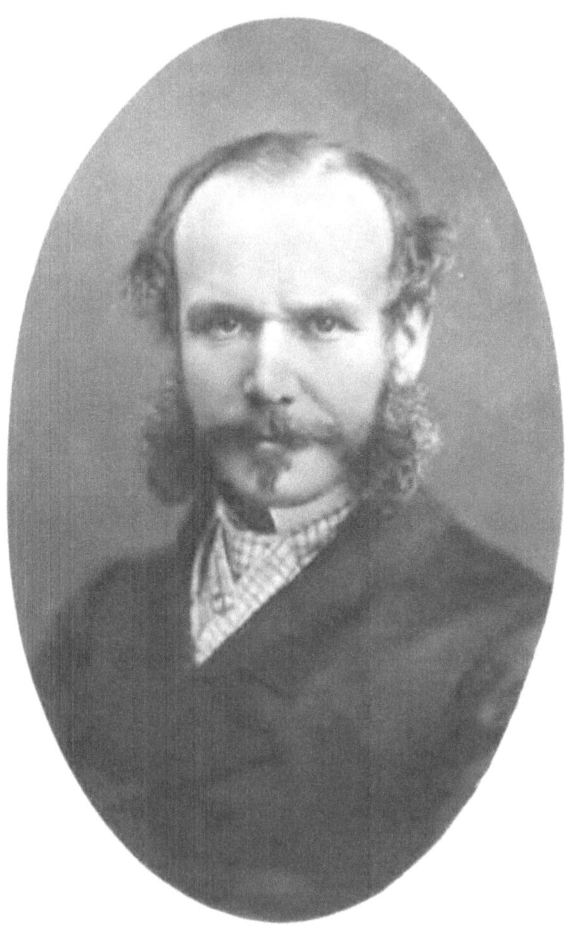

T. W. Bowlby,
photographer
unkown, c. 1855

Tientsin which lay close to the mouth of the Peiho River. By disembark-
ing all cavalry and artillery at Tientsin, the British could then march up
the Peiho to Peking. All the way from Tientsin to Peking the Chinese—
mostly cavalry, under the command of Prince Seng—harried the Europeans. In a difficult campaign that involved numerous small encounters as
well as several pitched battles, the Allies had to carefully advance against
an enemy with much superior numbers operating on their own soil.

Bowlby provides many interesting observations of the proceedings between his embarkation in England and mid-September when he was captured by the Chinese army:

The Narrative

April 26: Left London for China by the morning mail train and reached Folkestone about 11. Crossed at 1 to Boulogne—rough and lively sea and midst drenching spray, the passage lasting rather more than two hours. About 10 reached Paris where Lumley met me, and after an excellent supper at his rooms in the Pavillon Rohan I turned in and slept soundly until morning, not having been in bed for the three previous nights.[226]

In due course, having departed from southern France, Bowlby, Elgin, and Baron Gros arrived at the port of Galle in Ceylon, but all was not well:

May 21: Arrived at Galle at 11 A.M. after a frightful night. It blew a gale as we went into harbor and the pilot had the greatest difficulty in getting out to us. Lord Elgin, Baron Gros and suite landed about noon in most tremendous rain, but the Governor's boat was well covered and they escaped a ducking. We remained on board until 2 o'clock, when the weather moderated a little, and we at once set out for the old Mansion House Hotel. Here we remained all night, the rain descending and the wind blowing with true tropical force.[227]

Bowlby lost all his luggage in the storm and had to beg and borrow to find clothes to wear:

Soaked to the skin, shirtless and trouser-less, I was indebted to Mr. Churchill, Chief Commissioner of Works for those necessary garments. However, as I am 6 feet high and he some 6 inches less, I resembled an overgrown charity boy and my appearance was more provocative of laughter than of sympathy.[228]

---

[226] Bowlby, p. 1
[227] Bowlby, p. 2
[228] Bowlby, p. 3

The party continued from Ceylon on to Hong Kong:

> June 5: Left Galle in the *Pekin* for Hong Kong. Posted my letters for England in the morning and embarked at the jetty about 2. How changed the scene and how different the day from that of the 22nd. The sun was shining bright, the bay smooth as glass and a gentle breeze tempered the heat of the atmosphere. Arrived on board, we found that the ship would not start until 3 in consequence of the quantity of cargo we had to take. At 3 punctually Lord Elgin and Baron Gros embarked, the first in the barge of the *Cyclops*, the second in that of a large French transport which came in this morning with a cargo of gunboats, gunpowder, sailors and sisters of charity. Both ships manned yards as the batteries thundered out their salutes. We are nearly 60 first and 20 second class passengers, in addition to some 30 sailors on deck, volunteers for the fleet. However, every one is disposed to make allowances and we sink into our places, I am getting the surgeon's cabin. Shortly before sailing one of the passengers went into the first officer's cabin and found him drunk. He reported the matter to Mr. Bailey who said it was not his business and he could not interfere. At half-past three we get under weigh and bid adieu to Galle.[229]

In the latter part of June they arrived in Hong Kong:

> June 21: Dined with Fischer, P. & O. agent [Peninsular & Oriental shipping line]. Arrived at Hong Kong at half-past 9 A.M. Landed with Mr. Fischer . . . and, being at once proposed and seconded at the club, found myself in most comfortable quarters. Called on Messrs. Dent, Jardine, Russell & Co. and Mercer. Learnt that, by the last news from Shanghai, the Imperialist troops sent to besiege Nankin, having been left without pay for a considerable time, sacked Suzhou, the second town in the empire, and then left it to its fate and to the mercies of the rebels[230]

---

[229] Bowlby, p. 11

[230] Bowlby, p. 15

> June 22: Meanwhile, wonderful stories arrive as to the defences
> of the Peiho [river, which Allies must secure before advancing
> toward Peking] and the army of Sang-ko-lin-sin [Chinese gen-
> eral]. The Canton cotton brokers have made a bet of 50,000 dol-
> lars that we shall again be defeated at the Peiho, which bet was
> at once taken by some patriotic individuals of Hong Kong.[231]

In due course the British left Hong Kong for Shanghai:

> As we near the mouth of the Yangtse, the sea becomes yellow
> and turbid with the slime deposited by the stream and brought
> down some 2,000 miles. Indeed, both this and the Yellow Sea
> are gradually filling up with the deposits of the Yangtse and Yel-
> low rivers. A tremendous current sets in towards the shore and
> we are carried full 10 miles out of our course, which we have to
> change in consequence.[232]

Sporadic looting began long before the army arrived in Peking:

> [The fleet came upon junks] laden with Manchester goods, rice,
> oil etc., but there were no munitions of war. Notwithstanding
> this, they were carried off to Ta-lien-hwan and there given over
> to loot. One midshipman has sent down sixty pounds' worth of
> Sycee silver to be placed to his account at the Bank here, and
> I learn that one gallant captain, noted for his exploits in this
> way, has made a large haul. However, from what I have heard of
> Admiral Hope, he is not the man to sanction these proceedings.
> I am sorry to say that this mania for loot has taken complete
> possession of the Navy, officers and men. Few commanders try
> to check it and there is nothing—not even the leading articles
> in *The Times*—more likely to loosen the bonds of discipline.[233]

Having arrived close to the mouth of the Peiho, the infantry, accompanied by Bowlby, disembarked:

---

[231] Bowlby, p. 16
[232] Bowlby, p. 20
[233] Bowlby, p. 27

At half past 3 the landing commenced, the Queen's and a party of French leading the way. We had hardly gone 100 yards when the boats were ashore and over we went, waist deep into water and mud. We soon got out of the water, but before us lay three quarters of a mile of soft sticky mud, through which we had to wade more than ankle deep. However, every one went gallantly at it, and most of us adopted the wise precaution of carrying our shoes and stockings and inexpressibles, and making ourselves Highlanders for the nonce. The men formed immediately on landing, the English force consisting of the 2nd (Queen's), 60th Rifles, and 15th Punjabees. The French had an equal force, 2,500 men. We had rockets and hand grenades, they small rifled field pieces and a few ponies.[234]

Once on land the army was subjected to very heavy bouts of rain that turned the soil to mud:

This squall lasted about an hour and a half, commencing about half-past 2 A.M. It was accompanied by tremendous rain which effectually soaked every one in tents at head quarters. I have taken half of an outhouse with Beato, the photographer, and was completely sheltered from its effects.[235]

After some success by the infantry, the artillery was landed:

Nearly all the guns were landed during the night, Armstrongs, heavy battery etc. The streets were literally knee deep in slush, filth and mire; but, without a single accident, the guns were drawn right through the town and packed at the extremity of the causeway, along which they must advance. Every one turned out to see them, and there was but one opinion as to their entire efficiency. The way in which these Armstrong guns which came overland have been embarked 9 or 10 times without the slightest damage, and under the most disadvantageous conditions, reflects the greatest credit on every officer and man employed

---

[234] Bowlby, p. 63

[235] Bowlby, p. 67

with them. I was introduced to Captain Stirling, out of whose battery I am to have a mess.[236]

The first military objective for the Allies was the capture of the forts that lined the Peiho River:

August 16: Sir Hope Grant and General Napier rode along the newly constructed road and reconnoitered the North Fort. Its position was unquestionably strong; but, by aid of the heavy guns, success was all but certain. As it formed the key of the whole affair, it was determined to strike the blow there, and to do it as speedily as possible. The whole division is at work making roads etc. but the French object to the attack, and refuse to take part in the necessary preparations. Our force is ample for the purpose and the work will be done without their assistance.

This afternoon there was an extraordinarily high tide which completely flooded the lower part of Tungchow . . . the place itself is miserable. There is no tree, herb or vegetable in its neighbourhood; nothing but a sea of mud in every direction. The water is brackish and the sooner the North forts are taken, and everyone off, the better.[237]

A party of English crossed to the south side this afternoon. The village, wherein the French had established themselves, was completely looted, and a woman was found dead from a bayonet wound. Never, never did I see anything like the brutality of these men [the French infantry]. They destroy out of mere wantonness what they cannot carry off, and seem to have an absolute pleasure in taking life. When they cannot kill Tartars, they set to work with cats and dogs. God forbid they should ever effect a landing in England. Up and at 'em, volunteers.[238]

Keen attention to combat and proximity to it. Lieutenant M'Gregor gave the word to charge, and away went the Sikhs in

---

[236] Bowlby, p. 69

[237] Bowlby, p. 77

[238] Bowlby, p. 80

most gallant style. No flinching, no craning; every spur was well in the horse's side, when one-half the Tartars met them in full shock. The effect was instantaneous. One of the leading Sikhs ran his spear right through the body of a Mongol horseman, the head entering at his chest and going out at his back. The spear broke in the middle, the Mongol fell to the ground spitted, and never moved a limb. Lieutenant M'Gregor singled out his man, and was in the act of spearing him, when another Tartar fired his matchlock within ten yards point blank. The slugs hit the Lieutenant in five places, three lodging in his chest, two in the forehead. For a moment he was blinded by the fire, which burnt his face, but the work was done. The Tartars dispersed in every direction, the whole affair lasting little more than a minute. I am happy to say that Lieutenant M'Gregor is fast recovering from his wounds . . .[239]

Today [August 20] General Montauban served Sir H. Grant with a written protest. Since he is determined to attack the North Fort, the French Commander-in-Chief must send a force to co-operate with the English, but he places on Sir H. Grant the entire responsibility of an act so contrary to the rules of war. To this Sir Hope quietly replied that he should take the fort tomorrow morning.[240]

Bowlby became famous for his account of the storming of the Taku Forts on August 21. His story shows that he must have been close to the action as well as the fact that the fighting was far from the one-sided affair that critics of the British would have it. With less determination and less skill, the Allies could have easily been defeated by their stubborn and courageous foe:

The ladder party was ordered to advance and throw a bridge over the outer ditch. Two had been prepared, made of Blanshard's light infantry pontoons, under charge of Lieutenant Pritchard, R.E. They were carried by 82 Royal Marines, accompanied by 12 sappers of the Royal Engineers. The scaling-ladders and the

---

[239] Bowlby, p. 250
[240] Bowlby, p. 81

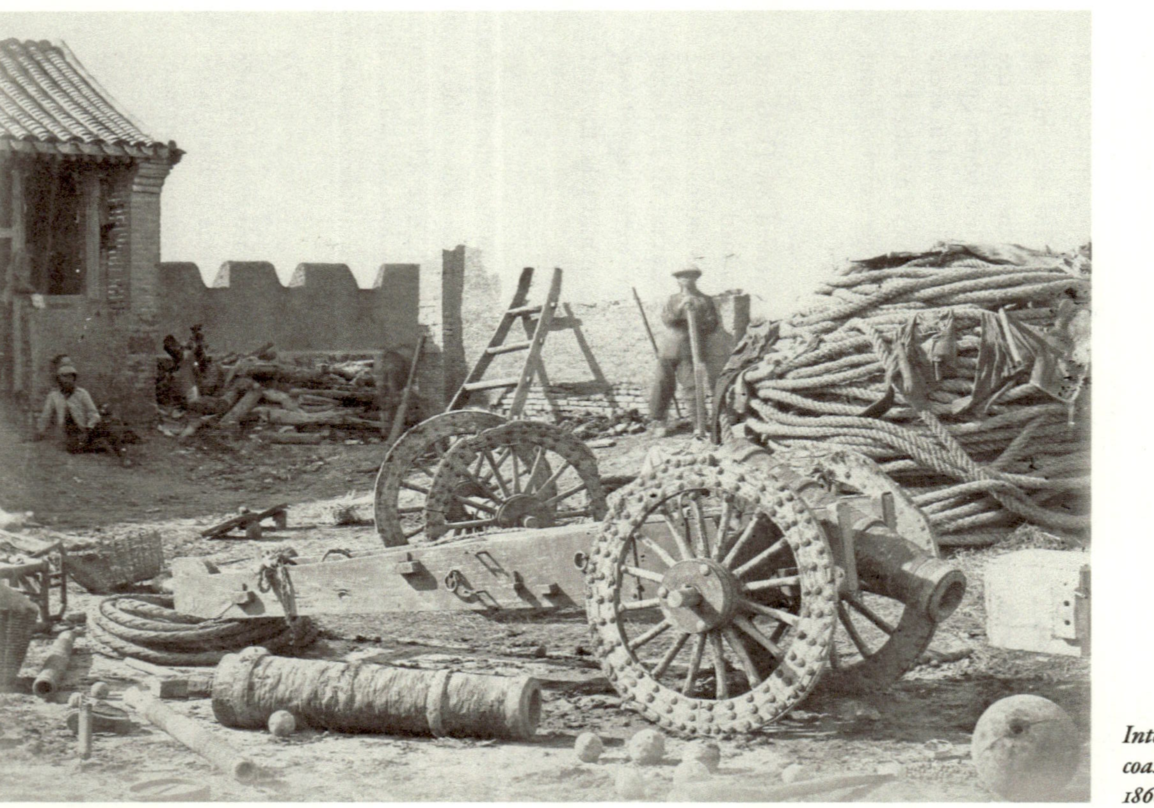

Interior of a captured coastal fort, August 1860, Felice Beato

powder bags for blowing in the gate followed the pontoons. The first pontoon was, after much difficulty, carried up to the causeway over the water, leading to the main gate of the fort. Hence the road up to the ditch was narrow, and crowded with killed and wounded. The pontoons were heavy and unwieldly; one of them was shot through, and, despite the struggles and exertions of the marines and sappers, who did all that brave men could, the pontoons could be advanced no further. Major Graham, Royal Engineers, was wounded while leading on his men. An officer and 11 men of the marines, and two of the sappers, were also wounded. One of the sappers is since dead. Meanwhile two companies of the 44th, one commanded by Captain Gregory, the other by Lieutenant Rogers, had rushed to the ditch to keep down the enemy's galling fire of gingals and matchlocks.

There was no cover against the bullets, spears, and arrows flying about in every direction, so Captain Gregory placed his men up to their middle in water and commenced a fusillade against the Chinese on the parapets, himself seizing a rifle from a wounded soldier and using it with excellent effect for 30 rounds. Man after man of the 44th continued to drop, and still there was no bridge. Lieutenant Rogers rushed through the ditch, pulled out the spikes, and succeeded in reaching the berm under the parapet wall. About the same time the storming companies of the 67th went at the ditches with a will. Some swam, some struggled through, and a few succeeded in reaching the berm. There they found the French, who had already crossed over light bamboo ladders carried by their coolies. These ladders bent when placed across the ditch. In jumped six coolies up to their necks. The ladders were supported across their shoulders, and the French quickly crossed over. 'These men should have a riband,' said Colonel Du Pin, himself conspicuous in the front, 'their gallantry is marvellous'.

A plank was now placed across the ditch in front of the main gate over which very rickety bridge many soldiers passed one by one. The English ladder party was also sent to the salient angle of the fort near the spot where the French had crossed. Here their ladders were laid and the troops got over. All this time the fire of the enemy continued incessant. Cold shot, hand grenades, stinkpots, and vases of lime were showered on the crowd of besiegers who stood upon the berm. The ladders placed against the wall were pulled into the fort, or thrown over, and in vain did man after man attempt to swarm through the embrasures. If the defence was desperate, nothing could exceed the gallantry of the assailants. Between English and French there was nothing to choose.

A Frenchman climbed to the top of the parapet, where for some time he stood alone. One rifle after another was handed to him, which he fired against the enemy. But his courage was unavailing, and he fell back speared through the eye. Another, pickaxe in hand, attempted to cut away the top of the wall. He was shot, and Lieutenant Burslem, of the 67th, caught hold of his pick and continued the work. Lieutenant Rogers attempted to force his way through an embrasure, but was driven back. He ran to another, but it was too high for him. Lieutenant Lennon, 67th, came to his assistance, forced the point of his sword into the wall, and, placing one foot on the sword, Lieutenant Rogers leaped through the embrasure just after Jean Fauchard, drummer of the French 103rd, had got over at the right angle. Lieutenant Rogers acted with conspicuous gallantry. He was the first Englishman in the place, and was afterwards of the greatest service in assisting others through the embrasures. He was wounded in the side by a matchlock ball, but is doing well. Jean Fauchard was followed by many of his own countrymen, and by Lieutenant Pritchard, R.E., Lieutenants Lennon and Burslem, 67th, who assisted their own men across the ditch, and were both wounded; Captain Prynne, R.M., and Lieutenant Hume, R.E. In addition to them, among the first in the fort were Colonel Knox and Ensign Chaplin, 67th; Captain Gregory, 44th; Brigadier Reeves (wounded in three places), Lieutenant Kempson, 99th; Colonel Mann, R.E., and Major Anson, Aide-de-Camp. Colonel Mann and Major Anson cut the ropes, and lowered the draw bridge over which the mass of the English crossed; and now, after half-an-hour's tremendous fighting under the parapet wall, the allies were in the fort.

Still the Chinese made a desperate resistance under cover of their casemates. Ensign Chaplin ascended the ramp almost alone, racing against a French soldier. Half-way up he was knocked over by a bullet, but, quickly recovering himself, he was up again, and won by a head. A second shot struck him through the leg as he placed the Queen's colours of the 67th at the top of the cavalier, and Private Thomas Lane, 67th, took his place by the flag. Lieutenant Kempson, who had a tourniquet in his pocket, bound up Mr. Chaplin's arm. Lieutenants Rogers and Burslem and Ensign Chaplin have been recommended for the Victoria Cross, which they right well deserve. And now the soldiers came rushing in, but still the Chinese fought. Captain Prynne shot the commanding officer with his revolver. The 67th caught the enemy on the left of the ramp, and bayoneted 27 in one mass. The French rushed at them on the other side as they vainly endeavoured to escape. At the proper left angle of the fort lay 17 bodies, blown up by a shell from Govan's howitzers, which General Napier had brought up in support of the French column as they stormed the fort. On the stakes outside were dozens of Chinese, 'hoist with their own petard'. One had fallen on his eyes, another was staked right through the body.

'They lie in sections, Sir,' said a 44th man. One hundred and thirty-seven were buried in the fort in one grave. For days the dead were floated from the ditch into the river, borne backwards and forwards with the tide. Their wounded were carried off in a most ingenious manner. A rope passed under their arms let them down into the ditch. They were then towed to the river, and thence along the edge of the stream to the lower northern fort, where they were passed across in junks. The Chinese loss in killed and wounded cannot have been less than 1,500 men. The English had 200 casualties—17 men killed, 22 officers and 161 men wounded. The 44th and 67th, having provided the storming parties, were naturally the greatest sufferers. The former had ten men killed, two officers and 50 men wounded; the 67th had six men killed, eight officers and 62 men wounded . . . The French list of casualties was a little over 100.[241]

From the top of the northern bastion Sir Hope Grant and General Montauban took a survey of the surrounding country, and a wretched scene of desolation it presented. To the east was the sea and the mouth of the river with its soft mud banks. North,

---

[241] Bowlby, pp. 275–278

south, east, and west one great muddy morass extended in every direction, not a trace of vegetation being visible within a circuit of six miles. But one road could be discovered—the causeway on which the troops were halted. It therefore became a sad necessity to take possession of the town and to house the troops at the expense of the inhabitants. Pehtang is intersected by one main street, nearly in the centre.[242]

The enemy is very different from the wretched rabble hitherto opposed to us in the South. These Tartars seem to be brave resolute men, well commanded, well disciplined, and well mounted on strong active galloways. They moved in good order. Their supports came up rapidly, and it is quite clear that their leader knows something of his business. However, so far as is known, they have no field artillery, and I cannot but think they will fall an easy prey before such infantry, cavalry, and artillery as are about to meet them. What can a gingal, however well directed, avail against an Armstrong shell? Moreover Sang-ko-lin-sin [Prince Seng] himself could hardly hold his own against such swordsmen as Probyn or Fane. Immediately after their return the commanders-in-chief determined to disembark the whole force immediately, and, as soon as the necessary precautions were made, to advance, storm the Tartar camp, and follow them up with vigour.[243]

Landing at Tientsin

Colonel Stephenson, Deputy-Adjutant-General, and his staff, were also indefatigable, and in due course the whole of the cavalry and artillery were landed without a single accident, except that a favourite mule of Sir Hope Grant, which had followed his fortunes in India for many years, got staked and was shot. Let it be remembered that these horses and guns were brought from ships lying some miles out at sea, towed in open boats across a dangerous bar and up a narrow tortuous river, in which the tide runs like a mill-stream, and landed on a narrow mud wharf; that the horses are over 2,000 in number, and the baggage animals as

---

242 Bowlby, pp. 228–229
243 Bowlby, p. 238

many more, and it will be evident that the staff of this little army is most thoroughly efficient.[244]

I am writing this letter in an outhouse which forms my quarters, the slate roof of which affords better protection against the sun than the canvas of a tent. My domicile is built of mud, the roof of wood and matting with a substantial tile cover. There is neither door nor window, for the oiled paper which I found doing service for the latter, excluded both light and air, and was pulled out at once. My apartment is paved with brick, and is ten feet by eight. It is unfortunately occupied by a numerous tenantry, whom all my exertions have been unable to eject, and who feed on my poor body nightly. For the rest, it keeps out the rain, except when the wind is due East, and it lets in the sun at 5 in the morning, so that I am driven perforce to very early hours.[245]

Amid ropes, wooden gun carriages, and debris of every description, the coolies are cooking their dinner, a most mysterious and unsavoury mess, and behind them are the artillery, just leading out their horses to water. Signor Beato, whose photographs of Indian camp life are so well known, has just asked for 'steadiness' while he takes a photograph of the scene. To the right are Probyn's Horse with their little square tents, their lances glittering in the sun, their red and blue pennants flaunting in the wind, their magnificent Arabs fighting, squealing, and kicking in every direction, their syces and beesties, their goats, dogs, mules, and asses. A more picturesque scene was never witnessed.[246]

August 22: Rode with Major Taylor over the ground and carefully inspected the North forts. The ditches, outside the one which was attacked, were full of dead Tartars, and the space between the two forts quite encumbered with their bodies. In the centre embrasure of the cavalier of the lower fort was a mass

---

[244] Bowlby, p. 239
[245] Bowlby, p. 240
[246] Bowlby, p. 241

of brains and blood smelling most foully ... The Tartar loss must have been frightful, at least 1,500 to 2,000 men.[247]

The Tartar wounded were brought in from the fort yesterday and placed in houses and tents. Rutherford told me he had never seen such frightful wounds as are made by the Armstrong shells. Wherever they hit, the bones are smashed in every direction, and such a shock is given that very few of the amputations have saved the life. They are grateful for the attentions they receive, and one offered Rutherford a small piece of Sycee silver.[248]

August 28: Visited every sick and wounded man on board the *Sir William Peel, Mauritius, Melbourne* and *Lancashire Witch* (for account see paper). Nothing could possibly be better than the arrangements made for their comfort.[249]

August 30: At 1 o'clock we arrived at Tientsin and, without guide or leader, plunged into the intricacies of a Chinese town of a quarter of a million people. After getting through the suburbs we reached a walled city and, knowing that the head-quarters were on the river, we tried to make for that part, skirting the wall. The place is enormous and the streets narrow. After an hour's wandering about, we struck into the city, rode through it and found we were at the cavalry camp. We were then directed on the road and went through another mile or two of streets without success.[250]

Beato's coolies run away and leave him at Peokhu with only three men. Wade is at an inn with his bloke. One of men comes to the inn in search of coolies.[251]

---

247 Bowlby, pp. 82–83

248 Bowlby, p. 86

249 Bowlby, p. 87

250 Bowlby, p. 89

251 Bowlby, p. 100

Capture

During September there were protracted negotiations between the Allies and the Chinese authorities, neither of whom for different reasons wanted the Allied army to advance as far as Peking. Discussions seemed to be progressing well and terms appeared, at least from the British point of view, to be close to agreement. Never-the-less the British army had continued to advance in the direction of the capital and the Chinese army continued to stand in their way. It was at this juncture that Harry Parkes, the British representative in Shanghai and a fluent Mandarin speaker, advanced to Tungchow half-way to the capital with Loch, Elgin's secretary, and an escort of cavalrymen. Bowlby, anxious to see the proceedings, and not perceiving imminent danger, joined the group. In Tungchow the party was well received by the Chinese officials and were in the process of returning to British lines under flag of truce when they came upon a mass of Chinese cavalry in line of battle blocking the British advance. Seeking permission to by-pass the Chinese lines and to rejoin the British by a circuitous route, they were detained and made prisoner by Prince Seng, who did not approve of the peace negotiations and was prepared to ignore the protected status of these envoys. It was a pivotal moment in the life of the captives and in the prosecution of the campaign, for it effectively stalled all peace negotiations for weeks and the Allies continued their advance to Peking and the Summer Palace. Indeed, it changed the course of history.

One of the Sikh cavalrymen who was captured with Bowlby relates what happened to them after their group (the prisoners were in two groups, one that was taken to a prison in Peking, and one that was taken to the Summer Palace) was taken prisoner and taken north:

> The first day we stopped at a joss house on the side of the road to Peking; we tied our horses up, and went inside. The Chinese then took them away, but brought them back in the morning, and we again mounted. Here two gentlemen left us; we went through Peking to the other side, and pulled up at a *serai*; here one of the Chinamen went to ask if we should dismount, and on his return we were taken to some tents. This place had barracks inside, and we went through a large doorway. We had been there half an hour when we were ordered out one by one to wash our hands and faces. They took out the gentlemen first, threw them

down, and fastened their hands behind them. They then made us kneel down in the middle of the yard, tied our hands and feet behind, and threw us over on our backs. From this position, if we attempted to rest on our right or left side, they kicked and beat us.

We remained in this position all night, during which time they poured water on our bonds to tighten them. Mr. De Norman spoke to one of the Chinese officers during the night, and told him that we came to treat and not to fight, and they then gave us a little water and rice. The Hindus would not eat it until Mr. Anderson [a cavalry lieutenant with Fane's Horse] persuaded them to do so, when some of them did. The next day a white button mandarin came to see us. He had many orderlies with him, and he took down in writing some answers to questions put by him to Mr. De Norman. About two hours after he was gone we were loaded with irons; got nothing more to eat or drink for three days; Mr. Anderson's hands were swollen to three times their proper size, and as black as ink; the whole weight of his body—chains and all—was thrown on his hands, they looked ready to burst.

As long as he was sensible he encouraged us, and rebuked us for calling out; when he became insensible he constantly called out Major Fane, Maclean, and others; he became delirious when the chains were put on. On the afternoon of the third day from this, they took four of us away in carts; travelled all that night, gave us no food or water, and beat us when we asked for any. Mr. Bowlby's hands were not so much swollen; he spoke no Hindustani, and so we could not understand him; at 10 A.M. next day we arrived at a fort, with a few buildings near it, there was no town. Another cart was with us containing Duffadar Mahomed Bux, a French Officer, very tall and stout, with a brown beard, and a dragoon named Pisa (Phipps). We were taken into the fort, and for three days were out in the open air in the cold. They then pulled us into an old kitchen and kept us there eight days; they never allowed us to stir for three or four days. Mr. Bowlby died the second day after we arrived. The next day the Frenchman died. Two days after this Jawalla Sing (first Sikh) died. Four days afterwards, Phipps, King's Dragoon Guards, died; for ten days he encouraged us in every way he could. Mahomed Bux, duffadar, died ten days ago; he remained very well till then, and abused the Chinese for bringing him pig to eat. I should have died had not my chains been taken off. The Chinaman who brought us here was very kind, he dressed our wounds and gave us what we wanted; when he was absent we got nothing.[252]

Commentary—Why Were the Emissaries Captured and Killed?

I don't recall ever reading an explanation as to why the emissaries were captured or why they were treated the way they were. I did read comments by one young Chinese gentleman stating that it was not a big deal since the emissaries were simply treated like any Chinese criminal, and Europeans should not make anything of it. This is not correct—Chinese prisoners were not put to death by having their hands bound so tight that they mortified, which is undoubtedly what happened to Bowlby et al. The central questions are: why were the emissaries captured, and why were they tortured and killed? Perhaps in the Imperial Archives there are documents explaining everything. Excepting this direct evidence, the ostensible reason why the emissaries were detained was because Prince Seng wished to resume fighting and drive the foreigners into the sea. Whatever the rationale, this in-of-itself would not have been especially controversial, especially if Seng had communicated the fact to the Allies that the emissaries had been detained but that they would be well treated and returned once the Allies were prepared to withdraw from Chinese soil.

What does not seem to make sense from the point of view of Chinese interests is the ill-treatment of the prisoners. What did the Chinese hope to achieve; how did it serve their objectives? If they simply wanted to kill the emissaries they could have had them executed. The emissaries were important members of the European expedition, and the Chinese authorities knew this, and they knew that the well-being of these men would be a matter of greater sensitivity than common soldiers captured in battle. There seems to be no clear reason for the ill-treatment that occurred, except pure vengeance, which might make sense on a personal level, but not on a diplomatic one.

It was assumed by Lord Elgin and the Allied officers that the ill-treatment of the prisoners was the capricious plan of the Chinese Emperor. Perhaps it was. In the absence of official documents, it is not

---

[252] Bughel Sing, 1st troop Fane's Horse, Bowlby, pp. 350–351

clear. But it may be an incorrect assumption. It could just as easily have been the work of a capricious jailer or an angry captain of the guard. Ironically, the Emperor may have had no idea about how the prisoners were being treated. But whoever's decision it was, it proved an unfortunate choice that caused the Allies to demand financial compensation and was the ostensible reason for the burning of the Summer Palace—significant consequences indeed.

Aftermath

The murder of the Allied prisoners had nothing to do with the looting of the Summer Palace, which followed as a direct consequence of the Allied capture of the place on October 6. However, it was one of the two reasons why the British felt that the Emperor should be punished and the Palace burned. It therefore had great consequence not just for the men who died but for the entire course of history. Had it not been for the death of the prisoners, Elgin may have yielded to French protests against the burning.

Captain Brooke, ADC to General Hope Grant wrote to Bowlby's brother:

> The Chinese authorities [are] sending to us five coffins which they informed us contained the bodies of those of our prisoners who had died while in imprisonment. When these were opened one of them proved to contain, I grieve heartily to say, the remains of your poor brother who we have since learnt expired on the day after his capture [*sic*]. Most truly do I, and his friends, who are numerous in this army, sorrow for his untimely end, and deeply do we sympathize with his bereaved family, to whom his loss must be a cruel and unexpected blow. During his stay amongst us he had made many friends and no enemies, and was a heartily welcomed guest wherever he went. I saw a good deal of him and I shall not easily forget his kindness and attention to me when confined to my bed by the wound I received at the storming of the Taku forts.[253]

---

[253] Letter to Mr. A. G. T. Bowlby, brother of T. W. Bowlby, from Captain H. Brooke, A.D.C., Bowlby, pp. 397–398

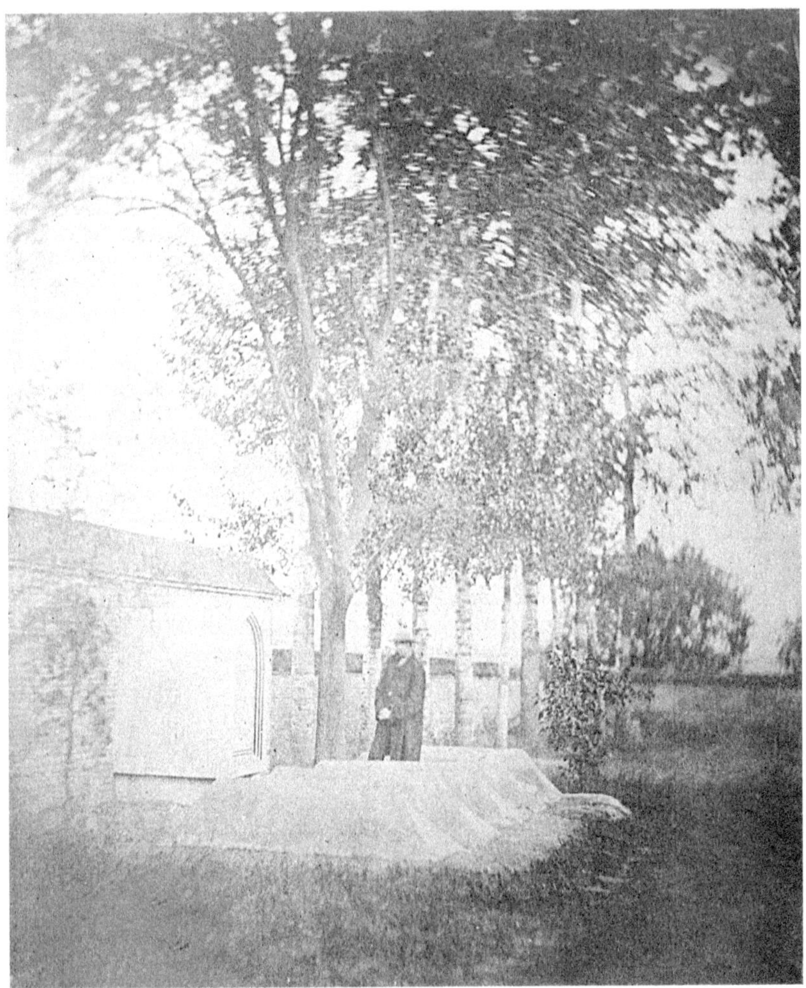

The graves of the four British prisoners, including T.W. Bowlby, in the Russian Cemetery, Igireff photographer, October 17, 1860. Image courtesy of Terry Bennett

The British were buried in the Russian cemetery:

> Wednesday, the 17th [October], was the day arranged for the burial of those whose bodies had been surrendered. The place selected was the Russian Cemetery, which is about a mile from

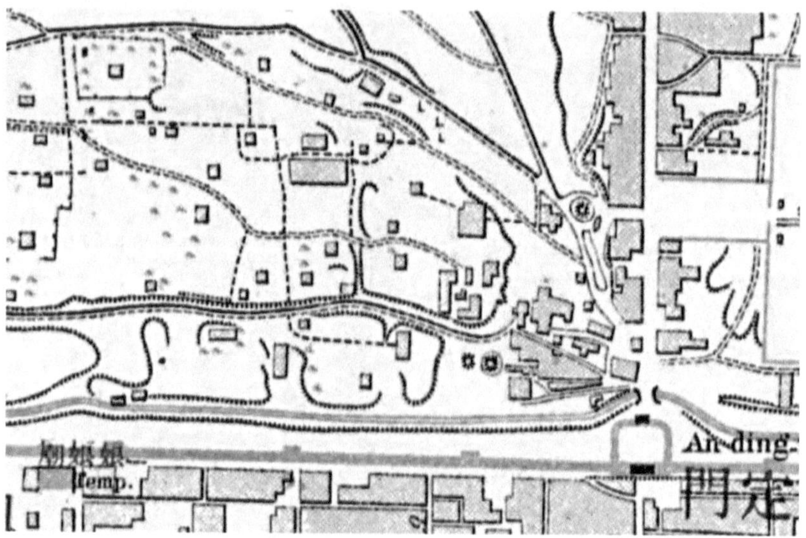

Area Around the Russian Cemetery

The Russian Cemetery, outside the city walls, northwest of the Anting (An ding) Gate. The site of the cemetery is not marked, but is described as being one quarter-mile northwest of the gate (bottom right). The small enclosure in the top left of the map seems to fit the description of the construction

the north-east angle of the city wall; officers and men from every regiment attended; the coffins were conveyed on gun-carriages; General de Montauban and many French officers were present. The procession moved slowly across the plain. Lord Elgin and Sir Hope Grant were the chief mourners, Parkes and myself next. A long trench had been dug, and the coffins were placed side by side, and, when at the close of the service the earth was thrown in, the unusual sight was witnessed of Protestant, Roman Catholic and Greek Church priests meeting in Christian charity and praying together over one grave.[254]

Lord Elgin wrote:

It was a mournful and affecting ceremony to witness these poor Christian victims of heathen barbarism laid in their untimely

---

[254] Bowlby, pp. 347–348

232

graves. The cemetery is about a quarter of a mile outside the northern wall of the city. The grave is on high ground just within the inner gate. The coffins were laid side by side from north to south—Private Phipps, then Lieutenant Anderson, then Mr. de Normann, then Mr. Bowlby. The Royal Engineers are to place a tomb over the poor fellows, and if the British Government does not erect a monument to their memory, it is to be hoped that it will be done by private subscription.[255]

Extract from a Letter to Mr. Delane, Editor of *The Times* from the Earl of Elgin and Kincardine. Private. Camp near Peking, October 25, 1860:

My Dear Mr. Delane, It is with very sincere grief that I have to announce to you that our worst fears have been confirmed and that it is now only too certain that Mr. Bowlby died under the effects of the ill treatment which he experienced as a prisoner in the hands of the Tartars. I saw much of him both on our voyage out and since our arrival in China; and I felt a real interest in and regard for him, not only because I had found him to be an accomplished and agreeable companion, but also because, from the conscientious and liberal spirit in which he took to his work, I believed that he would have done much to enlighten public opinion in England on Chinese affairs. I consider the loss of such a man at this conjuncture to be a great calamity.[256]

Letter, Lord John Russell, H.M.'s Secretary of State for Foreign Affairs. Pembroke Lodge, December 25, 1860:

My Dear Sir, I am sorry to find by the dispatches just received that no doubt whatever remains about the death of Mr. Bowlby. I am told his mother is living. May I ask you to carry to her my condolence upon the death of a son whose talents and energy gave such a promise of a brilliant career. His description of the taking of the Taku forts was one of the most interesting narratives of a war achievement I ever read. Lord Elgin, in one of his dispatches, gives a testimony far more valuable than mine to Mr.

---

[255] Bowlby, p. 402. Note, the monument was never erected in China

[256] Elgin, in Bowlby, p. 403

Bowlby's merits. It will remain as a public record. I am, Yours very truly, J. RUSSELL.[257]

Monument to the late Thomas W. Bowlby:

There is now in course of erection, in Bishops Wearmouth parish church, a monument to the late Thomas William Bowlby, of this town, *The Times'* correspondent in the late Chinese war, whose horrible sufferings and death, after being captured by the enemy, will be remembered by all. It has been designed by Mr. J. Pennethorne, architect, of London, and executed by Mr. Wren, of Pimlico, and will be placed in the south aisle of the church, near the chancel. It is executed in Aubigny stone, the tablet being polished black marble. The design is in the pointed Gothic, and is most chaste. Upon the tablet, in gilt letters, is placed the following inscription, written by Mr. Bowlby's schoolfellow and fellow townsman, Mr. Tom Taylor: 'In memory of Thomas William Bowlby, son of the late Captain Thomas Bowlby, R.A., born at Gibraltar, and educated at the Grange School, in this neighbourhood, who, while fulfilling the duties of correspondent to *The Times* newspaper in the Chinese war of 1860, was captured by the enemy, and, with his fellow-prisoners, died under the barbarous treatment of his captors, on the 25th September, 1860, in the 43rd year of his age. This tablet is erected by a body of his friends and schoolfellows as a tribute of respect and affection.'[258]

In 1906 Bowlby's son published *An Account of the last Mission and Death of Thomas William Bowlby* based on his father's reports to *The Times* and the letters and accounts of his death. In October 2014 Christopher Bowlby, great-grandson of T.W. Bowlby and a journalist with the BBC was in China making a radio documentary about the Summer Palace. He went to find the grave of his great-grandfather. The Russian Cemetery no longer exists, and what in 1860 was countryside, now forms the hub of a giant urban wheel. Sadly, no grave markers exist anymore. All that Chris was shown were some soccer fields.

---

[257] Russell, in Bowlby, p. 404
[258] *The Sunderland Times*, 1861, in Bowlby, p. 406

The Russian Cemetery was established in the 18th century and according to Robert Swinhoe of the British Consular Service, "The Russian cemetery is outside the city to the right of the Anting gate, situated about a quarter of a mile off the northern wall. It is a small piece of ground enclosed by a wall, with a gate on the side facing north."[259] Robert M'Ghee noted: "The Russian burial-ground is outside the north wall of the city, about a quarter of a mile from it, and on the verge of that . . . [a] parade ground."[260] It appears that the cemetery was destroyed during the Cultural Revolution and the land used for a public park. There are no signs today of where it lay, commentators say it is either beneath a driving range or a lake.

Bibliography

Bowlby, C.C., *An Account of the Last Mission and Death Of Thomas William Bowlby*, Probethain, London, 1906

---

[259] Swinhoe, Robert, *The North China Campaign of 1860*, p. 324
[260] M'Ghee, Robert, *How We Got to Pekin*, p. 256

The Soldier's Eye

Garnet Wolseley

"Some blackened gables and piles of burnt timbers alone indicating where the royal palaces had stood. In many places the inflammable pine trees near the buildings had been consumed with them, leaving nothing but their charred trunks to mark the site."

—Garnet Wolseley

Garnet Wolseley was one of the great British generals of the Victorian era. His life in the army was full of colorful events in various overseas theatres of operation. A man of energy and tremendous ability, as a young officer he was Deputy Assistant Quartermaster General to the British expeditionary force in China, an endorsement of his abilities and the attention to detail necessary to make this critical campaign a success. Like a number of other intelligent observers who were part of the expedition, Wolseley published an account of his experiences and observations—*Narrative of the War with China in 1860*, London, 1862. These detailed observations from the 'soldier's soldier', the man who in part organized the British campaign, are perhaps more sanguine than his fellow authors, reflecting his personality and training, but at the same time authoritative and honest.

Wolseley was born in County Dublin on June 4, 1833 into an Anglo-Irish family. He was the eldest son of another army officer, Major Garnet Joseph Wolseley of the 25th Regiment of Foot, and Frances Smith, the daughter of an Irish landowner. Wolseley inherited strong religious beliefs from his Protestant mother, and a deep passion for the military from his father.

Wolseley was not related to the famous chancellor of Henry VIII, but instead traced his ancestry to Danish invaders from before the Norman Conquest. In *The Story of a Soldier's Life* he wrote, "The fact of knowing that I inherited a very old name had a marked influence upon my boyhood and early life. It was a spur to the boundless ambition that filled my brain in my youth, and it has been an active factor in the events of my subsequent career." He had a sense of destiny which inspired him to bravery, believing that God would protect him, and to be a man of action at every opportunity, even when placed in 'staff' positions. During the course of his long career with the British army Wolseley was to win almost every possible honor that a soldier could earn.

Wolseley's father died when his son was just seven years of age. This resulted in financial hardship for the family. His mother had to raise seven children with little income, but she managed to send Garnet to school and as a youth he went to work for a surveyor. The call to arms was never far away and in 1852 Wolseley was awarded a commission as ensign with the 12th Regiment of Foot. Rumor has it that Wolseley received his commission at no cost (his family could not afford to *buy* him a commission, as was customary) because of his mother's appeal to the Duke of Wellington, who was also of Anglo-Irish stock. Action followed quickly afterwards when Wolseley transferred to an Indian regiment and fought in the Burma Campaign. He was severely wounded in March 1853 during the attack on Donabyu where he refused to leave the field of battle until his men had achieved victory. He almost died from his wounds.

Wolseley, not for the first time, was mentioned in dispatches for his bravery in Burma and promoted to the rank of lieutenant. In 1854 he was sent to the Crimea. During the siege of Sevastopol he was wounded twice, including losing an eye, as an officer with the Royal Engineers. In Russia Wolseley met fellow engineer officer Charles Gordon, another fearless fighter and devout Christian, whose qualities automatically appealed. Wolseley would serve with Gordon in China and would later try to rescue him in the Sudan. In 1855 he was promoted to captain, awarded the *Legion de Honeur* and mentioned in dispatches multiple times. Wolseley's regiment was sent to China to fight in the early stages of the Second Opium War but was shipwrecked in the Indian Ocean and when the troops were rescued they were sent to India to fight in the Indian Mutiny.

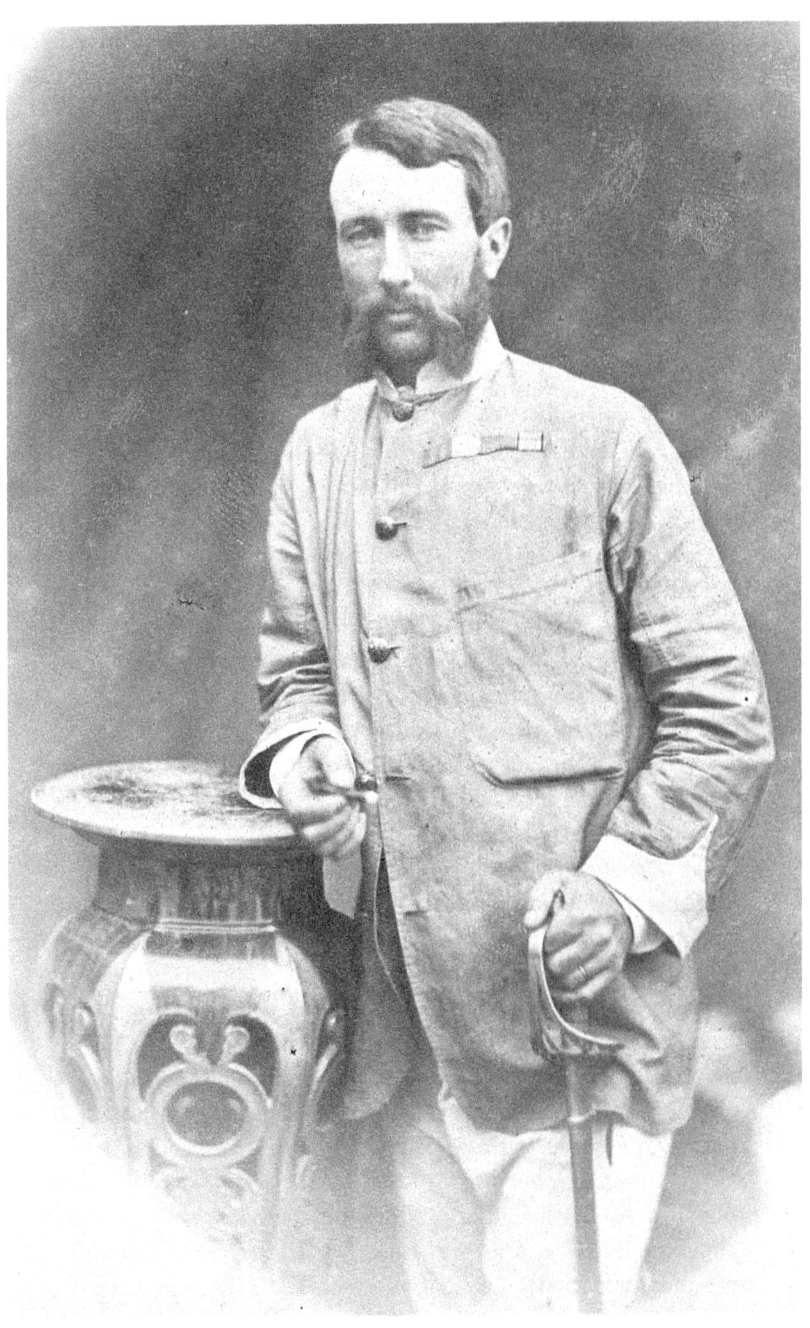

Lieutenant-colonel Wolseley, China, 1860, Felice Beato

In India, Wolseley was involved in almost all of the major actions of the war and seemed to distinguish himself at every turn. He was part of the first relief of Lucknow, the defense of Alambagh, and the final siege of Lucknow, and served under James Hope Grant in all of these engagements. He was again mentioned in dispatches, five times, and promoted to brevet Major and Lieutenant-Colonel before the end of the campaign. After his service with Hope Grant, the general selected Wolseley to be his deputy-assistant quartermaster general in China; he was just twenty-seven.

The Narrative

Wolseley, with a clinical pragmatism, no doubt the product of his training, carefully analyses the capture and looting of the Summer Palace, and provides an invaluable perspective.[261]

> General Montauban, who said that as soon as he learnt [of] Sir Hope Grant's intention of marching upon Yuen-ming-yuen, he also made for that place, and fell in with our cavalry during his march, when both proceeded together until they reached the large village of Haitien, which is situated close by the Palace.
>
> A mine of wealth and of everything curious in the empire lay as a prey before our French allies. Rooms filled with articles of virtue both native and European, halls containing vases and jars of immense value, and houses stored with silks, satins and embroidery, were open to them. Indiscriminate plunder and wanton destruction of all articles too heavy for removal commenced at once. Guards were placed about in various directions; but to no purpose. When looting is once commenced by an army it is no easy matter to stop it. At such times human nature breaks down the ordinary trammels which discipline imposes and the consequences are most demoralizing to the very best constituted army. Soldiers are nothing more than grown-up schoolboys. The wild moments of enjoyment passed in the pillage of a place live long in a soldier's memory. Although, perhaps, they did not gain sixpence by it, still they talk of such for years afterwards with pleasure. Such a time forms so marked a contrast with the

---

[261] Wolseley, pp. 224–279, inclusive

ordinary routine of existence passed under the tight discipline, that it becomes a remarkable event in life and is remembered accordingly.

I have often watched soldiers after the capture of a place, wandering in parties of threes or fours through old ranges of buildings, in which the most sanguine even could scarcely hope to find anything worth having; yet every one of them bore about them the air of enjoyment which is unmistakable. Watch them approach a closed door; it is too much trouble to try the latch or handle, so Jack kicks it open. They enter, someone turns over a table, out of which tumbles perhaps some curious manuscripts. To the soldier these are simply waste paper, so he lights his pipe with them. Another happens to look round and see his face represented in a mirror, which he at once resents as an insult by shying a footstool at it, whilst Bill, fancying that the 'old gentleman' in the fine picture-frame upon the wall is making faces at him, rips up the canvas with his bayonet. Some fine statue of Venus is at once adorned with a moustache, and then used as an 'Aunt Sally'. Cock-shots are taken at all remarkable objects, which, whilst occupying their intended positions, seem somehow or other to offend the veteran's eye, which dislikes the 'in statu quo' [*sic*] of life, and studies the picturesque somewhat after the manner that Colonel Jebb recommends to all country gentlemen who are desirous of converting their mansions into defensible posts. The love of destruction is certainly inherent in man, and the more strictly men are prevented from indulging in it, so much the more keenly do they appear to relish it when an opportunity occurs. Such an explanation will alone satisfactorily account for the ruin and destruction of property, which follows so quickly after the capture of any place; tables and chairs hurled from windows, clocks smashed upon the pavement, and everything not breakable so injured as to be valueless henceforth.

Soldiers of every nation under heaven have peculiarities common to all of the trade, and the amusements which I have just described are amongst them. The French most certainly are no exception to the rule. If the reader will imagine some three thousand men [the approximate size of the French army at the

Yuen-ming-yuen], imbued with such principles, let loose into a city composed of Museum and Wardour Streets [antique shops], he may have some faint idea of what the Yuen-ming-yuen looked like after it had been about twenty hours in possession of the French. The far-famed palaces of a line of monarchs claiming a celestial relationship, and in which the ambassador of an English king had been insulted with impunity [in 1793 and 1816], were littered with the debris of all that was highly prized in China. Topsy-turvy is the only expression in our language which at all describes its state. The ground around the French camp was covered with silks and clothing of all kinds, whilst the men ran hither and thither in search of further plunder, most of them according to the practice usual with soldiers upon such occasions, being decked out in the most ridiculous-looking costumes they could find, of which there was no lack as well-stocked wardrobes of Imperial Majesty abounded in curious raiment. Some had dressed themselves in the richly-embroidered gowns of women, and almost all had substituted the turned-up Mandarin hat for their ordinary forage cap. Officers and men seemed to have seized with a temporary insanity; in body and soul they were absorbed in one pursuit, which was plunder, plunder.

I stood by whilst one of the regiments was supposed to be parading; but although their fall in was sounded over and over again, I do not believe there was an average of ten men a company present. Plundering in this way bears its most evil fruit in an army; for if, when it is once commenced an effort is made to stop it, the good men only obey; the bad soldiers continue to plunder, and become rich by their disobedience, whilst the good ones see that the immediate effect of their steadiness is to keep them poor. I do not believe that it is attended with such demoralizing effects in a French army as it is in ours. The Frenchman is naturally a more thrifty being than the careless Britisher, who squanders his money in drinking, and 'standing drink' to his comrades. Three days afterwards when the French moved into their position before Peking, they seemed to have regained discipline, and their men were as steady under arms as if nothing had occurred to disturb the ordinary routine of their lives.

Description of the Palace

Proceeding due west for about a mile, you reach a well-made road ... being slightly raised in the centre and having good drains upon either side. Were it not that it is unmetaled, one might fancy it an English thoroughfare ... Continuing through that town [Haitien] and debouching from it towards the north, the road passes through the parks and gardens belonging to the many smaller houses which surround the imperial residence. At the distance of about half a mile, the road passes over a small stream by a handsome bridge with richly-carved parapet walls, surmounted by grotesquely designed figures. Beyond it is the broad road, running parallel with the little river, which sweeps round the southern face of the park, within which stand the summer palaces of Yuen-ming-yuen.

The park is of considerable extent, and is enclosed upon all sides by a high wall substantially built of granite, but not meant for defence. At about the distance of every quarter of a mile stands a good-sized guardhouse in which the faithful Tartar watchman kept guard both days and night over the person and property of their celestial master.

Immediately within every park wall there was a high earthen embankment, thickly planted with pine and cedar trees, which effectively screened the wall from view upon the inside, giving the place a secluded air.

There are two entrances to the imperial residence one eastward, the other westward of the bridge ... There was the usual screen wall in front of the door, coloured deep red, with a coping of yellow tiles on top, adorned here and there with long-tailed dragons. In front was a large square, partially enclosed with *chevaux-de-frise* [medieval wooden defensive spikes] ... There are several pretty granite bridges over the little river, which trickled along its pebbly bed in front of the entrance. If ... you made for the other entrance ... the road ran alongside the river, over which well-designed bridges led here and there to houses or gardens upon its opposite bank. Lofty trees, whose gracefully-drooping branches almost touched the water, stood along the edge, and were reflected in the running stream below them. On the right of the road was the high park wall of the Palace, which continued for some distance in a straight line, turned then sharp to the right disclosing an open expanse of water, through which the road was carried along a raised causeway, edged upon both sides by rows of trees ... At the further end of the causeway stood a fine joss-house, well shaded from the sun by lofty trees, which towered high above the mandarin poles in front of the building.

General the Baron Jamin had fixed his head-quarters there; the main body of the French army, and General Montauban's camp, being upon the opposite side of the road in a fine grove of trees. The grand entrance to Yuen-ming-yuen lay immediately beyond the paved road leading up to the gate, upon either side of which was the colossal representation of a lion mounted on a granite pedestal. As they were of a bronze colour, no one took the trouble ascertaining the nature of the metal of which they were composed, taking it for granted that they were of the ordinary alloy ... some months afterwards, when in Shanghai, some Chinamen asked a friend of mine ... whether they had removed the golden lions from the gates of the Yuen-ming-yuen ... and the fact of their being gold was well known to all the nation.

The gateway was at one end of a courtyard, enclosed upon three sides with ranges of guard-houses, handsomely ornamented outside with curious carving, and roofed with variegated tiling. The eaves were studded with small representations of birds and beasts. There was a well-arranged combination of red, white, green, blue and gilding about them, which gave a great richness of effect, without in any way palling upon the eye as heavy or gaudy. The gateway itself, like all those in the various public buildings of the country, was a curious combination of brick and woodwork, the former being used as sparingly as possible, with due regard to the stability of the building.

The doors were of massive woodwork coloured in red and picked out with gilding. The entrance was not intended for wheeled conveyances, the gate sills being some two or three feet above the adjoining pavement, with gently-sloping ramps of granite upon either side ... Within the gate as you entered there was a guard room to the right and left, in which the French sentries had taken the place of the Tartar household brigade ...

The gateway opened into a long, narrow courtyard, paved, or rather flagged over with utmost exactness.

Audience Hall

The floor of this grand hall was of highly polished marble, each piece cut into the form of some mathematical figure, and all joined so closely . . . An immense painting covered the upper portion of the wall upon the left hand as we entered; it was representation of the summer palaces and surrounding gardens done in isometrical projection . . . The imperial throne was a beautiful piece of workmanship, made of rosewood. It stood upon a platform, raised about eighteen inches above the other part of the hall, and was surrounded by an open-work balustrading, richly carved in representation of roses and other flowers.

Upon each side of the throne stood a high pole screen decorated with blue enamel and peacocks' feathers, upon which small rubies and emeralds were strung. Handsomely carved tables and sideboards were ranged along, around the room, upon which were numbers of enamel vases, porcelain bowls, jars of crackled china and other curiosities for which the empire is famous. Several large, gilt, French time-pieces were also in the hall. Piled up in one place were all the Imperial decrees published during the past year, and large quantities of the Chinese classics were arranged so as to be at hand. All these were beautifully printed, and many had autograph marks upon the margin, made by the emperor.

Palace Grounds

To leave the hall and get into the gardens, you passed out behind a screen at the back of the throne. You then found yourself in a labyrinth of neatly laid out walks, with high, grassy mounds bounding them upon either side, the tops of which were thickly studded with trees of all the various kinds to be found in the empire. Beneath their shade there were, at various intervals, some rustic-looking stone benches, or well-arranged piles of rockery, from the interstices between the stones of which sprang lichens and ferns of various sorts. Quaint shrubs and dwarf trees, stunted after the most approved fashion of Chinese gardeners, grew upon all sides. Upon proceeding some short distance along these winding paths, crossing over rustic bridges, ascending and descending many rural-looking steps, the walk opened out upon a tolerably sized pond [the Front Lake], on the further side of which were the private apartments of his Majesty, surrounded by the houses of his many wives, concubines, eunuchs, and servants. The suite of rooms from which Hien-fung [the Emperor] had fled only some fourteen days before, were one and all a vast curiosity shop . . . The French had placed a guard over those apartments, and none were at first admitted but their own officers, so that when we arrived most of the furniture, etc., still remained as it had been when Hsien-fung had occupied them.

His small cap, decorated with the character of longevity embroidered upon it, lay upon his bed; his pipe and tobacco pouch was upon a small table close by. In all the adjoining rooms were immense wardrobes filled with silks, satins, and fur coats. Cloaks covered with the richest golden needlework, mandarin dresses, edged with ermine and sable and marked with representations of the five-clawed dragons, showing they were intended for royalty, were stored in presses. The cushions upon chairs and sofas were covered with the finest yellow satin embroidered over with figures of dragons and flowers . . . In some rooms large chests were found filled with cups, vases, plates, etc. made of jade stone.

As you left these buildings and wandered through the maze of walks and winding paths, which led seemingly nowhere in particular, one soon became lost amidst the multiplicity of turnings, marble bridges, canals and fish-ponds met with everywhere, and literally covering the park. Upon some of these little sheets of water there were Lilliputian junks armed with small brass cannon, with which a naval fight was sometimes represented for the amusement of his Majesty, who watched the show from a neighbouring tea-house.

Numbers of our officers had consequently an opportunity of visiting the Palaces and securing valuables; but our men were carefully prevented from leaving camp. These officers who were fortunate enough to have carts and time for amusement, brought into camp large collections of valuables.

Burning of the Palace

Upon the 18th October, the 1st division, under the command of Major-General Sir John Michel, marched from our camp near Peking to Yuen-ming-yuen, and set fire to all the royal palaces which lay scattered about in that neighborhood. Throughout the whole of that day and the day following a dense cloud of black heavy smoke hung over those scenes of former magnificence. A gentle wind, blowing from the north-west, carried the mass of smoke directly over our camp into the very capital itself, to which distance even large quantities of the burnt embers were wafted, falling about the streets in showers, as silent but unmistakable evidences of the work of destruction and retribution going on in the palace of the Emperor. In passing between our camp and the Yuen-ming-yuen, upon both of those days, the light was so subdued by the overhanging clouds of smoke, that it seemed as if the sun was undergoing a lengthening eclipse. The world around looked dark with shadow.

Wolseley adds that the destruction of the Palace warned the Chinese "what they might expect in the capital itself, unless they accepted our ... terms", and as such he supported its destruction as an effective means of ending the war:

The destruction of the palaces appears to have struck the Peking authorities with awe. It was the stamp which gave an unmistakable reality to our work of vengeance, proving that Lord Elgin's last letter was no idle threat, and warning them of what they might expect in the capital itself unless they accepted our proffered terms. The imperial palace within the city still remained untouched; and if they wished to save that last remaining place for their master, it behoved them to lose no time. I feel convinced that the burning of Yuen-ming-yuen considerably hastened the final settlement of affairs and strengthened our ambassador's position. Our allies, who had looted all, and destroyed some of the buildings of that place, objected to our putting the coup de grace to their work. It was averred that the complete destruction of the palaces would be a Goth-like act of barbarism. It seems strange that this idea did not occur to the generally quick perceptions of our Gallic allies before they had shorn the place of all its beauty and ornament, by removal or reckless destruction of everything that was valuable within its precincts, leaving us, indeed, little more than the bare shell of the buildings on which to wreak our vengeance for the cruelties practiced therein upon our ill-fated countrymen.

After the fire, visiting the site, Wolseley notes, solemnly, ". . . some blackened gables and piles of burnt timbers alone indicating where the royal palaces had stood. In many places the inflammable pine trees near the buildings had been consumed with them, leaving nothing but their charred trunks to mark the site."

Wolseley does not mention taking any loot from the Palace, but at a minimum he took one piece. An exquisite set of watercolours with a zitan wood cover is now with the British Army Museum, donated by Wolseley. Its title (in English) is 'Famous Views in Wu-Lin Vol. 2' and it is attributed by the museum to Dong Gao (1740–1818) and dated to between 1780 and 1800. On the inside of the album is written a note, "I found this in the Summer Palace near Peking 1860, Wolseley." It is the type of item that one can imagine in the Imperial Apartments.

Canada, Africa

"After less than nine years [in the British Army], Wolseley had served with distinction in four campaigns, been mentioned in official army dispatches nine times, and had risen to the rank of lieutenant-colonel. In an age where noble birth and the purchase of rank for money yielded many officers, he had risen by merit alone. For his bravery or foolhardiness, as well as his ingenuity and calmness under fire, his superiors had taken notice. During his time in the military, Wolseley witnessed the lack of organization and training of the British army and felt it his duty to rectify this situation,"[262] notes a biographer.

"In 1861 Wolseley was posted to the Canadian command as assistant quartermaster-general at the time of the *Trent* crisis. He arrived, on Jan. 5, 1862, after the immediate threat of war with the United States had passed. In garrison in Montreal, he was drawn to amateur theatricals, to

---

[262] *Encyclopedia of World Biography*

squiring the ladies, and to the study of military theory,"[263] according to O.A. Cooke.

Wolseley was promoted to colonel in June 1865 and after being on duty to face a possible invasion from the United States, "He was loaned to command the camp of instruction at La Prairie, near Montreal. The camp was designed to provide practical experience for the graduates of the schools of military instruction operated in Canada by the British army. It was inspired by Colonel Patrick Leonard MacDougall, adjutant-general of the militia and military theorist, but the practical application was Wolseley's."[264] Wolseley trained 1,100 officer cadets during a three week period. He had them "employed in turns upon all military duties, from that of regimental field officers down to that of private sentinels", he noted in his diary.

"Much notice was taken of the activities of the camp. Most important, Sir John Michel [who had been a division commander in China], lieutenant-general commanding in British North America, sent a favourable report to his superiors, noting, 'It is difficult to speak too highly of this talented, energetic young officer.'"[265]

"At the expiration of his appointment as assistant quartermaster-general, Wolseley returned in April 1867 to England, where he was married. But he was called back in September as deputy quartermaster-general, at 34 the youngest officer ever to assume this senior staff post in Canada. His first years in Canada had marked the beginning of Wolseley the writer, with the publication of accounts of the war in China and of a visit he had made to the Confederate forces in Virginia in 1862. More important for Wolseley was the book he published during his second posting, *The soldier's pocket-book for field service* (London, 1869) … a pragmatic staff officer's compendium,"[266] confirming once again that Wolseley was the 'soldier's-soldier'. Wolseley's wife Louisa (1843–1920), was the daughter of Mr. A. Erskine. They had one child together, Frances (1872–1936), who was herself an author.

In 1870 Wolseley was a key officer and the mind behind the Red River Expedition to Western Canada. "He moved a force consisting of nearly 400 British troops, over seven hundred Canadian militia, and a

---

[263] Cooke, *Wolseley, Dictionary of Canadian Biography*

[264] Ibid.

[265] Ibid.

[266] Ibid.

large party of civilian voyageurs and workmen from their port of embarkation at Collingwood, Ont., to the Red River between May 3rd and August 24th, without losing a man. Altogether the expedition made 47 portages and ran 51 miles of rapids."[267]

Wolseley returned to England in October 1870 as assistant adjutant-general at the War Office, ". . . where he immediately became identified with the reforms initiated by Edward Cardwell, the Secretary of State for War. When the possibility of conflict with the Ashanti in West Africa arose, Wolseley wrote to Cardwell outlining a plan of campaign and again became identified as the officer to carry it out. He departed for West Africa in September 1873 with the local rank of major-general and with 35 specially selected officers, a number of them, such as William Francis Butler, from the Red River expedition. The resulting successful campaign captured the Ashanti capital of Kumasi (Ghana)."[268]

In 1882 Britain made the decision to intervene in Egypt following a revolt against the Turks. Wolseley commanded 31,000 troops against the Egyptians. He master-minded a night attack at Tell el Kebîr in September which was decisive in routing the Egyptian rebels and essentially left Britain in charge of Egypt. He returned home to Britain to much popular acclaim. The War Department promoted Wolseley to full general and he was made Baron Wolseley of Cairo and Wolseley.

Two years later, in 1884, Wolseley was sent to rescue his old brother-in-arms from China, General Charles Gordon, who was besieged at Khartoum by the 'Mahdi'. Wolseley wrote of Gordon, "I admired him with a reverence I had never felt for any other man." His relief force arrived just two days too late to save Gordon and British forces were forced to withdraw. In 1885 Wolseley was made a viscount. From 1890 to 1894 he commanded the British Army in Ireland and was promoted to field marshal in May 1894. In 1895 he became commander-in-chief of the entire army. He retired from active duty in 1900.

"Lord Wolseley was among the foremost of the Victorian generals," writes biographer Cooke. "Forced by lack of family wealth to make his own way, he was also driven by ambition to reach the highest levels in his profession."[269] He had great success as a junior officer in the field, but "he never proved himself as a commander of the first rank, for he never faced

---

[267] Ibid.

[268] Ibid.

[269] Ibid.

a first-class adversary using modern technology and never commanded the bulk of Britain's army in the field . . . [but] he became identified with the progressive element in the British army and a spokesman for army reform at a crucial period in that institution's history."[270]

In 1903 Wolseley published his autobiography. He began to live a somewhat reclusive life and died in Mentone, France, on March 26, 1913, before the outbreak of the war that would tragically destroy the army he had created.

> Almost single-handedly, Wolseley transformed the British army from a gentleman's army into a modern fighting machine. While intelligent, capable, and farsighted, he was also rather vain and arrogant. Wolseley was an extremely popular leader. Gilbert and Sullivan lampooned him in song as 'The Very Image of a Modern Major-General' in *The Pirates of Penzance*. An automobile, the *Garnet Wolseley*, was named for him. Although of humble origins, Wolseley ended his life as a viscount, socializing with some of the most influential people of his age.[271]

Bibliography

Wolseley, Garnet, *Narrative of the War with China in 1860*, Longman, Green and Roberts, London, 1862

---

[270] Ibid.

[271] *Encyclopedia of World Biography*

India

Dighton Macnaghton Probyn

*"My Lord—The 1st Sikh Irregular Cavalry, under Major Probyn,
and Fane's Horse under Captain Fane, have performed their work
most admirably. On more than one occasion these regiments have been
opposed to, and have successfully charged, a vastly superior force of the
enemy's cavalry; and their conduct in the field excited the admiration
of the French as well as of the English troops."*

—James Hope Grant

Dighton Macnaghton Probyn was the kind
of warrior that could probably not exist within the modern military
structure. As a young man he was a legendary irregular cavalry commander, a cavalier in the 17th century tradition. Like George Armstrong
Custer he was a general at a young age. As an elderly man he was a stalwart of the old military, an equerry to the Royal Family. He is one of
the most remarkable men featured in this narrative, and yet one of those
about whom we know the least. His views of the China War were never
recorded, nor his impressions of the Summer Palace. He can only be
known vicariously through his daring acts and the words of other men.
His personality, his involvement in the campaign, and his role in the
looting are all significant. He also represents an important element in the
British expeditionary force in China—the Indian Army.

Probyn is a name of Welsh origin, derived from *Ap Robyn* or *son of
Robin*. Probyns were landowners in the Welsh borders in North Wales,
South Wales, and in Gloucestershire. There is a record of a Probyn in

Newland, Gloucestershire in 1570. A Sir Edmund Probyn, a prominent lawyer, acquired the manor of Longhope on the road to Ross-on-Wye and the manor of Huntley near Newent. He seems to be a direct ancestor of Dighton. Dashing, handsome and savvy, extraordinarily brave—perhaps Probyn inherited these qualities from the ancient Welsh princes from whom he was descended.

Probyn was born in London on January 21, 1833, the son of George Probyn and Alice Macnaghten. Alice was the daughter of Sir Francis Workman-Macnaghten, 1st Baronet. Probyn's great-grandfather was Edmund Probyn (1731–1812), and his grandfather was William Probyn (1762–1825), rector of Longhope. He was the 3rd son in the family and one of nine children.[272] Dighton was the last name of a great uncle. Macnaghten was his mother's maiden name.

India

Nothing is known of Probyn's youth. He would be expected to have had a private education. And by virtue of his not being the eldest son he entered the British Army at an early age. In 1849 as a sixteen year old he joined Bengal Service in the light cavalry arm as a cornet. Why he chose the 'Indian Army' is not quite clear—his family does not appear to have had any prior connection with India. He was assigned to the 6th Light Cavalry. Three years into his military service he was made adjutant of the newly formed 2nd Punjab Cavalry under Captain Sam Browne. The 2nd was part of the 11,000 strong Punjab Irregular Force that had the responsibility for policing the Indus frontier and the turbulent tribes living there. Sir John Lawrence, Chief Commissioner in the Punjab, had ordered the creation of two regiments of Sikh irregular cavalry. The 1st was formed by Captain Wale out of the 18th Irregular Cavalry. Both regiments were dressed irregularly and discipline was unique, but the men were experienced fighters and horsemen. Wale was killed on March 1, 1858 during the Indian Mutiny in an ambush while leading the regiment in pursuit of the enemy.

When the Mutiny commenced at Meerut in May 1857, Probyn was at Jullundur, where his parent regiment, the 6th Bengal Light Cavalry, was stationed. For the next year Probyn's squadron of the 2nd Punjab Cavalry were involved in a series of actions in which he was mentioned

---

[272] Research thanks to the Dighton family tree at Ancestry.com

in dispatches many times. It was at this time that the 2nd Punjab Cavalry began to be referred to as *Probyn's Horse*, a moniker they were to maintain unofficially until 1904 when the title became official.

"Two bodies of irregular Sikh cavalry are attached to the main army," notes E.H. Verney, speaking of the Indian Army at the time of the Mutiny, "one is distinguished by wearing red turbans, is commanded by Captain Hodson . . . and is known as Hodson's Horse; the other wears blue turbans, is commanded by Lieutenant Probyn . . . Their dress consists of the whitey-brown 'kharki', each man is armed with a tulwa and brace of pistols, and one or two troops with lances. To command a regiment of these semi-barbarous troopers requires no small ability, tact, and personal courage, as well as knowledge of the native character, and both Probyn and Hodson are beloved by their wild horsemen. They are generally splendidly mounted, and each horse is the private property of his rider."[273]

During the final days of the capture of Lucknow in early 1858, the 2nd Punjab Cavalry was continually engaged in patrolling and was frequently sent in pursuit of fleeing enemy soldiers. By this time, Probyn, exhausted by the rigors of continual campaigning, was sent back to England on the advice of surgeons, to convalesce. He traveled down country starting on March 18, 1858. Three days before his departure for England, Lucknow fell. Probyn was promoted to Brevet Major and at the recommendation of Sir Hope Grant, Probyn was awarded the Victoria Cross in 1858 for conspicuous gallantry during the Indian Mutiny:

> 2nd Punjab Cavalry, Captain (now Major) Dighton Macnaghten Probyn. Has been distinguished for gallantry and daring throughout this campaign. At the battle of Agra, when his squadron charged the rebel infantry, he was some time separated from his men, and surrounded by five or six sepoys. He defended himself from the various cuts made at him, and before his own men had joined him had cut down two of his assailants. At another time, in single combat with a sepoy, he was wounded in the wrist, by the bayonet, and his horse also was slightly wounded; but, though the sepoy fought desperately, he cut him down. The same day he singled out a standard bearer, and, in the presence of a number of the enemy, killed him and

---

[273] Verney, E.H. Lieutenant RN, *The Shannon's Brigade in India*

captured the standard. These are only a few of the gallant deeds of this brave young officer." Despatch from Major-General James Hope Grant, K.C.B., dated January 10, 1858.[274]

He was invested with the Victoria Cross in Portsmouth, England on August 2nd, 1858.

China

On his return to India, Probyn's parent regiment, the 6th Bengal Light Cavalry was replaced by the 3rd European Light Cavalry. As a further reward for his service during the Mutiny, Probyn was given command of Wale's Horse—the 1st Sikh Irregular Cavalry, Wale having been killed.

The British cavalry brigade that was to be sent to fight in the China War of 1860 included the 1st King's Dragoon Guards together with Probyn's Horse (the 1st Sikh Irregular Cavalry) and Fane's Horse, two Indian units. Fane's Horse was raised especially for the campaign, taking many of the men from the recently disbanded regiment of Hudson's Horse. Probyn's Horse went to China armed with lances.

Probyn was the consummate man of action, very handsome, very brave and very patriotic, and the ideal cavalry commander for the China War. It was no coincidence that his regiment was one of the units selected to go to east. Hope Grant's command included four infantry brigades of British and Indian troops and the above mentioned cavalry brigade. At the outset of the campaign Probyn's Horse consisted of 18 officers, 454 men and 466 horses. Service in China was strictly voluntary and each man was asked if he wanted to go. The entire regiment agreed. They had to march from their post at Lucknow to the railhead at Raneegunge, 600 miles, and on April 1 embarked for China. The expedition arrived in Odin Bay and disembarked August 1.

Hope Grant, a cavalryman himself, noted in his journal at the outset of the campaign, "The two irregular cavalry regiments were really magnificent. They were composed of fine handsome men—Sikhs—becomingly dressed, well mounted, and commanded by two excellent officers—Major Fane and Major Probyn, both of whom I had known well in India during the Mutiny."[275]

---

[274] *The London Gazette*, June 18, 1858
[275] Hope Grant in Knollys, pp. 15–16

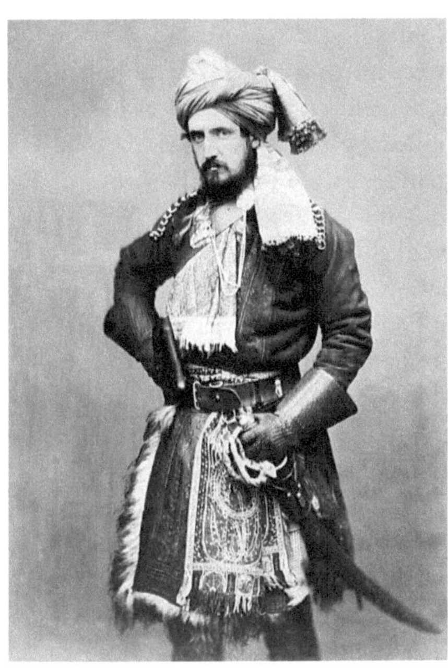

*Dighton Macnaghton Probyn,
India, 1857, photographer
unknown, possibly Felice Beato*

"Probyn's Horse had been landed," noted Hope Grant, "and I had posted them within the fort of Pehtang. On August 5, heavy rains and violent squalls flooded the horses up to their knees in mud, and, moreover, we were in great straits for drinking-water."[276] They withstood these difficulties.

The cavalry were not involved in the storming of the coastal forts, which was carried out by British and French infantry. There were small cavalry actions on August 3, 12 and 14 involving Probyn's men. They were put in the field against Manchurian horsemen ('Tartars') equipped as mounted archers. In the early fighting six officers and men were wounded:

> Probyn ordered his men not to charge too soon, and pursued the enemy quietly, saving his horses until he neared them. At length, when within 200 yards, the Sikhs became impatient and difficult to restrain. The chief Rissildar could contain himself no longer. He shouted his war yell at the top of his voice, the others followed suit, and down they went full speed after the Tartars.

---

[276] Hope Grant in Knollys, p. 61

Away they rushed helter-skelter, along the causeway, but the little galloways of the enemy were nearly a match for the splendid Arabs after their day's fatigue; and, to use the words of one of the officers engaged, they killed awfully few, not more than 50 or 60. Of these no fewer than seven fell before the sword of Lieutenant Anderson, whose blood was fairly up. Sowar Wayeer Khan, of Fane's Horse, was killed, as he manfully stood by Lieutenant Anderson. Duffadar Berjon Singh, of Probyn's, was dismounted early in the fight, but he refused to leave the field, and on foot had two desperate encounters with several of the enemy. He was severely wounded, and his life was only saved by several sowars going to his assistance. Sowar Khowajah Mahomed was cut off with Lieutenant Anderson. He charged the enemy several times, heedless of numbers, and when Anderson's right arm was disabled by a blow he rushed to his assistance. Lieutenant Anderson saw him slay four of the enemy. In another direction Fane maintained his well-earned reputation as a skillful swordsman and leader of irregulars. He was the first to get at the Tartar horsemen, of whom he gave a good account, though they escaped rather too quickly for his wishes across a canal.[277]

On September 8 a mixed force of troops began the advance from Tientsin to Peking. The entire cavalry brigade of six hundred men was part of this exploratory force. Following the Peiho River north, on the 11th the British force reached the town of Ho Si Wu which was approximately mid-way to Peking. On the 15th Parkes and Wade in their back-and-forth negotiations with the imperial emissaries observed that a force of about 2,000 tartar cavalry had been sighted near the town of Tungchow. On the 17th the army advanced still further toward Peking, reaching the city of Matow. On the 18th, after marching a further three miles, the British were confronted with a large force of Chinese infantry and cavalry blocking the route forward. At this place—Chan Chia Wan—the Chinese established a three mile front and were attempting to outflank the British on both wings and made prisoners of the British envoys.

The peace process had broken down and, before long, a pitched battle broke out. Sir John Michel and his troops on the left front of the British were particularly hard pressed as were the French artillery also on

---

[277] Bowlby, p. 252

the left wing, and the Chinese mounted a frontal assault. Michel's force were having difficulty holding their position in the face of such large masses of Chinese troops. There were no cavalry on the left wing and they faced the prospect of fighting a huge body of tartar horsemen. At this point Hope Grant ordered the Sikhs into action and Probyn, with just a few men, launched one of his famous charges: "Probyn, who had only 100 of his regiment with him at the time, was ordered to charge to the front, which he did in most gallant style, riding in amongst them [the Tarter cavalry] with such vigour and determination that they could not withstand his attack for a moment, and fled in utter consternation. The Musbees then advanced in a steady line carrying everything before them, and taking several guns,"[278] noted a proud Hope Grant. Soon after the Chinese were in full retreat and the Allies occupied both the town of Chan Chia Wan and a large encampment beyond.

On September 21 the Allied army resumed its march toward Peking. The Chinese had occupied a well defended position around Palikao. The Europeans drew up an offensive front with the cavalry on the left. While reconnoitering the enemy position General Grant was almost captured, "As I was quietly riding back, I saw some cavalry on the left front of our allies, which I at first took for some of their skirmishers, when they suddenly approached me, and I found that they were Tartars. I immediately galloped off to Stirling's guns, and opened fire with case at a range of 200 yards, which quickly made them retire. The King's Dragoon Guards and Fane's Horse, with Probyn's regiment in support, now advanced to the charge; the first-named taking a bank and ditch on their way, and, attacking the Tartars with the utmost vigour, instantly made them give way. Fane's men followed them in pursuit, and on reaching the margin of a road jumped into it over an imposing high bank and ditch. The front rank cleared it well; but the men in rear, unable to see before them owing to the excessive dust, almost all rolled into the ditch. Nevertheless, the Tartars had but a poor chance, and suffered severely. The whole of their cavalry retreated, and we followed them up for some time, occasionally firing long shots at them with our Armstrongs with good effect."[279]

The French then "attacked the bridge of Palikao," continues Hope Grant, "with great gallantry. The *elite* of the Chinese Imperial Guard was

---

[278] Hope Grant in Knollys, p. 113
[279] Hope Grant in Knollys, pp. 116–117

drawn up to resist them, but had to give way before European discipline. The French took the bridge and twenty-five guns."[280]

The way now seemed clear for an advance to Peking itself. After a brief rest-bite, on September 24 Hope Grant "sent the irregular cavalry to make a reconnaissance up to Peking; and on their return, Probyn, who was in command, told me that, along the whole distance, he had seen neither troops nor camps, but that report stated that the Chinese army were in position to the north of the town. He had ridden up to within 200 yards of the walls, which he described as being very high and in excellent repair."[281]

Over the next two weeks the British cavalry were used frequently to scout out the position of the retreating Tartar forces and where necessary to engage them. On one such reconnaissance, "I had ordered Probyn, with the 1st Irregular Cavalry, to make another reconnaissance, and to ascertain the whereabouts of the Tartar camp, a task which this excellent officer performed with great judgment. He came upon their pickets, drove them in, and discovered their camping-ground to be to the northeast of the town."[282]

Having encircled Peking from the east, the Allies advanced north of the city on October 6. The British cavalry brigade traveled with the French army that day and reached the Summer Palace at 7 P.M. that night. Although their encampment was not as close to the Palace gate as the French infantry, the British cavalry had much greater access to the Palace than the rest of the British army, camped five miles away outside the Anting Gate, during the two days of looting that followed. The corollary to this is that it is generally assumed that the cavalry collected much loot. The only information as to Probyn's loot is recorded by Robert M'Ghee:

> At each end [of the Audience Hall] stood one of those enormous and splendid enamelled bowls, which the army has presented to Her Most Gracious Majesty, at Major Probyn's request, who took them from the hall himself—minor spirits, being deterred from touching them by their vastness, were contented with some smaller and more suitable memento. But a difficulty is just the

---

[280] Hope Grant in Knollys, p. 117
[281] Hope Grant in Knollys, p. 120
[282] Hope Grant in Knollys, p. 122

thing for Probyn; he contrived to get them away when no one else thought of attempting it.[283]

This loot was then surrendered by Probyn to be sold at the Prize Sale: "There were two beautiful large enamels which had been given up by Major Probyn, and they were so handsome that I requested him and the prize committee to allow me to send them to the Queen, to which they readily agreed,"[284] notes Hope Grant.

The work of reconnaissance and defense was not over until a truce was signed and this involved Probyn and his cavalry in more work: "A large force of the enemy was encamped on the west side of the city . . . I sent Major Probyn, with the two Irregular Cavalry regiments, to reconnoiter in the direction alluded to. The force suddenly came upon an intrenched camp, where further progress was stopped by infantry lining a bank, and who with levelled matchlocks threatened to open fire. As Probyn had obtained all the information that was necessary, and as nothing was to be gained by bringing on a collision, he very wisely retired,"[285] states Hope Grant.

In due course, as has been described elsewhere, hostilities were concluded and at the beginning of November the British army retired from Peking to Tientsin. When time came for the British army to withdraw from Tientsin to the coast, Hope Grant had a special concern for the well-being of the cavalry:

> I . . . gave orders that the whole distance [from Tientsin to the mouth of the Peiho] should be accomplished in one day's march, somewhat to Brigadier Pattle's dismay, who was apprehensive for the wellbeing of his horses. I was confident the journey would not hurt them; and on the November 23, the two regiments, the King's Dragoon Guards and Probyn's Horse, marched independently, each commanding officer taking his own time and making his own arrangements.[286]

---

[283] M'Ghee, Robert, pp. 203–204

[284] Hope Grant in Knollys, p. 194

[285] Hope Grant in Knollys, p. 207

[286] Hope Grant in Knollys, p. 213

The following extract is from a dispatch by Hope Grant to Lord Canning relating to the services of the two Sikh irregular cavalry regiments. Headquarters, Tientsin, Nov. 21, 1860:

> My Lord—The 1st Sikh Irregular Cavalry, under Major Probyn, and Fane's Horse under Captain Fane, have performed their work most admirably. On more than one occasion these regiments have been opposed to, and have successfully charged, a vastly superior force of the enemy's cavalry; and their conduct in the field excited the admiration of the French as well as of the English troops. It is not only on the field of battle that their services have been so important during the recent campaign, but in performing the numerous other duties required of them of an infinitely more harassing nature—patrols, escorts, reconnaissances, as well as the task of carrying letters almost daily between Tientsin and Peking (a distance of 75 miles) for upwards of a month, during which they were frequently fired upon—their services have been of the utmost value to the expedition. I beg to recommend Major Probyn and Captain Fane to your Excellency's most favourable notice.
>
> I have, &c. J. Hope Grant, Lieut.-General, Commander of the Forces."[287]

After China

Probyn's Horse returned to India after the China War. Officially its name changed to the 11th Bengal Cavalry in 1861. Although Probyn relinquished command in 1866, a year later he sat for his portrait in his old uniform, such was his pride in the regiment.

Probyn was promoted to the rank of brevet lieutenant-colonel in the Bengal Army on February 15, 1861. Then again he was brevetted to colonel on February 15, 1866, and finally to major-general on July 25, 1870. He was 37. He was made Aide-de-Camp to the Viceroy of India, Lord Mayo. In 1872, on returning to England, such was the esteem in which he was held, Probyn was invited to be personal equerry to the Prince

---

[287] Hope Grant in Knollys, p. 262

of Wales. In 1875, appropriately, Probyn accompanied the Prince on a tour of India, designed to demonstrate that the power of the East India Company had been surmounted by the authority of the British Crown. The triumphant tour terminated after seventeen weeks.

Probyn's bravery in Asia had earned him honorary 'Sikh status'. On his return to England he could be seen at court, and in official portraits, in the native costume of his adopted land—complete with turban and a beard that he refused to trim. The beard allegedly became so long that it completely obscured his Victoria Cross that he wore when he became private secretary to the Prince of Wales (later King Edward VII). He was considered an eccentric in court circles.

In 1872 Probyn married thirty-six year-old Letitia Maria Thelusson, the daughter of Thomas Robarts Thellusson and his wife Maria. Sadly Laetitia died in 1900. They had no children.

Equerry

Probyn's fame and glamour made him attractive to the Royal Family. He served in the capacity of personal assistant to the Royal Family for the rest of his life. "He was knighted as a Knight Commander of the Order of the Star of India (KCSI) on March 7, 1876 ... He was promoted to the substantive rank of lieutenant-colonel in the Bengal Cavalry on April 1, 1881 ... He was appointed a Knight Commander of the Order of the Bath, Civil Division (KCB) in the 1887 Golden Jubilee Honours. On December 1 1888, he was promoted to the local rank of general in the British Indian Army while unemployed, and was promoted to the substantive rank of colonel in the Bengal Cavalry on April 1, 1893. He was appointed one of the first Knights Grand Cross of the Royal Victorian Order (GCVO) on May 26, 1896."[288]

> Probyn [as] secretary to the Prince of Wales and took-up residence at Marlborough House and subsequently the Prince's Norfolk estate, Sandringham House. In Jane Ridley's biography Bertie: A Life of Edward VII (2012), the author transcribes a letter from the Princess of Wales revealing Probyn's chivalrous courtly love for the woman he called 'the blessed lady'. Princess

---

[288] Wikipedia article, *Dighton Macnaghten Probyn*

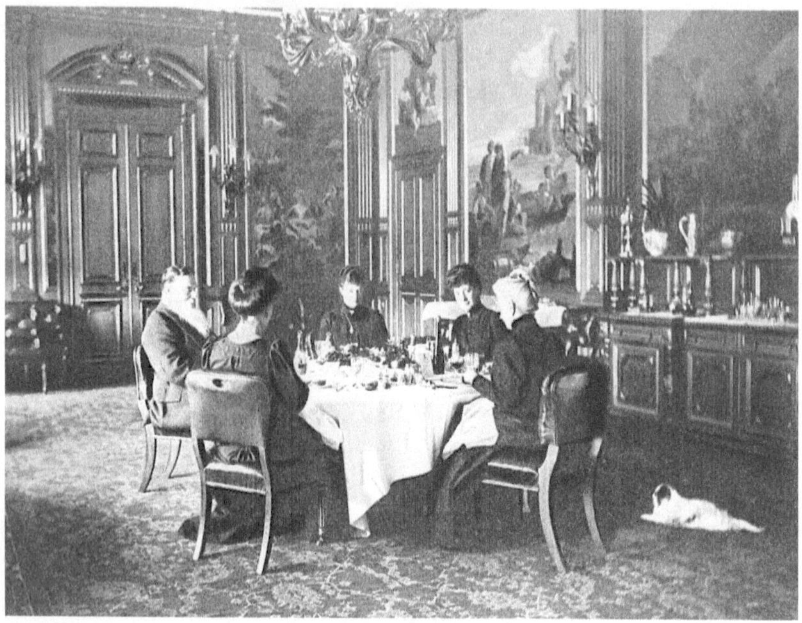

Probyn dining with royalty, 1910, photographer unknown

Alexandra was a keen huntress much to the disapproval of her mother-in-law Queen Victoria. When thrown from her horse, the Princess writes 'one of the gentlemen, Probyn, jumped off and pushed me into the saddle and then everything was well and I hurried on!!![289]

Probyn became the Prince of Wales's most trusted courtier and averted scandal in 1888 by allegedly tipping off Lord Arthur Somerset concerning a matter that could have become public. He served as messenger between the Prince of Wales (for whom Somerset was Master of the Horse) and Prime Minister Lord Salisbury.

The Prince of Wales was the authority on correct dress and decorations and would often publicly upbraid courtiers who erred sartorially. He chastised the Duchess of Marlborough for failing

---

[289] Ibid.

to wear a tiara at dinner and his own wife for pinning a decoration on the incorrect shoulder. Probyn's orders in the Henry Poole & Co ledgers reflect the courtier's obsession with wearing the correct orders to please his master. In 1903, Probyn gives Poole Buckingham Palace as his address to send a blue household tunic upon which new order loops had been added to attach 'six new ribbons'. He subsequently asks Poole's to add 'a long Order of St Olaf ribbon', 'five (more) decorative new ribbons' and 'a short ribbon for a red Eagle of Prussia first class' order to a blue superfine household tunic work at Sandringham.[290]

The Prince and Princess of Wales were spendthrifts and it was Probyn's responsibility to keep their affairs in order and introduce the Prince to wealthy financiers who could underwrite his expenses. When the Prince became king in 1901, it is to Probyn's credit that his debts were all paid. Probyn's love and loyalty towards Queen Alexandra remained true after King Edward VII's death in 1910. Ridley describes him thus: 'with his neck bent double, his chin and long white beard nodding on his chest, he fought a losing battle against the compulsive extravagance of the blessed lady'. Probyn predeceased the Dowager Queen Alexandra by a year. A monument to his love for Queen Alexandra still stands in the grounds of Sandringham. It is a folly overlooking a lake known as 'the Queen's nest' and is inscribed to 'the Blessed Lady' from General the Rt. Hon Sir Dighton Probyn.[291]

Probyn cut an impressive figure in old age with his very long white beard. Film of him with Queen Mary can be viewed at: www.britishpathe.com/video/a-great-soldier-passes-2. He was taken ill at Sandringham and died in June 1924 and was buried in Kensal Green Cemetery.

The Sikh cavalry continued to be an effective part of the Indian Army after 1860. Neither regiment was exclusively Sikh and had admitted men of other Punjab martial classes. Probyn's Horse saw action in the Second Afghan War of 1878–80. During WWI the regiment served in Mesopotamia. Major General 'the Right Honourable Sir Dighton Probyn VC' who had given up his command of the regiment in 1866 was

---

[290] Ibid.

[291] www.henrypoole.com

made honorary colonel in 1904, and his name was officially restored to their title. He retained this post until his death. The unit is now part of the Parkistani Army under the designation '5 Horse'. Probynabad, a town in Punjab, now a province of Pakistan which includes large farmlands owned by the regiment, is named after Probyn.

In 2005 Probyn's Victoria Cross came up for auction. According to *The Times* it was bought on September 24, 2005 for £160,000. It had been part of the Brian Ritchie collection of medals.

Bibliography

Knollys, Henry, *Incidents In The China War Of 1860, Compiled From The Private Journals Of General Sir Hope Grant G.C.B. Commander Of The English Expedition*, Blackwood, Edinburgh, 1875

The Wand of Victory

Charles 'Chinese' Gordon

*"You can scarcely imagine the beauty and magnificence of the palaces
we burned. It made one's heart sore to burn them . . . It was wretchedly
demoralizing work for an army. Everybody was wild for plunder."*

—Charles Gordon

In Churchill's words: "It is impossible to study any part of Charles Gordon's career without being drawn to all the rest." He portrays Gordon as a man "sustained by two great moral and mental stimulants: his honour as a man, his faith as a Christian."[292] Gordon was in many ways the embodiment of the Victorian Age and an exceptionally brave man whose actions captured the public imagination over a period of twenty-five years in various exotic locations.

For the Victorian public General Charles Gordon's death in a remote corner of Africa in 1885 was one of the great martyrdoms of and for the British Empire. But long before he became a famous general and a tragic figure Gordon made his reputation in China.

He almost missed the campaign completely, noting in September 1860, "I am rather late for the amusement, which won't vex mother." But although he may have been late to the 'party', such would be the extent

---

[292] Churchill, Winston, *The River War: An Account of the Re-conquest of the Sudan*, (1899; repr., Mineola, N.Y., Dover Publications, 2006), p. 13. quoted in *Major General Charles 'Chinese' Gordon: Saintly Soldier and Devoted Diplomat*, William Baker, 2008

of his eventual involvement in the fighting in China in the 1860s that the young officer would forever after be known as 'Chinese Gordon'.

Gordon was born in Woolwich, the son of General Henry Gordon (1786–1865), Royal Artillery, and Elizabeth Enderby (1792–1873). He went to school at Fullands, in Somerset, later Taunton School, and then the Royal Military Academy in Woolwich. In 1852 he was commissioned into the Royal Engineers as a second lieutenant. In 1854 he was promoted to full lieutenant. His family were Scots, of the Gordon clan, and had fought for Bonnie Prince Charlie at Culloden. They were a "family of soldiers" according to his biographer, and as soldiers the family redeemed themselves by fighting for the Crown in North America in the *French and Indian Wars.*

At the outbreak of the Crimean War Gordon was put to work at the siege of Sebastopol and later the assault of the Redan. At Sebastopol he served alongside another very promising young officer, Garnet Wolseley, with whom he also fought in China as part of General Hope Grant's staff:

> Gordon's first experience of war was in the Crimea, whither he went as an Engineer officer when he was about twenty. An incident which happened before Sebastopol may suffice to indicate his spirit at this early age. Some soldiers in a trench, who were not under Gordon's command, had suffered so severely that not even a non-commissioned officer survived to command them. Gordon, seeing the danger of the men, sprang in among them, armed only with a stick—which may have suggested the use of the 'wand of victory' at a later time in China. He at once raised his head above the earthworks, thus freely exposing himself to the fire of the enemy and he did not quit the trench until he had enabled the men to understand exactly what they were to do.[293]

After the end of the conflict Gordon served the commission that set the new borders between Russia and Turkey and it was not until 1858 that he returned to Britain as an instructor at Chatham. In 1859 he was promoted to captain in the Royal Engineers.

Gordon's biographer, Egmont Hake, states in the preface to his work that Gordon's "One aim in life has been to do his duty, and that without incurring the penalty of fame, the displeasure of being called a hero. He

---

[293] R.H. Barnes, *Charles George Gordon, A Sketch*, pp. 49–50

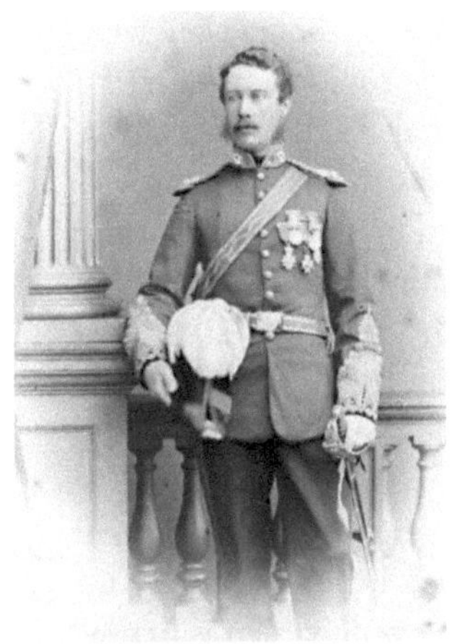

Captain Charles Gordon,
China, 1860, Felice Beato

has always abhorred publicity, he has never courted renown; yet he is among the most renowned of men, and to the peoples of three continents his name is almost a household word. Though fully conscious of irresistible strength of purpose, he claims no merit for himself. He, 'with celestial vigor armed, and plain heroic magnitude of mind', regards no feat of war as due to his efforts . . ."[294]

In July 1860 Gordon was sent to China. Sixty-eight days later, after traveling through Paris, Marseilles, Malta, Alexandria, Aden, Ceylon, Singapore, Hong-Kong, and Shanghai, he arrived in Tientsin. From there he proceeded overland to Peking.

Gordon did not write much about it in his diaries and letters of the time (perhaps because he did not witness the looting of the Summer Palace), and because there were so many interesting chapters in his life, there is not much in his biography, based on his diaries, about the sack of the Yuen-ming-yuen. What there is, is worth examining.

The Narrative[295]

[Gordon writes:] 'On the 11th October we were sent down in a great hurry to throw up works and batteries against the town [Peking]. As the Chinese refused to give up the gate, we required

---

[294] Hake, Egmont, *The Story of Chinese Gordon*, London 1884, Preface
[295] Hake, Egmont, *The Story of Chinese Gordon*, chapter III, pp. 23–25

them to surrender before we would treat with them. They were also required to give up all the prisoners. You will be sorry to hear that the treatment they have suffered has been very bad. Poor De Norman, who was with me in Asia, is one of the victims. It appears that they were tied so tight by the wrists that the flesh mortified, and they died in the greatest torture. Up to the time that elapsed before they arrived at the Summer Palace they were well treated, but then the ill-treatment began. The Emperor is supposed to have been there at the time.

'To go back to the work—the Chinese were given until twelve on the 13th to give up the gate. We made a lot of batteries, and everything was ready for the assault of the wall, which is battle-mented and forty feet high, but of inferior masonry. At 11.30 P.M., however, the gate was opened, and we took possession; so our work was of no avail. The Chinese had then until the 23rd to think over our terms of treaty, and to pay £10,000 for each Englishman and £500 for each native soldier who had died during his captivity. This they did, and the money was paid and the treaty signed yesterday. I could not witness it, as all officers commanding companies were obliged to remain in camp. Owing to the ill-treatment the prisoners experienced at the Summer Palace, the general ordered it to be destroyed, and stuck up proclamations to say why it was ordered. We accordingly went out, and, after pillaging it, burned the whole place, destroying in a vandal-like manner most valuable property, which could not be replaced for four millions.

'We got upward of £48 apiece prize-money before we went out of here; and although I have not as much as many, I have done well. Imagine 'D' giving 16s. for a string of pearls which he sold the next day for £500 . . . The people are civil, but I think the grandees hate us, as they must after what we did to the Palace. You can scarcely imagine the beauty and magnificence of the palaces we burned. It made one's heart sore to burn them; in fact, these palaces were so large, and we were so pressed for time, that we could not plunder them carefully. Quantities of gold ornaments were burned, considered as brass. It was wretchedly demoralizing work for an army. Everybody was wild for plunder.

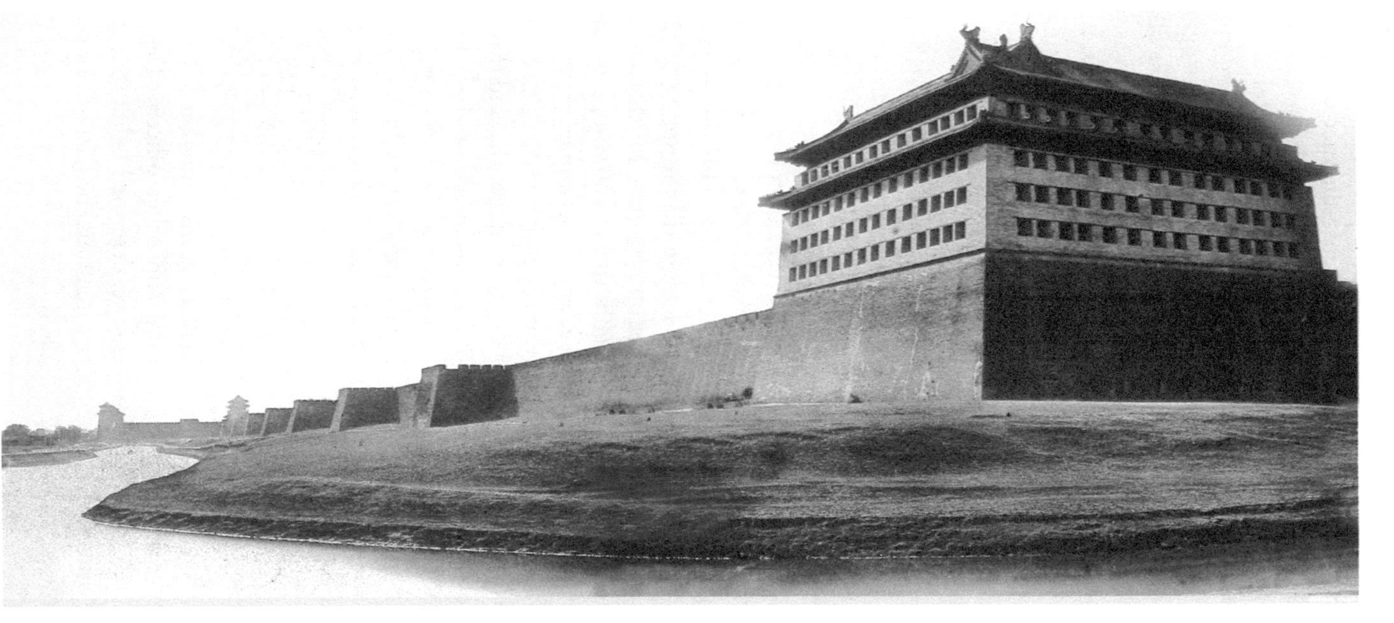

Panorama of the massive walls of Peking, Felice Beato, October 1860

'You would scarcely conceive the magnificence of this residence, or the tremendous devastation the French have committed. The throne and room were lined with ebony, carved in a marvelous way. There were huge mirrors of all shapes and kinds, clocks, watches, musical boxes with puppets on them, magnificent china of every description, heaps and heaps of silks of all colors, embroidery, and as much splendor and civilization as you would see at Windsor; carved ivory screens, coral screens, large amounts of treasure, etc. The French have smashed everything in the most wanton way. It was a scene of utter destruction which passes my description.'

For a month after these events Gordon remained in camp before Peking, paying occasional visits to the capital, and making his observations on the Chinese and their modes of living. On November 8 the two armies left for Tientsin, there to take up their winter quarters; and Gordon went as commanding royal engineer. His stay there was protracted, however, over a much longer period than he had expected; for, with the exception of a few excursions, he remained there till the spring of 1862. During this time he was engaged in providing for the wants of his troops, in surveying the neighboring country in parts where no European had ever been seen, and in occasional rides to the Taku forts and back, a distance of 140 miles; indeed, his longest absence from Tientsin did not exceed two months, and this was on the occasion of an expedition he made on horseback to the Outer Wall, with his comrade Lieutenant Cardew—a tour full of adventure, and for which they gained great credit, having visited, in the course of their journey, regions before unknown to Europeans.

Loot

The Royal Engineers Museum in Kent contains a number of items taken from the Summer Palace by Gordon and other officers. The primary point of interest is the emperor's throne, described below, but there are also a white jade bowl, a gilt-bronze ceremonial bell, Buddhist statuettes and silk throne fabrics.

Gordon's loot from the Summer Palace is clearly identifiable because he donated it to his regimental mess. Principal among his loot is the famous 'Gordon Throne'. There are various descriptions of what witnesses saw at the Palace before its destruction. The following is Wolseley's description of the principal one in the Audience Hall:

> The Imperial throne was a beautiful piece of workmanship, made of rosewood, stood upon a platform, raised about eighteen inches above the other part of the hall, and was surrounded by an open-work balustrading, richly carved with representation of roses and other flowers. Upon each side of the throne stood a high pole screen decorated with blue enamel and peacocks' feathers, upon which small rubies and emeralds were strung.[296]

Whichever throne Gordon chose, he did not have the means to transport the entire object back to England as it was. He had to dismantle it. He took it apart and shipped the individual panels back to England along with parts of another throne. Back in England Gordon had it reassembled for the officers' mess.

It is not conclusive from which part of the Yuen-ming-yuen the Gordon throne was taken. There were many thrones throughout the Palace for the emperor's use. The most magnificent was the one described by Wolseley that sat in the Audience Hall. It is most likely that this was the Gordon throne.

Gordon did not leave a record of where he found the throne or when he took it. But it is probable that he obtained it on October 18 while his men and men of the 1st division were burning the Palace, building-by-building. These are other descriptions of the throne in the main Audience Hall:

> Robert M'Ghee: "the chair of state, richly carved in dark wood, and cushioned in rich embroidery."[297]
> Robert Swinhoe: "We entered its central door, and found ourselves on a smooth marble floor, in front of the Emperor's ebony

---

[296] Wolseley, Garnet

[297] M'Ghee, Robert, pp. 203–204

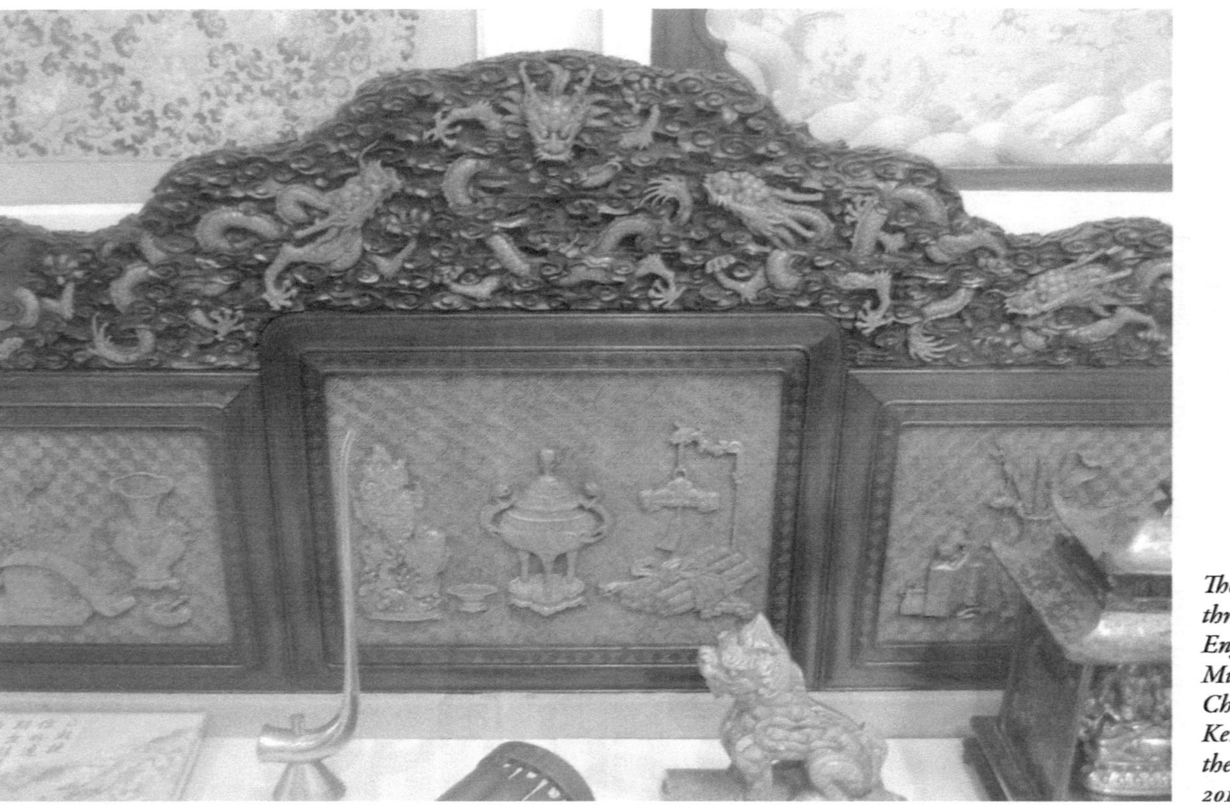

The Gordon throne, Royal Engineers Museum, Chatham, Kent, copyright the Author, 2016

> throne. The carvings on the throne consisted of dragons in vari-
> ous attitudes, and was quite a work of art . . ."[298]
>
> Colonel Du Pin: "We climbed the wide, white, marble steps and
> entered a huge hall. At the far side stood a throne made out of
> black wood, marvelously sculpted, a wonderful work of prodi-
> gious size."[299]
>
> Maurice Irisson: "The throne faces the screen; it stands on top of
> about ten steps. It is formed of a pile of silk cushions and mat-
> tresses in an alcove"[300]

The Royal Engineers Museum has determined that the panels used to construct the current throne came from two different thrones from the Summer Palace. The rear panels are from one throne which was square in nature, according to the museum, and the lower front and side panels are from a different throne. Close examination reveals that although the front and rear panels are similar in style, the light colored backgrounds are indeed different, which is consistent with this explanation.

At least three types of wood were used in the construction: On the lower panels, the interior portions are of a golden colored burl wood, most likely burled rosewood. The upper panels, which form the back of the throne, have had the most workmanship, and have been heavily carved out of what appears to be the finest zitan wood, in high relief showing inter-twining dragons and some contrasting golden wood, or cinnabar elements. It is an extremely fine and well planned piece of furniture and exquisitely carved, most likely from the 1760–80 period—the height of the reign of the great Emperor Qianlong when China was very wealthy and when the fashion was for more ostentatious pieces to glorify the emperor.

The Taiping Rebellion

Gordon's involvement in the Taiping Rebellion is quite remarkable and worth looking at in some detail. The Taipings were a nominally Christian force who had succeeded in 'freeing' several provinces in South China from Imperial control. Their army had defeated the soldiers of local

---

[298] Swinhoe, Robert, pp. 294–295

[299] Du Pin, *Expédition de Chine*, 1862, p. 233

[300] Irisson, Maurice, p. 310

governors and armies of the Emperor. For the purposes of the Second
Opium War the Allies found the Taping Rebellion quite useful because it
forced the Imperial army to fight on two fronts—against themselves and
the Taipings—and thus weakened the defense of Peking. And the Allies
had no concern about the rebellion per se, viewing it as a civil war. However, they became concerned when the Taipings reached Shanghai and
sent before them a huge wave of refugees. The foreign 'powers' wanted
to keep Shanghai and their own citizens living there safe from the rebels,
and make sure that trade was not interrupted.

The foreign authorities in Shanghai organized a militia of Europeans and Chinese to defend the city, under the command of Frederick
Townsend Ward, an American army officer. A British force under General
Staveley also arrived from the north, and the two foreign armies cooper-
ated. Staveley decided to drive the rebels back at least 30 miles from the
city, and this he did. By the end of 1862 the area around Shanghai was
secure. Gordon was attached to Staveley's staff. The American, Ward, was
killed in the fighting and Li Hongzhang the governor of Jiangsu Province wanted Staveley to find a replacement. In March 1863 Staveley sent
Gordon to command the militia, which by now was composed mostly
of Chinese conscripts and mercenaries and had adopted the name 'Ever
Victorious Army'. Gordon, with the unofficial rank of general, led the
unruly force to relieve the besieged town of Chansu. He then began re-
organizing the army, based on his own ideas, and led them against the
city of Kunshan which they also recaptured from the rebels.

Gordon, "a driven man, who like [governor] Hong had had a religious experience that gave him an unbending Christian duty to all less
fortunate than himself. Gordon was just the person that was needed to
remodel the army. Military discipline of the firmest kind was instilled
into his soldiers, they were to be paid a salary in place of a share of the
pillage. They were issued with uniforms. In the early days of his strict
regime the whole Army mutinied against the changes he had instituted,
but with summary execution for desertion and selfless leadership he
gradually won them over."[301]

To Governor Li Hongzhang, who had been faced with utter defeat
and had no answer for the rebels, Gordon was a hero:

---

[301] *The Baldwin Project, Charles Gordon*

It is a direct blessing from Heaven, the coming of this British Gordon ... He is superior in manner and bearing to any of the foreigners whom I have come into contact with, and does not show outwardly that conceit which makes most of them repugnant in my sight. What an elixir for a heavy heart—to see this splendid Englishman fight! ... If there is anything that I admire nearly as much as the superb scholarship of Zeng Guofan, it is the military qualities of this fine officer. He is a glorious fellow![302]

Gordon ... knew how best to fight a campaign. He planned expeditions using every benefit that the countryside could afford him. He went on dangerous mapping sorties to reconnoitre enemy territory. He devised his own form of gunboat to navigate the shallow creeks of the Yangtse. Like the Duke of Wellington, Gordon was a highly professional soldier. Looking after his troops he epitomises the hardworking, selfless military life. Meticulous and daring he inspired idolatry among his men.[303]

Most remarkably, Gordon led his troops from the front, unarmed, "treating with disdain the bullets that flew around him. Such brave (or stupid) behaviour was bound to cause some degree of veneration, and it is said that the Taiping rebels were ordered not to shoot at the faintly smiling Englishman leading their enemies. The 'Ever Victorious Army' now lived up to its name, and the rebels were repeatedly beaten back towards Nanjing."[304]

"Gordon, in his mild way, would take one or other of [the Chinese officers] by the arm and lead them into the thick of the fire. When he was once wounded in battle, and his men wished to carry him out of it, he would not allow it, but went on leading them till he fainted from loss of blood,"[305] notes biographer Hake. They captured the ancient city of Suzhou. Having promised the rebel leaders that they would be spared if they gave up the city, Gordon was hopping mad when Li Hongzhang

---

[302] Research by *The Baldwin Project*

[303] *The Baldwin Project, General Charles Gordon*

[304] Ibid.

[305] Hake, *The Story of Chinese Gordon*

executed them. And it was only after considerable begging that Gordon was convinced to stay on as commander.

> When offered the command, Gordon had said he would finish the 'business' in eighteen months. He was true to his word ... the job was done and the Qing Emperor was enormously grateful. Gordon was sent heaps of gold in bowls carried by the emperor's men. Believing this was some sort of bribe he sent them away but only after giving the bearers a flogging for the perceived insult he had received. Such was the empire's wish to reward that he was then given gifts he would accept: the highest possible military title of field marshal and the imperial yellow jacket (Huang Ma Gua) with a peacock feather. A special heavy gold medal was struck by imperial decree and presented to him.[306]

May 10, 1864 Gordon wrote to his mother, "I do not want anything, either, money or honours, from either the Chinese Government or our own. As for the honours, I do not value them at all. I know that I am doing a great deal of good, and, liking my profession, do not mind going on with my work ..." He continues, "I shall leave China as poor as I entered it, but with the knowledge that through my weak instrumentality upwards of eighty to one hundred thousand lives have been spared. I want no further satisfaction than this."[307]

> On return to England he was fêted by the British Press who had portrayed him as a hero and 'Chinese Gordon' but his distaste for 'show' meant he quickly retreated into a fairly squalid, lonely existence at Gravesend. Who could use someone like Gordon in a military role? He had shown himself as an independent fiery spirit who was no-one but his own master—under God's guidance. The gifts he had received from the emperor were given to his artillery regiment [*sic* engineers].
>
> Gordon has to be given considerable credit for the defeat of the Taiping Rebellion which very easily could have toppled the Qing regime. In the wider Chinese context, the Tongzhi

---

[306] Ibid.

[307] Ibid.

restoration (1861–1874) sought some overdue reforms through the 'Self Strengthening Movement' to rejuvenate the Qing dynasty. This was considered not as a wholesale adoption of Western principles but rebuilding on sound Confucian doctrine: 'Western function and Chinese essence'. This included Zeng Guofen's use of European style military organization to build his unit of 'Hunan Braves', it should be remembered that Zeng had worked with Gordon on the Shanghai defenses. Mao Zedong revered Zeng Guofan and Mao's military campaign in Jiangxi against the Guomindang must surely have looked back to the exploits of Gordon.[308]

After China

Gordon returned to an enthusiastic welcome in Britain in January 1865. He was given command of the Royal Engineers base at Gravesend. Here he spent most of his colonel's salary and much of his time on the poor, the sick and the dying. When he had free time, he taught at a school for poor children.

"His house [in Gravesend]," according to Hake, "was school, and hospital, and almshouse in turn. The troubles of all interested him alike. The poor, the sick, the unfortunate were ever welcome, and never did supplicant knock vainly at his door. Many children he rescued from the gutter, cleansed, clothed, and fed them, and for their benefit established evening classes, over which he himself presided."[309]

In the book, *Eminent Victorians*, Lytton Strachey states that for Gordon: "The easy luxuries of his class and station were unknown to him: his clothes verged upon the shabby; and his frugal meals were eaten at a table with a drawer, into which the loaf and plate were quickly swept at the approach of his poor visitors." The only book he read was the Bible. According to Strachey, Gordon was possessed of inherent contradictions which became exacerbated as time went by, "He was an English gentleman, an officer, a man of energy and action, a lover of danger and the audacities that defeat danger, a passionate creature."

Starting in 1873 Gordon began a series of overseas postings of a political nature. His first assignment was as governor of one of the provinces

---

[308] Ibid.

[309] Ibid.

of Sudan. He used his time there between 1874 and 1876 to map the upper reaches of the Nile River. He was promoted to Governor-Geneeral of the Sudan, and in that capacity was engaged in suppressing rebellions and trying to stamp out the slave trade. In 1880 ill health forced him to return to England. Between 1880 and 1883 he was sent on various assignments to South Africa, India and China.

The Mahdist Uprising

In 1882 Britain's hold over the Sudan began to be threatened and the Egyptian army was not able to restore order. A large army of Sudanese led by a fanatical Muslim leader called the *Mahdi* was bent on driving the Egyptians and the British out of the Sudan. The British government's response was to instruct the Egyptians to withdraw and concentrate on stabilizing Egypt. Gordon was ordered to Khartoum, the capital of Sudan, not to defend it but to supervise a withdrawal.

In 1884 Gordon reached Khartoum and began to organize the withdrawal of civilians to Egypt. But before the task of complete withdrawal could be accomplished, the Mahdi's army threatened to capture Khartoum. The Egyptian forces still in Sudan under British command were engaged in fighting yet another revolt in eastern Sudan and so Khartoum was largely unprotected militarily. Against orders, Gordon decided to organize a defense of the city, and in March 1884 the Mahdi's army began a siege of Khartoum against Gordon's defences. Prime Minister Gladstone's administration was against sending troops back into the Sudan and was prepared to leave Gordon to his fate. The British public, however, were in uproar and demanded that Gordon be rescued, with even Queen Victoria lending her support to the cause. Finally, under intense public pressure, Gladstone relented and sent a relief force under Gordon's old comrade, Wolseley, to save him.

As the siege dragged on, food in the city began to run low. Even so, they might have held out longer but on January 26, 1885 a traitor inside Khartoum opened the gates and let the rebel forces in. The British relief column set off in November 1884 and by January had reached the upper Nile. An advance force reached Khartoum on January 28, but found that the city had already fallen and the defenders had been massacred. Under attack from the rebels, they were forced to withdraw.

Death

Gordon's death was perhaps the great Victorian romantic tragedy. Caught in a barbarian land, thousands of miles from home, defending British interests, the virtuous general sacrificed himself rather than surrender to the savages that besieged him. Help came tragically too late.

Gordon was apparently killed about an hour before dawn, at the Governor-General's palace. As recounted in Bernard M. Allen's article *How Khartoum Fell* (1941), the Mahdi had given strict orders to his three Khalifas not to kill Gordon. However, the order was not obeyed. Gordon died on a stairway in the northwestern corner of the palace where he and his personal bodyguard, Agha Khalil Orphali, had been firing at the enemy. Orphali was knocked unconscious and did not see Gordon die. When he came to, he found Gordon's decapitated body covered with flies. A merchant, Bordeini Bey, glimpsed Gordon standing on the palace steps in a white uniform looking into the darkness.

> Reference is made to an 1889 account of the General surrendering his sword to a senior Mahdist officer, then being struck and subsequently speared in the side as he rolled down the staircase. When Gordon's head was unwrapped at the Mahdi's feet, he ordered the head transfixed between the branches of a tree . . . where all who passed it could look in disdain, children could throw stones at it and the hawks of the desert could sweep and circle above. His body was desecrated and thrown down a well. After the re-conquest of the Sudan, in 1898, several attempts were made to locate Gordon's remains, but in vain.[310]

In the course of the capture of Khartoum the Madhi's troops killed an estimated 10,000 civilians and soldiers. A painting was produced by George Joy entitled *General Gordon's Last Stand* currently hangs in the Leeds City Art Gallery. The 1966 film *Khartoum*, starring Charlton Heston, immortalized Gordon's last battle.

Aftermath

"On February 5th, news reached London that Khartoum had fallen, and that Gordon was dead. A frenzy of public mourning ensued. Pictures

---

[310] Wikipedia article—*General Charles Gordon*

of the dead hero, draped in black, appeared in countless shop windows, and not merely in Britain, but also in Paris, Berlin and New York. Queen Victoria sought out her lady-in waiting to tell her in grief-stricken tones, 'Gordon is dead!' She expressed her outrage more formally by sending Gladstone an angry telegram. Gladstone himself was reviled as the 'Murderer of Gordon', and stones were hurled through the windows of 10 Downing Street by incensed patriots. Far away in South Africa, Cecil Rhodes repeatedly bewailed the fact that he had not been at Gordon's side when disaster struck. Gordon songs and Gordon poems poured from the printing presses."[311]

In Britain, a day of mourning—March 13—was declared. And the public demanded revenge. A few weeks later Wolseley and his troops defeated the Mahdi and recaptured Khartoum, in the public mind righting some of the wrong that had been done.

Honors

A statue of Gordon was set up in Trafalgar Square, London, and the following year one in Melbourne, Australia. Another statue of Gordon was put on display in the town of Chatham, home of the Royal Engineers. Schools in Vancouver, Canada and in the city of Khartoum itself have been named after the general.

As a military officer Gordon was impetuous, strongly opinionated, yet also decisive and resolute. These qualities ended up being both his strengths and weaknesses.

Bibliography

Hake, A. Egmont, *The Story of Chinese Gordon*, Vol. I, John W. Lovell & Co, New York, 1863

---

[311] Ibid.

Burning of a Palace

James Bruce, Earl of Elgin

"Having, to the best of my judgment, examined the question in all its bearings, I came to the conclusion that the destruction of Yuen-ming-yuen was the least objectionable of the several courses open to me . . ."
—James Bruce, Earl of Elgin

James Bruce, 8th Earl of Elgin was the senior diplomat and the Crown representative in China in 1860, and the man who ordered the burning of the Summer Palace. No protagonist in these events has generated more controversy for his role in the affair, and he and his family have been beset with criticism for his actions in China ever since. It is curious how a mild-mannered British aristocrat whose resume is otherwise notable for his diplomatic successes in the Americas and Asia came to earn this reputation. Elgin has left a full record of his thoughts concerning the campaign and especially his reasoning for burning the Palace. On this basis alone his life and comments about the sack are vital to this story.

His biographer, Walrond, aptly describes Elgin's career as "a record of stirring incidents, of difficulties triumphantly overcome, or novel and entangled situations successfully mastered."[312] He was born James Bruce, in 1811, into a very old and distinguished Scottish noble family. Records

---

[312] *Elgin*, Letters and Journals of James, Eight Earl of Elgin, Theodore Walrond, Editor, 1872. John Murray, London (Publisher)

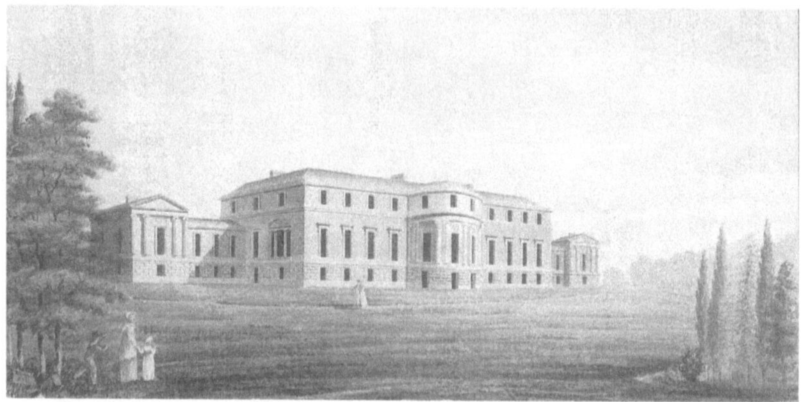

Broomhall, c. 1780, artist unknown

show that there were several *De Bruce* who accompanied William the Conqueror on his invasion of Britain in 1066, and from whom the Bruce family are descended. Over the course of time the Bruces became Scottish landowners and peers, earls of Elgin from 1633 and earls of Kincardine from 1643. Lord Elgin's family are directly related to Robert the Bruce and the earl is recognized as the head of the Bruce Clan.

In 1704 the Bruce family built a grand Palladian mansion on lands that had once belonged to the Abbey of Dunfermline. *Broomhall*, on the north shore of the Firth of Forth in eastern Scotland has since been the home of the Earls of Elgin. Thomas Bruce, the 7th Earl (1766–1841), father of the man who commanded the British expedition to China, inherited an estate that was plagued with financial difficulties. He was obliged to find an 'occupation' to provide an income for himself and his family. Through royal connections he was able to secure the post of British Ambassador to the Sultan of Turkey. And it was in this capacity that he brought the family into controversy by acquiring the famous *Elgin Marbles*—approximately half of the marble frieze which formed the upper decoration of the Parthenon. Getting the marbles back from Athens to Britain, given their substantial size and weight, proved logistically difficult and expensive. In the process the 7th Earl was imprisoned in Napoleonic France for three years and this indirectly resulted in his wife leaving him for another man. On his return to Britain he was beset with criticism from his countrymen, found himself without employment, and his reputation in tatters.

Having lost his first wife, the 7th Earl married for a second time to Elizabeth Oswald, who was to bear him seven children—three sons and four daughters. Out of financial necessity the 7th Earl lived out the remainder of his life (after 1815) in France, where the cost of living was much lower, and where the couple's children were largely brought up. But his earlier lavish spending on Greek antiquities, capital investment into the business operations of the Broomhall estate, and substantial repairs to the house itself, had increased the family's debts, which were only marginally reduced when he did finally sell The Marbles to the British Museum in 1816. In that year his total debts were estimated at 100,000 pounds—a vast sum.

The Broomhall estate was put into the hands of trustees of the creditors to ensure effective management of the assets and repayment of funds, while Elgin and his family lived in financial exile.

James was the eldest son of the 7th Earl and his second wife Elizabeth Oswald. For most of his early years his elder brother—Lord Bruce, son of Mary, the 7th Earl's first wife—was the heir to the earldom and it appeared that James was destined for a relatively minor role in public service.

Elgin and his younger brother Frederick were educated at Eton, where Elgin was a contemporary of William Gladstone, the future prime minister, and a number of other embryo political leaders. Gladstone became a close friend, as did William, later Lord, Canning. Elgin went up to Oxford in 1829 where he was considered the leading scholar of his year, obtaining a First in classics in 1832. It would have been a *Double* First had he not suffered a collapse due to over-work in his last year—a trait that would follow him into his career—he was a stubbornly dedicated worker. Elgin was a fundamentally serious man but also possessed an innate charm with both men and women, as evidenced by his ability to win the respect and friendship of international leaders and to woo eligible females. He was elected a Fellow of Merton College in 1832.

After his brilliant university career it would have seemed natural for the young Elgin to go into Parliament and begin what would perhaps be a distinguished political career. He had an active interest in politics and government policy, but *money* was to be the principal barrier to this course of action. In the 1830s MPs were unpaid and it might take years before he became a (salaried) minister. Younger brother Robert went into the army and Frederick the navy, but Elgin could not decide what he wanted to do, and for the next eleven years he lived in a sort of limbo at Broomhall as the de facto manager of the estate. There he developed a paternalistic view of society in which he saw that the proper role of the aristocracy and other men of learning was to rule beneficently on behalf of the people as a whole, and it was this view that translated later in his career to his leadership in colonial and international affairs.

By all accounts Elgin was a thoughtful man, anxious to act responsibly and use his authority appropriately. He was a conservative, a Christian, and willing to adopt progressive policies where he felt they were fair, based on sound principles, and necessary for the advancement of British interests.

In 1837 Elgin stood as Tory candidate for Parliament in the local constituency of Fife. Disorganized, and with no money to support his campaign, he was comfortably defeated by the Whig candidate.

In early 1840 he met Elizabeth Mary Cumming Bruce, the very beautiful daughter of a highland kinsman, and in 1841 they were married. In the parliamentary election of 1841 a friend of his father's, Sir Robert Preston, paid the election expenses for Elgin to stand for Parliament a second time, on this occasion for the seat of Southampton. This time he was victorious. But his political career was cut short by the death in quick succession of his elder half-brother in 1840 and then his father in November 1841, leaving him as the heir to the earldom. As a peer, Elgin was barred from sitting in the House of Commons. All was not lost, however. Through his sister Augusta's connections to Queen Victoria, the Bruce family had once again found favor at Court and James, now 8th Earl of Elgin, was appointed Governor of Jamaica in 1842—a minor but significant diplomatic post. It was not be an easy or prestigious position, but it was a necessary one.

Jamaica

In May 1842 Elgin and his new bride arrived in Jamaica, after a fashion. Their ship was wrecked in the West Indies and the seven month pregnant Elizabeth never fully recovered from the traumatic experience. She gave birth to a healthy daughter and even became pregnant again, but her health declined and she died in Jamaica in June 1843. The loss was a devastating one for Elgin who now found himself alone, a widower, with a young child, thousands of miles from home, in a troubled political and economic environment.

Elgin saw his job as governor not to *rule* Jamaica as an autocrat but to *lead* the government through the elected national assembly—a much more delicate and precarious operation. Jamaica, once very propserous, was in economic decline due to the recent abolition of slavery on the island and competition from other sugar-producing islands. Sugar was the colony's primary product, and for the time being her future was tied to it. In addition to having to compete with lower prices from sugar produced elsewhere, the Jamaican sugar planters found themselves struggling to find workers. Many former slaves preferred to work their own small holdings, eking out a basic living rather than work for wages on a plantation. The white plantation owners were also in political trouble, on the cusp of losing control of the island's assembly.

The government in Britain favored the abolition of trade tariffs on the import of foreign sugar. When this happened it left Jamaica to compete on the global stage without help from the mother-country.[313] Despite honorable and wise suggestions about how the planters could return their enterprises to profitability, Elgin was unable to raise the funds from London to assist with capital investment (to modernize equipment), and so ultimately his ideas came to nought. He was left frustrated and the planter community felt abandoned and betrayed by Britain and her governor.

Elgin disliked Jamaica, the heat, and his bachelor lifestyle, and in January 1845 he announced to the Colonial Office that he was leaving the island for good. Back in England he set himself the task of finding a suitable wife, the kind of woman that did not exist in Jamaica. And here he demonstrated his very considerable charm. In what he later described as one of the 'four great triumphs' of his life, each taking just two weeks to accomplish, he met and courted Mary Louisa Lambton, an attractive young woman of twenty who became his second wife. Mary Louisa was also well connected at Court, the daughter of a former Governor of Canada, and niece of the Colonial Secretary.

Elgin's Jamaican reports to the colonial office, his obvious abilities, and now his family connection, paved the way for the Colonial Secretary to offer him the appointment of Governor General of British North America (Canada), a much more prestigious and substantial position

---

[313] Traditionally Britain's colonies had traded with Britain free of import duties whilst foreign producers were subject to tax. Prime Minister Robert Peel was a believer in abolishing import duties on all goods, no matter their place of origin. His policies benefited British consumers by lowering prices, but hurt her colonies who lost their commercial advantage and were often undercut by foreign suppliers

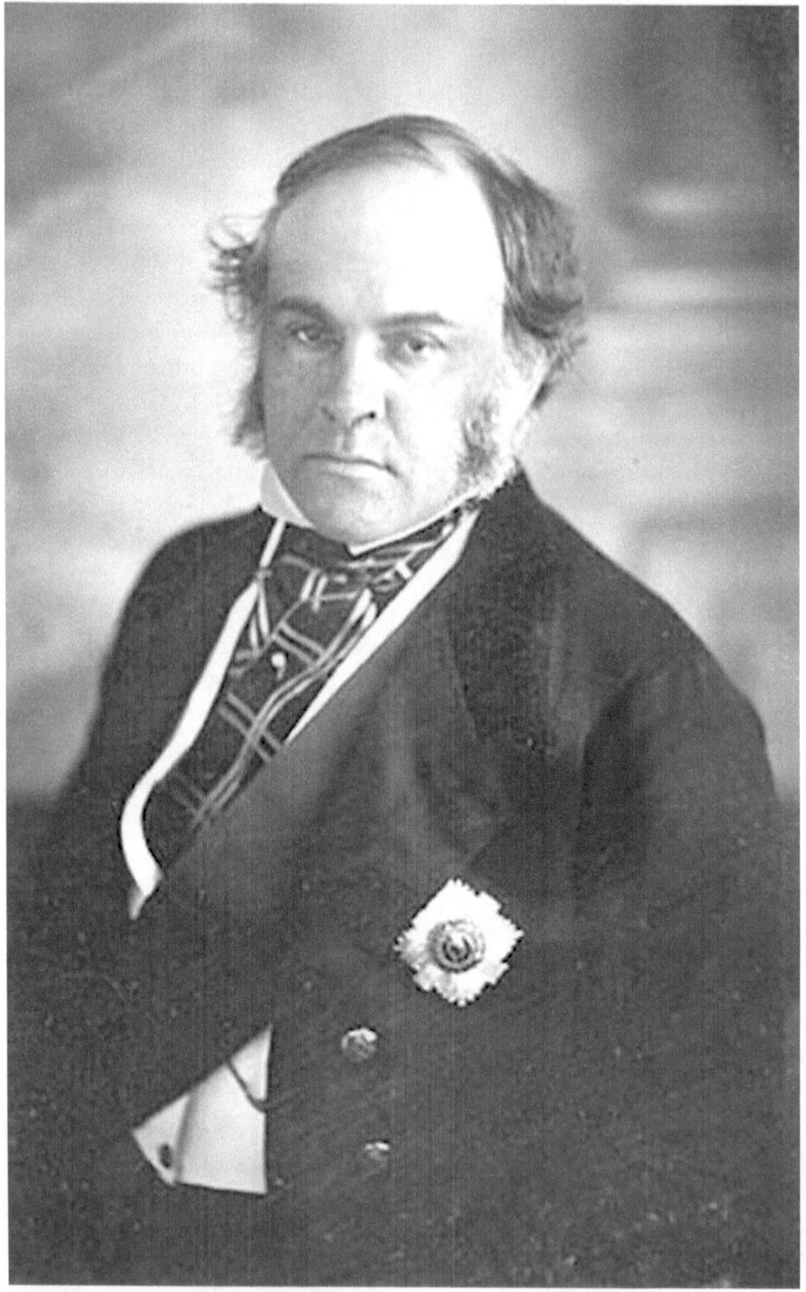

Lord Elgin as a young man, 1840's,
early daguerreotype photograph, photographer unknown

within the colonial diplomatic service. Again, Elgin was unhappy to be posted far from London, but he had little choice if he must earn a living to support his family and to pay down his family's debts.

Canada

The governorship of Canada, like Jamaica, was a challenging assignment. At the time of his sailing—January 1847—Elgin's new wife was already pregnant and Elgin sailed ahead of her in rough seas, to avoid the catastrophe which had befallen his first wife in the Caribbean. Robert Bruce, Elgin's younger brother, now a lieutenant colonel with the Grenadier Guards, accompanied him as his military secretary.

It was not a simple or pleasant role for Elgin. He inherited a colony that was deeply divided along national and linguistic lines. The French and British colonists were at odds with each other. Whilst the French resented British rule, they believed that they deserved a say in the running of the colony. The British settlers felt that British dominance over the French entitled them to the leading role in government. Elgin took a progressive line, one that had been posited by the previous governor, that French citizens must be allowed to take part in Canadian politics on an equal footing with the British. Again, his approach was to allow the colony to govern itself, with the governor acting as head of state, but removed from policy and politics. He initiated free elections with French and British citizens able to vote on equal terms. The representatives of the French and British sections of the colony must then come together to form a government. It produced an administration dominated by French representatives and a few liberals from the British community. The established British leaders and their supporters were furious. After the passing of legislation to compensate French citizens who had suffered losses in the rebellion of 1837, there were riots in Montreal and the parliament building was burnt to the ground. Elgin handled it all very calmly, with a soft touch, and weathered the storm. He refused to intervene and set up his own administration, insistent that the electorate must decide who would be their leaders. And it proved a success. After talk of joining the United States subdued and died away, the growing British population of Canada came to accept this new form of greater autonomy and greater democracy. But at the time Elgin was a popular man with neither the British or French communities in Canada.

To further solidify the equality of all Canadians, Elgin decided to move the capital away from Montreal, to Ottawa. The enfranchisement of French Canadians and the relocation of the capital city were events of great constitutional significance for Canada and made Elgin one of the most important governors in Canadian history.

Elgin's governorship culminated in a very important trade agreement with the United States. Until that time (1854) there was still lingering animosity between the North American colony and the United States stemming from the War of 1812. In a two week visit to Washington, Elgin charmed his American hosts and came away with a comprehensive trade agreement—the The Reciprocity Treaty. It was perhaps his greatest achievement while Governor, and he classed it as the second of his four greatest achievements in his lifetime, all accomplished within two weeks.

In 1855, after eight years as Canada's governor, Elgin returned to Britain hoping to find employment closer to home. He had earned the respect and esteem of the politicians in London, had managed the family's finances prudently, and it appeared he was going to be able to return to Broomhall and finally spend time with his young family. He was appointed Postmaster General by Lord Palmerston—an important, minor, but 'paying' cabinet appointment.

That was until the Arrow incident that sparked off the Second Opium War and called for a major military presence in the East and a diplomatic mission to China.

China

When troubles arose, Lord Palmerston needed a steady hand to guide his policy in China, and Elgin, with his international experience and considerable diplomatic skill, was considered a cool head who could secure Britain's interests in the region without unnecessary use of military force. In 1857 Elgin set sail for China, stopping in Egypt along the way, and then India. He arrived in Singapore only to learn that the Indian Mutiny had broken out and that his friend the Viceroy, Lord Canning, was in short supply of troops and in danger of losing the colony. Elgin immediately redirected his soldiers from Singapore to Calcutta, and sent orders for soldiers *en route* to China also come to the assistance of Canning. His decisive action was critical in allowing Britain to defeat the uprising and stabilize her hold on India.

It was not until 1858, therefore, that Elgin received his troops and began his campaign against the Chinese. With the assistance of naval forces commanded by his brother, Elgin succeeded in capturing the Taku forts and advancing to Tientsin. The Chinese government, having to fight the Taiping Rebellion as well as the British, were in no position to make war. They reluctantly signed the Treaty of Tientsin which opened five additional ports to trade with Britain, agreed to an indemnity of six million taels of silver, and, crucially, allowed the British to send diplomatic representatives to Peking to negotiate directly with the Chinese court.

Treaty with Japan

At the end of his dealings with China in 1858, Elgin continued on to Tokyo where in two weeks of negotiating he succeeded in obtaining the first trade agreement between Britain and Japan. It was the third of what he felt were the four great achievements of his life, all accomplished in two weeks. Elgin was no puppet, but a keen observer who was able to see the irony and also the injustice in his government's policies. But he was also a loyal servant of the Crown. Speaking of the Japan he encountered in 1858 he noted, admiringly, and with a word of caution:

> There is no luxury or extravagance in any kind, no jewels or gold ornaments, even a Court, but the nobles have handsome palaces, and large bodies of retainers. A perfectly paternal Government; a perfectly filial people; a community entirely self-supporting; peace within and without; no want; no ill-will between classes. This is what I find in Japan in the year 1858, after a two hundred years' exclusion of foreign trade and foreigners. Twenty years hence, what will be the contrast?[314]

Return to England

All appeared well in the East and Elgin returned to Britain content that he had secured the agreement that Palmerston was seeking with minimal military conflict. His happiness, however, was short-lived. The Chinese Emperor was persuaded by the more hawkish factions at court to flout

---

[314] Elgin, in Wrong, p. 146

the Tientsin agreement, and the British plenipotentiaries who wanted to advance to Tientsin and then to Peking were sent away by Prince Seng. Palmerston was furious and determined to impose his will on China. He sent Elgin as the leader of a second expedition. But in order to ensure a clear demarcation between civil and military affairs, General Sir Hope Grant was made commander of the expeditionary army. It was an unenviable position for Elgin to be in—the responsibility for a great army and for the fair treatment of the Chinese people.

France insisted on sending their own diplomatic representative and their own army to fight alongside the British. This was a complicating factor in what already was a difficult diplomatic situation, but Elgin, to his credit, managed the relationship effectively. The two armies were a formidable combination of infantry, cavalry and artillery. The artillery forces of both armies were a cumbersome and slow moving element and hard to transport from ship to shore and then from shore to Peking, but they proved to be a crucial component in the defeat of the much larger Chinese army and in posing a credible threat to Peking. Without them victory would not have been assured.

China Revisited

Elgin, as always conservative, did not want to fight the Chinese any more than he had to. From the start of the campaign, it is clear that his objective was to bring China to the negotiating table, get her to ratify the 1858 treaty, and go home. In no way did the Allies want to conquer China, rule China, or occupy China. Elgin considered war an unpleasant and brutal business.

As has been outlined in other chapters, the British army landed on the North China coast, captured the coastal defenses, and occupied Tientsin. Then followed a period of prolonged negotiations which went nowhere. Elgin rightly surmised that delaying tactics were being employed against him and at the beginning of September he ordered the army to continue its advance toward Peking. As the Europeans advanced, negotiations continued, and appeared to be bearing fruit, but then at the crucial moment the emissaries were captured and imprisoned. Quite apart from their treatment and the death of 15 of them (facts which would not be known until mid-October), Elgin was dismayed at what he considered the dishonesty and lack of good faith of the Chinese government. He felt the conflict had been concluded in 1858 and it was at great inconvenience to himself that he was forced to return east in 1860. The capture of the emissaries undermined any confidence Elgin had in the fair-dealing of the representatives of the Emperor. This was still uppermost in his mind when later he determined to destroy the Summer Palace. He had lost patience with negotiation and wanted both to avenge the treatment of the Crown representatives and instill a sense of fear in the Chinese government.

The imprisonment of the Allied emissaries effectively ended negotiations between the two sides for the time being and Elgin ordered the army to advance on Peking with a view to capturing it if necessary. Seng, having been defeated decisively at Tungchow and then at Palikao by the French, withdrew his forces north of the capital and the Emperor and his court fled beyond the Great Wall to Chengde, well out of reach of the invading force.

Elgin's concern from the start was a protracted campaign. Supply of food and munitions would be a serious issue if the army was forced to camp through the winter in North China. The morale of the men would likely fall and the invasion force would lose its impetus and be highly vulnerable to defeat from winter attack or in the spring. In Elgin's mind, and correctly so, one feels, it was vitally important to conclude the military campaign quickly, reach an agreement with the Chinese government and exit before the winter began and the Peiho Rover froze over preventing either reinforcement or supply from the sea. The need to end the campaign quickly was another driving force in the destruction of the Summer Palace.

Seng withdrew his troops north of Peking, relying on the city's massive walls to keep out the invaders while he harassed them with cavalry attacks. His army was still largely intact, and so Elgin must still fight, threaten, and negotiate to get a treaty signed. But with the Chinese army now unwilling to come to battle, this proved problematic.

The Allies waited for two weeks, short of Peking, for their supporting troops and heavy guns to catch up. Then on October 6 they marched north of the city with a view to putting themselves between the Chinese army and the Capital. The French reached the Summer Palace along with the British cavalry contingent. The next day (October 7) Elgin, General Hope Grant and their staffs arrived at the Palace:

Sunday, October 7th. We hear this morning that the French and our cavalry have captured the Summer Palace of the Emperor.

All the big-wigs have fled, nothing remains but a portion of the household. We are told that the prisoners are all in Peking ... Five P.M. I have just returned from the Summer Palace. It is really a fine thing, like an English park, numberless buildings with handsome rooms, and filled with Chinese curios, and handsome clocks, bronzes, but, alas! Such a scene of desolation. The French General came up full of protestations. He had prevented looting in order that all the plunder might be divided between the armies, etc. etc. There was not a room that I saw in which half the things had not been taken away or broken to pieces. I tried to get a regiment of ours sent to guard the place, and then sell the things by auction; but it is difficult to get things done by system in such a case, so some officers are left who are to fill two or three carts with treasures which are to be sold ... Plundering and devastating a place like this is bad enough, but what is much worse is the waste and breakage. Out of 1,000,000 pounds worth of property, I daresay 50,000 pounds will not be realised. French soldiers were destroying in every way the most beautiful silks, breaking the jade ornaments and porcelain, etc. War is a hateful business. The more one sees of it, the more one detests it.[315]

Elgin has nothing further to say about the looting that ensued. It is evident from items he acquired in China that he did, in due course, obtain loot from the Palace, the most significant of which was an exquisite pair of bronze cranes, a gift from the Emperor of Japan to the Emperor of China, but he records nothing of how this happened in his diary.

During the coming three weeks Elgin was preoccupied by the desire to save the prisoners, which included his personal secretary and the journalist from *The Times*, Thomas Bowlby—friends as well as colleagues—and at the same time obtain the Emperor's signature on a new treaty, then leave a core of diplomats in Peking, protected by soldiers. He was under a short time-frame—winter was on its way and he must conclude matters and have his army out of North China before conditions became impossible for fighting. The Allies were haunted by the collective memory of Napoleon's invasion of Russia in 1812 and the Allied invasion of the Crimea in 1854, both of which caused great suffering and loss of life

---

[315] Elgin, in Walrond, pp. 361–362

to their respective armies. Winter in Peking would be a disaster for British policy. From the point of view of British policy Elgin's ability to get a favorable treaty signed and his forces withdrawn in good order before winter was a triumph.

Elgin's journal reveal his personal horror when he discovered that despite his threats and his diplomatic efforts most of the prisoners had died while in the hands of the Chinese: "Camp near Peking. October 14th. We have dreadful news respecting the fate of some of our captured friends. It is an atrocious crime, and, not for vengeance, but for future security, ought to be severely dealt with."[316]

The Destruction of the Summer Palace

After the dishonesty of the Chinese in negotiating the peace treaty, the capture of the prisoners under dishonorable circumstances, and finally their torture and death, much of the British army were clamoring for the destruction of Peking itself. Elgin was cool in his assessment and took a more measured approach. This was the reason that he was made leader of the expedition, to carefully exercise power and authority and not overreact to every event. Terms were more or less settled with Prince Gong by October 16, but Elgin was anxious that Chinese treachery and murder of the prisoners should not go unavenged.

According to Cordier, of the thirty-seven members of the Allied expedition captured by the Chinese on September 18, only nineteen survived. And all of them underwent torture.[317]

On October 16 Elgin first communicated to Baron Gros, the French minister, his desire to include an article in the peace treaty explicitly requiring the burning of the Yuen-ming-yuen. Baron Gros opposed this as a condition of peace and as an inappropriate act. His feeling was that it would not achieve anything constructive and would send the wrong message to the Chinese people:

> As for the destruction of the Summer Palace, a defenseless country site, it would have, in my opinion at least, such an Unhappy vengeance, since, unfortunately, it could not remedy any of the cruel misfortunes which we deplore, that we ought not to think

---

[316] Elgin, in Walrond, p. 365

[317] Cordier, p. 370

of, and it seems to me that in the eyes of Europe, as for the peoples of China, of the palace of Peking after having removed the archives, a palace which, in the capital, is the seat of the sovereign power, would be an expiatory act more striking than the burning of a house of pleasure.[318]

Gros was convinced that including the destruction in the terms of peace would only delay reaching an agreement with Prince Gong:

> Without having attained the goal which has been pointed out to us by our governments. I am convinced that we shall be able to finish in a few days, if you do not mention in your letter to Gong, the destruction of Yuen-ming-yuen, and the atoning expedients which the Chinese government will have to make at Tientsin. All the other conditions which you impose, such as those which I stipulate, will be accepted, I believe at least, and I shall be happy, I confess, to come out of an impasse. . . . I slept little last night and I thought for a long time about our position and the solution we can give it. I cannot find any better than the one I propose. The means we have at our disposal, the advanced season which, from one moment to the next, can make the roads impracticable, the manner in which the Commanders-in-Chief speak of the situation—and the fear.[319]

On October 17, Baron Gros re-iterated in his correspondence that the idea of destroying the Palace was repugnant to him and he would not agree to it.[320] According to French historian Cordier, "The English, and they were right, wanted to punish this great culprit personally; General Grant and Lord Elgin believed it to be a sensible blow to him [Gong] by destroying his summer residence at Wan-cheou-chan, beside the walled enclosure of the Yuen-ming-yuen; I do not think the solution was honorable; We gave the Chinese the feeling that we were really Barbarians."[321]

---

[318] Baron Gros, letter to Lord Elgin, October 16, 1860, Cordier, pp. 370–71, translation by the author

[319] Baron Gros letter to Lord Elgin, October 16, 1860, Cordier, p. 372, translation by the author

[320] Cordier, p. 374, translation by the author

[321] Cordier, p. 384, translation by the author

"Les Français se trouvèrent en désaccord sur ce point avec leurs Allies: pillards, mais non incendiaires."[322]

Elgin in a letter to Gros outlined his reasons for wanting to take the momentous decision of destroying the Palace and why he rejected other options:

> I confess that I attached more importance to the impression which we might leave behind us on our departure from this place, than to any formal stipulations by which the Chinese authorities might bind themselves. It was necessary, therefore, to discover some act of retribution and punishment sufficiently severe to produce the required effect, and yet capable of such rapid execution that it would be possible after it had been accomplished, to complete, before the 1st of November, the Treaties of Peace, and such further measures as might be immediately necessary to put them into operation. This had to be done without attacking Peking, or anything within Peking, and in such a manner as to make the blow fall on the Emperor, who was clearly responsible for the crime committed; without, however so terrifying his brother, whom he had left behind him to represent him, as to drive him from the field. The destruction of the Yuen-ming-yuen palace, coupled with the exaction, as a step preliminary to negotiations, and in name of compensation to the sufferers, of such sum of money as could be raised on the spot by the government, seemed to me to be the only combination which fulfilled all these conditions.
>
> I had also at one time I resolved to require that a monument should be erected at the expense of the Chinese Government stating the circumstances of the arrest and murder of the British subjects illegally captured, who had died from the effects of their ill-treatment in prison, and the penalty which had been inflicted for the deed; but this proposal I finally abandoned for reasons which I have explained elsewhere. As the destruction of Yuen-ming-yuen is, however, *an act to which exception may with great apparent reason, be taken,*[323] it is my duty before closing this despatch to say a few words respecting the only modes of

---

[322] "The French disagreed on this point with their Allies: looters, but not arsonists," Cordier, translation by the author

[323] Emphasis added

inflicting a specific punishment for the crime in question which, limited as were my means of action for the reasons above stated, I could have adopted as substitutes for that measure. I might, perhaps. have demanded a large sum of money, not as compensation for the sufferers, but as a penalty inflicted on the Chinese Government. But, independently of the objection in principle to making a high crime of this nature a mere money question, I hold on this point the opinion which is, I believe, entertained by all persons, without exception, who have investigated the subject, that, in the present disorganized state of the Chinese Government, to obtain large pecuniary indemnities from it is simply impossible, and that all that can be done practically in the matter is, to appropriate such a portion of the 'Customs' revenue as will still leave to it a sufficient interest in that revenue to induce it to allow the natives to continue to trade with foreigners. It is calculated that it will be necessary to take 40 per cent of the gross Customs' revenue of China for about four years in order to procure payment of the indemnities already claimed by Baron Gros and me, under instructions from your Lordship and the French Government. Embarrassing questions respecting the occupation of Chinese territory are involved in this arrangement, and I do not think that it would be advisable to bind the Chinese Government by engagements which would cause the term of liquidation of the indemnities to be indefinitely extended. Or, I might have required that the persons guilty of cruelty to our countrymen, or of the violation of a flag of truce, should be surrendered. But if I had made this demand in general terms, some miserable subordinates would, probably, have been given up whom it would have been difficult to pardon, and impossible to punish. And if I had specified Sang-Ko-lin-sin [Prince Seng], of whose guilt in violating a flag of truce evidence sufficient to ensure his condemnation by a court-martial could be furnished, I should have made a demand which, it may be confidently affirmed, the Chinese Government would not have conceded, and mine could not have enforced. I must add that, throwing the responsibility for the acts of Government in this way on individuals resembles too closely the Chinese mode of conducting war to approve itself altogether to my judgment. Having, therefore, to the best of my judgment, examined the question in all its bearings, I came to the conclusion that the destruction of Yuen-mingyuen was the least objectionable of the several courses open to me, unless I could have reconciled it to my sense of duty to suffer the crime which had been committed to pass practically unavenged. I had reason, moreover, to believe that it was an act which was calculated to produce a greater effect in China, and on the Emperor, than persons who look on from a distance may suppose. It was the Emperor's favourite residence, and its destruction could not fail to be a blow to his pride as well as to his feelings.

To this place, as appears from the depositions of the Sikh troopers, copies of which were inclosed in despatch to your Lordship of October 13, he brought our hapless countrymen in order that they might undergo their severest tortures within its precincts. Here have been found the horses and accoutrements of the troopers seized, the decorations torn from the breast of a gallant French officer, and other effects belonging to the prisoners. As almost all the valuables had already been taken from the Palace, the army would go there, not to pillage, but to mark, by a solemn act of retribution, the horror and indignation with which we were inspired by the perpetration of a great crime. The punishment was one which would fall, not on the people, who may be comparatively innocent, but exclusively on the Emperor, whose direct personal responsibility for the crime committed is established, not only by the treatment of the prisoners at Yuen-ming-yuen, but also by the Edict inclosed in my despatch of October 21, in which he offers a pecuniary reward for the heads of the foreigners, adding, that he is ready to expend all his treasure in these wages of assassination.[324] [325]

Cordier's comments on the destruction seem closer to the mark: "In 1860, the burning of the Wan-shou-shan, by order of Lord Elgin, and the pillaging of the Yuen-ming-yuen by the French, are perennial in the memory of the Chinese. Sad acts that tarnished the brilliance of a campaign;

---

[324] Contrary to some accounts of the war, it is clear from Elgin's explanation that the destruction of the palace was *not* a device to end the conflict. Prince Gong was agreeable to peace terms before the burning of the Palace

[325] Elgin, Letter to Baron Gros, October 19, 1860, Cordier, pp. 388–389

the work of the incendiaries began; the fire continued on the 19th; a black smoke formed above the flames, a cloud which floated towards the capital, striking Prince Gong with terror; the latter, terrified, fearing to be chosen by the Allies as an expiatory victim of the crimes of his brother Hien-Foung, thought of escaping. If he had been able to put his project into execution, we were condemned, for lack of authorized negotiator, to do a winter campaign. Twelve days later we visited Lord Elgin's work of ruin; Nothing more melancholy than the bronze pagoda surmounting the great staircase, devastated, and the pavilions and temples surrounding them in the state in which they had left the destructive scourge. And as a contrast to this landscape of desolation, the calm of the lake, covered with lotus flowers, with its large marble bridge."[326]

Commentary–Why Was the Summer Palace Destroyed?

Some comment about the burning of the summer palaces and other imperial properties is germane. The dialogue between Lord Elgin and Baron Gros, it is fair to say, dispels the myth that the destruction had anything to do with ending the China War or getting a treaty signed. Peace negotiations were far along at the point when Elgin decided to burn the Palace. And although this situation could have changed, that was not contemplated by the Allies as they debated the destruction. In fact, not only was the destruction nothing to do with obtaining a settlement, but quite the reverse, Gros was afraid that it could actually delay or derail negotiations.

So if not to obtain peace and end the war, then what was the rationale for the burning? The ostensible answer to this question is *retribution*. Elgin and the British contingent were enraged at the deaths of their emissaries and their escorts. But although the treatment of the emissaries gave Elgin the rationale he needed, and maybe appeased his conscience, this does not appear to be the true underlying reason. One has to look at the overall context. Elgin had been fighting and negotiating with the Chinese since 1856. He had had to make not one, but two unwelcome and lengthy voyages to China, and fight two campaigns. He wanted to be sure that he did not have to fight a third campaign. Personally, he was exasperated with dealing with the Chinese and, as he saw it, their 'double-dealing'. For himself, it is clear he wanted to make a statement,

---

[326] Cordier, p. 392, translation by the author

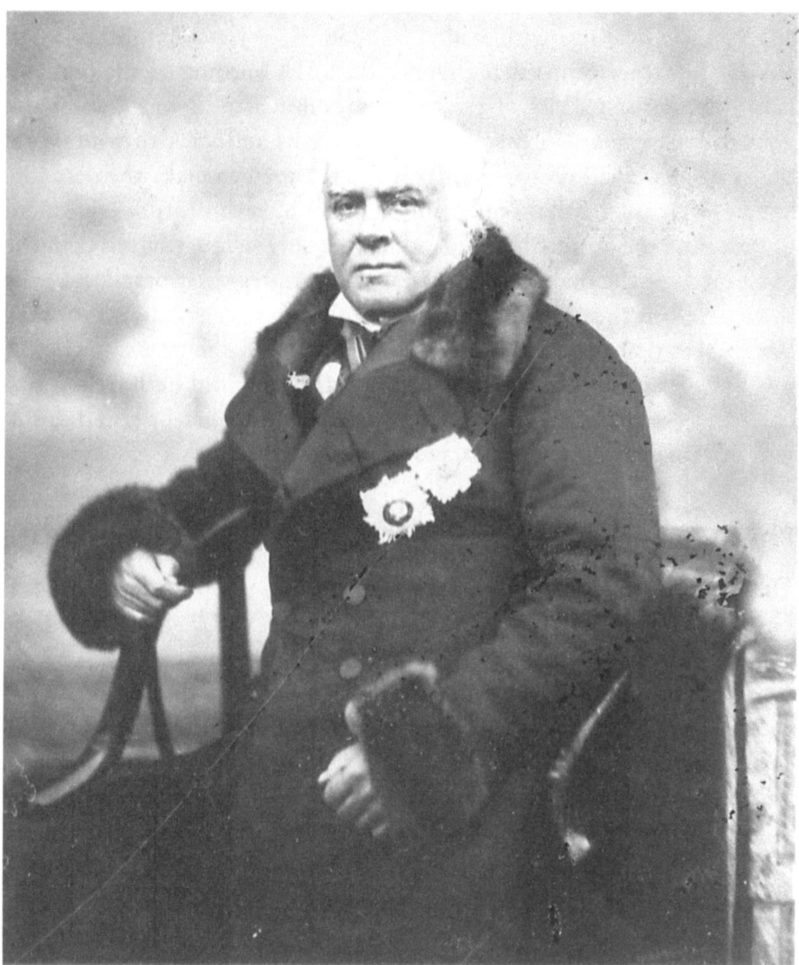

Lord Elgin, Peking, November 2, 1860, Felice Beato

put a full-stop to the whole affair, and force the Chinese to accept that Britain, and he, Elgin, had won. But on an even larger level what this was really about was not the lives of a few emissaries or even Lord Elgin's frustrations, but about one country trying to establish their dominance over another.

Wars and treaties and negotiations and even alliances and membership of organizations have a track record of establishing lines of power and influence, in a word, *control*. Britain was not trying to be fair and just in their dealings with China in 1860, they were simply trying to obtain the treaty terms that they wanted. The burning of the Summer Palace was Britain's way of establishing dominance. It was a cruel and powerful statement—'if you do not respect us and stick to your word, this is what we will do to you'. Elgin was the man to make the decision, but he was doing Britain's bidding. It was the 19th century equivalent of dropping the atomic bomb. And, if you only judge it in terms of the outcome (not the barbarous act itself), as a strategy, it worked. Burning the Palace had the desired effect on China and from that point forward Britain was dominant in the relationship between the two countries. It was not nice or kind or friendly or respectful of world heritage—it was cruel and destructive. This is not a justification for what Britain did. But it is an explanation that appears to be close to the truth.

Peace

On the 19th Prince Gong formally agreed to all the peace terms. Baron Gros to the French government, October 19:

> This morning we saw from here the fire which devoured the Palace, and the fire was pressed . . . You will see through my correspondence with Lord Elgin that I did not wish to associate myself with him in acts of vengeance useless on the one hand and dangerous on the other. He wanted to raze to the ground the Palace of Yuen-ming-yuen, I asked him to abandon this idea and I then refused to take part. General de Montauban did as I did. At the moment I write this despatch to you, there is a fire which devours the Palace. Lord Elgin also wanted, I believe, that we should destroy the imperial residence in Peking, but we shall not go to this end.[327]

There were those in Britain that criticized it as an act of barbarity, but the French writer Victor Hugo was the most eloquent opponent of the burning of the Palace:

> You ask my opinion, Sir, about the China expedition. You consider this expedition to be honourable and glorious, and you

---

[327] Cordier, p. 393, translation by the author

have the kindness to attach some consideration to my feelings; according to you, the China expedition, carried out jointly under the flags of Queen Victoria and the Emperor Napoleon, is a glory to be shared between France and England, and you wish to know how much approval I feel I can give to this English and French victory.

Since you wish to know my opinion, here it is: There was, in a corner of the world, a wonder of the world; this wonder was called the Summer Palace. Art has two principles, the Idea, which produces European art, and the Chimera, which produces oriental art. The Summer Palace was to chimerical art what the Parthenon is to ideal art. All that can be begotten of the imagination of an almost extra-human people was there. It was not a single, unique work like the Parthenon. It was a kind of enormous model of the chimera, if the chimera can have a model. Imagine some inexpressible construction, something like a lunar building, and you will have the Summer Palace. Build a dream with marble, jade, bronze and porcelain, frame it with cedar wood, cover it with precious stones, drape it with silk, make it here a sanctuary, there a harem, elsewhere a citadel, put gods there, and monsters, varnish it, enamel it, gild it, paint it, have architects who are poets build the thousand and one dreams of the thousand and one nights, add gardens, basins, gushing water and foam, swans, ibis, peacocks, suppose in a word a sort of dazzling cavern of human fantasy with the face of a temple and palace, such was this building. The slow work of generations had been necessary to create it. This edifice, as enormous as a city, had been built by the centuries, for whom? For the people. For the work of time belongs to man. Artists, poets and philosophers knew the Summer Palace; Voltaire talks of it. People spoke of the Parthenon in Greece, the pyramids in Egypt, the Coliseum in Rome, Notre-Dame in Paris, the Summer Palace in the Orient. If people did not see it they imagined it. It was a kind of tremendous unknown masterpiece, glimpsed from the distance in a kind of twilight, like a silhouette of the civilization of Asia on the horizon of the civilization of Europe.

This wonder has disappeared.

One day two bandits entered the Summer Palace. One plundered, the other burned. Victory can be a thieving woman, or so it seems. The devastation of the Summer Palace was accomplished by the two victors acting jointly. Mixed up in all this is the name of Elgin, which inevitably calls to mind the Parthenon. What was done to the Parthenon was done to the Summer Palace, more thoroughly and better, so that nothing of it should be left. All the treasures of all our cathedrals put together could not equal this formidable and splendid museum of the Orient. It contained not only masterpieces of art, but masses of jewelry. What a great exploit, what a windfall! One of the two victors filled his pockets; when the other saw this he filled his coffers. And back they came to Europe, arm in arm, laughing away. Such is the story of the two bandits.

We Europeans are the civilized ones, and for us the Chinese are the barbarians. This is what civilization has done to barbarism . . .

This, Sir, is how much approval I give to the China expedition."[328]

Treaty and Conclusion of the War

Obtaining peace and concluding a treaty was the fourth and last of what Elgin considered his four great accomplishments, all achieved in two weeks. On October 13, faced with the threat of bombardment, Peking opened its gates to the British and Prince Gong (now in the ascendency amongst the Chinese factions at Court) agreed to British terms for an ending of the conflict on October 19, as mentioned previously. On October 24 Elgin and his commanders entered the Forbidden City and signed the Convention of Peking. The French did likewise on October 25.[329]

The Convention, among other things, confirmed the terms of the Tientsin Treaty, awarded 8 million taels of silver in indemnity to the Allies, established a permanent diplomatic presence in Peking, and the legalization of the opium trade. It was a decisive and dramatic change in the relations between Britain and China and established Britain firmly

---

[328] Hugo, Victor, letter to Captain Butler, Hauteville House, November 25, 1861

[329] The precise dates of the surrender, when China agreed to terms and when the convention as signed, are often mis-quoted. The dates stated here come from the National Palace Museum, www.npm.gov.tw, and are considered accurate

as the dominant party in the relationship. In the context of world affairs of 1860, diplomatically, Elgin had much to be proud of. The war may not have been his idea, and certainly he did not want to be in China, but he had done his job for the British Government very effectively.

Having secured peace, Elgin waited in Peking for his brother to arrive as the first British ambassador to the Imperial Court. During this hiatus he left a description of Jingshan Hill and the Forbidden City:

> We obtained access to two enclosures, forming part of the impe-
> rial palace appendages: both elevated places, the one ascended
> by a pathway in regular Chinese rockwork on a large scale, and
> really striking in its way; and the other being a well-wooded
> park-like eminence, crowned by temples with images of Buddha.
> The view from both was magnificent. Peking is so full of trees,
> and the houses are so low, that it hardly had the effect of looking
> down on a great city. Here and there temples or high gateways
> rose above the trees, but the general impression was rather that
> of a rich plain densely peopled. In the distance the view was
> bounded by a lofty chain of mountains, snow-capped. From the
> park-like eminence we looked down upon the Imperial Palace, a
> large enclosure crowded with yellow-roofed buildings, generally
> low, and a few trees dotted among them.[330]

Surprisingly, Prince Gong and Elgin developed a cordial, even friendly, relationship after the truce. Gong made gifts to the British aristocrat including some bottles of fine wine. "November 7th. There has not been much to report since the 2nd. I returned Gong's visit the next day, and we had a more coulant conversation than I have before had with any Chinese authority."[331] Elgin handed over representation to his brother Frederick, and he and his escort left Peking on November 10, just in time to avoid the ice and snow of winter and be able to move the army back to Tientsin in good order. He then sailed home for what turned out to be a brief visit. It would be his last.

---

[330] Elgin, in Walrond, p. 369
[331] Elgin, in Walrond, p. 370

Viceroy

Elgin would get no happy sojourn with his family. After China his life seemed doomed. Walrond notes:

> He had not been more than a month at home when the Viceroyalty of India, about to be vacated by Lord Canning, was offered to him, in the Queen's name, by Lord Palmerston. The splendid offer of the most magnificent Governorship in the world was accepted, but not without something of a vague presentiment that he should never return from it. This feeling was expressed with his usual frankness and simplicity, when in the course of an address delivered at Dunfermline, some months before his departure, after referring to former partings, uniformly followed by happy meetings, he said 'Gentlemen, I cannot conceal from myself, nor from you, the fact that the parting which is now about to take place is a far more serious matter than any of those which have preceded it; and that the vast amount of labour devolving upon the Governor-General of India, the insalubrity of the climate, and the advance of years, all tend to render the prospect of our again meeting more remote and uncertain.'[332]

It is clear why Elgin did not welcome his new appointment. Many years posted away from home, the effort he had already expended on his two expeditions to China, the very hot climate in Calcutta. Why Elgin did not refuse the offer of the Viceroy of India is not made explicit. Perhaps a sense of duty to the Crown that once asked, he must not refuse. No doubt an offer refused would mean no other offer of a government position, and he needed an income. Perhaps the prestige of the position was too much to walk away from—it certainly represented the pinnacle of his or any career in the diplomatic service.

> Independently of any such forebodings, there were sorrows on which it is hardly necessary to dwell, but which were felt keenly by one so devoted to that peaceful home-life towards which he was always aspiring, the pain of tearing himself again from the children now growing up to need in an especial manner a father's presence, and of leaving the mother of these children,

---

[332] Walrond, pp. 395–396

for a time at least, to contend alone with cares and anxieties from which it would have been his greatest happiness to shield and protect her. Something, too, there may have been of the depression which breathes in the poet's complaint, the roll of mighty poets is made up a feeling that the work of pacifying and settling India had been so thoroughly accomplished by Lord Dalhousie and Lord Canning, that the field no longer contained any laurels to be reaped by their successor ... For some time he remained in London; after which he spent several pleasant months in Scotland, laying up a store of happy recollections to which his thoughts after days often turned. Early in January 1862, a visit accompanied by Lady Elgin, he went to Osborne House on a visit to the Queen; who even in those early days of widowhood, roused herself to receive the first Viceroy of India ever appointed by the sole act of the Crown. On the 28th of the same month he quitted the shores of Sails for England; and, after a rapid and uneventful journey, reached Calcutta on March 12. As Lady Elgin was unable to accompany him [she was to follow later and join her husband in India], he resumed the habit of conversing with her, so to speak, through the medium.[333]

In his correspondence Elgin shows a gentle, human side that perhaps a Chinese audience might find strangely at odds with the actions of the same man in Peking two years before. He sorely missed his family, "It is very lonely to be spending this Sunday evening by myself, after the many happy ones I have enjoyed with you and the children during the past three months; and yet I would not forego the recollection of those happy days though it deepens the gloom of the present. Surely, whatever may happen to us all, it is something gained to have this retrospect in store."[334] On February 12, 1862 he wrote, "I have been thinking of the past, and remembering that just twenty years ago, at this same season, I set out on my first visit to the Tropics. What a strange career it has been. How grateful I should be to Providence for the protection I have enjoyed. How wild it seems, to be about, at the close of twenty years, to begin again."[335] Four days later he added, "Feb 16: It has been a sad time

---

[333] Walrond, p. 397

[334] Walrond, p. 398

[335] Elgin, in Walrond, p. 398

... I could not read, and have been lying down, thinking over so many things! ... But there may, please God, be a good time beyond. I have been thinking of the little party in your room on this day, and endeavouring to join with you all."[336]

On August 9, 1862 Elgin was formally installed as Governor-General of India in Calcutta. He had much to do. The weather in early 1863 was cool enough but then it became very hot and it was a great burden to Elgin. He wrote from Barrackpore, where he had gone to seek the change of air which his health now began imperatively to require: "This place looks wonderfully green. At the end of the broad walk on which I am gazing from my window, is Lady Canning's grave; it is not yet properly finished. Who will attend to it now?"[337] he noted with prescience of the grave of the former governor-general's wife. "While still oppressed with these sad thoughts, he received a blow which went even deeper home, in the intelligence of the death of his brother Robert."[338]

In February 1863 Elgin left Calcutta for a tour of India. They reached Agra: "The six days spent at Agra, Lord Elgin was disposed to rank among the most interesting of his life, 'nothing that will give you' an idea of an Indian Durbar. The exhibition of costly jewels, the display of wealth in priceless ornaments and splendid dresses, the strange mixture of wealth and poverty, the means of accomplishing magnificence and splendour enjoyed to such profusion, yet rendered almost void to this end from want of taste!"[339] Then on to Dehli. In April he reached Simla. "The hills on which Simla stands are well clothed by trees, not of great stature generally, though of much beauty; ilexes of a peculiar kind, deodars, and rhododendrons being conspicuous among them; but there is little wood on the surrounding mountains."[340]

On September 26 Lord Elgin left Simla *en route* for Sealkote, where he was to rejoin his camp and proceed with it to Peshawur, the most distant station on the North-West frontier, before making his way to the great rendezvous at Lahore.

October 18, he wrote to Sir Charles Wood: "Thus far our expedition through the mountains has been very pleasant and interesting. The

---

[336] Ibid.

[337] Ibid.

[338] Walrond, p. 403

[339] Elgin, in Walrond, p. 436

[340] Elgin, in Walrond, p. 443

scenery has been magnificent and the climate enjoyable, though the changes of temperature have been considerable. We are now at Sultan-pore, in Kuloo, at an elevation of about 4,000 feet above the sea. But Rotung a few days ago we (the men of the party) scaled the Rotung Pass, which divides Kuloo from Lahoul, and attained in so doing a height of 13,000 feet, with a temperature low in proportion. This pass is on the road from these provinces to Ladak and China."[341]

"Although he had suffered often from the unhealthy and depressing climate of Calcutta during the summer and autumn of 1862, and thus, to the eyes that saw him again in 1863, he looked many years older than when he left England," notes biographer Walrond,

> Yet it was not till he entered the hills that any symptom manifested itself of the fatal malady that was lurking under his apparently stout frame and strong constitution. The splendid scenery of those vast forests and snow-clad mountains inspired him with the liveliest pleasure; but the highly rarefied atmosphere, which to most residents in India is as life from the dead, seemed in him to have the exactly reverse effect. It was on the 12th of October that he ascended the Kotung Pass, and on the 13th he crossed the famous Twig Bridge over the river Chandra. It is remarkable for the rude texture of birch branches of which it is composed, and which, at this late season, was so rent and shattered by the wear and tear of the past year as to render the passage of it a matter of great exertion.
>
> Lord Elgin was completely prostrated by the effort, and it may be said that from the exhaustion consequent on this adventure he never rallied. But he returned to his camp, and continued his march on horseback, until, on the 22nd, an alarming attack obliged him to be carried, by slow stages, to Dhurmsala. There he was joined, on the 4th of November, by his friend and medical adviser, Dr. Macrae, who had been summoned from Calcutta, on the first alarming indications of his illness. By this time the disorder had declared itself in such a form as to cause the most serious apprehensions to others, as well as to himself the most distressing sufferings . . . on the 6th of November Dr. Macrae came to the conclusion that the illness was mortal. This

---

[341] Elgin, in Walrond, p. 455

intelligence, which he communicated at once to Lord Elgin, was received with a calmness and fortitude which never deserted him through all the scenes which followed. It was impossible not to be struck by the courage and presence of mind with which, in the presence of a death unusually terrible, and accompanied by circumstances unusually trying, he showed, in equal degrees and with the most unvarying constancy, two of the grandest elements of human character. He was startled, he was awed; he felt it 'hard, hard, to believe that this life was condemned'; but there was no looking backward. Of the officers of his staff he took an affectionate leave on that day. 'It is well,' he said to one of them, 'that I should die in harness.'

On the following morning, Lady Elgin, with his approval, rode up to the cemetery at Dhurmsala to select a spot for his grave; and he gently expressed pleasure when told of the quiet and beautiful aspect of the spot chosen, with the glorious view of the snowy range towering above, and the wide prospect of hill and plain below. His death was on November 20, and on the 21st he was privately buried, at his own request, on the spot selected beforehand."[342]

His wife and daughter were there with him at the last.

Walrond praises the diplomat and minister, "The varied ability, the steady conscientious industry, the genial temper, the combination of fertility of resource with simplicity of aim, of firmness with tact, of cautious sagacity with prompt resolution, which might have found even larger scope in the government of India than in the active and eventful life which has been described. He sleeps far away from his native land, on the heights of Dhurmsala; a fitting grave, let us rejoice to think, for the Viceroy of India, overlooking from its lofty height the vast expanse of the hill and plain of these mighty provinces a fitting burial beneath the snow-clad Himalaya range, for one who dwelt with such serene satisfaction on all."[343]

One is left with a profound sense of sadness. Here was a man who wanted nothing more than to be in Scotland and spend time with his

---

[342] Walrond, p. 464

[343] Walrond, p. 467

family. Duty required him to travel the world in the service of his country only to die and be buried far from home at a comparatively young age. And yet he is only known for an act which has come down to us as one of infamy. He was a devout man who hated war and valued art, but in the course of his responsibilities destroyed something great and beautiful, for which he personally has had to shoulder the blame, a cruel aftermath to the life and work of a statesman. This brief account is not an apology for the architect of the destruction of the Summer Palace. Elgin lived in the real world, a harsh world, and he was forced in time of war to make some very unpleasant choices, ones which inevitably were going to mean massive damage to property, possibly great loss of life. He navigated those choices as best he knew how. One could argue that war, conflict, and disputes between nations were the root problem, he was merely the man sent to implement the solution.

Limekilns

According to the current Lord Elgin, after the death of the 8th Earl, Broomhall was 'shut-up' and Lady Elgin, suffering greatly, was in mourning for a long period. The family had lost their guiding light.

Limekilns in Fifeshire, Scotland is a village of quiet charm. Nestled gently on the north shore of the Firth of Forth, it's within easy reach of Edinburgh, but a world away. The old painted cottages, the views south across the water, dark silhouettes of mountains in the distance, a peaceful haven, an oasis of calm on an island of 60 million people. It's an unlikely setting for the home of one of the most castigated men in Chinese history. On top of a stone escarpment crowning the village, lies the estate and impressive Georgian mansion of the Earls of Elgin. Broomhall was the family home of James Bruce, the 8th Earl and where he grew up. The setting is seemingly a million miles from the plains of North China.

As one wanders around the Elgin estate on a meandering public footpath, the land has probably not changed much since the days of the 8th Earl. In June it is impossibly green, heavily wooded around its open fields, and pleasantly rural. Although 5,000 miles from Peking, it reminds one a little of the gardens of the Summer Palace. The tranquility is the same, the trees—huge beeches and chestnuts remind one of the vision of the designers of the Yuen-ming-yuen. In the distance from the western part of the estate the mountains are eerily similar to Peking's Western Hills in whose shadow the Summer Palace was built.

In a sense the 8th Earl should have appreciated and felt distantly at home when he stepped into the gardens of the Summer Palace on October 7, 1860. The 8th Earl was not an ambitious or greedy man, his goal, always, was to serve his country to the best of his ability.

Robert the Bruce had strong connections to Fife but it was only in the late 16th century that one line of the Bruce family acquired land which had previously been in the hands of religious institutions on the north bank of the Firth of Forth. The Elgin Broomhall estate literarily towers above the village of Limekilns sitting at the water's edge. The village, formerly little more than a row of artisans cottages along the banks of the Forth estuary, is joined to its neighbor Charlestown (a planned village laid out by Charles the 6th Earl). Woods grow thickly all the way up and on top of the stone escarpment behind the cottages, the same escarpment where lime was excavated to make ingredients for cement and additives for agriculture.

The Elgin estate is still a working farm, its hedgerows are imposing and the fields populated by sheep and pheasant. Broomhall House is reached by private road entered past a disused lodge, passing through a series of large fields growing hops and where sheep graze, to the flat top of the escarpment. As you cross the final cattle grid at the end of the final field the Georgian house comes into view, sitting facing the mountains to the north and the estuary to the south, set amongst a group of large trees. Viewed from amongst the massive oaks adjacent to the gravel roadway it is magnificent, an imposing and plainly noble façade that exudes an energy quite unlike those stately homes open to the public. There is a privacy and a dignity about this house that commands immediate respect. The gravel forecourt gives way to the very tall and imposing windows of the house's reception rooms. There are mighty stone steps up to the ground floor rooms (mimicked in so many urban 18th century British town houses).

On my visit the Countess of Elgin comes out onto her front porch, a massive Greco-Roman portico, to greet me with a dignified handshake. The front door originally pierced the front wall in the center of the portico in the dead center of the front façade of the house. Long ago the old doorway has been glazed over giving the inside of the portico an airy feel and the reception hall plenty of light. The modern door has been set off to the side to protect the house from wintry blasts and to brighten the interior. The front hall is a massive, palatial room, very tall and very long, like the inside of a Roman temple, filled with modest 19th century furniture, large pieces of marble statuary and a gallery of huge ancestral portraits. The floor is still paved in stone and covered with warming oriental rugs to give it something of a homely feel.

Andrew Bruce, the 11th and current earl of Elgin is a quiet, unpretentious man with large, soft, blue eyes and a soft rounded face reminiscent of the 8th Earl. He is a brave man, having fought and, as a young tank commander, been seriously wounded when his tank was hit by a German anti-tank gun in Normandy in 1944. A graduate of Eton and Baliol College, Oxford, the present earl served with distinction on boards of directors and in the House of Lords. But in spite of his position of social responsibility, an extremely distinguished pedigree, many obvious talents and a remarkable memory concerning the events in the lives of his ancestors, he is resolutely unassuming. He has a warm smile and a dignified but generous way about him. Although advanced in years now he still knows more about his ancestor than anyone else probably ever will. He understands his family and the challenges and obstacles they have faced.

The 11th Earl has inherited several very interesting mementos from his great-grandfather's expedition to China. He has a number of engravings and sketches done by Colonel Crealock, military attaché to the Earl, depicting various scenes, including the fleet moored at Tientsin and the Earl and his party entering Peking on horseback. There are no images of the Palace itself. The family originally owned a set of photographs made by Felice Beato, which the 11th Earl had sold. Amazingly the large, heavy, black fur trimmed coat (and matching fur hat) that were worn by Lord Elgin in October 1860, that he had made in Canada in the 1850s, the one he was wearing in his famous photographs taken by Beato on November 1, a few days after the signing of the Convention of Peking in the Forbidden City has survived. There is also the remarkable gift from Prince Gong—one of several original flasks of wine, in a dark blue porcelain vase with a feint gold decoration, unopened since 1860. Lord Elgin also has all of the original letters and journals written by the 8th Earl during his time in China. These are the tangible remains in Scotland of an expedition for which the 8th Earl has gained so much notoriety. He himself sleeps far away in India.

Bibliography

Checkland, S.G., *The Elgins 1766–1917: A Tale of Aristocrats, Proconsuls and Their Wives*, Aberdeen University Press, Aberdeen, 1988
Cordier, Henri, *L'Expedition de Chine de 1860*, Alcan, Paris, 1906
Oliphant, Laurence, *Narrative of the Earl of Elgin's Mission to China and Japan, 1857–8–9* (2 volumes), 1859 (reprinted by Oxford University Press, 1970)
Walrond, Theodore, ed. *The Letters and Journals of James, Eighth Earl of Elgin*, John Murray, London, 1872
Wrong, George M., *The Earl of Elgin*, Methuen & Co., Toronto, 1906

A Scene of Destruction

With the loot from the Palace mostly in Europe being auctioned off[344] in the immediate aftermath of the war, the ruins in of the Yuen-ming-yuen remained behind as a sad reminder of what used to be. What follows are several accounts of the destruction and Palace ruins, including from Chinese writers.

The Chinese scholar Wu Kedu noted in his diary, dated October 18, 1860: "A vast column of smoke arose from the northwest direction ascertaining that the Barbarians had burnt the Summer Palace. [I learned] that the Three hills were not spared, leaving the area absolutely bare."[345]

After a tour of the ruins of the Palace in 1871, scholar Wang Kaiyun composed the following poem:

Burned in the windswept smoke,
The country royal estate has been ruined.
The Jade spring flows as usual,
But with sighing sounds.
Alas! Kunming Lake has silted up.
I come, but what can I see?
Buried in thrones are the broken bronze rhinoceros.
The great Green Rocks become
The hideouts for crying wolves;

---

[344] For more information on the aftermath of the art objects taken from the palace, see *Loot*, by the same author, Forbidden City Books, 2018

[345] Wu Kedu, Diary, Oct. 18, 1860, in Wong, *Paradise Lost* p.150

And the fish under the Bridge of the Embroidered Ripples
Seem to be sobbing.
Alas! An old eunuch at the Happy Garden Gate
Had once attended His Majesty.
The buildings here all disappeared,
Gone also the loud excitements of crowds of people.
The lonesome visitors stand in the garden's solitude.
The exciting past, the sorrowful present,
Distinguished guests shall never come.
Not any more!
When I peep behind the scenes
Of the Inner Palace Gate and the Main Audience Hall,
I find a lot of broken bricks.
None of the crumbling walls,
Gone is the Clear Sunshine Belvedere facing the lake,
Where the late (Xianfeng) emperor often enjoyed the morn.
They said His Majesty once had a strange dream,
An old man who says he is the guardian of the garden,
He wants to quit because peace can no longer be maintained.
The Buddha statues inside the Sravasti Wall,
Thousands of them,
Where are they now?
Look around from side to side,
Cattail leaves grow wild in the lakes.
Mugwort grass rustling in the air, blocking stairways.
Some burned trees blossom anew,
But are cut and taken away for firewood.
The startled fish jump in the stream,
Trying to avoid nets.
The wonderful Peony Terrace,
Where three great rulers once met,
None of them could foresee misfortune.
The bamboo trees grow so disorderly
Out of the messy mosses.
One can no longer see in the spring days
The dropping dew and the blossoming peony.
Westward to the Smooth Lake,
A chamber is still there,
But where is its window paper?

Behind the bursting Chinese chives,
Emerged the gradually elevated road.
But where are the footprints of beautiful ladies?
The beauties left behind their block pigment makeup,
Imprints on windows in green everywhere[346]

The poem captures the feeling of the Chinese people at the loss of the Palace.

The following account describes the journey of Catherine de Bourboulon, wife of Alfonse de Bourboulon, the French ambassador to the Chinese court who visited the French cemetery and the Summer Palace grounds in late 1861, just twelve months after the fire:

Leaving Peking, departing through the Pin-tse gate, one finds oneself on the grand road northwest which takes one to the Summer Palace . . . Several kilometers further on one finds the French cemetery which contains the monument consecrated to the memory of the officers and soldiers killed during the China Campaign. There is nothing sadder than the sight of this necropolis! One arrives there by a dilapidated gate through encircling walls in ruin; a Catholic priest, who is the guardian of the cemetery and school master . . . [the graves] are aligned equal distance apart and all constructed of the same model adopted by the missionaries . . . The white head stones are gloomy.

The funeral monument raised by the French army under the supervision of Captain Bouvier, is found close to the entrance. It is square, quite tall and large, and decorated very simply; an iron grating encircles the base, and protects the approach. On the front is an imperial eagle, behind two crossed swords embraced with the Legion of Honour; one side has the inscription, 'To the memory of the officers and soldiers killed during the China Campaign of 1860'.

Mme. de Bourboulon accompanied by several other Europeans, went to visit the Yuen-ming-yuen. The village of Haitien still bore many traces of destruction; some Tartars were barracked in the gardens of the Palace whose burnt main gate was boarded up with logs and large stones. The visitors found a

---

[346] Wang, Kaiyun, in Wong, *Paradise Lost* pp. 163–164

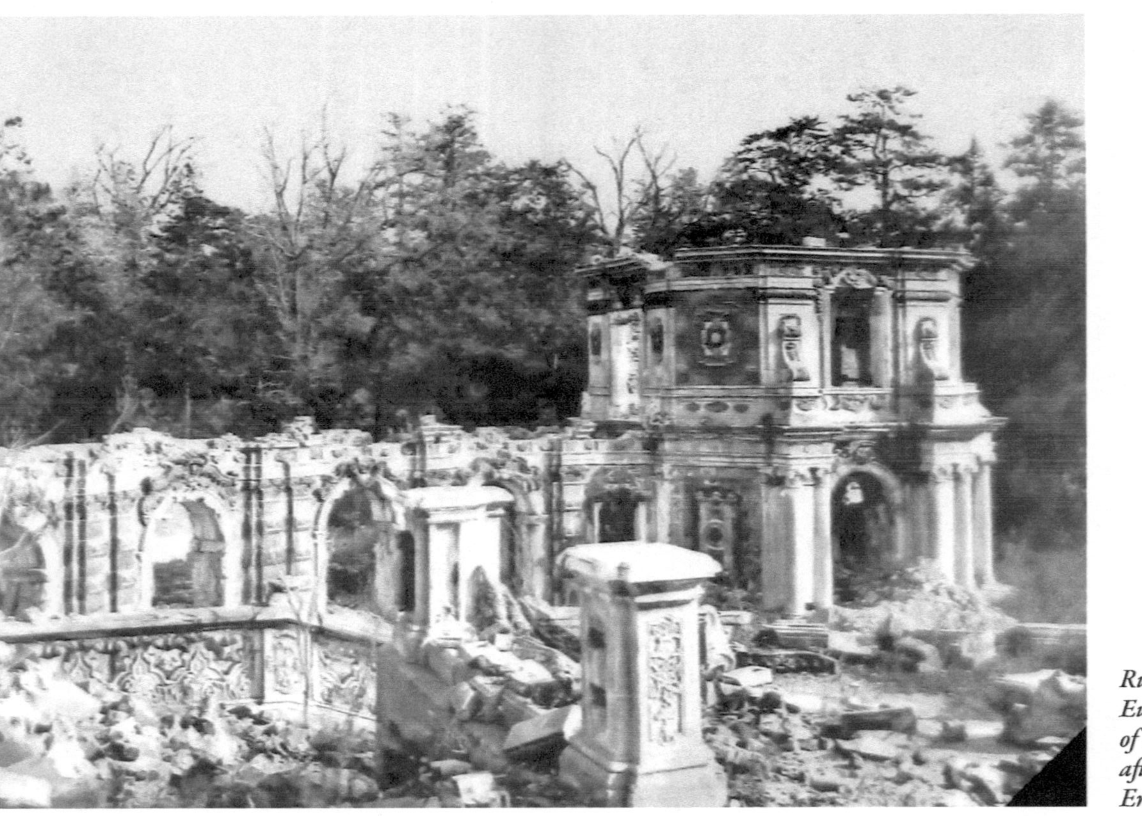

*Ruins of one of the
European Palaces, part
of the Yuen-ming-yuen,
after the destruction,
Ernst Ohlmer, 1873*

wooded terrain northwest of the walled enclosure [of the Palace], to avoid the Chinese troops, and after having crossed a lake on the ice, strong enough to carry them, they arrived at the foot of a double marble balustraded staircase covered by charred wood. Once in the Palace enclosure they mounted a high hill which dominated the whole valley of the Yuen-ming-yuen. The view was magnificent, hovering above the lakes, the forests and the prairies therein; several pagodas, forgotten by the destructors, rose their pinnacles above the countryside, but debris of all kinds, charred beams, fire-scarred stones of marble and alabaster, alone marked the places where at one time were the thirty-six palaces of the splendid residence of the emperor of China.[347]

Ludovic de Beauvoir, another foreign traveler, viewed the ruins in 1866, before any rebuilding or further destruction had occurred, and left this account of what he saw:

> Here we are before the famous Yuen-ming-yuen, the Summer Palace! To left and right, avenues once lined with porticos and monuments, and pavilions are now no more than a heap of ruins. Also ruined and hideous rubble are the hundreds of adjoining residences that formed a whole town of the imperial palace. Only two huge bronze lions, the most beautiful pieces found in the Celestial Empire, remain intact and guard the threshold of what was the Versailles of the great emperors descended from fire! (or from the sky?). These lions are the only objects that the Allies had respected, for good reason, it is true, that there was no way to transport them, and that it would need special construction to carry by cart over fifteen bridges, to reach Tientsin!
>
> Ah! This palace must have been splendid! Imagine a lake surrounded by green trees and beautiful granite and marble terraces; fifteen artificial hills forming a natural wall of such elegant line of shade and verdure; a mountain whose side is black cut stones, dominates these vast gardens; it is crowned by a temple

---

[347] Poussielgue, A., *Voyage en Chine et en Mongolie de M. de Bourboulon, ministre de France, et de Mme de Bourboulon, 1860–1861*, Paris, 1866. Translation from the French by the author

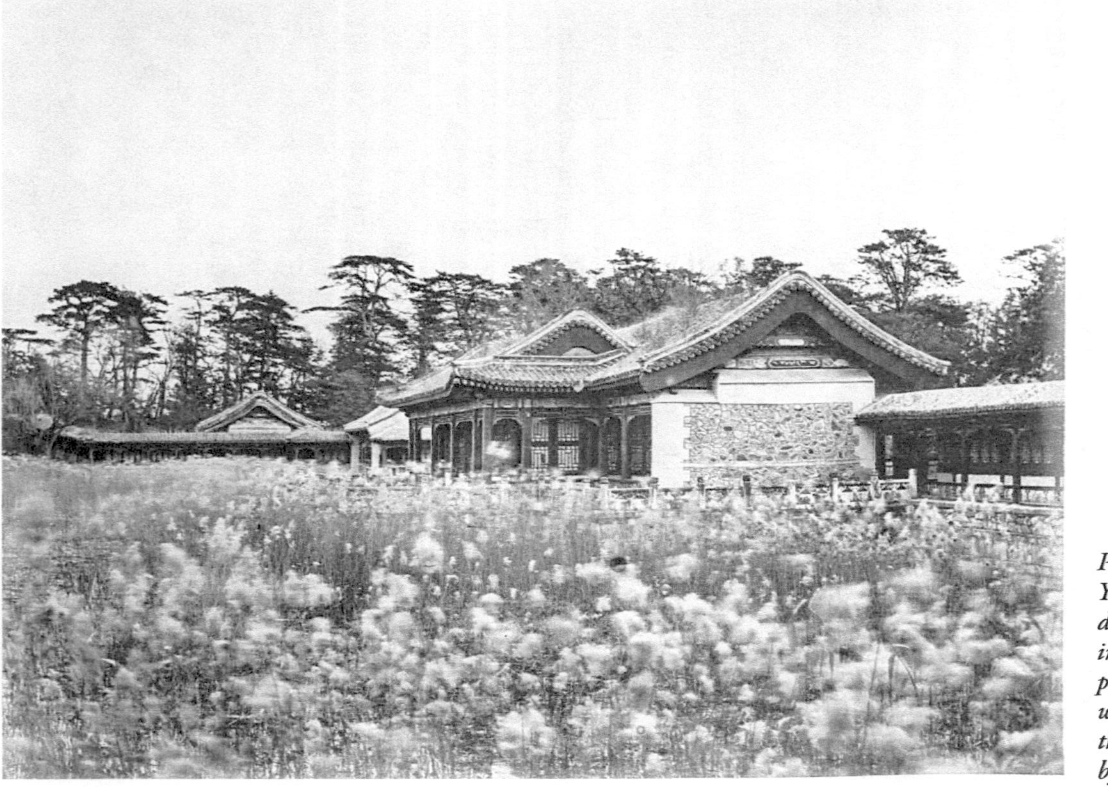

Palace buildings at the Yuen-ming-yuen after the destruction, photographed in 1879 by Hong Kong photographer, Afong. These were among the buildings that escaped destruction by the British in 1860

in glazed tiles which leads to a gigantic double stairway of tall stones.

An island covered in pavilions—in the past!—is connected to the mainland by a bridge of tall arches and most picturesque terraces. This is what remains of so much grandeur: the whole 'town' of the palace which was situated in these surroundings was destroyed by flames, and now there are just-collapsed sections of walls, masses of sulfur coloured bricks, heaps of statues and broken vases, groups of trees blackened and charred!

It is this that has become of the magnificence of emperors, and the pavilions of the innumerable empresses, and the chests full of pearls, and the columns of gold, and the cloisonnés, the crackled porcelains, the jades, the red lacquer, in a word, all the most admirable marvels of fifteen centuries of civilization, of art and craftsmanship. Good heavens! It's too painful to see such a dismal annihilation! I believe I also in the same way have been affected by the flames of the destruction, wandering amongst the formless rubble; one feels the desolation it also touches your heart: to see the ruins of the Summer Palace and not shiver, it is against the forces of an honest man!

I think I could repeat twenty extraordinary anecdotes told here on these unheard days, where the horses of the army had left litter half a foot of imperial silk in thickness; but silence is only decent to the ruins, and I bring you only the view of the Palace chapel, located on a rock so high that the flames could not reach it. There I spent long hours thinking about the sad end of this expedition begun so boldly, so bravely and so wonderfully for the honor of the French arms until the unlucky day of looting and arson; to contemplate what was the Summer Palace, and blush in spite of myself in front of beggars who pointed and seemed to call us thieves and arsonists.[348]

The following are notes from an early English guidebook concerning the state of the Yuen-ming-yuen in 1866:

---

[348] Ludovic de Beauvoir, *Voyage autour du monde: Australie, Java, Siam, Canton, Pékin, Yeddo, San Francisco, Paris, Plon*, Paris, 1867, original research by Bernard Brizay, translated from the French by the author

In its present state the traveller will be struck with the thorough demolition effected by the troops 'not one stone being left upon an another' in many places, to quote the old saying. Those who wish to visit this gigantic memorial of Chinese perfidy—as it may now be well called—must be careful to ask for Wanshoushan and not for Yuen-ming-yuen as that portion of the grounds open to the visitor is known by the former name. Yuen-ming·yuen proper is now closed, and parts of it are even said to be inhabited by persons attached to the Court. It will however require the work of a lifetime to restore this once magnificent palace to its former grandeur.[349]

---

[349] Dennys, Nicholas Belfield (1840?–1900). Notes for tourists in the North of China, 1866.

Acknowledgments

Bill Yin, my good friend in Beijing came up with the idea for this book in the first place. I am grateful for his friendship and vision. I would like to thank Lu Wu and Liu Yang for making it possible for me to visit the site of the Yuanming Yuan which as a result I have been able to do many times, and which has been invaluable in helping me to understand this magnificent palace as it was and is after its destruction. I would like to offer my sincere appreciation to Colin Youngs for translating Maurice Irisson's narrative.

I would also like to thank:

Lord and Lady Elgin for their wonderful hospitality and the insights they have given me into the life of the 8th Earl and his command of the British expedition to China.

Vincent Drouget, Head Curator at Le Palais de Fontainebleau.

Terry Bennett for his assistance with 19th century Chinese photographs.

Chris Bowlby for his help making introductions and with help researching the life of his ancestor T. W. Bowlby.

Dr. John Finlay for his help understanding many aspects of the Palace from his vast knowledge and sensitive appreciation of it.

Martin Fiennes for his hospitality, generosity, and help researching the life of Sir John Hart Dunne.

Dr. James Hevia for his professional consultation and advice about loot.

Alexandra Harrer for introducing me to colleagues in China and greatly helping my understanding of the Yuen-ming-yuen.

Sally Goodsir at the Royal Collection in London for information about Her Majesty the Queen's holdings.

Kathy Roote, Annette Rose, Nigel Giles and John Bradney for reviewing my manuscript.

Mayapriya Long with Bookwrights for her professionalism and kindness in laying out this book and guiding me through the publication process.

All images used in this book are in the public domain, unless otherwise noted.